DRYDEN AND THE PROBLEM OF FREEDOM

DAVID B. HALEY

Dryden and the
Problem of Freedom

The Republican Aftermath
1649–1680

Yale University Press   New Haven and London

Published with assistance from the Kingsley Trust Association Fund established by the Scroll and Key Society of Yale College.

Designed by James J. Johnson and set in Monotype Ehrhardt Roman type by Tseng Information Systems, Inc., Durham, North Carolina. Printed in the United States of America by BookCrafters, Inc., Chelsea, Michigan.

Library of Congress Cataloging-in-Publication Data

Haley, David, 1936–
    Dryden and the problem of freedom : the republican aftermath, 1649–1680 /
    David B. Haley.
    p. cm.
    Includes bibliographical references (p.   ) and index.
    ISBN 0-300-06607-4 (alk. paper)

    1. Dryden, John, 1631–1700—Political and social views.   2. Politics and literature—Great Britain—History—17th century.   3. Great Britain—Politics and government—1649–1660.
4. Great Britain—Politics and government—1660–1688.   5. Political poetry, English—History and criticism.   6. Republicanism in literature.   7. Freedom in literature.   I. Title.
PR3427.P6H34   1997
821'.4—dc20   96-43964

A catalogue record for this book is available from the British Library.

The paper in this book meets the guidelines for permanence and durability of the Committee on Production Guidelines for Book Longevity of the Council on Library Resources.

10   9   8   7   6   5   4   3   2   1

CORNELIAE UXORI

Contents

Acknowledgments

This book was fostered at its earliest stage by the encouragement of two scholars I can no longer thank. The late Samuel Monk and William Frost generously criticized my initial essay on Dryden's slip about "Queen Gorboduc." Earl Miner, also, hailed my explanation of that notorious error (see chapter 5), the source of which was uncovered by Thomas Clayton in his definitive edition of Suckling's poems. During the years that I taught the Dryden course inherited from Professor Monk, the germ of this unpublished essay grew into the present book. Several of its arguments have been aired in different forums. I thank the editors of *Cithara* for permission to use materials from my article of 1991 on the Rose Alley beating.

Achsah Guibbory and Steven Zwicker, and my colleagues Peter Firchow and Joel Weinsheimer, each read substantial chapters, as did my brother, Brian Haley, who spotted the Ciceronian construction in Lisideius's name. A fuller version of the manuscript was reviewed by Emrys Jones and Barbara Everett, and particularly by Maximilian Novak. Another congenial critic, Sandy Budick, introduced me to Yale University Press, whose anonymous reader recommended the chronological presentation that I have adopted. While I naturally hope the book answers to their expectations, I must point out that none of these scholars has read or approved the final version.

My debt to the monumental California Dryden and to James Winn's biography will be obvious. The work of J. G. A. Pocock showed me the political dimension of early modern literature, and the biography of Shaftesbury by K. H. D. Haley (no kin) armed a mere literary scholar against Tory revisionism and Whig history alike. The present study owes most to Cornelia Deemer Haley. In my pursuit of early modern reflexivity, from the epic of the Shakespearean court to the Civil Wars and the Restoration stage, I have taken my cue from the unfailing intelligence she brings to bear on this vital topic from cultural history.

Two McKnight Summer Fellowships awarded by the University of Minnesota's Graduate School allowed me to finish the book. I am grateful to Jonathan Brent and Richard Miller of Yale University Press, and especially to Lawrence Kenney, for shaping the final product.

DRYDEN AND THE PROBLEM OF FREEDOM

Introduction: The Public Poet

Twentieth-century criticism has restored John Dryden to his rightful status of public poet. The achievement is academic, though, because modern society rates poetry and rhetoric very low among civic pursuits. The two kinds of speech are no longer compared as classical genres, yet a poet giving a public reading is never mistaken for a political orator. Poetry and rhetoric have drifted apart with the steady professionalization of all civilized activity. The private nature of poetry has become its characteristic mark. Poetry has withdrawn from its commitment to politics because the public sphere in which human beings were wont to seek their common good has gradually withered away, and we cherish our privacy instead. Poetry has become our voice for sharing a private world isolated from politics. We no longer ask poetry to show us a fuller civic life, and it is least welcome to do so in behalf of a public interest we deem chimerical.

In these circumstances, the driving force behind much of Dryden's poetry is easily lost. Given a little information, readers can still hear the personal voice in *Mac Flecknoe*, in *The Medall*, in *Religio Laici*, or in the "Defence of An Essay of Dramatic Poesy" and some of Dryden's prefaces. But this is not the same as relishing Dryden the public writer. On the other hand, to point out that Dryden wrote for the king or for court patronage is to awaken the old charge that his pen was mercenary. The hint quickly empties his rhetoric of its moral excellence and civic purpose.

Recent literary theory has reduced all speech to a kind of *writing* that transcends its historical context. This hypothesis, by methodically ignoring

the public sphere, collapses the distinction between public and private writing that governed Renaissance and early modern literature. The ideological
premises of postmodernism cannot be reconciled with Dryden's theory and
practice because his public poetry, including some that Samuel Johnson considered "encomiastick homage," is grounded in consciously political ideas.
These ideas in turn are born of the historical moment. Against the new
literary historicism that lumps historical narrative with rhetoric as perfor-
mative modes of "representation," I shall reaffirm the traditional standing of
historiography as mimesis. Mimetic theory is the Achilles' heel of poststruc-
turalist approaches to literature, all of which rest upon a concept of literary
autonomy that is not germane to Renaissance culture.[1]

Indeed, the belief that literature is autonomous lies at the heart of the
problem of freedom, and Dryden's mistrust of the antinomian imagination
is the subject of my three last chapters. As my subtitle indicates, however,
the problem of freedom is political in origin. The first two chapters examine
the Interregnum matrix of radical ideas that not only bred Dryden's reactionary outlook but, well into his Restoration career, continued to leaven
the poet's historical self-understanding. Because political ideas were bound
up with religion in the seventeenth century, I preface the fourth chapter on
republicanism with a chapter devoted to Dryden's religious views, although
discussing these meant overstepping the book's chronological limits to examine *Religio Laici* (1682), the earliest writing in which Dryden made his
religious opinions known.

The progression in my chapters from politics and religion to literature
reflects the broad contours of Dryden's earlier career. The movement also
corresponds to poetry's retreat from the public life already noted. Since
that retreat continues today, with poetry farther removed than ever from the
public deliberation discussed in my first chapter, this book makes some attempt to understand our own historical situation as well as Dryden's. The
passage of three centuries has not resolved the questions he raised about our
freedom and its limits. Posed in moral or Kantian terms, the problem lies
in our individual autonomy—the modern form of the same doctrine of free
will that drew Augustine's rebuke. Dryden first ran into the problem when
he encountered a republicanism hostile to monarchy. By the 1670s he was
beginning to realize that antinomianism in the guise of critical relativism
threatened the sovereignty of poetry as well. In his writings, he relates the
problem variously to criticism, to politics, and to religion, but nowhere does

he formulate it more succinctly than in the non-Miltonic lines he added to *The State of Innocence*. In act 4, Dryden's Adam, a far more anxious, Augustinian figure than his Miltonic original, has been debating free will with Raphael and Gabriel. Unable to disabuse Adam of his "impious fancies," the two angels simply exclaim, "Our task is done: obey." The stage direction then has them "*fly up in the Cloud*," leaving Adam to his quest for obedience. "Why am I not tied up from doing ill?" he soliloquizes. " 'Twould show more grace my frailty to confine." [2]

The freedom that Adam so ungraciously deprecates was more eagerly embraced by humanists like Pico della Mirandola, whose *Oration on the Dignity of Man* (c. 1486) proclaimed man "a creature of indeterminate nature" and imagined God addressing Adam as follows: "Neither a fixed abode nor a form that is thine alone nor any function peculiar to thyself have we given thee, Adam, to the end that according to thy longing and according to thy judgment thou mayest have and possess what abode, what form, and what functions thou thyself shalt desire. The nature of all other beings is limited and constrained within the bounds of laws prescribed by Us. Thou, constrained by no limits, in accordance with thine own free will, in whose hand We have placed thee, shalt ordain for thyself the limits of thy nature." [3]

More than politics and time separate Dryden's Restoration London from Pico's republican Florence. Florentine humanism was heretical and needed protecting by secular patrons like Lorenzo de' Medici. At first, the same was true of Erasmian humanism in the north. Then came the Reformation, which proved a refuge for heretics like Lelio Sozzini, the Unitarian disciple of Erasmus. The antihumanist doctrine of Martin Luther and John Calvin obscures the fact that Calvinist societies, in Huguenot France and in Holland as well as in Switzerland and Scotland, harbored intellectuals who criticized both the Roman Church and Calvinist dogma itself. Humanists like Milton's hero, George Buchanan, and the Arminian John Cameron, who took over the Huguenot academy at Saumur, kept alive Erasmus's teachings. These included free will in theory, tolerance in practice, and the amenability of religious problems and texts to reason—all within a reformed, visible Christian church. In England, "Arminian" ideas like these were denounced because they came from the pens of liberal theologians like William Chillingworth and Archbishop William Laud, who were thought to be soft toward papists. In a wide-ranging essay entitled "The Religious Origins of the Enlightenment," H. R. Trevor-Roper traces liberal humanism through each of its three brilliant stages. He shows that it flourished every time the Catholic danger abated and "the tolerant, sceptical rationalism of the Erasmians" broke free of "the intolerant, predestinarian, scholastic doctrines of the Calvinist clergy [to] whom political necessity had joined them."[4]

Dryden's discovery of this mixed and even contradictory heritage undoubtedly had much to do with his conversion, and I shall argue that a strain of Puritan radicalism runs through the first half of his career and can still be discerned beneath the Tory propaganda of *Absalom and Achitophel*. The "radical Protestantism" that Trevor-Roper paradoxically explains was embodied in Dryden's grandfather Erasmus Dryden, who "In bonds retain'd his Birthright Liberty, / And sham'd Oppression, till it set him free." Dryden himself abstained from active partisanship as long as he could while witnessing the collapse of three regimes and the ascendancy of a fourth. Yet as the public elegist of Henry Hastings and Oliver Cromwell, as the chronicler of the Restoration and the *mirabilis annus*, and as the leading playwright during the first half of Charles's reign, he could not avoid political sentiments in his writings.[5]

And he did not wish to. On the contrary, he exploited the public and rhetorical side of his profession. Throughout most of his career, political authority was hobbled by the constitutional struggle, and the nation was held together mainly by its fear of renewed civil war. The lack of a consensus such as that which began to form after 1688 meant that any public utterance might be hazardous to the civic peace. A professional writer who kept silent about his private life, however, managed thereby to safeguard neither his contemporary reputation nor his posthumous fame, as Dryden found and as the critical heritage has borne out. His latest biographer tartly observes that "Dryden has proved to be all too easy a victim for those who think that they know what integrity must look like, and whose suave derision costs them nothing. Both speech and silence cost Dryden dear."[6]

Scholars have usually accounted for the tensions in Dryden's public role by outlining his notoriously reserved personality against a background of political and cultural instability. The outline was originally sketched by Sir Walter Scott, the first critic who saw fit to assert the integrity of "Dryden's moral powers" while relating them to his public career. "As he wrote from necessity," Scott explained, Dryden "was obliged to pay a certain deference to the public opinion." In the advertisement of his monumental edition of the poet, Scott acknowledged Johnson's criticism and Edmond Malone's biographical researches, while making room for his own ambitious project: "Something seemed to remain for him who should consider these literary productions in their succession, as actuated by, and operating upon, the taste of an age, where they had so predominant influence; and who might, at the same time, connect the life of Dryden with the history of his publications, without losing sight of the fate and character of the individual."[7]

Scott's very readable introductory volume is the first literary history of Dryden's era, and its hero figures as the legislator of Restoration culture. T. B. Macaulay, covering part of the same ground four decades later, would have none of this. The grand Whig historian denied any keeping to Dryden's character: "Self-respect and a fine sense of the becoming were not to be expected from one who had led a life of mendicancy and adulation. Finding that if he continued to call himself a Protestant his services would be overlooked, he declared himself a Papist." W. D. Christie endorsed this stinging indictment of Dryden's motives in the memoir he prefixed to the Globe volume (1870) that became the standard edition of the poet for generations.[8]

His integrity impugned, Dryden fell from the ranks of serious poets. Critics who upheld his craftsmanship, like Mark Van Doren and T. S. Eliot, merely wrote large the Victorians' contempt for his "moral powers." During the first third of the twentieth century, no effort was made to vindicate Dryden's moral integrity until Louis Bredvold, in the most original study of its kind since Scott's, examined afresh Dryden's intellectual milieu. Having shown that Dryden received only half of his pension during the crisis of 1677–84, Bredvold tried to scout once and for all the notion that Dryden turned to politics out of mercenary considerations: "The time has come when it is possible to reconsider the question of Dryden's character, both intellectual and moral, with a more open and receptive mind." Bredvold's thesis is that Dryden's "philosophical skepticism" and inherent distrust of reason drove him "toward conservatism and authority in religion, and ultimately to the Catholic Church, just as his distrust of the populace was one reason for his increasing conservatism and Toryism in politics."[9]

By taking Dryden's conversion seriously and seeking to locate his deliberations in a context of Renaissance Pyrrhonism and Catholic apologetics, Bredvold restored much of the poet's intellectual character, missing from criticism since Johnson and Scott. Dryden was more responsive to history than to political ideology, according to Bredvold, and saw that the crisis of 1678–81 threatened "the stability and honor of the nation"; for the sake of the common quiet he was ready to invoke pragmatically an absolutist doctrine like *jus divinum*. What his detractors called opportunism becomes, on this reading of Dryden's motives, a historic occasion that awakened the genius of the greatest Tory apologist. Not his interest or ambition called forth *Absalom and Achitophel*, but the poet's resurgent zeal for "his national traditions of freedom." Bredvold acknowledged the paradox in this reading of Dryden as a Burkean Whig concerned for the Englishman's ancient, constitutional liberties: "There was in Dryden something even of the spirit of that Revolution [of 1688] which he never could bring himself to accept." This is a shrewd insight into the problem of Dryden's relation to republicanism. Bredvold pursued the question no further, however, concluding instead with a general formulation: "The perpetual problem of politics is to preserve both the freedom of the individual and the continuity of the national traditions." At the time Bredvold wrote, Keith Feiling's influential history of the Tory party had recently defined an unbroken tradition of Anglicanism and Royalism to which an individual like Dryden could be assimilated as readily as could Eliot. Feiling's book did more than Eliot's criticism to break the monopoly that Whig history, with its saga of the Glorious Revolution and constitutional monarchy, had long enjoyed over the rhetoric of freedom.[10]

Bredvold described his book as *geistesgeschichte*, a history of ideas, and its final chapter on Dryden's politics is still echoed by scholars who challenge its other arguments. To Bredvold, who wrote in the exhilaration of a recuperated Toryism, Dryden appeared to have discovered himself as a public poet by articulating the crisis of his time. His Toryism could be equated with the zeitgeist. During the middle third of the century, between Bredvold's work and the publication of the first volumes in the California edition, the equation of Dryden with his times fell apart. As the details of his long career came into focus, it became harder to think of him as a latent conservative who suddenly discovered his true calling in 1681. Hugh Macdonald's bibliography and the biographical researches of James Osborn and Charles Ward all cleared away numerous misconceptions about Dryden the man. The figure of the public writer was replaced by a distinctly more individual personality.[11]

A kind of division of labor between critics and literary historians led to the disintegration of the portrait that Bredvold had left of Dryden in his milieu. The formalist critics of the postwar era brushed aside the parochial circumstances and the indeterminacy of public affairs from which Dryden's poetry emerges. They derived from *the poetry itself* its shaping structure.

They cast literary history in discrete periods, suppressing its dynamic relation to the present. These stereotypical periods still survive, preserving vestiges of the political isolationism and diminished historical awareness that characterized much New Criticism at midcentury. The truth is that once the Toryism rediscovered by Feiling and Bredvold and Eliot had lost its historical novelty, Dryden's expansively intellectual poems began to look forbiddingly time-bound when compared, for example, with the brilliantly generalized polemics of a poet like William Blake.

The New Criticism clung to the axiom that genuine poetry springs from the private life, even when the poet is a Renaissance courtier. He may use dialogue and irony, but such poetry can always be supposed to be overheard, as John Stuart Mill put it, in opposition to rhetoric, which is spoken to be heard. This New Critical axiom is singularly inappropriate to Dryden, who constantly addressed his readers as if they were in a public forum. For Dryden's audience, finding the right standpoint meant knowing the facts conveyed to us by the California edition or in James Kinsley's Oxford edition of the poems. Reviewing the latter in 1959, a critic mused that Dryden inspires little enthusiasm "because he is preeminently a public poet, and public poetry disappeared with Byron, [and] today there is practically no occasional or political poetry; there is only private worry or semi-public rant which excuses itself by espousing more or less worthy causes."[12]

In its traditions of Dryden scholarship, our own century splits up as neatly as the author of the *Secular Masque* could have wished, dividing into three phases. Bredvold's work appeared in 1934; in 1967, K. G. Hamilton observed that "Dryden has thus far mainly escaped the attention of the 'new criticism,' and there have been no really sustained attempts to analyze the qualities that go to make up his poetry. . . . Alan Roper's *Dryden's Poetic Kingdoms*, and Bernard Schilling's *Dryden and the Conservative Myth*, both seem to draw their inspiration ultimately from an interest in the ideas and the thought rather than from the poetry itself." While preferring "close analysis of the poetry itself," Hamilton entered a caveat against New Critical methods. He wrote, "I do not believe that this kind of analysis, particularly when it is applied to poetry of an age other than our own, can be as autonomous as some exponents of the new criticism would like to make it." And he suggested "the need for a renewal of interest in the now generally outmoded concept of poetry as 'imitation,' as the soundest basis for an appreciation of the kind of poetry that Dryden excelled in writing."[13]

By 1967, the time for studying the poetry itself had indeed passed. Notwithstanding the fine appreciation of Dryden's craft in the books by Earl Miner and by Paul Ramsay shortly after Hamilton wrote, most scholarship in the closing third of the twentieth century seems to have focused on the content of the poet's ideas, or what one influential study calls "contexts of Dryden's thought." In this way, criticism has swung back to the approach taken by Scott and Bredvold, who tried to understand Dryden within his culture. Dryden's poems, with or without a preface, usually refer the reader to their public occasion. Having proved recalcitrant to New Critical analysis of its "autonomy," such highly contextualized poetry might be expected to withstand the subversion of this putative autonomy by deconstruction, whose guiding purpose is to uncover what has been omitted or suppressed by the poetry itself.[14]

The break with New Critical autonomy in the final third of the twentieth century obviously has not revived public poetry, and we may well ask why this is so. When Dryden's works are contextualized, their public side quickly stands out, but their political import is assessed quite variously. For Schilling, Dryden's Toryism is less problematic than it was for Bredvold, and he is able to analyze "conservative mythology" entirely in terms of "figurative language" or controlling metaphors. Miner pursues a different tack, examining the poet's attempts "to accommodate the personal with the public." "Most of his poetry," Miner writes, "is radically public and engaged, which is to say that it is personal in commitment rather than private in exploration." Miner's focus on Dryden's personal commitment, however, tends to divorce it from the genuinely public life to which Miner refers in his epigraph from Hannah Arendt. He says the poet of *Annus Mirabilis* gives us "the sense of man before an audience, freed from the accidentals of private life to assume a full personal character in his world that makes historical poetry, or poetry imbued with history possible. Dryden brings that collectively public and personal experience into poetry and makes it convincing, true." The trouble with this description is that "collectively public" experience is not the same as the historically specific experience that inspires an orator. A historical event, even when it affects the entire nation, still misses the universality of tragedy — the ultimate "collective" experience that fuses individual and public. Miner has this fusion in view when he discusses the epic or tragic elevation of *Annus Mirabilis* and *All for Love*. He relates public to private in a way that suggests public is built up from private life. That is, he does not make public experience historically antecedent to private, as Arendt does. The distinction, to which I will return, is important for understanding Dryden's public role.[15]

Miner, by stressing Dryden's historiographical bent, touches on a classic preoccupation of orators. Roper had anticipated Miner in his book, *Dryden's Poetic Kingdoms* (1965). Like the New Critics, Roper organizes his chapters by the several major analogies or "kingdoms" the poet invokes; unlike them, he is prepared to rethink the political context of the poetry and to weigh the contemporary import of its topical references. He calls attention to "the greater freedom of invention permitted [Dryden] by the nature of historical allusion than by other available analogies." Historical inventiveness enables Dryden to gloss events by specific historical correspondences, as in *The Duke of Guise* or in the parallels between 1641 and 1681. Roper observes that *Absalom and Achitophel* takes on the nature of a tertium quid between fact and fiction: "It reconciles fact with interpretation by elaborating fact in accordance with interpretation." This last remark is crucial for the present study. Roper assumes that Dryden's poetry rises to political and historical hermeneutics, the supreme ends of oratory.[16]

Despite Roper's historical originality, many critics continued to discuss the formal marks of Dryden's oratory, much the way earlier scholars had been content to refer Dryden's ideas to his zeitgeist without assaying their political force. L. C. Knights, never one of Dryden's admirers, complains that the political poems, despite their vigorous language, "have not the seminal power of the imagination in politics that can inform and nourish the thoughts of men in later ages." He bases this judgment upon a narrow conception of style as metaphor, tone, and "shading." Not surprisingly, he finds Dryden lacking the "resonance" of a Marvell. Knights admits to his audience (for the Clark Lectures of 1971) that he means to take the microscopic view of politics and to deal only in passing "with the political *content* of particular works and their relation to immediate issues of the day. What I most want you to think about is *the nature of political language, of ways of talking about politics* . . . in the context of our own present."[17]

Self-assured judgments like these began to seem incongruous by the 1970s, when the "context of our own present" had become a problem that the academies could no longer ignore. Something of the restless self-criticism or self-transcendence of the times informs Steven Zwicker's essay *Dryden's Political Poetry,* which is not about historical politics but about

Dryden's "rising and falling belief in the possibility of political redemption that parallels Dryden's changing religious attitudes." Locating Dryden in a seventeenth-century tradition of scriptural typology, Zwicker reads the poetry as "a metaphoric presentation of sacred history." The public poet who emerges from Zwicker's reading is a much more dramatic figure than the "occasional poet" presented by Saintsbury and Van Doren.[18]

A very different, highly integrated reading of Dryden, "the last English poet to be interested in history," is offered by William Myers, who discerns no "rising and falling belief" in Dryden's attitude to human institutions. He assumes rather that Dryden was from the start wed to authority wherever it should be found, and that he recognized it finally in the Catholic Church. This is of course Bredvold's thesis, and it is based moreover on a reading of Dryden's character that goes back at least to Johnson's *Life of Dryden*. Giving Dryden's skepticism a new currency, Myers interprets the poems as moments in an ongoing struggle with tradition, particularly the generic traditions that Dryden inherited from Elizabethan literature. He seeks to ground Dryden's public writing not in the zeitgeist but in the poet's *reflections upon* historical events. Here again, as in Roper's book, we approach Dryden's hermeneutic enterprise. Myers implies that the enterprise is not very successful, however. Dryden subordinates his ideals to historical fact because history, although inadequate to our desires, is providential. His attitude to history thus contrasts with the later, liberal attitude. He "insists that even immoral government can witness to an essentially divine order of things provided it is 'royal'; that is, providentially constituted by time." This intellectual ability to separate personal conviction from providential dispensation is the source, Myers holds, of Dryden's authority when he speaks as public poet.[19]

In a sense, Myers inverts Bredvold's earlier synthesis by stressing the conflict between poet and zeitgeist. His inversion points to the subsequent course of Dryden studies. By the 1970s, the imposing historical and philological achievement of Bredvold's and Ward's generations loomed like the work of a giant race before the flood. Both formalism and historicism, commonly opposed during the middle part of the century, came to be regarded as twin aspects of a scholarly consensus that had grown stale. Cultural change, politics, history—in a word, the generational revolution—had laid bare the unsuspected ideology of university faculties. Philologists immersed in history's diachronic ebb and flow were out of sync with the quicker and more superficial pulse of sociological change. In English studies particularly, established scholars were bewildered by the clamor over ideology and critical theory, which younger academics were not always above using as a shibboleth to rid themselves of much oppressive learning. At its worst, the generational revolution was contemptuous of living traditions and did not bother to distinguish them from blind reaction.

We can highlight the problem of freedom by drawing a momentary parallel between the crises of literary authority in the late seventeenth and late twentieth centuries. Our recently fashionable postmodernism is a reprise of the modernism to whose rise Dryden somewhat reluctantly contributed. Literature as an institution changed radically when, early in the modern era, it began to claim autonomy and asserted its freedom of imagination, making itself independent of its strong rival, scientific rationalism. The Kantian basis of this autonomy is complex but tolerably clear; what is obscure is the relation of literature to politics. For Kant, politics is essentially a prudential activity which he differentiates both from the determinism of science and from the freedom of the imagination. Where politics and literature combine forces, as they conspicuously do in historiography, the result carries the double imprint of prudence and imagination. Prudential action, as Aristotle before Kant observed, never achieves a definitive outcome—never brings about a situation in which prudence is finally superfluous. Political action leads always to more political action. For this reason, literature, with its everlasting indeterminacy, lends itself naturally to politics, the art of the possible.

If politics uses rhetoric to project a desirable future, historiography is no less dependent on prudential rhetoric. Historiography took its orthodox formulation from Leopold Ranke, who conceived it as a realistic narrative in contrast to the romances of Sir Walter Scott. For nearly a century, historiography downplayed its literary affiliations and flirted with ideals of scientific positivism. When positivism itself came under attack after World War II, the subjective, relativistic side of historiography was exposed as well. Like politics, historiography relies upon imagination and prudence in its effort to grasp *facta*, deeds. Philosophers of history had always taken for granted the political nature of historiography. It remained for Hayden White to demonstrate, in his *Metahistory* of 1973, that historiography, from its very origins, is intertwined with rhetoric. Public poetry resembles historiography in that it, too, combines history with rhetoric. What White calls the modern "crisis of historicism" was foreshadowed by the fate of the public poet in the eighteenth century. White's structuralist analysis of historiography amounts to an assault on traditional historicism and is part of the postmodern attack on the scientific rationalism born of the Enlightenment. This attack springs from the supposedly recent (but in fact originally Kantian) perception that modern rationalism, far from presenting us with an inevitable or a unique path to truth, represents an essentially political program. To institute rationalism as a method is therefore an act of *prudence:* when we as moderns acknowledge the preeminence of "reason," we adopt the rhetoric of the Enlightenment.[20]

The prudential and arbitrary nature of the Enlightenment and its rhetoric of reason would have been transparent to Dryden. He regularly exploits the same rhetoric, for instance in the opening lines of his poem "To Dr. Charleton":

> The longest Tyranny that ever sway'd,
> Was that wherein our Ancestors betray'd
> Their free-born *Reason* to the *Stagyrite,*
> And made his Torch their universal Light. . . .
> *Columbus* was the first that shook his Throne:
> And found a *Temp'rate* in a *Torrid* Zone.   (1:43)

Dryden implies that "Reason" was overshadowed by the Aristotelians' pretense of furnishing us with a "universal Light." The reader who is too quick to identify the enfranchised reason with the all-powerful arbiter of modern scientific investigation, however, will miss Dryden's real point: that our reason guarantees our freedom of inquiry within the limits of the *saeculum* but does not warrant the discovery of truths lying beyond those limits. Because reason is secular, its light cannot pretend to universality, whether it radiates from Aristotle or from modern science (which in Dryden's time was not accorded the absolute authority that has dazzled subsequent eras). Changing one pretended revelation for another would merely subject "free-born" individual reason to a novel but equally dogmatic methodology — for example, the logic of scientific uniformity or patterns of historical determinism. Dryden's free reason is *deliberative:* it implies a choice of alternatives. He declines to foreclose prudential action by dwelling on the prospect of theoretical certainty.

The late–twentieth century's postmodern attack on reason, then, cannot touch Dryden because he never gave his assent to the rationalistic program of the Enlightenment. Reason for Dryden was properly free only when exercised within limits found out by experience and verified by custom. Columbus discovered the fallacy in Aristotle's "Torrid Zone," but he would have been mad to look for new worlds in infinite space, as some enthusiasts did. Dryden valued liberation from settled errors of the imagination equally with liberation from dogmatic scholasticism. A "free-born Reason" that enlarged its scope only to tyrannize over the other faculties would disserve both its owner and society. Its freedom depended on its being integrated into the quest for knowledge, which continued to rely upon nonrational sources, notably experience and faith. In the same way, an integrated civilization depends on the coordination of its several arts. Our post-Cartesian stress on methodology makes us exaggerate the importance of one or another function in the community or of a single faculty in the individual.

Dryden's model for integrating both the human faculties and the arts was the traditional figure of Cicero's orator, from whom the public poet descends. Classical and Renaissance discussions of poetry always correlate it with the other arts, and the cinquecento critics, especially, harmonize the poet's role with all the offices of society. As the Enlightenment bestowed autonomy upon literature, however, and as Kantian aesthetics freed the imagination to pursue its own truth, poetry withdrew from the public realm, and ceremonial laureates retired to the academy. We no longer take seriously the social function of poetry, in the older, inclusive sense meaning all fiction. Ever since Kant, the most searching theoretical discussions of poetry have ignored its public function and have focused instead on its source in the imagination or on the laws of its organic unfolding: in sum, on its autonomy.

In the broad view I am taking of literary modernism, the twentieth century marks an extreme swing of the pendulum toward autonomy, and recent challenges to literature as an institution might seem to indicate a cyclical return to the pre-Enlightenment estimate of poetry. In that case, the postmodernism of the 1970s would be a liberation, not from the tyranny of Aristotelianism but from three centuries of modern rationalism. The historical parallel fails, though, because the new reformers of poetics conceive of politics in a fashion radically divergent from Renaissance humanists. Michael McKeon, for example, introduces his book on the context of *Annus Mirabilis* with a tightly argued theoretical chapter on "political poetry"—a phrase, he notes, that has become almost "a contradiction in terms." McKeon asks why literary criticism separates poetry and politics: "What are the broadest consequences of such a separation for the understanding of the nature and function of poetry? What might be the benefits of a literary criticism which perceives all poetic achievement as a complex function of political achievement, rather than as a negation or transcendence of it?"[21]

This "negation or transcendence" is the literary autonomy we have been reviewing. McKeon criticizes likewise the formalism in midcentury rhetorical criticism, noted above. If modern readers agree that "Dryden's poetry is in some manner peculiarly 'public' or 'occasional,' that it occurs, and therefore should be read, 'in context,'" why has so little attention been paid to "the perspectives of Dryden's contemporaries who are taken to constitute his audience"? McKeon concludes that critics interested chiefly in classical rhetoric have created or "objectified" an ideal audience answering to Dryden's own fiction of a public persona. Rather than asking why the audience proved resistant to persuasion, critics run through the formal repertory of satire, with its victim, scene, action, masks, ironies, and so forth. McKeon's sharpest quarrel is with critics who ignore the clash of ideologies inherent both in a rhetorical occasion and in their interpretation of the occasion. Public discourse occurs on two levels simultaneously: at a "primary" level of commonplace or "myth," such as the eschatology in *Annus Mirabilis;* and at a "secondary" level of "ideology," which calls into play "the interests of one social group against the interests of other social groups."[22]

The principle of McKeon's "dialectical criticism" is the reflexive, Hegelian principle on which Marx grounded his critical theory: by becoming aware of your prejudices—of your historical present, work of material production, or scholarly criticism—you transcend them and rejoin the larger movement of society, history, or Absolute Idea toward its self-realization. McKeon's analysis, however, denies this reflexivity to Dryden. The public poet is despoiled of his moral leadership and is made the mouthpiece of a "historical event" that in turn is dissolved into a clamor of competing ideologies. His oratorical prudence is of no account and must be dragooned into a dialectical contest in which deliberative, civic precepts are unlikely to prevail. The truth is that McKeon's analysis of Dryden's public poetry is dialectical rather than rhetorical. His conception of a poem's "original rhetorical capacity" sets up a polar opposition between the poet and his audience. "Rhetorical analysis assumes at the outset the oppositional nature of the audience addressed, and attempts to discover the quality and the degree of this opposition to the poet's ideology," McKeon says. This definition of the rhetorical situation is nearer to Marxism or to medieval scholasticism than to Ciceronian humanism, which rather than polarize the elements of the community emphasizes its organic wholeness.[23]

The reaction against literary autonomy has so far not overtaken the best recent work on Dryden, which follows in the historical and mimetic tradition of Scott and Bredvold with occasional digressions into New Critical analysis. Two books in particular have added to our biographical knowledge of the poet: George McFadden's *Dryden: The Public Writer* and James Winn's *John Dryden and His World*. Both of these books reject the limits that Ward placed on his biography when he "excluded, in general, critical pronouncement upon Dryden's work." On the contrary, McFadden and Winn evaluate each poem, play, and prefatory address not only in the light of Dryden's private circumstances but also in view of his literary ambitions and his critical or generic consciousness. Insisting that Dryden kept his eye on his audience, they concentrate their attention on what he actually said and on its probable rhetorical effect. Their interchangeable focus, however, alternating between his private thought and his public figure, leaves us with a Dryden curiously lacking in historical self-consciousness: a public poet who seems imperfectly aware of his immediate oratorical role.[24]

Such reticence about Dryden's historical and political reflexivity is an inheritance from Bredvold, who dichotomized the poet's ideas and emotions in an effort to preserve his moral integrity. Dryden's "saturnine" personality remains a problem for his biographers, as it was for his contemporaries. What Renaissance philosophy would have called his melancholy frequently creates an impression of diffidence, if not sullenness; yet out of this impassive condition an agile wit explodes, fully conscious of its power. Ideas seem to spring from Dryden's brain wholly formed; we never see their gestation. "I am of opinion," he says, "that they cannot be good Poets who are not accustomed to argue well," while he confesses in the same essay that "my Conversation is slow and dull, my humour Saturnine and reserv'd: In short, I am none of those who endeavor to break Jests in Company, or make reparties" (9:12, 8). That is, Dryden was incapable of arguing extempore, but he could pen cogent arguments for an imaginary occasion. This characteristic discrepancy makes it very difficult, in any given instance, to know his real forum as well as to specify the precise arguments to which he is responding. As McKeon demonstrates, critics have quietly embraced Dryden's own construction of his audience; they inadvertently have been won over to his position and speak as "converts."[25]

The paradoxical result of espousing Dryden's political arguments in their finished form is that such partisan sympathy effectively walls the poet off from the reflexivity of historical politics, to which he looked for inspiration. The public poet loses his dynamic poise or active deliberation and seems to echo opinions already formed, particularly when they are Tory views. His distinctive insight into the moment and into his own role dies away. McFadden, especially, portrays a Dryden who formulated magisterial pronouncements on human society while shrinking in disgust from actual politics: snubbed by the court, Dryden retreated to his dream of writing a great Stuart epic.

McFadden makes better use than anybody else has done of the poet's dedications. His comments on Dryden's self-revelation in the epistle to Mulgrave (prefixed to *Aureng-Zebe*) show the virtues and deficiencies of his approach: "When one thinks of it, it was amazing that he should have spread in public print the account of his proposing an epic to Charles and James, and it was ironic that he should also have included the expression of his personal need for intimacy and ease and affection, to say nothing of his need for money. Dryden, having become the object of a public, which to a great extent he had helped to create, had for some time been offering his inner self to that public in his prefatory essays. The development seems to have been unconscious." Naked self-disclosure by a public poet would indeed be amazing. McFadden is dismayed at the spectacle of an "unconscious" Dryden giving "expression" to his "need for intimacy" and all this in public, *coram populo*. Because McFadden's notion of Dryden's public is so indefinite, one cannot tell what connection to make, if any, between Dryden's "inner self" and the "public [that] he had helped to create." McFadden compares Dryden with Montaigne because he finds in both writers "the same sense, not so much of addressing a single and therefore ephemeral audience, but rather of speaking to humanity at large."[26]

Speaking to humanity at large must surely be fatal, however, to the orator who aims at persuading a specific audience. The meditation on retiring to private life that Dryden shares with Mulgrave continues an epistolary tradition reaching back through Abraham Cowley, whom Dryden quotes, to Horace and Cicero. The fact that the meditation is generic does not negate the personal expression in Dryden's epistle, but it does block our view of Dryden's unconscious motives. He is abundantly conscious of the liberty he takes with the epistolary mask. He finds himself reflected in the epistle, and this self-reflected speaker has to be distinguished from any biographical Dryden whose unconscious we seek to fathom. We cannot do that without first explaining the reflexive persona thus created. When he speaks as public poet, Dryden's reflexivity does not arise from his unconscious, it is produced entirely by his conscious response to politics.

Winn's outstanding biography pays attention to Dryden's reflexive persona, but, like McFadden's book, it largely ignores the political source of Dryden's reflexivity. Winn's narrative oscillates between Dryden's political hopes and his disappointment by events, without bringing the alternate phases of Dryden's experience into consistently political alignment. McFadden had repeated the charge that Dryden is "the only great poet who never succeeded in creating a 'world.'" Whether or not Winn intends his title as a rejoinder, his book goes far toward refuting the charge. The spacious world that Winn spreads before us, however, excludes an important element: the historical actuality of political conflict, in which McKeon locates his dialectic of history and which I have identified as political reflexivity. For instance, instead of analyzing *Aureng-Zebe*'s dynastic issues politically and historically, Winn follows McFadden in treating the play as domestic allegory. Similarly, Winn interprets *Absalom and Achitophel* on the basis of a parallel he draws between King Charles and Dryden. For both critics, the king and his brother James are essentially father figures, not heads of state. From a political standpoint, this Freudian conception merely psychologizes the patriarchalism of Robert Filmer.[27]

Although it seems to promise novel insights into Dryden's political opinions, a structuralist approach based on psychology inevitably takes on board conventional notions of the Restoration zeitgeist. Notwithstanding the pharisaism of our politically correct and voluble academies, metaphor is not effectual politics: the figure of a patriarchal king always falls short of the historic reality. Up to a point, Dryden certainly responded to political metaphors. But his rhetorical flourishes had to withstand new and vigorous ideas. Republicanism emasculated the patriarchal metaphor, just as John Locke castrated Filmer. Because Dryden's monarchical figures in his poems and plays are always flawed, McFadden thinks that "Dryden obviously had some block that prevented him from creating a true hero-king." McFadden and Winn scan Dryden's psyche to find the epicenter of this widespread flaw, ignoring the dialectic content of his political reflections. They assume that his world is a structure of necessary or else of voluntary relationships, not a complex of political ideas. For the latter they substitute sexual and familial metaphors. Even the energetically "Hobbesian" ideas of *The Conquest of Granada* become an enervated "ideology" teased from "the psychological reality of sexual desire." Winn grants that this masterpiece "is indeed 'full of ideas,' but part of its greatness lies in Dryden's dramatization of the limits of ideology. . . . What finally sets *The Conquest of Granada* apart from Dryden's earlier plays is his success in integrating materials drawn from political philosophy, prose romance, and epic poetry into a coherent dramatic whole."[28]

The last sentence suggests what Winn and McFadden prize most in Dryden's art. Just as he worked literary materials into a coherent whole, they claim, so Dryden overcame personal crises and political conflicts by transforming these experiences into great literature. This approach to literary value rests upon the assumption McKeon criticizes: the notion that literature transcends politics. McFadden and Winn do not consider that by making the autonomy of literature a refuge from politics, they are following the path marked out by Bayes in *The Rehearsal*. That path leads inward to the solipsism of metaphor, not to the politically explicit reflexivity of the public writer.

Whatever their estimate of Dryden's politics, critics can no longer ignore the public meaning of his writing. He was the first English poet after Shakespeare to reflect widely upon his own culture and to bring home to his audience the meaning of their historical experience. Dryden's latest biographer, Paul Hammond, deprecates the search for Dryden's private life in his works. "Commentators," he remarks, "have inadequately imagined the precariousness of public life and public speech in the late seventeenth century, and neglected to consider that in any age there is no secure and privileged position outside the structures of language where a man's private self may reside. . . . We can have no access to a secret or even stable self; there are only texts, and the interpretations which we make of them." Hammond pays close attention to Dryden's own "struggle for hermeneutic control, for authority over the interpretation of politics and religion." For Dryden, hermeneutic control made no sense unless it was a public achievement. The public poet's struggle was not for aesthetic autonomy, but for civic freedom and historical integrity.[29]

Praise and Deliberation
under the Republic

Critics have long set forth the contradictory opinion that Dryden gained his status of public poet through the aesthetic freedom of his poetry. Until recently, they hailed Dryden's ability to overcome the constraints of parties or of the times by raising his subjects to enduring art. Since at least the 1970s, scholars have noticed an alloy of satire in this artifact, and some have argued that aesthetic transcendence means the loss of political meaning. Before reading Dryden's earliest poem, I propose to look at the public poet as an orator unaffected by the modern prejudice in favor of aesthetic autonomy—the public poet, that is, whose work antedates our Kantian separation of art from politics. Where Michael McKeon wants to replace modern aesthetic canons with a dialectical criticism generated by the clash of ideologies, I shall focus on the orator's prudence, which bridges the gap between political action and rhetoric. The disparity between them is undoubtedly pre-ideological, but that does not make it less historical: the poet who adopts a civic pose has always needed the prudence of the classical orator.[1]

RHETORIC AND THE *KAIROS*

The public poet answers to Cato's definition of the orator as *vir bonus, peritus dicendi,* "a good man skilled at speaking." With the decline of public poetry since the Renaissance, rhetorical analysis has regularly disjoined the two elements in Cato's description and has produced contrasting stereotypes opposing the glib sophist to the honest man of few words. Considered as formal strategies, either rhetorical stance has its use. The pose of the good man is known as the ethical argument because it relies on the speaker's character (*ēthos*). In a judicial situation, where proof depends upon an appeal to reason (Aristotle's *logos*), ethical argument is not particularly effective. But in the popular or public forum, the appeal to ethos and the appeal to *pathos*—the other two kinds of proof distinguished by Aristotle—both have their place.[2]

Criticism of Dryden's rhetoric in his plays as well as his poetry has concentrated overwhelmingly on his ethical argument—whether we understand by ethos the poet's own character, the character of his audience, or that of his panegyric subject or even of his dramatis personae, whose decorum he maintains. Critics have usually ignored other kinds of persuasion unless Dryden calls attention to the occasion, as he does in the preface to *Religio Laici:* "A Man is to be cheated into Passion, but to be reason'd into Truth" (2:109). Even here, however, critics overlook the task laid on the reader's prudence because they assume that the alternative to irrational (ethical or emotional) appeal is logical demonstration.

This bare dichotomy of reason and passion comes from disjoining Cato's formula. The "good man" is contrasted with the skilled speaker who plays upon our irrational *pathos*. The dichotomous scheme falsifies the tripartite hierarchy of reason, emotion (appetite), and will in a Renaissance poet like Milton:

> Understanding rul'd not, and the Will
> Heard not her lore, both in subjection now
> To sensual Appetite, who from beneath
> Usurping over sovran Reason claim'd
> Superior sway.   (*Paradise Lost*, 10.1127–31)

Lapsed from their happy state into time and passion, "our grand parents" struggle unsuccessfully to bring their Will back under Reason's "sovran" direction. Milton's hierarchical scheme focuses attention upon our will, which always seeks its own good while being subject to the passions and to reason. In the same way, the will is the chief object of the orator and public poet, whose rhetorical efforts are bent on persuading the audience to choose a specific form of action. The true sign of a prudential choice is neither passion nor reason, but deliberation.

Cato's succinct definition—if we resist breaking up its elements to suit a post-Renaissance dichotomy of the faculties—yields the essential meaning of the prudential poet's role. The skilled speaker is also a good man. And *good* here does not mean morally exemplary, as it does when disjoined from speaking. In a public forum, the audience of the good speaker ordinarily does not separate his character from his style. He is good in that he articulates the common good. This kind of rhetoric Aristotle calls deliberative (*symbouleutikon*) because it consults the common interest and debates the means to that end. It draws upon both reason (required for *dikanikon*, or judicial rhetoric) and imagination (needed for *epideiktikon*, or encomium). The deliberative orator has to present a rational, sober account of actual conditions as well as provide an appealing vision of the future. More than this: he must persuade the audience that his paramount interest is their good.

Phronēsis (prudence)—the gift of finding out and expediting the common good—is obviously a political virtue. Kant, we recall, held prudence to be the characteristic virtue of politics. It is a virtue distinct from both science and art. Political activity does not follow the rational laws of science, and it does not enjoy the imaginative freedom of art. In most civic crises the law, whether positive or moral, is not definitive. That this indeterminacy should frustrate our patience indicates how deeply the illusion of rational uniformity and objectivity has infected the modern soul. When politics shatters that illusion, we seem to be left to the mercy of chance, or we sink into moral relativity. Either way, we give up our freedom, which was in jeopardy from the moment we made an idol of reason.

Prudence and the prudent orator reaffirm our political freedom. For Aristotle and Cicero (or for Machiavelli and Milton) prudence, practical wisdom, is rooted in praxis. Praxis and theory are not antithetical, as are the human faculties in Kant's schema. Kant categorically opposes pure reason to practical reason and then subordinates the first to the absolute command of the second. The orator does not exalt any single faculty, and he does not pretend that his art, disjoined from praxis and theory, can lead us to the desired goal. *Theoria, praxis,* and *poiēsis* (or *technē*) are alternate aspects of our experience, and our political freedom depends on their coordination, not the autonomy of any one of them.

The orator can exercise his prudence only in a civic or political forum. For that reason, it is a distortion of his role to abstract the public poet from the historical conditions of his deliberation and to impose an aesthetic resolution on his work. Genuine deliberation is an act of weighing alternatives. Given a politically dynamic and rationally indeterminable set of circumstances, no authority or rule can help. Deliberation begins where uniform calculation leaves off, but it stops short of mere heuristics. Its guide is neither rule nor chance, but *phronēsis*.

Rhetorical deliberation interprets the past in the light of present needs, either to discover the best course of action or to form a probable expectation of the future. It is obviously allied to historiography in some of the ways described by metahistorians like White (see Introduction). In a public poem such as *Absalom and Achitophel*, we are particularly reminded of that alliance and of the close analogy between rhetorical deliberation and historical hermeneutics, an analogy to which I will return.

Because the public poet deliberates upon courses of action, his imagination is governed by prudence. At first glance, certain Renaissance doctrines of "wit" (*ingenium*, imagination) resemble the modern theory of an autonomous imagination. Sir Philip Sidney, for instance, describes the poet "freely ranging only within the zodiac of his own wit"; and Thomas Hobbes says that when the imagination "seemeth to fly from one *Indies* to the other, and from Heaven to Earth, and to penetrate into the hardest matter and obscurest places, into the future and into her self, and all this in a point of time, the voyage is not very great, her self being all she seeks." Neither writer envisages the unlimited freedom claimed for the imagination in post-Kantian poetics, however. The basis of modern autonomy is spontaneity, and the imagination, especially, is grounded in nothing higher than itself. This is another way of saying that the imagination's autonomy is political in the way that Kantian reason is essentially political: both are self-grounding, or willed. For Sidney and Hobbes, by contrast, the imagination, like the other human faculties, is limited by natural laws. Neither writer supports the inference to which the modern doctrine of artistic autonomy gives rise—the suggestion that our imagination is the guarantee of our freedom.[3]

The Enlightenment belief in spontaneity sharply differentiates the modern era from the Renaissance. The autonomy both of the reason and of the imagination is based on spontaneous self-assertion. Those faculties are literally *autonomous:* they legislate for themselves. As one historian of the Enlightenment writes, "An extreme pressure toward self-assertion gave rise to the idea of the epoch as a self-foundation. . . . The legitimacy of an epoch is supposed to consist in its discontinuity in relation to its prehistory."[4]

For Hobbes or Dryden, to say nothing of Sidney or Shakespeare or Milton, a legitimacy based on historical discontinuity and spontaneous self-assertion would be nonsense. Each national revolution, from the Tudor Reformation to the establishing of the Protectorate and from the Restoration to the Revolution of 1688, went forward on the plausible pretext of restoring an institution to its original form and authority, whether that institution was the primitive church or England's Ancient Constitution. The most radical of these innovations, the republican Rebellion which abolished monarchy and set up a Commonwealth, was justified by Milton on the grounds that the king had violated an original contract with the sovereign people limiting his "tenure" as their ruler. None but fanatics or enthusiasts asserted a spontaneous authority, and even fanaticism claimed to be divinely inspired, unlike the modern, purely autonomous imagination.

The fact that *prudence* can now be opposed to spontaneity indicates how much of the word's original meaning has been lost. If spontaneity and neglect of historical continuity prompt our most creative actions, it follows that whatever impedes them is timid or reactionary, and caution and prudence must be rooted in blind conservatism. In that case, deliberation implies paralysis rather than freedom. Effective political action, as Hegel said of popular philosophy, begins like a shot from a pistol. Public councils no doubt can be swayed by prudential rhetoric, but nowadays skillful speakers are seldom commended for their prudence. Their success is attributed to their vision, rather, or to their command of the facts, or their appeal to partisan interests and common prejudice. A modern speaker would find no advantage in reminding a deliberative body of its freedom as distinct from its self-interest, as Milton does when he addresses parliament at the opening of *Areopagitica:* "Be assured, Lords and Commons, there can no greater testimony [of your excellence] appear than when your prudent spirit acknowledges and obeys the voice of reason . . . and renders ye as willing to repeal any act of your own setting forth as any set forth by your predecessors." Today, this style of public address would cry out for decoding in terms of one group interest or another. Free debate is automatically presumed to be a mask for power, which cynically awaits the moment to cut off all deliberation.

I am not arguing that a citizen of the Commonwealth like Milton or a subject of the crown like Dryden enjoyed greater political liberty than someone living in a modern democracy. My point is that public writing was freer simply because it was authentically public. We have since made it into a mirror of our private anxieties that reminds us of the mortality we share with our leaders. "We must not," says Aristotle, "follow those who advise us, being men, to think [*phronein*] of human things, and, being mortal, of mortal things, but must, so far as we can, make ourselves immortal, and strain every nerve to live in accordance with the best thing in us." Hannah Arendt remarks of this passage that Aristotle intends the *polis* as the proper theater of our immortal striving. The *polis* is the space protected "against the futility of individual life," as the *res publica* is for Rome and for Renaissance humanists. She notes how much of this attitude has been lost already by the time of Adam Smith, who mentions "that unprosperous race of men commonly called men of letters [for whom] public admiration . . . makes almost the whole" of their reward. "The point," Arendt concludes, "is not that there is a lack of public admiration for poetry and philosophy in the modern world, but that such admiration does not constitute a space in which things are saved from destruction by time." [5]

The classical orator's prudence led his audience to ponder (*phronein*) the highest good, beyond the horizon of the immediate present: the immortality of city or nation. The modern alternative to civic prudence is the privacy of the individual life, which is liable to the futility Arendt mentions. Spontaneity uses fantasy to relieve this futility. It offers a momentary escape from time and history but not the enduring hope of immortality among our earthly community. Spontaneity has its own rhetoric, and in fact the kind of oratory that survived longest into the modern era was not prudential and deliberative, but epideictic. Epideictic, or encomiastic, oratory is closest to modern poetic canons of spontaneity and linguistic free play, and it remains the most accessible part of the mock-orations in *Mac Flecknoe* and *The Rape of the Lock*. Scholars who have dwelt on Dryden's formal rhetorical practice have not always respected the distinction between public deliberation and public praise. We can outline more definitely the poet's civic or public role by discriminating the prudential element in his panegyrics.

Deliberation always points beyond the rhetorical occasion to a historical moment in the nation's life. Deliberative oratory can express this moment because it imports an immediacy and sense of crisis missing from an epideictic exercise. Deliberative urgency plunges us into the flux of history, whereas encomium merely puts us in the actual or memorial presence of its subject. Deliberative rhetoric is *occasional* in a different sense from epideictic. For the latter, decorum is everything. Its nature or life is in the ideal. By contrast, a truly deliberative occasion cannot be brought under the rule of decorum without losing what makes it unique: its *kairos*, or special historical instant. *Kairos* is a time of opportunity and crisis both. It represents that awkward individuality in events which decorum tries to neutralize or to control through seemly generality.[6]

When poet and orator address the moment of *kairos*, their emphasis on contingency serves to distinguish the active hero from the decorously inert subject of praise. *Kairos* is not imposed unexpectedly on passive humanity, like chance. In order to happen, *kairos* has to be recognized and grasped: someone must apprehend the crisis as opportunity. Out of this nettle, danger, we pluck this flower, safety. As one theorist of historiography has put it, "The occurrence of *kairos* times is essentially related to historical decision and action, to history 'in the making.' " In this moment of deliberation, the prudent orator can show the way to heroic action. Until the hero appears on the scene, the orator may act as the historiographer or interpreter of events; but his rhetorical hermeneutics should not be confused with the real historical order of happenings that he is interpreting. *Kairos responds* to the hero and to the prophet whereas it merely *inspires* the public poet or historiographer.[7]

The public poet of *An Horatian Ode upon Cromwell's Return from Ireland* depends implicitly on the distinction between hermeneutics and action. At the end of his poem, Andrew Marvell assumes the role of prudential orator addressing the heroic Cromwell:

> But thou the Wars and Fortunes Son
> March indefatigably on,
> > And for the last effect
> > Still keep thy Sword erect:
> Besides the force it has to fright
> The Spirits of the shady Night,
> > The same *Arts* that did *gain*
> > A *Pow'r* must it *maintain*.

When Dryden wrote his *Heroique Stanzas* (see chapter 2), his most important Interregnum models were the Cromwell poems of Marvell. Marvell first taught Dryden to respect Cromwell's providential role. Dryden's *Heroique Stanzas* borrow their prosody from Sir William Davenant and their note of Virgilian epic from Edmund Waller, but neither of these royalist authors hints at Marvell's conception of an active, messianic Cromwell. Waller indeed tells Cromwell he was like the shepherd David in his private life, in which, though "Born to command, your princely virtues slept." Waller passes over his hero's providential tribulations, however, to present the fortunate King of Israel, whom he likens to an equally blessed Joseph receiving his full measure of homage from contrite brethren. "We'll bays and olive bring," Waller concludes, "To crown your head; while you in triumph ride / O'er vanquished nations, and the sea beside; / While all your neighbour-princes unto you, / Like Joseph's sheaves, pay reverence, and bow." Such cavalier triumph precludes serious deliberation. For that, Dryden had to turn to the politically more complex *Horatian Ode*.[8]

Douglas Bush called Marvell's ode "the only English poem, except some of Milton's sonnets, in which the tone of Horace's heroic odes is recaptured with original strength." Marvell's severe Roman decorum presents Cromwell as a warrior chief, or *dux bellorum*, whose ongoing conquests will strengthen the young Commonwealth. Written presumably between Cromwell's return from Ireland in May of 1650 and his entering Scotland in late July, the *Horatian Ode*, however impenetrable its ironies, is clearly a deliberation about whether or not to invade the north. At year's end, after God's "mighty and strange appearance" at Dunbar had confirmed England's cause, Cromwell's supporters had no difficulty justifying the action. Writing in the early summer, however, Marvell could offer no political argument besides that of expedience ("The same Arts that did gain / A Pow'r must it maintain") along with the aggressive emblem of prudence that closes his poem: Cromwell with his sword.[9]

An Horatian Ode upon Cromwell's Return from Ireland has generated considerable disagreement among those who seek a consistent political theory beneath its celebrated irony. Amidst all the debate over Marvell's notorious allusiveness—a debate I shall pass by, reserving my discussion of Marvell's hermeneutics for another Cromwell poem—the large political ideas in the poem have been trivialized as literary commonplaces. In particular, the overt republicanism of the *Horatian Ode* and its hero's antithetical career have been compared with Lucan's epic of a brutal Caesar destroying a slightly less objectionable Pompey on his furious path to the crown. With that general literary parallel in mind, the reader will detect almost a sneer in the lines referring to the "asham'd" Irish whom Cromwell subdued in less than a year:

> They can affirm his Praises best,
> And have, though overcome, confest
> How good he is, how just,

> And fit for highest Trust:
> Nor yet grown stiffer with Command,
> But still in the *Republick*'s hand.   (77–82)

By the same token, the thoroughly Machiavellian remarks (37–40) on state prudence — "Though Justice against Fate complain, / And plead the antient Rights in vain: / But those do hold or break / As Men are strong or weak" — have been deflated by setting beside them the scornful lines on the republican poet Tom May, who published a continuation of the *Pharsalia* in Latin and English. May is addressed by the formidable shade of Ben Jonson, who bids him "Go seek the novice Statesmen, and obtrude / On them some Romane cast similitude, / Tell them of Liberty, the Stories fine, / Until you all grow Consuls in your wine." Jonson's ghost disparages May by comparison with a true public poet who would courageously maintain the "antient Rights" Marvell had named in the *Horatian Ode:*

> He, when the wheel of Empire whirleth back,
> And though the World's disjointed Axel crack,
> Sings still of ancient Rights and better Times,
> Seeks wretched good, arraigns successful Crimes.[10]

The aspect of Marvell's political theory that I wish to emphasize is to be sought not among these literary allusions, however, but in his reflexive concept of himself as public poet. Politics implies reflexivity, which is merely to say that political thought differs from other kinds of theory in that the act of thinking becomes part of the political situation contemplated. A political thinker like Arendt always places herself in her conceptual polity. To overlook oneself is to lapse from politics into utopia, like old Gonzalo in *The Tempest* (II, i), who declares that if he were king of his ideal commonwealth, he would admit no sovereignty. The latter end of his commonwealth forgets the beginning. Critics too often discuss the political views in Marvell's poetry, as in Dryden's, without regard to the poet's reflexivity, which is an indefeasible attribute of the public writer. In Marvell's poem, the poet's reflexivity illuminates the allusions by raising them from literary footnotes to a politically dynamic context. His peculiarly deliberative process is seen in the poem's famous opening:

> The forward Youth that would appear
> Must now forsake his *Muses* dear,

> Nor in the Shadows sing
> His Numbers languishing.
> 'Tis time to leave the Books in dust,
> And oyl th'unused Armours rust:
> Removing from the Wall
> The Corslet of the Hall.
> So restless *Cromwell* could not cease
> In the inglorious Arts of Peace.

Critics remark on the one hand that Marvell associates himself with Cromwell, since either man gives up his privacy to engage in political action or in public poetry; on the other hand, they note Marvell's familiarity with Lucan (in May's version). The reflexivity is much more brilliant, though, if the passage from the original *Pharsalia* (1.225f.) is used to interpret the reluctance that the poet projects. Caesar crossed the Rubicon by night and seized the first town, Rimini, whose young men awoke and "snatched down the arms that hung beside the household gods," arms corroded by "the bite of black rust. But when they recognized the glitter of Roman eagles and standards and saw Caesar mounted in the midst of his army, they stood motionless with fear, terror seized their limbs," and they silently lamented their city's fate. As John Wallace observes, "The title of the poem suggests that Marvell is to be another Horace to Cromwell's Augustus, while the exordium could imply the poet's hostility towards his subject."[11]

Marvell's dilemma as public poet is like that of the youths of Rimini faced with their hard choice. If he remains silent or acquiesces in events by praising the dictator, he ceases to be a civic orator. If he criticizes Oliver Cromwell, he joins the detractors—Levellers, Fifth Monarchists, Tom May republicans—and incidentally spoils any chance of serving in his government. For Marvell, the figure of Cromwell is both exemplary and problematic. Cromwell resolved the earlier, parliamentary dilemma by taking arms against Caesar, and "Did thorough his own Side [party] / His fiery way divide." Marvell's deliberation imitates that of his hero, up to a point. He accommodates his political theory to the rhetorical demands of the moment:

> What may not then our *Isle* presume
> While Victory his Crest does plume;
> What may not others fear,
> If he thus crown each year!

> A *Caesar* he ere long to *Gaul*,
> To *Italy* an *Hannibal*,
> And to all States not free
> Shall *Clymacterick* be.   (97-104)

By this reading of history, Marvell acknowledges the "Clymacterick" that Cromwell's actions have wrought in his own political outlook, which is derived from the Puritan vision of England as God's Elect Nation. He can now view Cromwell as another Gustavus Adolphus leading a Protestant alliance against the pope. He predicts Cromwell's intimidation of France and the papacy, but not his wresting maritime dominion from the Dutch. Marvell apprehends the *kairos* the only way the orator can: reflexively. In affirming Cromwell's potentially messianic destiny, he simultaneously, as public poet, defines the historical moment. At this point, however, Marvell's Horatian irony and his ostensible impartiality and judiciousness mask from the reader his deliberation and choice. Prudence is choice, and the poet of the *Horatian Ode* leaves his audience in doubt as to whether he actually embraces "the Wars and Fortunes Son."

As a public poem, therefore, the *Horatian Ode* is imperfect. Later, in his *First Anniversary of the Government under O.C.*, Marvell would discharge his role of orator less introspectively. Deliberation about the common good always implies psychological extroversion. Deliberation is *political* self-transcendence—the reflexivity characterized above.[12]

To fill out the political context from which Dryden's poetry would emerge, we may look briefly at Milton's stance during the fateful year of Regicide and the birth of the republic. In his prose and his public sonnets, Milton consistently projects a distinct idea of the citizen having a role in the national epic. The citizen's self-awareness as *zōon politikon*—as a being created for political association—acquired a further, temporal dimension during the Civil Wars and Interregnum. Until then the doctrine of the Elect Nation, born of Tudor millennialism and the Marian persecution, throve mainly outside of politics. A godly prince—an English Constantine such as Henry VIII or Cromwell—would usher in the Christian Millennium. All retrograde forces opposing its advent were summed up in the name of Antichrist: the pope, Queen Mary, Arminian bishops, and, most recently, Presbyterians. When the Presbyterians were overthrown in consequence of the second Civil War in 1648, the army and its supporters in Parliament saw their path clear to godly rule. In the early months of 1649 they proceeded to execute the king, abolish monarchy and the House of Lords, and set up a Commonwealth.[13]

Milton tried to make his audience reflexively aware of their status as free citizens—a status as ancient as it was new. His initial tract justifying regicide, *The Tenure of Kings and Magistrates*, appeared within weeks of the king's execution and argued forcefully that the Presbyterians had already broken their oath as loyal subjects to the king by their original rebellion against him. According to Milton, the king's authority rests wholly upon "those two Oaths of Allegeance and Supremacy [over the church] observ'd *without equivocating, or any mental reservation.*" The king on his side undertakes to uphold the law as constituted and not command new things unlawful:

> Therefore when the people or any part of them shall rise against the King and his autority executing the Law in anything establish'd civil or Ecclesiastical, I doe not say it is rebellion, if the thing commanded though establish'd be unlawful, and that they sought first of all due means of redress (and no man is furder bound to Law) but I say it is an absolute renouncing both of Supremacy and Allegeance, which in one word is an actual and total deposing of the King, and the setting up of another supreme autority over them. And whether the Presbyterians have not don all this and much more, they will not put mee, I suppose, to reck'n up a seven years story fresh in the memory of all men.

In the *Horatian Ode* of sixteen months later, we saw Marvell's deliberations about the cause Milton espoused. Dryden was completing his nineteenth year in that summer of 1650. Even though he was elected to enter Trinity College as one of five King's Scholars from Westminster, he too would have been required to take the Oath of Engagement to "be true and faithful to the Commonwealth of England as it is now established, without a king."[14]

The republic that lasted eleven years between the beheading of King Charles I and the Restoration of his son to the throne was a unique moment of political opportunity, a *kairos* extraordinarily protracted. Although he published only two poems over its course, this period was the matrix of Dryden's public poetry. The obviously great works of philosophy and historiography from the second half of the century—leaving aside the ideas of scientists like Thomas Burnet or the subtle researches of a jurist like Sir Matthew Hale—all bear the impress of the midcentury crisis. The Earl of Clarendon's *History of the Rebellion* and Hobbes's *Behemoth* expressly examine the causes of the revolution, while James Harrington's *Oceana* is an original work of farseeing political genius. In many respects, the crowning meditation on the Interregnum experience is *Paradise Lost*. Every public writing by Marvell and Dryden is stamped with the consciousness of this decisive epoch, which never left their memory. Dryden's first poem was born with the republic in 1649. One does not expect political reflexivity from a juvenile effort, but Dryden's elegy on Hastings makes up for that deficiency by its energetic engagement with secular change. The youthful Dryden was not a republican in the sense that Milton or even Marvell was, but he fully shared their commitment to reforming the old order.

PURITAN RADICALISM

The problem of freedom always confronts the revolutionary, who is a political innovator. To be sure, *innovation,* in the early modern vocabulary of Dryden and Shakespeare, meant what we call revolution. The word normally bore the radical sense given it by one of the tribunes in *Coriolanus,* for example:

> *Sicinius.* Go call the people, in whose name myself
> Attach thee as a traitorous innovator,
> A foe to th' public weal.   (III, i, 173–75)

As the tribunes later complain, Coriolanus's innovation is fundamental and therefore subversive. His refusal to obey them means that he sets himself above the officers of the plebs, by that gesture flouting the Roman constitution:

> *Sicin.* We charge you, that you have contriv'd to take
> From Rome all season'd office, and to wind
> Yourself into a power tyrannical,
> For which you are a traitor to the people.   (III, iii, 63–66)

When they undertook "innovation," the "people" in turn became tyrannical. In the scene from *Sir Thomas More* ascribed to Shakespeare, the mob is urged to consider "how horrible a shape / Your innovation bears." " 'Tis a sin," More admonishes them, "which oft th' apostle did forewarn us of, urging obedience to authority, / And 'twere no error if I told you all you were in arms 'gainst God."[15]

The scriptural text to which More refers, Paul's epistle to the Romans, is a locus classicus of Renaissance political theory: "Let every soul be subject unto the higher powers. For there is no power but of God: the powers that be are ordained of God. Whosoever resisteth the power, resisteth the ordinance of God" (Rom. 13:1–2). Luther initially gave this text a narrowly Augustinian interpretation, restricting all subjects whoever they might be to spiritual, or passive, obedience (that is, disobedience) even if that meant suffering under a tyrant. Barely a century after Luther's death, *The Tenure of Kings and Magistrates* inverts the meaning of Paul's injunction. Milton glosses Romans 13 using a companion text from 1 Peter 2:13, "Submit yourselves to every ordinance of man for the Lord's sake": "*There* is no power but of God, saith *Paul*, Rom. 13. as much as to say, God put it into mans heart to find out that way at first for common peace and preservation, approving the exercise therof; els it contradicts *Peter* who calls the same autority an Ordinance of man. It must be also understood of lawfull and just power. . . . Therefore Saint *Paul* in the forecited Chapter tells us that such Magistrates he meanes, as are not a terror to the good but to the evil; such as beare not the sword in vaine [Rom. 13:4], but to punish offenders, and to encourage the good." In Milton's interpretation of the Pauline text, kings and magistrates, just like statutes, are "ordinance[s] of man" enacted for the good of the commonwealth. The power of God resides not in the king himself but in the commonwealth, and the king can claim authority from God only through the vox populi, whose servant he remains in common with the other magistrates.[16]

This reversal of the meanings read into Paul's text over the course of the sixteenth century reflects the political maturing of Protestant thought. Marian exiles elaborated the doctrine of lawful resistance found in Luther's writings after 1530, and, in France in the seventies and eighties, Huguenot scholars, taking as their cue the final paragraphs that Calvin added to his *Institutes* (1559), worked out a "constitutional" theory of resistance that owed much to the postscholastic, or Jesuit, conception of natural law. The Calvinistic magistrate's *duty* to resist became, in the thinking of Buchanan and his seventeenth-century successors from Johannes Althusius to John Locke, the celebrated *right* to resist. Consequently by 1600, as Quentin Skinner observes, the concept of "the State—its nature, its powers, its right to command obedience—had come to be regarded as the most important object of analysis in European political thought. Hobbes reflects this development when he declares in the Preface to his *Philosophical Rudiments*, first published as *De Cive* in 1642, that the aim of 'civil science' is 'to make a more curious search into the rights of states and duties of subjects.' "[17]

Inquiry into the ends of the political state by thinkers like Hobbes and Hugo Grotius had largely replaced the older discourse on the ends of providence. Whereas Calvinists derived the magistrates' collective duty to resist from their God-given responsibility to reform a community of reprobates, Hobbes and Harrington, followed by Locke and Anthony Ashley Cooper, first earl of Shaftesbury, grounded the individual subject's right to resist on the freedom enjoyed by each of us in our hypothetically "natural" condition antecedent to the state. In either case, resistance was not a right that one enjoyed passively. If reformation had seemed a divine imperative in the sixteenth century, it was now considered the end for which society was formed according to natural law. Properly understood, the right to resist awakened in everyone a certain responsibility for the commonwealth and encouraged them to pursue the common interest.

Accordingly, by the middle of the seventeenth century the Calvinistic goal of reformation had given way to specifically political innovation. The English revolutionaries knew they were venturing into uncharted waters when they deliberately altered the constitution. "We will cut off the King's head with the crown on it," Cromwell was reported to have said; and a week after the Regicide, members of the purged Parliament (later known as the Rump) resolved to abolish the monarchy. By October, they promulgated an Oath of Engagement based explicitly on the new constitution: all government officers (including Richard Busby, Dryden's schoolmaster at Westminster) had to promise to "be true and faithful to the Commonwealth of England as it is now established, without a king or House of Lords." Three months later this Engagement was extended to every adult male. The notoriety of the oath, even if it was not universally enforced, would induce any man over eighteen—such as the young John Dryden, hoping soon to stand for a fellowship at Cambridge—to reflect on his personal stake in the national innovation.[18]

Unlike Marvell, who was ten years his senior and traveled abroad during the first Civil War, evidently without returning to England until after 1646, the adolescent Dryden watched the whole scene unfold. From his ninth year until he entered Westminster, and thereafter during every vacation until he went to Cambridge, Dryden would have heard his father and the rest of the family discussing with his uncle, Sir John Dryden, and his cousin, Sir Gilbert

Pickering—the two M.P.s for the shire—the progress of the fighting as well as the maneuverings in Commons. If he was still living at home in June 1645, some immediate impressions of the war may have reached him from the decisive royalist defeat at Naseby, twenty miles from Titchmarsh. Exactly two years later in Westminster, he witnessed the extraordinary violence of Presbyterian mobs besieging Parliament; or, if he was still in Northamptonshire, he felt the nation's shock when army troops seized the king from Holdenby House near Northampton. Any of these events would have brought home to him some of the practical difficulties impeding a negotiated settlement and religious and constitutional reform—the chief ends sought by each of Charles's parliaments and by three generations of Dryden's family.

Dryden's earliest lessons in communal responsibility no doubt harped on the need for church reform. All doors from religion opened onto politics, however, so that by the time he left home for London he would have learned to identify the honor and welfare of his family with the "country" interest. The matrix of his political thought, therefore, was Presbyterianism, meaning that he knew the bishops were corrupt and that the king needed a push from his more godly subjects to help overcome the backsliding of courtiers and others willing to abuse king and constitution for their own interest. His biographers always acknowledge Dryden's Presbyterian heritage, but they generally treat it as an ungainly cocoon he quickly discarded—if not in 1649 or 1658, then certainly in 1660. A more grievous mistake is to confuse Presbyterianism—heir to the robust tradition of disciplined, Puritan radicalism under Elizabeth—with democratic or sectarian movements. Quite to the contrary, Dryden's native religion was aristocratic, which would nicely explain his disdain for sectarians and Levellers, and it was consistent with his subsequent royalism, since the "Presbyterian" party in the Long Parliament had never sought to depose the king, much less execute him. What the label of Presbyterian does not explain is Dryden's pronounced anticlericalism and his skeptical approach to religious doctrine.

The characteristic mark of religious Presbyterians, as of their enlightened Calvinist predecessors, was their zeal for a reformed church that would include the entire Christian community. This Erasmian vision was the original goal of Puritan radicalism, and it would remain the dream of Unitarians and other secular movements after the seventeenth century. In the very broadest sense, Dryden cleaved to this ideal by finally becoming a Roman Catholic. The one specifically Presbyterian tenet that runs through all his

writings is his lifelong deprecation of sectarianism. Although it has been dis-
counted as merely an aspect of his cosmopolitan distaste for parochial views,
Dryden's animosity toward the sects reveals a curious ambivalence: much
as he deplores their spiritual license, he refuses to join their Establishment
oppressors. His family remained radically Puritan or Calvinist in rejecting
the doctrinal uniformity imposed by Scots Presbyterians in 1645. That very
act of imposition turned Presbyterianism into a tyrannical sect resembling
its Laudian predecessor, as Milton remarked. The Westminster Assembly's
high-handed exclusiveness was a betrayal of Calvinistic comprehension in
that it forced a choice between denominations. The only alternatives to a
lame Erastian Presbytery were the several outlawed forms of dissent or, after
1660, the narrow legitimacy of Anglican conformity. Over time (see chapter 3), Dryden came to realize that the Church of Rome alone provided a
corporate form that resembled his inherited Puritan ideal of a visible, truly
catholic Church Militant: a universal communion of the saints which had
been the goal of his fathers.

In his early years, Dryden had before him an example of a Presbyterian
who lapsed into sectarian uniformity: Thomas Hill, the rector his father installed at Titchmarsh. After ten years at St. Mary Virgin, Hill left to join
the Assembly of Presbyterian divines convened at Westminster in 1643 for
the purpose of devising a national church to replace the episcopalian system that had just been dismantled "root and branch." In 1644, preaching
before Parliament under the watchful eye of the Scottish Baillie, Hill denounced the licentious books that had brought down God's punishment,
naming Roger Williams's *Bloody Tenent of Persecution* and Milton's *Doctrine
and Discipline of Divorce*. In 1645, when Cambridge was purged of its Fellows who refused to take the Covenant, Hill was made Master of Trinity,
where he continued "to haunt Dryden" when the young King's Scholar was
sent up five years later.[19]

The dialectic of sectarian exclusion and catholic comprehension animates Dryden's religious sentiments and doctrinal reflections right down to
his conversion, but it is not a sure clue to his earliest political views. Religious Presbyterianism, except in the case of a member of the Westminster
Assembly such as Hill, did not automatically lead to affiliation with the
"Presbyterian" party in Commons. The discrepancy, long unsuspected by
historians, was exposed years ago by J. H. Hexter in his essay "The Problem
of the Presbyterian Independents." Hexter's explanation, which has been

confirmed by Valerie Pearl and David Underdown, supposes that the Long
Parliament's impulse to reform came from a "godly party" of Puritan radicals (including, presumably, Sir John Dryden and Sir Gilbert Pickering).
Toward the end of 1644, at a crisis of command recalled years later in the
Heroique Stanzas, the godly party demanded a more vigorous pursuit of the
war and fell afoul of the Presbyterians—the moderate Anglican reformers
and the outright Erastian Presbyterians—who, now that the episcopacy had
been uprooted, wanted to make peace with the king.[20]

Fourteen years later Dryden remembered this crucial parting of ways
between "war" and "peace" parties, and his comment leaves no doubt that
his family stood with Cromwell and the political "Independents" who opposed the earls of Essex and Manchester, supreme generals of Parliament's
forces until the embarrassment of Newbury in October 1644:

> Our former Cheifs like sticklers of the Warre
> First sought t'inflame the Parties, then to poise;
> The quarrell lov'd, but did the cause abhorre,
> And did not strike to hurt but make a noise.
>
> Warre our consumption was their gainfull trade,
> We inward bled whilst they prolong'd our pain:
> He fought to end our fighting, and assaid
> To stanch the blood by breathing of the vein.
>
> (1:12; lines 41–48)

Dryden's last two lines of course do not refer to the Regicide but to Cromwell's getting rid of the dilatory earls ("sticklers" are umpires) by the Self-
Denying Ordinance, and to his subsequently refashioning their feudal levies
into a professional, New Model Army under Parliament's command. The
poet's enemies who later quoted these lines against him were nevertheless
right in detecting a certain hostility to the king. These stanzas record a key
moment in the political deliberations of Dryden's family—although the poet
himself was only thirteen. They found their "cause abhorre[d]" by Manchester, one of the Montagu family (with whose local branch, I suspect, the
Drydens were not on good terms); and they swung their support to Manchester's rival, Cromwell, who refused to compromise with the king over the
godly party's original goals of reform. Two years of grinding war, leading to
Marston Moor and the anticlimax of Newbury, had raised an alarming prospect: if the king should refuse to own himself beaten, what then?[21]

"The cause" from which the Presbyterians in Commons first drew back
in 1644 was carried on by the Independents under their leaders Oliver St.
John, Cromwell, and Sir Henry Vane. It became identified, over the course
of 1645–46, with the demands for religious Independency and a military
permanently under parliament instead of king. It was during these two years
that the original "cause" of godly reform to which Dryden refers was elevated to the Good Old Cause by those at either end of the Independent spectrum: the religious Independents and their preachers at one extreme and
at the other the secular republicans. Later, after the experience of 1659–60,
Dryden would detest the name of the Good Old Cause and associate it with
anarchy. But until 1659, Dryden identified Cromwell's power with the cause
of reform in which the young poet had been raised to believe. Cromwell
was evidently of God; bishops evidently were not. Kings should be godly,
but, ominously for England, King Charles may not have been: that was the
agonizing question during three whole years from 1646 to 1649. Dryden's
family were certainly not republicans. If they came to doubt the monarchy, as they probably did, their doubt was that of the Calvinist "magistrate"
responsible for godly reform of the community. In this respect, Presbyterianism resembles a political aristocracy or even feudalism, as has often been
remarked. Puritans tended to find every monarch wanting in comparison
with their One Sovereign Lord.

The poem Dryden wrote in his eighteenth year abounds with sentiments
befitting a young Puritan of magistratical bent. The elegy *Upon the Death
of the Lord Hastings*, published in the summer of 1649, preserves Dryden's
earliest reflections on history and religion. The young author's political orientation, though, is not obvious. Critics have assumed that "the Nations sin"
in line 49 refers to the Regicide in January, and that Dryden combines grief
for his schoolmate with the sentiments of an incipient royalist. I think this is
a misreading and that Dryden, even after at least three years under the epis-
copal Busby, remained as unsympathetic to the Cavalier cause as his family
had been to the bishops or to the king's government. A review of events
from about the time Dryden went up to Westminster School will put us in
a better position to read the Hastings elegy.

After the king surrendered to the Scots at the end of 1646, Parliament
compounded with them to hand over the king and withdraw from England.
The Presbyterians, led by Denzil Holles, wanted to disband the New Model
Army and come to terms with the king. The Independents were led by mem-

bers of the former war party who deplored a disbandment that gave up on the constitutional goals of 1641. The tactics of these leaders—Cromwell, Henry Ireton, Vane, St. John, Lord Say and his son Nathaniel Fiennes—followed "those of Pym in 1643: war, in order to negotiate, not negotiations in order to avoid war, of which the outcome would be probable surrender" on the king's terms. Sir John Dryden and Pickering, like the seven Northampton-shire borough M.P.s, voted consistently with the Independent group during the tumultuous events of 1647. Among those events were the army's petition to Commons impeaching their Presbyterian foes, the counterrevolution of "king and kirk" mobs orchestrated by City Presbyterians, the army's occupation of London in August, and the debates at the end of the year (both in Parliament and among the Army Council of Officers at Putney) over how to deal with the king, who had fled to the Isle of Wight and was negotiating with the Scots to prepare a royalist invasion of the country.[22]

In the next year, 1648, the struggle between the City-backed "peace" party and the army allied with the Independents spread to the counties. The gentry now rose in reaction against the entire revolutionary machinery of taxes, the New Model Army, and above all the committees that had been set up by Parliament and were answerable to the central government instead of to those families who traditionally exercised local rule. "Many of the revolts of 1648 occurred in formerly Parliamentarian counties," a fact, according to Derek Hirst, that "reflects the growing realization of property-owners that what many had taken to be a godly cause was not worth the sacrifices it entailed." In Dryden's Northamptonshire, where the greater gentry like Pickering and Sir John had cooperated with Parliament from the start, re-sentment against the County Committee was perhaps not great, and Sir Gilbert was not a man to be upset by the proliferation of sectaries. Still, vir-tually everyone wished to see the army curbed and the taxes that supported it reduced. Dryden would remember these chaotic two years chiefly as a period when the army surged unpredictably out of control.[23]

In May of 1648, the nation's reaction came to a head. Mammoth petitions signed in Kent, Essex, and Surrey demanded not only an end to Parliament's county committees but disbandment of the army and immediate treaty with the king. Underdown describes how "a great throng of Surrey men" marched on Westminster: "Neither the petition's inflammatory royalist tone, nor the tumultuous manner of the delegation, pleased the Commons. The petition-ers were kept waiting for several hours in and around Westminster Hall, some of them being plied with drink and Cavalier slogans by the bystanders. Insults were hurled at the Parliament's guards, and in the end several people were killed when the troops cleared the hall. The first blood had been shed in the Army's conflict with the county communities, otherwise known as the second Civil War."[24]

If Busby, across the way in Dean's Yard, wanted his scholars to savor the royalist spirit in full reaction, here was a prime exhibit. Three months later, when Dryden was home for the vacation and had just marked his seventeenth birthday, he would hear of the Scots being destroyed by Cromwell at Preston, followed by the news ten days later that Sir Thomas Fairfax had reduced Colchester. These melancholy examples of blind reaction and of royalist heroics, both caused by the chronic obliquity of the king, must have helped to shape Dryden's concept of "the Nations sin," about which he would write before his next birthday.

The army now renewed its demand of May that "Charles Stuart, that man of blood," be brought to justice. The moderates in Parliament were forced to choose between the army and settlement with the king, and they chose settlement. As Underdown shows, the spring and summer of 1648 brought the collapse of the Independent party. During the fall, while the new parliamentary majority was desperately negotiating yet again with the king, the army was enlarging its demand for justice to include constitutional reform. The *Agreement of the People* that had been put forth by the Levellers at Putney the previous autumn was now restated in the form of a *Humble Petition*. With Cromwell still in the North, Fairfax and Ireton had to deal with the soldiers' radical demands that the king be removed and the sovereignty of the people constitutionally recognized. Ireton carried the army's Remonstrance to Parliament on 20 November. This document, through which ran the refrain *salus populi suprema lex,* argued that punishing the king was the only way to show that he was not above the law. Parliament, after justice was done, was to be dissolved and a new government established on the basis of contract and natural law, replacing the old constitution founded on customary law and the three estates of king, lords, and commons.

The moment of innovation now exploded. Presbyterians in the House furiously spurned the Remonstrance. One M.P. demanded that "the doors be locked and that everyone present solemnly deny his complicity in the Remonstrance. A gang of 'sectaries in arms' were trying to dictate to Parliament, one member thought, while another saw in the Remonstrance an argument for immediate agreement with the King." Ireton returned to the Council of Officers and urged them to disperse Parliament by force if it should refuse to dissolve itself. Snubbed by the Commons and fearing that the cause for which they had fought was being sold out, the council, on 28 November, decided to move the army from Windsor slowly into London.[25]

Young John Dryden, Kings Scholar, possibly had missed the army's occupation of the City after the Presbyterian demonstrations of 1647. He now had a second chance to see the army at close quarters. Ignoring a plea from the Common Council to keep the troops out because their presence "would make provision grow dear, decay trade," Fairfax installed them in Westminster on Saturday, 2 December. They were well-enough behaved over the next few days, even if some thought they "swaggered about the streets." On Monday, defying intimidation, Commons sat in a record-breaking, all-night session. By eight o'clock on Tuesday morning, 5 December, a majority of 129 to 83 voted to keep up the negotiations with the king at Newport. In this marathon debate, says Underdown, "most of the accustomed spokesmen for the extreme factions managed to have their say." Opposed to the Presbyterian majority were the radicals and the friends of the army. The old party of moderate Independents may have joined the latter group, but "after Fiennes's speech on the 1st, there is no record of any major intervention in the debate by the middle group." It would appear that "they had given up. The time for speech-making was over."[26]

The Army Council of Officers, who had also been in all-night session, at this point overruled Ireton and ordered Colonel Thomas Pride to purge the Parliament rather than dissolve it. On Wednesday, 6 December, "a dry, blustery day," John Dryden, by looking out from Westminster School upon the Palace Yard, might see this scene unfolding:

> The regiments duly paraded at seven o'clock, and in the cold light of dawn the noise of marching men and shouted orders echoed through the otherwise empty streets . . . Parliament's normal guards, the innocuous City trained bands, came marching down to Westminster to perform their daily service. In Whitehall they found their way blocked by a thousand men of the New Model. . . . By eight o'clock, when the members began to assemble, the dispositions were complete: Rich's horse and Pride's foot were stationed in the Palace Yard, Westminster Hall, the Court of Requests, and on the stairs and lobby outside the House of Commons. Two other regiments patrolled the neighboring streets.

The worried M.P.s must have guessed what was afoot by the time they reached the Palace Yard. On the stairs leading to the House they encountered Col. Pride, flourishing his list of the members to be secured.

To the young Dryden, the soldiers seemed out of control. In particular, he would never forget their misconduct in St. Stephens Chapel, where the House of Commons sat.[27]

Upon the Death of the Lord Hastings appeared the following summer at the end of a funereal volume commemorating the heir of the earl of Huntingdon. The nineteen-year-old Hastings had died of smallpox on 24 June 1649, and his connection with Dryden is unclear; possibly he was a Westminster schoolmate, a circumstance that would explain the presence of Dryden's poem along with five or six more Westminster offerings in *Lachrymae Musarum*. Among the other thirty-odd poems, including nine by literary men like Robert Herrick, Sir John Denham, and Richard Brome, a few associate Hastings's death with the Regicide five months earlier. Most of them, however, echo the grief felt for the charming young nobleman by his talented and witty mother, Lucy, daughter of Sir John Davies.[28]

Dryden's poem is thoroughly Puritan in its content and in much of its language. He blames Hastings's premature death on "The Nations sin"—a standard explanation for calamity: God visits his wrath on his elect people, who have failed in some respect of their covenant with him. The poem's classical elements come from a schoolboy's mythology; Dryden correlates Seneca, Cato, Numa, and Caesar with learning, virtue, piety, and greatness, but he has yet to grasp the humanist concept of *virtù* found in the *Heroique Stanzas*. Indeed, virtue is as perishable as Hastings:

> Must *Vertue* prove *Death*'s Harbinger? Must She,
> With him expiring, feel Mortality?
> Is *Death* (Sin's wages) Grace's now? shall Art
> Make us more Learned, onely to depart?
> If Merit be Disease, if Vertue Death;
> To be Good, Not to be; who'd then bequeath
> Himself to Discipline? (1:3)

The crudely Ramistic propositions and antitheses come straight out of a Puritan sermon, and so does the telltale word "Discipline." Doctrine and discipline are the twin poles of Calvinist Protestantism, and, for the godly party intent on reforming seventeenth-century England, discipline was the more important. "Discipline is the practic work of preaching directed and applied," Milton had written seven years earlier, paraphrasing Calvin: "There is not that thing in the world of more grave and urgent importance throughout the whole life of man, then is discipline. . . . The flourishing and decaying of all civill societies, all the moments and turnings of humane occasions are mov'd to and fro as upon the axle of discipline. So that whatsoever power or sway in mortall things weaker men have attributed to fortune, I durst with more confidence . . . ascribe either to the vigor, or the slacknesse of discipline." Milton goes on to elaborate discipline by using an astronomical analogy. Similarly, Dryden makes Hastings a figure of celestial harmony and unfallen knowledge, an "*Archimedes* Sphere." [29]

Dryden's callow poem is a serious effort of theodicy. Assuming that Hastings was perfect, the poet must somehow justify his untimely death. He decides that England's communal guilt made her unworthy of this divine "Pledge" that heaven has taken back and thinks the disfiguring blisters, which especially bother the poet, stand for our own mortal sins:

> Where was room left for such a Foul Disease?
> The Nations sin hath drawn that Veil, which shrouds
> Our Day-spring in so sad benighting Clouds.
> Heaven would no longer trust its Pledge; but thus
> Recall'd it; rapt its *Ganymede* from us.
> Was there no milder way but the Small Pox? . . .
> Blisters with pride swell'd; which th'row's flesh did sprout
> Like Rose-buds, stuck i' th' Lily skin about.
> Each little Pimple had a Tear in it,
> To wail the fault its rising did commit:
> Who, Rebel-like, with their own Lord at strife,
> Thus made an Insurrection 'gainst his Life.   (1:4)

"Dryden seems to have been out of sympathy with the execution of Charles I," the California editors comment on the last couplet. This reading is unwarranted; Dryden's elegy nowhere alludes to Charles. Thirty years later, Dryden might be able to look back on the Civil Wars as a rebellion; in 1649, the young Puritan understood the national trauma, which involved the king's death along with many besides, to be God's means of scourging a rebellious people. The latest stroke fell on the virtuous Hastings—on "his Life," not on the life of King Charles.

Dryden calls it smallpox, but he is thinking of the plagues brought on Israel by Korah's spiritual rebellion (Num. 16:46) and prophesied by Moses in the event that Israel should again break its covenant with the Lord: "If ye walk contrary unto me, and will not hearken unto me, I will bring seven times more plagues upon you according to your sins" (Lev. 26:21); "The Lord shall make the pestilence cleave to thee, . . . smite thee with the botch of Egypt" (Deut. 28:21, 27). England has rebelled against the covenant that incorporates them under the Lord as a godly people. The symbolic "Corps" (line 66) of Hastings, with its pox making "an Insurrection 'gainst his Life," mirrors the spiritual and moral rebellion of a nation sick unto death.

The metaphor of rebellion was no doubt suggested to the fledgling poet by the word "rising." This pun is the sole instance of political language in the poem, if we exclude the allusions to biblical rebellion (besides the "Nations sin," see the "falling Stars" in line 33) and the apparent anticlericalism of "Ghostly Fathers in the Street" (88). The figure of rebellious tenants rising against "their own Lord" better suits a feudal or biblical, premonarchical society than Stuart England; even the covenanting Presbyterian M.P.s did not think of Charles as their patriarchal lord, and not even the most super-annuated courtier would denounce the regicides as treacherous vassals.[30]

If the elegy on Hastings offers no political reflections, can we gather from other sources the young poet's response to the national cataclysm? Dryden seldom mentions the Regicide in his subsequent poetry, although he does refer to the military purge of M.P.s that preceded it (see chapter 4). A royalist alumnus later avouched that Dr. Busby at Westminster saw to it that "the King was publicly prayed for an hour or two before his sacred head was struck off," but that is no proof that the contumacious young Puritan bowed in spirit to the kingly image — the *basilikon eikon*. Dryden may have been more impressed by the power that brought the axe of justice upon "Charles Stuart, that man of blood" and may well have preferred the text chosen by his contemporary Samuel Pepys for the occasion: "And the memory of the wicked shall rot."[31]

The strongest personal accent in the elegy is heard in Dryden's out-burst against the "old three-legg'd gray-beards with their Gout" who outlive Hastings,

> Times Offal, onely fit for th' Hospital,
> Or t' hang an Antiquaries room withal;

> Must Drunkards, Lechers, spent with Sinning, live
> With such helps as Broths, Possits, Physick give?
> None live, but such as should die? Shall we meet
> With none but Ghostly Fathers in the Street?   (1:5)

"Grief makes me rail," as the poet says. Lamentation over the untimely death of youth, a theme treated with elegiac sincerity in later poems on John Oldham and Anne Killigrew, here sours into anxiety over a wasted patrimony. Dryden would touch this harsh string again at the Restoration. The poem of 1649 lacks political reflection, but it does express resentment of an older generation whom it makes parasitical on the youth of Hastings. The poet shows impatience toward old men and their "Discipline," which fails to reform those "spent with Sinning" while Hastings perishes. Perhaps Dryden had grown disgusted with hearing about the godly cause.

His adolescent impatience can be related to the nationwide reaction against seven years of revolution. Pride's Purge at the end of 1648, followed by the Regicide, climaxed an exhausting year of reaction and counterrevolution. From this year I would date the birth of Dryden's political awareness, even though his Hastings elegy is barren of reflections on the state. His subsequent comments on revolution are as deeply imbued with the memory of 1659 as of 1647 and 1648. After the *Heroique Stanzas* on Cromwell, he is apt to find rebellion fugitive and brief, while reaction is significant and lasting. Refusing to detach innovation from precedent, he will argue that authority not grounded in tradition lacks legitimacy. For this Puritan radical, the Miltonic hope that political change might lay the foundations of a new order was simply outside the pale of sober contemplation. To Dryden the public poet, revolution means historical discontinuity. It hails from the realms of Chaos and old Night.

Historians of the midcentury Rebellion have located its crest at different moments: in November 1647 when the Leveller movement at Putney was suppressed; early in 1649 when the republic was founded upon the Regicide; in April 1653 when Cromwell finally expelled the purged Long Parliament. For marking Dryden's first glimpse of the problem of freedom, the decisive moment is December 1648. Parliament's reactionary mood that fall spurred the army to renew the flagging *cause;* this renewal of rebellion provoked further reaction by Cromwell, who arrived on the scene the day after Pride's Purge to take over—or rather, to mount and ride—the wave that bore him on to Regicide within two months. Dryden, whether he viewed it as the providence of God or the prudence of men, never forgot this *kairos* moment of deliberation that tried Ireton, Cromwell, and the army as well as the Long Parliament and his elders. Dryden's subsequent plays and poems would reproduce the deliberative crisis time and again.

No sooner had the Good Old Cause of reform and revolution peaked in 1648 than innovation ushered in new worries about legitimate authority. The godly party that Dryden's elders supported had never doubted its aims, which had seemed modest at first. After 1646, the stakes were higher: nothing less than the righting of a constitution loosed from its moorings. Here was an unprecedented moment of freedom and opportunity, demanding extraordinary prudence. For Cromwell and the older generation, which at this juncture included Marvell, deliberation meant awaiting the promptings of divine providence, as Cromwell hung back from, then supported, Pride's Purge. Dryden, coming of age in an epoch of sustained crisis, was endowed with a historical reflexivity lacking in his more deeply engaged elders. Providence is never far from his thoughts, and it informs his epic view of history. But he keeps his eye on the foreground of human prudence and clearly distinguishes public *facta* and the results of deliberation from divine providence.

"Pride's Purge appears a dreadful blow to the independence of Parliament," says J. P. Kenyon, "but the opposite was the case; by proceeding to these lengths the army betrayed its absolute need of the sanction of the House of Commons, *some* House of Commons, any House of Commons." Even the radical republicans welcomed a limit on revolution. When some of the M.P.s allowed into Commons by Pride wanted to suspend the session in protest, Edmund Ludlow reminded them of the "inconveniences as might otherwise fall upon the nation, if the whole power should be left in the hands of an army." Great as the revolutionary act of Regicide was, Dryden was struck by the even more potent reaction that overshadowed that act and by the specter of monarchy that haunted the republic and Protectorate.[32]

Cromwell and the Millennium

John Pocock identifies the epochal *kairos* of England's republic and Inter-regnum as a "Machiavellian moment." Pocock's book of that title alludes not to the cynical author of *The Prince* but to the fervent admirer of Rome's republic. The classical republicanism that Machiavelli analyzes in his *Discourses on Livy* was first revived in quattrocento Italy, and it was rediscovered again under very different circumstances in seventeenth-century England and in revolutionary America. Long after his death, Machiavelli's fertile study of the moment of civic renewal *(rinnovazione)* caught the imagination of legislators and actors on the historical scene. The origin of a free republic is a potently ambiguous occasion. The prudential act that brings the new state into being is at the same time a historical return to immemorial principles. This Machiavellian reduction, or *ridurre ai principii,* closely parallels the Reformation quest for a primitive, Apostolic Church. If England's godly Presbyterians had nothing else in common with the agnostic Florentine, they shared his strong faith that human prudence is able to ordain an inclusive and lasting community. Politics and religion converge: the republic is a secular millennium, and the civic *virtù* that renders the citizen immortal corresponds to the grace that makes the saint invincible.[1]

Pocock shows that the writings of Milton and Harrington as well as those of Vane and Marchamont Nedham and the Fifth Monarchists all celebrate this original conjunction of Puritan saint with classical citizen. In these authors, prophecy is tempered by a new, historical reflexivity like that in early quattrocento Florence, leading them to conceive of England's midcentury experience in terms of "the rise, fall, and rebirth of republican virtue." Pocock takes his theme from the political *kairos* of 1647–59: "The present moment was one at which England had the opportunity to recreate the commonwealth . . . in such a form as had not existed since the days of Livian Rome. . . . The moment of recreating the republic, that society in which men were what they ought to be, was hard to conceive without adding the concept of the apocalyptic moment, or moment at which grace acted in history."[2]

In the debates at Putney in the fall of 1647, the army radicals found themselves at a moment "of freedom triumphing over necessity," whether they conceived the moment politically as "one at which a true millennium seemed imminent, or, more spiritually, one at which some liberation amounting almost to divinization of human capacities seemed to be taking place." Pocock's crucial point is that this liberation was not sectarian (in the sense of separatist), but catholic, in the sense of universally inclusive, and secular: the radicals' apocalyptic conviction fed on a new civic consciousness that impelled them to transform the world instead of spurning it. The extreme chiliasts among these reformers, notably those momentarily expecting a Fifth Monarchy of Christ that would supplant the ancient four named in the book of Daniel, repudiated all human law as a corrupt institution. With these fanatics, apocalyptic passed over into antinomianism. Extremists of a different stamp placed their trust not in Christ but in thoroughgoing communism and "the law of nature," deriving their republican New Jerusalem from a populism untainted by history and tradition. More formidable than these dreaming radicals were the Levellers, the basis of whose "power was the London mob, swelled by unemployment in years of slump."[3]

The 1650s in England were the *occasione* for radical innovation in the historical constitution and, more radically still, in godly rule. The Machiavellian moment tests the civic *virtù* of a nation while it calls forth and concentrates the individual virtue of its leaders. By praising Cromwell as the exemplar of prudence, Marvell and Dryden themselves exemplified that virtue in the public orator, sometimes exchanging their toga for the mantle of the prophet. The civic *virtù* of either public poet shows in their joint response to millenarianism. Their prudence is fully on display when they interpret Cromwell and the historical moment. The purpose of this chapter and the next is to sample Marvell's hermeneutics and contrast it with the hermeneutics later perfected by Dryden.

PRUDENCE AND PROPHECY

The poet who taught Dryden to interpret the Bible politically was not the royalist and visionary Cowley but Marvell. In the twenty years of public rivalry during which both poets, with the utmost deliberation, weighed the question of apocalypse, Marvell's chiliasm appears to have begotten a complementary antimillenarianism in Dryden. John Wallace has laid out Marvell's religious position with fine discrimination. When he characterizes Marvell's cautious millenarianism in the Cromwell ode, Wallace is describing his prudence. Marvell's view that the "climacteric" of the Cromwellian moment was "final and irreversible," Wallace notes, "was tempered by his aristocratic bias, his dislike of religious and political enthusiasm, his classical training and Horatian irony, and, perhaps above all, by his opinion of the poet's role. His function was to speak not himself but the truth, to mirror reality, not to express opinion, and the solemnity of the ode is in part derived from the effacing of personality. . . . Whatever their politics, or their past allegiance, or their religion, [the people of England] ought to recognize in Cromwell the man chosen by God to lead them forward to a future which He had prepared, and which He alone could discern." [4]

Much of this characterization of Marvell's religious liberalism fits the author of the *Heroique Stanzas* on Cromwell. Dryden's prudence as a public writer and occasional prophet should not be mistaken for religious conservatism. Both poets dislike *zealous* chiliasts, Marvell fearing their antinomianism and Dryden appalled by their separatism. Yet both are obsessed with millenarianism. Their first ventures into public poetry were inspired by the figure of Cromwell, suggesting that they wanted to bear witness to a leader they deemed historically unique. They were rediscovering as poets their identity with a national community unknown to their Caroline predecessors. Dryden learned to evoke this community by emulating Marvell's contemporary idiom, beginning with Marvell's Cromwell poems. In the second of these, Marvell deploys the biblical hermeneutics that opened up new paths for Dryden.

Despite their common Puritan heritage—Marvell was the son of an Independent (Congregationalist) minister, while Dryden was born into a family of Presbyterian squires—the two Cantabrigians diverge significantly in their response to the upheavals of the Interregnum. The divergence is partly owing to the decade that separated them. Attending the university in the 1630s, Marvell must have remembered a king who ruled his country in peace, albeit without a parliament. But the militant defiance of Charles, beginning in Scotland in 1639 and soon followed by the Irish uprising, meant that Dryden knew no example of an authoritative monarch until his own Cambridge years, when Cromwell took over the governance of the nation.

Quite apart from the circumstance that Dryden reached civic adulthood ten years after Marvell did, the two poets differ markedly in their intellectual temper. Marvell, who flirted with Roman Catholicism and seems to have briefly converted at the age of eighteen, was apt to embrace new ideas with unchecked conviction. The more reserved Dryden was slow to commit himself. The radicalism of his Puritan heritage was not strong enough wholly to overcome his innate distrust of novelty. Before assenting to an idea, he liked to know its pedigree. His later recollection of having rejected Joshua Sylvester and "the Darling of my youth," Cowley (4:84), shows a habit of critical reflection never found in Marvell. And although both poets were educated in the same traditional curriculum, Dryden's classical allusions from the beginning are scrupulously contextualized. The more playful Marvell cannot resist giving a witty turn to a familiar myth or parodying a Virgilian phrase merely for burlesque or incidental satire.

The fact is that Dryden eventually outstripped him as a public poet, even though Marvell's civic and poetic achievements, taken separately, appear to excel Dryden's. Probably Marvell would now be considered the more imaginative writer, while his public service as M.P. from Hull in the Cavalier Parliament seems more substantial, by any modern reckoning, than Dryden's civic contribution as laureate. But these modern judgments are based on the liberal aesthetics of the past two centuries that I discussed in my Introduction. The Whiggish bias of Marvell scholarship has naturally steered the bulk of it toward the most dramatic of his political poems, the Cromwell ode, whose contemporary events are accessible without the tedious spadework needed to understand Marvell's Restoration satires. The crises selected by Whig history are always familiar moments that can be dramatized without taxing the deliberation of historian or reader: the event has already been decided and its actors delivered up for judgment. In a word, Whig history is antihistorical, weaving a dramatic fabrication to replace the complex tissue of historical politics and prudence.[5]

Machiavellian prudence is falsified when it is dichotomized into moral reflection and dramatic action. Separating action from contemplation, especially in a public poet, vitiates the deliberative unity of his work. In the Cromwell ode, Marvell poses the moment of choice with brilliant irony yet without finally choosing. His mock-deliberation is a means of evading history. In *The First Anniversary*, by contrast, he offers a decisive and public deliberation that is worth close examination. Because the deliberation is conducted in terms of biblical typology, we need to analyze Marvell's hermeneutics. Doing so will reveal that *The First Anniversary* became Dryden's model for using Scripture in public poetry.

The First Anniversary is the only political poem Marvell allowed to be published and the poem in which he most nearly perfected his role of public poet. Nevertheless, to some of his critics, this poem is a retreat from the political commitment of the ode. Warren Chernaik believes that "the debate between withdrawal and involvement was resolved for Marvell (insofar as it can ever be resolved) by the decision to write a literature of commitment, which attempts to preserve the inner vision in the world of action." Whatever "literature of commitment" may be, the parenthetical disclaimer does not save Chernaik's remark from the Whiggish habit of interpreting rhetorical sentiments—responsibility, disappointment with an imperfect world, chastened hope—as the signs of inward enlightenment. Such Whig history is anachronistic and creates a derivative politics in which moral goals, characterized in terms of religious or psychological individualism, are devoid of real civic import. The poet is uprooted from the *vivere civile* and transplanted to a liberal utopia or to the *otium* of stoic self-sufficiency.[6]

Between the *Horatian Ode* and *The First Anniversary*, Chernaik supposes Cromwell to have been promoted from an example of Machiavellian *virtù* to "a Christian hero" through whom "millenarian prophecies may be realized." Chernaik extrapolates this shift of emphasis to an opposition between realpolitik and religion, despite the fact that republicans like Harrington, with whom Chernaik compares Marvell, went out of their way to deny precisely this opposition. Chernaik recognizes that the later poem is explicitly concerned with the problem of innovation, "founding a firm State by Proportions true" (line 248), but thinks it missed its aim as propaganda for the year-old Protectorate constitution, which crumbled at the very moment Marvell's poem appeared in January 1655. "Poets and constitution-makers can present their dreams of perfection, but reality exacts its revenges," says Chernaik. With this "difficulty endemic to the genre of panegyric," he contrasts the " 'Horatian Ode,' committed to nothing except the impersonal solidity of fact. . . . Its historical analysis remains valid, its balance of emotions convincing, even when the historical circumstances that produced it have ceased to exert any hold over the reader."[7]

This judgment typically misapprehends the public poet's role, substituting aesthetic or pseudoscientific autonomy ("the impersonal solidity of fact") for political experience. The *Horatian Ode* is praised for what is really deliberative paralysis ("balance of emotions"), while its historical indeterminacy is somehow understood as valid analysis of the event. *The First Anniversary*, on the other hand, in which the poet directly states his opinion on a topic gravid with the common interest, is pronounced an impractical dream, a failed political panegyric. This Whiggish judgment after the fact bespeaks a despair of reuniting Marvell's poetry with "the historical circumstances that produced it."

The despair is unwarranted. In the course of the past three decades, several readers of the poem, each building upon predecessors, have managed to restore *The First Anniversary* to something like its original context. Ruth Nevo and Joseph Mazzeo called attention to the biblical and physical imagery whereby Cromwell is raised to the status of a superhuman ruler who establishes the state as a *discordia concors* (harmonious discord). Wallace showed that Marvell's preoccupation with the figure of a millennial king arose out of current expectations that the Protector, who had ruled for a year under the Instrument of Government, would end by accepting the crown. Wallace argued accordingly that Marvell's poem may be considered an oration written to demonstrate Cromwell's extraordinary qualities as a Davidic monarch. Realizing more fully than he had in 1650 that Cromwell at this moment stood for the "two great possibilities [of] millennium and constitutional order," Marvell urged that the Protector be made king. His coronation, with its solemn unction, would join "High Grace . . . with highest Pow'r" (line 131). Marvell's chief aim is not to prophesy the millennium (of which the advent is unknowable), but to deliberate on the common good: authority and succession to the rule in a commonwealth whose previous orders have collapsed. He can publicly recommend this "wish'd Conjuncture" (line 136) because it would also be an election on the principle *vox populi vox Dei:* "the creation of a monarchy by popular consent was the natural apotheosis of Cromwell's glorious works."[8]

The historical orientation established by Wallace has guided subsequent readings of *The First Anniversary*. Zwicker questioned Wallace's accent on kingly title and chrismatory succession, emphasizing instead the "judicial model" of Gideon, one of Israel's judges who repudiated monarchy in favor of theocracy. The judges, furthermore, were types of Christ, a fact implying that Marvell denies "the propriety of kingship" and celebrates rather "Cromwell as the spirit of God healing the nation." The Old Testament, theocratic model of governance is confirmed in a brilliant New Testament figure at the end of the poem: the angel who heals the waters of the Commonwealth by troubling them.[9]

Shifting the focus away from the question of whether Marvell's allusions were historically congruent, Annabel Patterson examined instead their adequacy to Cromwell, astutely noting that Marvell relies on the panegyric topos of "inexpressibility" to characterize his hero's "indefinable selfhood." The poet is asking "what it is 'to be Cromwell.'" "No conventional category," she says, "and certainly not that of kingship, was adequate to delimit the 'One Man' [of the *Horatian Ode*] whose like had never been seen before." She finds that Marvell, to demonstrate this inadequacy, fits Cromwell both with traditionally royalist (or classical) figures of praise and with scriptural figures. Waller, in his poem *Upon His Majesty's Repairing of Paul's*, had compared Charles with Amphion. Patterson shows that Marvell deliberately emulates that poem when he contrasts Cromwell's work of reform (building the "Temples" of God, line 64) with the "earthy Projects" of time-bound, "heavy Monarchs" (15–22). Most of the biblical comparisons in *The First Anniversary*, on the other hand, serve to highlight Cromwell's *imperfection:* "There is no exact equivalence between the new Protector and Noah, Gideon, Elijah, and the hero of the Apocalypse; and if the use of royalist topoi had the effect of making Cromwell seem infinitely better than a king, the adjustment of biblical topoi seems, conversely, to make him seem less than perfect as patriarch, judge, prophet, or millennial hero."[10]

The imperfection, however, lies fully as much with the poet as in his subject, for Marvell doubts his own vision. Patterson begins and ends her discussion of *The First Anniversary* by stressing its apparent subversion of Christian prophecy. She notes that in lines 113–16, Marvell is more faithful than Milton to the ambiguity in the apocalyptic text at Revelation 17:16, which casually mentions that the "ten horns" of the Beast—for Milton, plainly the godless European kings—"shall hate the whore [Mystery or Babylon], and shall make her desolate and naked." This odd wrinkle in the divine plan is caught up and magnified in Marvell's lines (117–58) following, which are labeled by Wallace the poet's *divisio* or "most explicit avowal of his theme." Marvell there expresses his hope for a reformation not by war but through the truth revealed, by which he means revealed in an epic poem he will write to awaken the "unhappy Princes" from their "Errour." Yet at the same time he deliberately spells out the limits upon both his vision and Cromwell's action. These are substantial: the "thick Cloud" that lies about "the latest Day" and "intercepts the Beams of Mortal eyes," the indolence of men inured to sin, and—by no means the least impediment—"my Weakness," counterpart to the "Regal sloth" of the continental kings. Cromwell alone "outwings the wind" in pursuit of the Beast. The poet's mortal Muse joins in the cry and follows its "Angelique" leader but owns itself unable to discover all that it means "to be *Cromwell,*" admitting in the end that " 'tis the most which we determine can, / If these the Times, then this must be the Man."[11]

The arguments I have been recalling bear upon Marvell's deliberative intention, in line with which *The First Anniversary* needs to be read. To capture the deliberative moment of a public poem, scholars must invoke historical circumstances brought to light and interpreted by their predecessors. Their effort becomes, therefore, a work of collective prudence. This is as it should be, for historical truth is not apocalyptic, and hermeneutical scholarship is not prophecy. Its object, the Machiavellian moment of innovation, depends fully as much on tradition or custom as on revelation and grace. The recovery so far of Marvell's response to the public moment of *The First Anniversary* has quite properly been a *customary* accomplishment (to borrow the adjective Pocock uses to characterize English law). Wallace's carefully integrated argument furnished a standard that screened out fanciful and unhistorical interpretations of the poem. Patterson was able to devote closer attention to its deliberative aspect, and her rhetorical refinements upon Wallace's reading have in turn been tested and confirmed by the historical insights of Derek Hirst.

For example, Hirst clarifies the emulation between Marvell's "Amphion" and Waller's by pointing out that the "Temples" raised by Cromwell were the national church with its Triers and Ejectors of ministers, a loose but authentic order that was being set in place even as the newspapers in 1654 were describing "the progressive collapse of Charles's cherished cathedral." Hirst is able to bring a superior historical gloss to some passages by identifying more specifically the public topic Marvell had in view. Thus the allusion (249–54) to Gideon punishing the elders for refusing to supply his army had its exact counterpart in Cromwell chastening both parliaments in 1653, when they refused to meet the soldiers' demands for "indemnity and for pensions for widows and orphans" (Barebone's Parliament even sought to limit the army's pay). Hirst can with fair assurance refer the line "And *Is'rel* silent saw him rase the Tow'r" to Cromwell's boast, in September 1654, that when he had dissolved the purged Parliament eighteen months before, "there was not so much as the barking of a dog, or any general and visible repining [at] it."[12]

Marvell's poetic almanac might be expected to echo Cromwell's official speeches, particularly those of September 1654. A. J. N. Wilson has suggested that Marvell's final couplet addressed to Oliver "as the *Angel* of our Commonweal," who, "Troubling the Waters, yearly mak'st them heal," picks up Cromwell's declaration to the new Parliament that their great task was "healing and settling" the nation's divisions. And a week later, in his speech justifying his dissolution of the purged Parliament, Cromwell dwelt upon the fact that he was yielding up his "boundless and unlimited" power by stooping to become constitutional Protector under the Instrument. "I was arbitrary in power, having the armies in the three nations under my command, and truly not very ill beloved by them." This speech, Hirst maintains, is enough to explain the often glossed lines 225–28

> For to be *Cromwell* was a greater thing,
> Then ought below, or yet above a King:
> Therefore thou rather didst thy Self depress
> Yielding to Rule, because it made thee Less."[13]

Hirst is notably successful in delimiting the poem's millenarian argument, which he reads in light of the government's struggle against the Fifth Monarchists. Marvell, no matter how strong his millennial conviction, had to manage this topic with caution. When for instance Amphion builds Thebes, "Th'harmonious City of the seven Gates" (line 66), readers were not to imagine the New Jerusalem (which has twelve gates); they were to envisage the seven-gated London rebuilt by Cromwell. Once we grasp the seriousness of Cromwell's difficulty with militant Fifth Monarchists in 1654—some of whom were calling for his assassination—the poem's seeming digressions fall into place. For one thing, it becomes impossible to dismiss the coaching accident as "poetically inert." Men like John Simpson and Christopher Feake would have rejoiced mightily to see Oliver, the Little Horn of the Beast, removed to make way for the reign of the saints.[14]

In his opening speech to Parliament on 4 September, Cromwell confessed that "we all honour, wait, and hope for" the advent of Christ, who "will have a time to set up his reign." But that reign is to be "in our hearts." Quoting these phrases, Hirst explains that "the characteristic Independent, or Cromwellian, position was . . . that the millennium would only be achieved by an outpouring of Christ's word into the world, not by physical action." Marvell might long for that "happy hour" when "High Grace should meet in one with highest Pow'r" (131–32), but Cromwell deplored the Fifth Monarchists' call for violence to "found *dominium in gratia.*" Despite the poem's tirade (293–320) against Fifth Monarchists and antinomians, other lines apparently echo their millennial hopes, and Hirst wonders if "the irony of Marvell's performance lies in the degree to which the pot seemed to be calling the kettle black." [15]

Hirst thinks Marvell was harking back to the millennial excitement of 1653 and Barebone's Parliament in an effort to preempt the Fifth Monarchist leaders who were making overtures to the army in the autumn of 1654: "Marvell attempted to limit potential damage by reclaiming the high religious ground for the Protector, warning the radical saints that they had got the meaning of the 'holy Oracles' all wrong and that they should abandon their hostility, for Oliver was still the great captain." In other words, Hirst here reduces Marvell "to the role of publicist for the regime, albeit a publicist of unique perceptiveness." Hirst concedes only a secondary, deliberative purpose in the poet's "rhetorical posture" vis-à-vis Cromwell, namely, to counsel him to *resist* the monarchy advocated by reactionaries just as he rejected the anarchy of the radicals. Lines 145–48 echo the *Horatian Ode:* "And well he therefore does, and well has guest, / Who in his Age has always forward prest: / And knowing not where Heavens choice may light, / Girds yet his Sword, and ready stands to fight." These lines may have been spoken "*to* a doubting Cromwell," Hirst says, "as well as *of* Cromwell." [16]

In suggesting that *The First Anniversary* counsels Cromwell to decline the crown, Hirst would appear to have stood Wallace's interpretation on its head. Marvell's "panegyric tone," in Hirst's view, implies propaganda rather than deliberation: "Marvell's deployment of scriptural types reveals a brilliant exercise in casuistry. . . . It makes it impossible to see the poem as *doing* a single thing, other than celebrating the complex figure of Cromwell." But as Wallace and Patterson demonstrate, what the poem is doing is deliberating on what choice the public should make in the crisis of the moment. The poet and his audience are poised on the verge of assenting to—and "hollow[ing]" after—"Angelique *Cromwell* who outwings the wind." Hirst criticizes Patterson (and by implication Wallace) for slighting the millenarian warmth of Marvell's deliberation, which Hirst connects with the celebration of Machiavellian *virtù* in the *Horatian Ode*. Like the republican Nedham's *The Case of the Commonwealth* and *Mercurius Politicus,* Marvell's *The First Anniversary* makes Cromwell a *principe nuovo* founding a state, except that the state is identified with New Jerusalem.[17]

Hirst's bid to demote *The First Anniversary* from deliberative oration to "perceptive" propaganda needs to be countered if Marvell's poem is to serve as a touchstone for the public poetry written later by Dryden. Hirst is least convincing when he tries to expose the "casuistry" in the poem's "deployment of scriptural types." "Marvell uses Gideon to legitimate Cromwell's use of force in politics," Hirst claims, finding in the line (255) on Gideon's success—"No King might ever such a Force have done"—"a phrase charged with Machiavellian dynamic." The line by itself, however, is a mere proclamation of God's power; even in Harrington's hermeneutics, Gideon is the champion of theocracy, not a Machiavellian judge like Moses. Elijah and Noah, as Hirst wants to read them, are likewise used merely to exalt the Protector's moral significance.[18]

"THE VINE OF LIBERTY": MARVELL'S HERMENEUTICS

Noah as a type of Cromwell (*pater patriae*) in the poem is hard to explain, let alone the episode of Noah's drunkenness. Noah was invoked consistently in royalist pamphlets and of course by Filmer in *Patriarcha*. As Wallace says, "If the kingship of Adam was the cornerstone of patriarchal theory, the kingship of Noah was no less important, and, after the deluge of the civil war, a good deal more relevant to Marvell's poem." The phrase "That sober Liberty" in the title of Hirst's essay sends us to the Noah passage (279–92), which is where Patterson, too, begins her interpretation of the poem's scriptural allusions. All three critics, joined by Wilson, agree that the legitimacy Marvell evokes by thrusting in Noah is harshly qualified, if not erased, by the passage that directly follows on Noah's weakness and his unfilial, "Chammish issue."[19]

Two principles structure *The First Anniversary:* its annual organization and the myth of Noah's Flood. These principles are not casually related, but coordinate; both imply cyclical renewal. The great sign of renewal, found at the poem's beginning and end, is the sun, standing for Cromwell. The archetypal myth of renewal is the story of the Flood. That Genesis episode is artfully constructed to show a second creation rising out of chaos. As the waters cover the world in chapter 7, the six days of chapter 1 are reversed, and man and beast nearly relapse into the confusion of the original abyss. The ark riding upon the Flood is the only relic of the first creation—of the initial, formative parting of the universal waters. Chapter 8 begins the recreation, as "God remembered Noah." When read for their political equivalent, the first eight chapters of Genesis disclose the radical myth underlying Machiavelli's *ridurre ai principii*.

The poet in *Upon Appleton House* also contemplates this scriptural *renovatio*. There he imagines the river Wharfe opening its "Cataracts" near Denton and flooding the scene of life before him while he retreats to the green world of his imagination: "But I, retiring from the Flood, / Take Sanctuary in the Wood; / And, while it lasts, my self imbark / In this yet green, yet growing Ark" (466–84). This "easie Philosopher" studies "Natures mystick Book," reading in the leaves overhead a Pentateuchal "Mosaick" that presents a continuous "History" (561–84). The Flood and ark are recalled more strenuously in another poem, *Bermudas,* by the English landing party as they raise a psalm of thanksgiving for the new world:

> What should we do but sing his Praise
> That led us through the watry Maze,
> Unto an Isle so long unknown,
> And yet far kinder than our own?
> Where he the huge Sea-Monsters wracks,
> That lift the Deep upon their Backs. (5–10)

I quote these lyric passages to show that the oceanic Creation and Apocalypse, which are the Alpha and Omega of the Scriptures, were never far from Marvell's thoughts. At the opening of *The First Anniversary,* "the watry Maze" reclaims man, who sinks beneath the waters of "flowing Time." Marvell still is thinking of the primal deluge, from which springs suddenly the vigorous sun of Cromwell:

> Like the vain Curlings of the Watry maze,
> Which in smooth streams a sinking Weight does raise;

> So Man, declining alwayes, disappears
> In the weak Circles of increasing Years;
> And his short Tumults of themselves Compose,
> While flowing Time above his Head does close.
>   *Cromwell* alone with greater Vigour runs,
>   (Sun-like) the Stages of succeeding Suns. . . .
>   'Tis he the force of scatter'd Time contracts,
>   And in one Year the work of Ages acts.   (1–14)

This initial burst of Cromwellian energy recalls the lovers' strife with time at the end of *To His Coy Mistress* ("though we cannot make our Sun / Stand still, yet we will make him run"). Like the lovers, the "heavy Monarchs" struggle vainly against profane time, "Nor sacred Prophecies consult within" (line 35). They are mere jacks in the clock who strike the hour without using it ("useless time they tell," line 41), whereas Cromwell, running his course through "the yearly Ring" (line 12), has dynamically concentrated "the force of scatter'd Time."

At several points Marvell reminds us that he is focusing upon the year just ended ("yearly Ring"; "yearly song," line 182; "yearly" in the final line)—a year of innovation that saw the creation of a promising *novum ordo saeclorum*. This is the formal argument of *The First Anniversary:* the year from December 1653 to December 1654 is contrasted with the twelve-year deluge that preceded. "The Commonwealth then first together came" only in this year, "When *Cromwell* tun'd the ruling Instrument" (75, 68); before that it was a political chaos, or a discord of "hack[ing]" musicians, "tedious Statesmen." No specifically biblical figures appear until we reach lines 99–104, where Marvell reviews the powerful effect of Cromwell's new foreign policy. At that point, Marvell paraphrases Psalm 2 and makes the traditional identification of its messiah with the warrior Christ (Rev. 19:15) of "the latter Dayes." This is the mystic figure that Cromwell humbly but unscripturally serves as "Captain," meaning presumably that he leads one of the armies (Rev. 19:19) who oppose the forces of the Beast at the ultimate battle of Armageddon. Marvell recommends Cromwell to the "observing Princes" for a pattern of Christian service, but *not* as the Davidic king some readers have imagined:

> O would they rather by his Pattern won
> Kiss the approaching, nor yet angry Son;

> And in their numbred Footsteps humbly tread
> The path where holy Oracles do lead;
> How might they under such a Captain raise
> The great Designes kept for the latter Dayes!
>
> (105–10)

The poet then launches into his apocalyptic flight only to be checked, as we saw, by the recollection that he lives yet in the temporal world of anniversaries, where "still the Dragons Tail / Swinges the Volumes of its horrid Flail." The thought of sin leads right back to the "Watry maze" at the opening, now made explicit as the Flood:

> For the great Justice that did first suspend
> The World by Sin, does by the same extend.
> Hence that blest Day still counterpoysed wastes,
> The Ill delaying, what th'Elected hastes;
> Hence landing Nature to new Seas is tost,
> And good Designes still with their Authors lost.
>
> (151–58)

The first part of the poem (down through Wallace's *divisio*) is thus rounded by distinct images of Cromwell, initially as the sun and then as heroic warrior with ready sword (147–48), imposing order upon the sea—or its mythical equivalent, the "Dragon"—of moral and political chaos.[20]

The second part, lines 159–292 (comprehending Wallace's *confirmatio* and *refutatio*), begins with a matriarch, Cromwell's mother, and ends with the patriarch Noah. The "Saint-like" Elizabeth Cromwell lived an entire "age" (nearly a century; literally, a *saeclum*) but, even so, had to suffer the effects of time and sin, and her death points to her son's mortality. In this middle third of the poem, Cromwell, the heroic *pater patriae*, is revealed to be human: a patriarch with "Mortal cares." The "Angelic *Cromwell*" of the first part, the legendary "Amphion," becomes on closer view the Protector whose only visible aureole is his "Crown of silver Hairs" (179–80). And because he remains the chief support of the new order he created, the state is no less mortal than he. That is why Marvell dwells on the coaching accident, cleverly connecting it with Elijah ascending in the chariot and passing on his mantle to Elisha—easily the favorite biblical type of spiritual (that is, nonhereditary) succession.

Cromwell's brush with accidental death caused by innocent horses is contrasted with the assassination plots earlier in 1654, all of them the effect of "Our brutish fury struggling to be Free" (171–77). To bring out the moral and political meaning of the Protector's death, the poet imagines the "Panique groan" of the shipwrecked order Cromwell has sustained:

> It seem'd the Earth did from the Center tear;
> It seem'd the Sun was faln out of the Sphere;
> Justice obstructed lay, and Reason fool'd;
> Courage disheartned, and Religion cool'd. . . .
> When now they sink, and now the plundring Streams
> Break up each Deck, and rip the Oaken seams. (203–14)

The Elijah passage (215–38) comes next. We can pass over it for the moment and pursue the narrative of Cromwell's acts "since [he] o'r-took and wet the King"—a reference, I think, not to 1649 and the Regicide specifically, but to the historical suppression of England's temporal monarchy by a Cromwell who serves a greater king: "an higher Force him push'd / Still from behind, and it before him rush'd." A similar zeal for God's kingdom stirred Elijah and Gideon, with whom Cromwell is next compared. His military actions, too, were providential, "Though undiscern'd among the tumult blind, / Who think those high Decrees by Man design'd" (238–42).

Likewise providential were his political actions of 1653, "Here pulling down [sc. the purged Parliament], and there erecting New [the Nominated Parliament]." What looked like trial and error has resulted in his "Founding a firm State by Proportions true" (247–48). The Gideon passage (249–64), as we saw, refers explicitly to Cromwell's dismissing both Parliaments—the purged and the Nominated, "Rump" and "Barebone's"—in order to preserve theocracy, or God's commonwealth, in England. Oliver himself (the olive tree in Jotham's parable) declined to take over God's kingdom, but the spiritually conceited "Brambles" (Fifth Monarchist saints like Thomas Harrison) had no such scruples and were all clamoring to be "anointed" with the oil, which, *if* it belonged to *any* man—so I read Marvell's emphasis— was surely Cromwell's due for his "Labor."

In a theocracy, in which God is the acknowledged king, a tyrant is any party that offers to supplant him, including a rebellious, popular faction (see the quotation from *Sir Thomas More* in chapter 1, above). Consequently Marvell's next figure of the "lusty Mate" who seizes the helm—a famous simile drawn, perhaps, from the Huguenot *Vindiciae contra tyrannos*—refers to Cromwell's saving the theocracy from the tyrannical ambition of those republicans and saints who threatened to take over the commonwealth in 1653. The public, like "Passengers all wearyed out before, / Giddy, and wishing for the fatal Shore" (271–72), were unaware that England was steering upon the rocks of anarchy. Cromwell, seeing the primal chaos for which the ship of state was bound, seized control to "double back unto the safer Main." Marvell succinctly formulates the political lesson: where all command, it is not freedom but anarchy; where one withstands anarchy, it is not tyranny but godly service. Knowing the boundaries of resistance and command, Cromwell has rescued the ark of the state and therefore, like Noah, deserves the passengers' respect as "their Father" (279–82).

Marvell has made it perfectly clear by now that Cromwell, just like Noah, enjoys the authority of a *pater patriae* solely by virtue of serving as God's "Captain." Marvell himself was perhaps less a republican than a theocratically inclined constitutionalist, but nowhere in his works does he ascribe absolute authority to a mortal being. Therefore, he is not concerned to demonstrate either Noah's patriarchal sovereignty, as Filmer tries to do, or Noah's human "inadequacy." Noah is important not because he was our sire but because of the Machiavellian "orders" (as Harrington translates them: *ordini, principii*) that he transmitted to his heirs. Besides directing the ark and renewing the covenant with Yahweh, Noah first cultivated the vine. This last *innovatio* Marvell ingeniously adapts to Cromwell:

> Thou, and thine House, like *Noah*'s Eight did rest,
> Left by the Wars Flood on the Mountains crest:
> And the large Vale lay subject to thy Will,
> Which thou but as an Husbandman wouldst Till:
> And only didst for others plant the Vine
> Of Liberty, not drunken with its Wine.
>   That sober Liberty which men may have,
> That they enjoy, but more they vainly crave:
> And such as to their Parents Tents do press,
> May shew their own, not see his Nakedness. (283–92)

The final couplet here, as we shall see, is a deftly preemptive stroke against the false prophets whom Marvell goes on to assail.

The last third of the poem is shortest and simplest in structure, focusing entirely on the various responses to Cromwell's reported death. If we skip over the gloatings by his "Chammish issue," we find the two basic motifs of the sun and Noah's Flood brought to the fore. Noah and the sun are combined in "the great Captain" of line 321, who was momentarily thought to be "a Captain dead" (line 350) but now flames in the forehead of the morning sky: "So while our Star that gives us Light and Heat / Seem'd now a long and gloomy Night to threat, / Up from the other World his Flame he darts, / And Princes shining through their windows starts." Cromwell escapes from death, and the state from dissolution, by a renewal that is here made consonant with the poem's theme of rebirth out of the Flood and distinguished from the lesser, Amphion theme of political *discordia concors*. Having noted that the radical zealots "Tremble" at Oliver's recovery (321–23), Marvell describes two further responses.[21]

The nation's thankfulness is expressed in terms of primitive man's experience of night and sunrise. The night, of course, is Cromwell's rumored death, for which birds of ill omen (Feake and Simpson) "with their screeching noyse / Did make the Fun'rals sadder by their Joyes" (333–34). But the "great Captain, now the danger's ore . . . returning yet alive / Does with himself all that is good revive" (321–24). With his return, the scene of death and impending chaos is completely transformed. Following the long simile (325–45) of the day-star, the transformation is described from the standpoint of the startled princes. The metaphorical Flood has become a fertile ocean breeding battleships, "Arks of War," "A Fleet of Worlds, of other Worlds in quest." The reborn nation, animated by the "one Soul" of Cromwell, now declares, " 'The Ocean is the Fountain of Command' " (355–69, 379).

The rival prince's wonder at Cromwell's return from "death" is thus a testimony to England's renewal. This long, imputed speech (349–94), inspired by Cromwell's survival, glances back at England's recovery from "both Wars" (the Civil War and the Dutch war of 1652–54), but it mainly emphasizes what Cromwell has done over the past year: "rig a Navy," "rase and rebuild their State" (351–52). The note of admiring envy in the quotation intimates an expansive future for England. The speaker, however, cannot quite place "That one Man still" (line 375), this Noah founding his *novum ordo* upon the *imperium* of the sea:

> "He seems a King by long Succession born,
> And yet the same to be a King does scorn.
> Abroad a King he seems, and something more,

At Home a Subject on the equal Floor.
O could I once him with our Title see,
So should I hope yet he might Dye as wee."

(387–92)

The foreign prince is baffled by Cromwell's proudly republican status, noted in the middle couplet. The first and last couplets about traditional succession and regal mortality are more significant, though, because they echo the poem's chief public topic.

The poet begins his envoy (395–402) with an apology for quoting this praise inspired by malice: "Pardon, great Prince, if thus their Fear or Spight / More than our Love and Duty do thee Right." He thus artfully dissociates himself from the foreign speaker's perverse wish that Cromwell were crowned king. The gesture no more confirms Marvell a republican, however, than the closing allusion to the angel at Bethesda proves that Oliver is Christ. The final third of the poem falls apart, in fact, if we force Cromwell into either of these roles: either Machiavelli's founding legislator who abdicates, like Lord Archon in *Oceana;* or a Christian messiah heralding the millennium. The Machiavellian model of a republic of *buoni ordini* is realized only imperfectly in the *concors discordia* of "Amphion," and government cannot by laws accomplish the radical and dynamic *innovatio* overseen by this Noah. On quite different grounds, Marvell also rejects a Christic model for Cromwell.[22]

Fifth Monarchists and republicans alike feared that Cromwell might assume the crown. For a republican like Ludlow, reviving the monarchy would have been a shameful betrayal of the *cause,* to be corrected by assassination. The Fifth Monarchists, however, considered monarchy an affront to providence. A Cromwellian dynasty would perpetuate hereditary succession, the temporal reign of the Beast. Oliver's coronation would thus be the immediate signal for war with Christ's saints. Their millennial monarchy under Christ must differ from the previous four under historical monarchs. It would be an aristocracy of the spirit led by "saints" completely freed from the customary legal and moral restraints imposed on the unregenerate sons of Adam and Noah. Freedom to prophesy was a mark of their election. Caught up in the Pentecostal spirit of Acts 2, they forgot or brushed aside Christ's warning from Acts 1: "It is not for you to know the times or the seasons, which the Father hath put in his own power."[23]

Marvell introduces them immediately after Noah, characterizing them as parricides who had watched for Cromwell's fall and who rejoice at his apparent death. They are his "Chammish issue" — that is, illegitimate pretenders to his rule, renegade sons outside the line of true spiritual succession. Wallace points out that the biblical parallel was important to royalists who upheld patriarchal succession. For them, Ham "was a defection from God's original plan," an elective (and therefore inauthentic) king from whom Nimrod was descended. Wallace applies the scriptural parallel to 1654: "The sons of Cham, of whom the chief was Nimrod, are waiting to seize control of the state, and only Cromwell stands between them and the fulfilment of their designs; they are overtly contrasted with the noble family of Cromwell. If the crown is not to devolve on the Chammish issue, as it did in the Bible, it must descend to the worthy offspring." Noah and his "Chammish issue" do clearly signal the topic of succession here, but I doubt that Marvell is counseling Oliver to establish a dynasty. As the earlier passage on Elijah demonstrates, the succession and legitimacy the poet is most concerned with are spiritual.[24]

And it is not succession to a *monarchy*. Cromwell is not, and must not be, a king. The Gideon passage showed, and the heathen admiration of the foreign prince confirms, that "to be *Cromwell* was a greater thing, / Then ought below, or yet above a King" — "*above* a King" referring to the limitless authority of which Cromwell divested himself to become Protector. Cromwell must not be king because he holds a higher office: not the office of the Machiavellian new prince (the self-limiting founder) or that of the expected Messiah. It is the office that Marvell distinguishes simply by the title of "Captain": a unique but mortal leader whose charisma has been acquired by submitting to the rod of the supreme authority — that is, by his having "Kiss[ed] the approaching, nor yet angry Son" (line 106).

Marvell's title of captain has the same etymology (*caput*) and force as Milton's epithet in his sonnet when he salutes "Cromwell, our chief of men." Cromwell's unique office is primarily temporal, although Marvell is obliged to relate it to the spiritual order forecast by the Fifth Monarchists. While *The First Anniversary,* like Dryden's later *Annus Mirabilis,* is a reply to their prophecies, in either poem the eschatological polemic is secondary to the main historical purpose. Despite both poets' unmistakably political bias, their scriptural allusions have confused modern critics too apt to equate the Bible with the spirit and to ignore its historical or literal meaning, which was actually more relevant for their typology. Passages like Marvell's *confessio* ("Hence oft I think, if in some happy Hour / High Grace should meet in one with highest Pow'r") foster this confusion by introducing into a public oration what sounds like private religious sentiment.

Why he introduced the topic of the millennium becomes clear later, when we get to the diatribe upon the "Chammish issue." Marvell's poem celebrates the great Captain's feat of renewing the nation out of chaos. His basic fable of the Flood meant that sooner or later Noah, Captain of the original Ark of state, had to appear. But the Fifth Monarchists broadcasted their rival version of the same myth, with Christ replacing Noah as the innovator of a spiritual kingdom and rescuing the saints not from the Deluge but from the Beast out of the sea—a rescue that escapes the chaos of ocean and time's watery maze as neatly as it transcends politics and logic. The poet cannot allow these zealous fundamentalists to appropriate the scriptural text, any more than Cromwell might suffer Barebone's Parliament to seize the helm of government. Marvell's quarrel with the Fifth Monarchists is literally a *hermeneutic* struggle over biblical interpretation.

This sharp contest over scriptural meanings, which will become even more prevalent in Dryden's writing, drastically affects Marvell's poem. I focus my analysis on the way the poet uses Noah and Elijah to frame the question of succession. Cromwell had to face the problem of freedom not just among the fissiparous republicans but in religion: in the tendency of the Reformation spirit to split up into an anarchy of sects and schisms. The Fifth Monarchists are his "Chammish issue" because they benefit most from the "sober Liberty" that Cromwell extended to them by his notorious protection of religious Independents. Among fanatics, spiritual liberty quickly degenerates into antinomianism. The Christian liberty of Milton and Saint Paul, never a practical rule for political governance, was distorted and made the basis for a morally inane doctrine of *dominium in gratia,* to the great annoyance of Cromwell's regime.

What looked to Hirst like the pot calling the kettle black, then, is Marvell trying to wrest the hermeneutic tools out of uncouth hands. Ignorantly pretending to expound their Captain's historical role—a pretense Marvell curbed in his own poems on Cromwell—they rush into the tent of the *arcana imperii* to "see his Nakedness," and, in their vain rage, they expose their own. The bastard sons of liberty prove libertines. The text they would interpret becomes their snare, as Marvell demonstrates by turning its meaning against them. They fail to read Genesis reflexively as a mirror of their own spirit. If they misapprehend Noah's drunken nakedness at the beginning of history, no doubt they have misunderstood the end of history, too, hazily pre-figured in their fundamental text of the Apocalypse. Marvell hints at their mistake when he substitutes for their visionary fifth monarchy — "their new King" with his "fifth Scepter" — the plagues of the fifth trumpet (Rev. 9:1–11). These are the locusts whom Satan released from the bottomless pit with their king, Apollyon (311–12).

Marvell denounces enthusiasts in general here, but his satire takes par-ticular aim at false prophets, who are typified by Mahomet and his "Falling-sickness" (303–4). These are they — Marvell names Feake and Simpson — "who the Scriptures and the Laws deface" and who deride Cromwell's accident as a judgment; for "their Religion only is to Fall" (315, 302). Marvell apparently refers to their obnoxious assertion that Cromwell's fall confirms a national cataclysm. Drunk with the license of prophesying, they have lost all reflexivity and cannot see that by invoking Doomsday, they place them-selves, too, before the throne of judgment (Rev. 4). Feake and Simpson are like the two witnesses of Revelation 11:3–11: "And I will give power unto my two witnesses, and they shall prophesy a thousand two hundred and three-score days, clothed in sackcloth. . . . And when they shall have finished their testimony, the beast that ascendeth out of the bottomless pit shall make war against them, and shall overcome them, and kill them. . . . And after three days and a half the Spirit of Life from God entered into them, and they stood upon their feet; and great fear fell upon them which saw them." Of the many resurrections, both infernal and blessed, revealed to John in ex-pectation of the Second Coming, this is probably the most ghastly.

"THE FERTILE STORM":
MARVELLIAN PROPHECY

To counterbalance both the false prophecies of Cromwell's stumbling and this parody of the Fifth Monarchists' "falling," Marvell has provided the vision of Elijah ascending in the chariot. In that vision, Cromwell once again is imagined outsoaring the oceanic chaos of our "low World." Like the drowned Lycidas, he is borne above its "Panique groan,"

> Such as the dying Chorus sings by turns,
> And to Deaf seas, and ruthless Tempests mourns,
> When now they sink, and now the plundring Streams
> Break up each Deck, and rip the Oaken seams.

> But thee triumphant hence the firy Carr,
> And firy Steeds had born out of the Warr,
> From the low World, and thankless Men above,
> Unto the Kingdom blest of Peace and Love.
> We only mourn'd our selves, in thine Ascent,
> Whom thou hadst left beneath with Mantle rent.
>
> (211–20)

Had the great Captain abandoned the sinking ark or left "the headstrong People" without their charioteer, there would be nobody to succeed him.[25]

With these lines, the poet brings to an end the hypothetical "one Sorrow" that he chose to "interweave among / The other Glories of our yearly Song" and that he places exactly at the center of his poem (181–220). He returns to the historical destiny of his hero, going back to the point at which Cromwell abdicated from "all delight of Life" to assume command of the nation. The central figure of Elijah is kept before us, however, by the metaphor of the people's charioteer, which is immediately followed by the ambiguous assertion, "For to be *Cromwell* was a greater thing, / Then ought below, or yet above a King" (225–26). Unlike the quotation from the rival prince (389–90), these lines are not republican; the poet is not asking us merely to admire this Cato for leaving the contentment of rural sovereignty to serve his country. The stress is rather on Cromwell's obedience and humility in "Yielding to Rule, because it made thee Less" (line 228). Cromwell's classical prayer for "An healthful mind within a Body strong" was answered when "an higher Force him push'd / Still from behind, and it before him rush'd" (232, 239–40). Marvell remarkably blends servitude and potency into the single image of a cloud. His fertile storm heralds the Son of Man.

The cloud, like the horses, the charioteer, the mantle, and Cromwell's imagined ascent, are all connected with Elijah. In the span of twenty-four lines (215–38), Cromwell fictitiously ascends as Elijah and historically descends as Elijah's cloud that "wet the King." In the very center of the passage, Marvell hints at what it means "to be *Cromwell*." The "fertile Storm," like the original Deluge, can stand only for tempestuous innovation; Marvell signals his hermeneutic intent by veering from Scripture, where the cloud did *not* wet King Ahab. If Cromwell is a great Captain, a Noah and a judge, is he also something more—a prophet or even a messiah?

Wallace tries to explain Marvell's elusiveness here by quoting a political exegesis of the scriptural text that he finds "identical with Marvell's. . . .

Elijah was both chariot and charioteer because one is led while the other leads, demonstrating 'that he rules well who first is led in obedience.' " Wallace furthermore makes Cromwell out to be "both Elijah and the storm, just as in the ode he had been scourge and deliverer," while Hirst wants to link Elijah with Cromwell's prayers for relief from drought. I think these attempts to find a literal gloss for the allusions to Elijah are misguided. They ignore the poet's declared intention of embroidering ("purling," line 184) his annual history at this point by offering a more distant, memorial perspective. Supposing Cromwell had died, exactly what would have been his significance? The fiction of his Elijah-like death is made the clue to his life (221–42), which, read prophetically, can shed light on "those high Decrees . . . undiscern'd among the tumult blind."[26]

The meaning of Elijah's reappearance is stated in the penultimate verse of the Old Testament: "Behold, I will send you Elijah the prophet before the coming of the great and dreadful day of the Lord" (Malachi 4:5). Jesus (Matt. 11:10–11) tells his Jewish disciples that Malachi's prophecy refers to him, and that John the Baptist is the "Elijah" meant in the text; some Jews reportedly thought Jesus himself might be Elijah (Mark 6:15). In the interpretation eventually settled upon by Christian dogma, the Jewish messiah and the day of the Lord (Yahweh) became Christ's Second Coming (Parousia) and Doomsday. The Christian Apocalypse with its *returning* Messiah is at odds with the tradition of the Jewish messiah, who is merely Yahweh's agent of justice—another earthly King David who comes to reform the world, not to annihilate it and raise his faithful to a transcendent Heaven.[27]

Christ the Messiah was to appear in history twice. John the Baptist heralded the first advent, but the Gospels name no harbinger of the Son of Man's return. Their authors were not interested in its chronology. Expecting Christ's imminent arrival (Parousia), they never spoke of a historical *return.* Jesus himself compares it with Noah's Flood: "Heaven and earth shall pass away, but my words shall not pass away. But of that day and hour knoweth no man, no, not the angels of heaven, but my Father only. But as the days of Noe were, so shall also the coming of the Son of man be. For as in the days that were before the flood they were eating and drinking, marrying and giving in marriage, until the day that Noe entered into the ark, and knew not until the flood came, and took them all away; so shall also the coming of the Son of man be" (Matt. 24:35–39).

As they gradually realized that the Parousia is an event belonging to the indefinite future, later generations of Christians revived the Old Testament promise that Elijah would herald the Apocalypse. The standard doctrine came from Augustine. At the end of book 20 of *De Civitate Dei* 20, he describes the signs of Doomsday: "At or in connection with that judgment the following events shall come to pass, as we have learned: Elias the Tishbite shall come; the Jews shall believe; Antichrist shall persecute; Christ shall judge; the dead shall rise; the good and the wicked shall be separated; the world shall be burned and renewed. All these things, we believe, shall come to pass; but how, or in what order, human understanding cannot perfectly teach us, but only the experience of the events themselves." "Elias" (Elijah) will expound the law to the Jews, teaching them rightly to understand it as Christians and their own prophets do.[28]

By alluding to Elijah, Marvell associates Cromwell with the conversion of the Jews and the Second Coming. His poetic allusion avoids directly prophesying a millennium. It is a *reply* to such prophecies—to Fifth Monarchists like Hannah Trapnel, who attacked Cromwell and his government in 1654: "They are so taken up and wrapt up in their own mantles, that they have no eyes to look up for Elias his mantle." This rant from one of the "hypocritically strict" (line 317) draws a skillfully hermeneutic answer from the poet. Marvell weaves a "thred / Of purling Ore, a shining wave" (183–84) into his tapestry of the Cromwellian year. Elijah and Cromwell, ascension and mortality, Apocalypse and Flood, are brought together from sources lying far apart, just as Christ's words (above) on Noah and the Second Coming are distanced from the lover's words to his Coy Mistress: he would "Love you ten years before the Flood: / And you should if you please refuse / Till the Conversion of the *Jews*."[29]

Flood and Apocalypse are the limits of the providential time series from which the poet has selected his tributary year. All the actions of Cromwell are perfected within time. As the "great Captain" of his nation and the church, he is more like a Jewish messiah than a Christ, whom he merely serves. *The First Anniversary* was meant to be a public record of Cromwell's innovation. Pressures from the millenarians, however, warp the poem from its historical alignment and force its hero to confront the ultimate *innovatio* of the Apocalypse. The confrontation is staged by foreshadowing Cromwell's prophetic dimension in the figure of Elijah. The poet creates a moment of prophetic identification that overlaps England's crisis of historical succession: he meets the danger of a void in government by feigning an apocalyptic leap from time to eternity. I hear no suggestion that Marvell wanted Cromwell to found a dynasty, and I see a feebly republican hope, at best, that the constitution established by the Protector might outlast his personal rule. Marvell leaves the problem of succession hanging. If Elijah's appearance implies some wish for spiritual succession, the metaphor of the "Mantle rent" clouds that prospect, too. The torn mantle lends a touch of hermeneutic reflexivity. The public poet identifies himself with Elisha expecting a double measure of foresight from Elijah, but the metaphor confesses his frustration as the great Captain's official prophet.

As a celebration of Cromwell's new government, *The First Anniversary* proclaims a *novum ordo saeclorum* whose precise millennial significance is unclear. Historians since Charles Firth have usually regarded the Protectorate as an obvious move back to the old constitution. Marvell, however, concentrates on Cromwell's innovation. When he wrote, he probably knew that Cromwell had been offered the crown the year before, at the time of the Instrument of Government. Given Cromwell's refusal and the fact that Feake continued to preach up Gideon's example as a warning, the poem's allusion to Gideon is doubly ironical. Marvell seems to push the question of succession into the background, diverting our attention from the restoration of national monarchy to the Puritan epic of England's millennial hegemony and "The great Designes kept for the latter Dayes" (line 110). In that perspective, the "watry Leaguers [that] all the world surround" (line 366) are really mustering for Armageddon.

CLAIMING A TITLE IN CROMWELL: DRYDEN'S *HEROIQUE STANZAS*

Written during the Interregnum like Marvell's Cromwell poems, Dryden's first offering as a public poet registers the crosscurrents of millenarian and republican thought. Although he hesitates to adopt the apocalyptic view of Cromwell's rule just examined, Dryden learned much from the way Marvell used hermeneutics to deliberate upon the problems of monarchy and succession. The *Heroique Stanzas* are at one with *The First Anniversary* in acclaiming Cromwell's legacy of stable government. What is perhaps most remarkable is that Dryden goes further than Marvell in implying that Cromwell has established a new dynasty. Although he does not mention Cromwell's successor (as Marvell does in the unconvincing lines on Richard at the end of his "Poem upon the Death of O.C."), Dryden strikes the attitude of a public poet officiating at the ceremonial founding of the House of Cromwell. His *Heroique Stanzas to the Glorious Memory of Cromwell* culminate the last rites actually given to the Lord Protector. Those rites bore every mark of a royal funeral. Cromwell's "Vertue" was not poisoned "With the too early thoughts of being King," by which Dryden means Cromwell's birth was providential: he was destined to achieve the greatest historical *innovatio* of all, a new empire.[30]

Throughout their subsequent emulation as public writers, Marvell and Dryden repeat their contrasting estimates of the Protector's regal power. After the Restoration, their Puritan radicalism made both poets critical of monarchy in different ways. Marvell was skeptical of Charles but not of the crown, whereas Dryden, as we shall see, came to question the institution of monarchy itself. His political skepticism would become explicit only with the dedication of *All for Love* early in 1678, shortly after Marvell's death and nineteen years after the *Heroique Stanzas*. In Marvell's Interregnum poems, we can easily trace the Whig propagandist of the 1670s. On the other hand, we search in vain for an incipient Toryism either in Dryden's early work or in his poems and plays before 1678 (see chapter 7).

These observations will sound less paradoxical if one recalls that the opposition of royalist and radical, which is a modern opposition stemming from republican and liberal attitudes, cannot be applied without anachronism to the 1650s. Then, a *royalist* was a radical: someone who dared to revive monarchy when the institution had been pronounced officially dead. To Dryden, the crown would always be a novelty; he was suspicious of it and, I believe, never quite learned to submit to it with the wholehearted conviction of a born Tory. Marvell could at least remember the old order of kings who were presumably limited by divine and human laws. Dryden took his conception of monarchy from the formidable but unconstitutional example of Cromwell, who refused to spell out the extent of his powers. Apart from differences of temperament, it is no surprise that Marvell should have become the preliberal Whig, a rationalist in politics in contrast to his younger rival. Dryden professed obedience to a voluntaristic if not arbitrary rule and allied himself uneasily with the Tories only after he was driven to seek his political patrons among Cavaliers like Thomas Osborne, the earl of Danby.

Less superficial than the opposition of royalists to radicals is the conceptual contradiction between messianic millennium and secular restoration.

That historical contradiction enters the thinking of both poets, but only in Dryden's work does it generate a serious tension. For disappointed radicals like Milton, the Restoration of an earthly king meant forsaking the godly republic and returning to Egyptian bondage. Marvell sympathized fully with Milton's reforming vision but was prepared to defer the millennium; like Hobbes and modern liberals who inherit a godless state, Marvell divorced the Kingdom of God from the secular world. Dryden's more radical, Erasmian ideal of a church that was both visible and catholic barred his assent to this preliberal separation of church and state. Dryden was among the chorus of poets heralding the Stuart Restoration because he had first learned to celebrate the godly empire of Oliver Cromwell. The chief theme of his early Restoration poems, as we shall see, is the divine providence that forged the chain of events restoring England's throne. Less than eighteen months before writing *Astraea Redux,* Dryden had published a poem designed to "claime a *Title*" in the "*Heroïque Vertue* Heav'n set[s] out" in Oliver Cromwell. In that work too, the poet diligently acknowledged that the powers that be are of God. Only readers looking for the views of a nascent royalist in these two poems would complain that Dryden's political principles are slippery or nonexistent. His politics rest upon an immanent providence. Had he not already reflected, much like Hobbes, on the incomprehensible yet divine purpose that is manifestly active in secular affairs, he could not have celebrated the miracle of Restoration.[31]

Dryden's public interpretation of Cromwell comes eight and a half years after Marvell's ode. In contrast to the Horatian play of wit in the earlier poem, with its ironical wonder at "restless *Cromwel*" (line 9), Dryden offers an imperial garland of measured, "Heroique Stanzas" to crown the Protector's memory. Even though Cromwell is dead, Dryden's poem is not an elegy like Marvell's "Poem upon the Death of O.C." Cromwell's departure is regarded more as an apotheosis, a pagan deification. His public achievements are immortal and loom so large as to make grief appear indecorous. In contrast to the young Lord Hastings commemorated in Dryden's juvenile poem, Cromwell has bequeathed to the world a legacy more substantial than the Platonic ideas left to Hastings's "Virgin-Widow" (1:5). Hastings's life was untimely cut off by the smallpox, whereas Cromwell lived to perfect his life work and to attain "a *Fame* so truly *Circular*" that the poet cannot tell where to begin his praises or end them. "Our best notes are treason to his fame," the poet says. Those who praise him the highest "Add not to his immortall Memorie, / But do an act of friendship to their own" (1:11).

Whereas Marvell eight years before had introduced himself by saying, "The forward Youth that would appear / Must now forsake his *Muses* dear," Dryden steps forth as Apollo *musagetes* to begin the ceremony. Above all, he maintains the decorum of the public poet:

> And now 'tis time; for their Officious haste,
> Who would before have born him to the sky,
> Like *eager Romans* ere all Rites were past
> Did let too soon the *sacred Eagle* fly.

The poet must control by his ceremonial decorum the potentially disruptive topics of fortune and Cromwell's *virtù:* "His *Grandeur* he deriv'd from Heav'n alone, / For he was great e're Fortune made him so." Marvell, by contrast, swings violently between human and supernatural polarities: " 'Tis Madness to resist or blame / The force of angry Heavens flame; / And, if we would speak true, / Much to the Man is due" (lines 25–29). Adapting Machiavelli's remark on *Fortuna*'s capriciousness, Dryden works out the perverse symmetry between the rise of Cromwell and the fall of Pompey both in their forty-sixth year (Pompey reached his fifty-ninth year, like Cromwell, but was beheaded, like Charles):

> Fortune (that easie Mistresse of the young
> But to her auncient servants coy and hard)
> Him at that age her favorites rank'd among
> When she her best-lov'd *Pompey* did discard.
>
> (1:12)

The birth of *virtù* in Cromwell is a superhuman event respected by either poet, but Dryden is careful to separate it from ambition: "Nor was his Vertue poyson'd soon as born / With the too early thoughts of being King." Marvell leaves this *virtù* dangerously ambiguous, punning on the cosmic irony in the fact that Cromwell, before he manifested his prodigiously "industrious Valour," "liv'd reserved and austere, / As if his highest plot" were "To plant the Bergamot."[32]

Dryden's praise of Cromwell, always subordinate to the ceremonial occasion, is more politically reflexive than Marvell's. Because his poem is public and less self-revealing, Dryden avoids the paralysis that results from Marvell's conjunction of ironic detachment and his sense of the Machiavellian moment. Marvell, despite his seeming deliberation and his call for resolve, never takes a stand for or against Cromwell. The perplexing result is nicely described by Blair Worden: "Is the ode pro-Cromwellian or anti-Cromwellian? It is both, and it is neither, and yet we know not. A man who will not take sides in politics is an incomplete man. A man who takes sides in politics is a foolish man. This Marvell knows, as we can deduce from his later correspondence, for which there have been too few kind words." Marvell's judgment on the Civil Wars ("the Cause was too good to have been fought for") has won him sympathy for his Hamlet-like irresolution. I cannot agree with Worden, however, that "the sense of time that pervades Marvell's poetry, as a force that either masters or is mastered, brings him close to Machiavelli's teaching." While Marvell's "sense of time" lets him depict tragedy or pathos, neither in the Cromwell poems nor the later, Restoration satires does he approach the historical gravity of Machiavelli's viewpoint.[33]

By withholding the 1650 ode from print, Marvell showed greater political caution than Dryden and therefore a less decided commitment to the role of public poet. What Worden says of the Cromwell ode is quite true: "Marvell has given timelessness to a desperate and portentous moment in his country's history." But an unpublished poem on a timeless event hardly amounts to a significant gesture of public deliberation; as an example of rhetorical prudence, its importance is slight. Both Aristotle and Machiavelli warn expressly against trying to study prudence (*phronēsis*) by isolating the virtue from specific, *temporal* achievements.[34]

For this reason, I would insist upon the superior historical sense found in Dryden's poem on Cromwell. In chapter 1, above, I noted that panegyric is ruined by deliberation. In order to praise, one must take up a definite standpoint; personal anxiety is as much out of place as private irony, and so is the suggestion of crisis. If on the other hand the poet's rhetoric is deliberative, it should lead to resolve and public action. Marvell is prompted to exclaim, "What may not then our *Isle* presume / While Victory his Crest does plume" and to venture a millenarian prediction:

> A *Caesar* he ere long to *Gaul*,
> To *Italy* an *Hannibal*,

And to all States not free
Shall *Clymacterick* be.
                    (lines 97–104)

Dryden infers a more definite future from the past and present, as in *The First Anniversary*. From Cromwell's "high-spring" of heroic *virtù*, he says,

our forraign Conquests flow
Which yet more glorious triumphs do portend,
Since their Commencement to his Armes they owe,
If Springs as high as Fountaines may ascend.

He made us *Freemen* of the *Continent*
Whom Nature did like Captives treat before,
To nobler prey's the *English Lyon* sent,
And taught him first in *Belgian walks* to rore.   (1:15)

To the carefully articulated historical order of Dryden's poem correspond also the firmness of its rhythms and the solid coherence of its physical world. In *The First Anniversary*, Cromwell appears as the sun, but in Marvell's earlier ode, natural phenomena take on a transient, apocalyptic character. For example, Marvell had made a playful, punning transition from the predatory falcon (91–96) to plumed "Victory." The aviary figures that open and close Dryden's poem, the imperial eagle and the nesting halcyons, are identified with the same order of nature that has claimed Cromwell and that signalized his death by a storm, with the ocean sending him the extraordinary "tribute" of a beached whale. These portents, the poet gives us to understand, were merely nature's brief convulsion marking the translation of Cromwell's heroic *virtù* into the earthly immortality of his monuments:

No Civill broyles have since his death arose,
But *Faction* now by *Habit* does obey:
And *Warrs* have that respect for his repose,
As *Winds* for *Halcyons* when they breed at Sea.

His Ashes in a peacefull Urne shall rest,
His Name a great example stands.   (1:16)

Most important, Dryden reflects himself publicly in the poem's historical moment by venturing a political judgment. Marvell's ode attempts this his-

torical reflexiveness only in the opening and closing lines. We see the "forward Youth . . . appear" on the historical scene, roused from his shadows
by the Lucanic return of "restless *Cromwell*" (1–9), and he reappears at the
end of the poem to volunteer encouragement. Throughout the body of the
poem, he never really leaves his shade, preferring to participate intellectually
in the Cromwellian phenomenon by reflecting its various light, rather than
by establishing a civic presence. Dryden's persona, by contrast, is politically
defined and contemporary. He locates himself within the same order of history as Cromwell and the audience.

     This order is political, since the poet is deliberating about our com-
mon "interest" and claiming a title in Cromwell and the innovation he has
wrought. The *Heroique Stanzas* produce no dramatic scene like that in which
King Charles adorned "the Tragick Scaffold," "While round the armed
Bands / Did clap their bloody hands" (54–56). Such *ekphrases*, diverting us
by their wit or pathos, also rob us of political self-consciousness. Dryden's
persona, avoiding such distraction, moves easily among superficially neo-
classical similes whose immediate aptness can be admired without interrupt-
ing the rhetorical program: "His latest Victories still thickest came / As, neer
the *Center, Motion* does increase; / Till he, pres'd down by his own weighty
name, / Did, like the *Vestall,* under spoyles decease" (1:15–16). Dryden succeeds as public poet, in other words, by not getting too caught up in his
poetry. Putting this more constructively, Dryden maintains a suitably reflexive, public decorum. To do so, he must identify his political standpoint
and set before us his deliberations on the dead Cromwell's historical role.

     During the last decade of his life, Cromwell was the champion of reaction
and settlement. No council or institution could equal his authority because
nobody dared stand as near as he to the source of revolution. From December 1648 onward, Cromwell was for Dryden the man who held the army
and the radicals in check, who "disciplined" the delinquent king and malig-
nant royalists, and who made the "*Commons* sullenly obey" his "Heroïque
Vertue" that had been sent by "Heav'n" to recall a contentious England to
her imperial destiny. Looking back on ten years of Cromwell's achievements,
Dryden chose his phrases to suggest the Protector's providential gifts. Great
as these were, Dryden was even more impressed by Cromwell's prudence:

> When absent, yet we conquer'd in his right;
> For though some meaner Artist's skill were shown

> In mingling colours, or in placing light,
> Yet still the *faire Designment* was his own.   (1:14)

Dryden insists that Cromwell's prudence is something more than an occasional response to rebellion. His "faire Designment" lasts beyond the change of death. The figure is revealing. Art was Dryden's first and last metaphor for prudence. By making his poetic art a surrogate for providence, Dryden fashioned a versatile mirror in which he could reflect the historical world of human action — the *saeculum* — while containing it safely within a larger, providential design. In 1659, facing the potential chaos of innovation, Dryden opted to cash in on the Protector's legacy. The *Heroique Stanzas* were one way to claim a title in Cromwell's prudence. The other way, taken by Marvell four years previously when Cromwell was alive, was to interpret him as a messiah and to emphasize his charisma rather than his historical prudence. Dryden, with the example of Marvell's decidedly mythical interpretation before him, preferred to stress the lucky conjunction of piety and *virtù* at this historical, transient moment. His final, profoundly ironical heroic stanza affirms a fragile calm resting on nothing more than Cromwell's name and ashes. Cromwell's memory and fair design are all that remain of his active prudence — the sole force capable of harnessing rebellion:

> His Ashes in a peacefull Urne shall rest,
> His Name a great example stands to show
> How strangely high endeavours may be blest,
> Where *Piety* and *valour* joyntly goe.

In their two poems on the founding of Protectorate and empire that I have paired in this chapter, Marvell and Dryden converged more nearly than at any other point in their careers. Using a purely formal measure, one might compare their works at ten-year intervals — their difference in age. The Cromwell ode of 1650 has its counterpart in *Astraea Redux* of 1660, *The Rehearsal Transpros'd* foreshadows *Religio Laici*, and *An Account of the Growth of Popery*, begun in the midseventies, is answered by Dryden's translation of *The History of the League*. But in poems published at the start of 1655 and 1659, respectively, the two poets addressed the same historical questions. Marvell taught Dryden how to deal with innovation, specifically in the form of a monarchy for which there was no precedent and whose succession was doubtful. Marvell's example made an indelible impression on Dryden, and twenty years later such lines as

> *Cromwell* alone with greater Vigour runs . . .
> *Cromwell* alone doth with new Lustre spring
>
> (7–11)

still echoed in his memory, together with the key image of Elijah's ascension and torn mantle:

> *Sh*—— alone my perfect image bears,
> Mature in dullness from his tender years.
> *Sh*—— alone, of all my Sons, is he
> Who stands confirm'd in full stupidity. . . .
> He said, but his last words were scarcely heard,
> For *Bruce* and *Longvil* had a *Trap* prepar'd,
> And down they sent the yet declaiming Bard.
> Sinking he left his Drugget robe behind,
> Born upwards by a subterranean wind.
> The Mantle fell to the young Prophet's part,
> With double portion of his Father's Art.   (2:54, 60)

The mock coronation of *Mac Flecknoe,* conceived at the time of the Exclusion crisis, reflects at a generation's remove the two Cromwellian poets' joint analysis of monarchy under the destabilizing conditions of the Machiavellian moment.[35]

This Talking Trumpet:
Dryden's Hermeneutics

In contrast to Marvell's Cromwell ode with its vivid scene on the scaffold of Regicide, Dryden's *Heroique Stanzas* never mention King Charles or England's vanished monarchy. Instead, Dryden assimilates the Puritans' godly "cause" to Cromwell's half-accomplished mission as a Protestant emperor. He makes Cromwell the emulator of Alexander the Great and the nemesis of Pope Alexander VII:

> That old unquestion'd Pirate of the Land,
> Proud *Rome*, with dread, the fate of *Dunkirk* har'd;
> And trembling wish't behind more *Alpes* to stand,
> Although an *Alexander* were her guard.

In the "Heroïque Vertue" that sustained Cromwell's international conquests Dryden sees an omen of the providential future awaiting England:

> From this high-spring our forraign Conquests flow
> Which yet more glorious triumphs do portend,
> Since their Commencement to his Armes they owe,
> If Springs as high as Fountaines may ascend.
>
> (1:15; cf. line 50)

This is as close as the *Heroique Stanzas* get to prophecy. The final, conditional line is characteristically reserved, but it is enough to prove that Cromwell inspired in Dryden as in Marvell the Puritan vision of an Elect Nation under its godly ruler. Whereas Marvell, in *The First Anniversary,* imagines

Cromwell's messianic role at the coming Apocalypse, Dryden seeks to clarify Cromwell's historical role by suggesting that the Protector has founded a new cycle of the Roman Empire on the soil of a reformed England. Marvell's scriptural hermeneutics in *The First Anniversary* depends explicitly upon the book of Revelation, and many of his poems allude to apocalyptic events. Dryden's allusions point in another direction. He likes to find secular analogues to scriptural events; or, failing that, to historicize Scripture itself—and not only in *Absalom and Achitophel*. In contrast to the symbolic language of apocalypse, Dryden perfected a language that imitates the literal phenomena of nature and history. I shall call this literal imitation *providential mimesis*. Because it expounds the *saeculum* instead of revelation, Dryden's hermeneutics often seems to invert the older practice of interpreting history according to Scripture. For instance, when Dryden compares Cromwell—and later James II—with Constantine, the first godly emperor, the English rulers are not merely fulfillments of a figural type. Cromwell's strong example actually forces us to reevaluate his scriptural prototypes such as Moses or David or the captains in Revelation 19:19. Dryden's turn to a more historical or literalistic typology is in keeping with the trend of hermeneutics in early modern Europe. Moreover, his hermeneutic literalism accords with the directives for sermons given to clergy after 1660 by the restored Church of England, who sought to defuse the radical potential of certain scriptural texts by showing that the historical context of these incendiary passages made them irrelevant to the present.[1]

We saw Marvell engaged in a hermeneutic struggle with the Fifth Monarchists, who arbitrarily interpreted Cromwell's coaching accident as a providential sign. Marvell tried to turn the tables on them by linking the event with Elijah's chariot of fire. Given its Interregnum provenance, scriptural hermeneutics was a dangerous tool to handle. The biblical allusions in Dryden's Restoration poems up to *Annus Mirabilis*—for example, the figure of David in *Astraea Redux*—are carefully chosen so as not to disturb the aura of epideictic triumph. Dryden's overall achievement in satire can make us forget that he exercised this talent only in prologues and epilogues before he wrote *Mac Flecknoe* and *Absalom and Achitophel*. Not until *The Medall* of 1682 did he find his métier as scourge of the sectarians and their "talking Trumpet" (2:48). The hermeneutics of providential mimesis that he skillfully adapted to *Absalom and Achitophel* was in fact two decades in perfecting, and he employed it for satire because by 1681 his ends had become partisan.

I shall reserve his satires for my final chapter and concentrate here on his other major poem of 1681–82. *Religio Laici,* besides being his first explicit statement of religious opinions, is Dryden's fullest comment on hermeneutics. Together with *The Medall,* it registers his discovery that the historical origins of sectarianism were political and that republican anarchy flowed from a source close to his own Puritan radicalism.

THE ELECT NATION
AND THE ANGLICAN REACTION

Dryden never mentioned religion in his addresses to patrons until 1686, after he had turned Catholic. On the contrary, he liked to present himself as companion to the wits, to whom he dedicated several plays: to John Wilmot, earl of Rochester, to Sir Charles Sedley, and to John Lord Vaughan. So assiduously did he cultivate the role of *libertin,* or freethinker, that his sallies into religion struck the public as incongruous. When he published *Tyrannick Love* in 1670, Dryden had to fend off the imputation of godlessness; twelve years later Narcissus Luttrell, upon buying a copy of *Religio Laici,* added the word "Atheisticall" to its title. His public character has some bearing on Dryden's biblical hermeneutics. For thirteen years following the Restoration, Dryden remained pretty much at the fringe of a court society whose dramatic taste he learned to gratify. His earlier writings show none of the partisanship that would agitate public life in the 1670s and would energize his poems of the 1680s. His dedications to patrons other than the royal family, although self-interested, were politically inept. Having offered the *Heroique Stanzas* to a tottering dynasty, Dryden paid homage after the Restoration to several fading suns: to Walter Charleton and Roger Boyle, earl of Orrery, to Clarendon and Lady Castlemaine, to Sir Thomas Clifford and William Cavendish, duke of Newcastle. The only rising politician among his patrons was Sir Robert Howard, who became his brother-in-law at the end of 1663 and with whom he quarreled irreparably in 1668.[2]

Only with the political crisis of 1678–81 did Whigs and Tories appear on the scene, and no cohesive parties were formed before the eighteenth century. Most historians nonetheless identify two persisting ideological causes that contributed to the emergence of political partisanship: first, the old division between court and country, intensified at the Restoration by a new wave of office-seekers and later exploited by Danby with his system of clientage; and second, the still older fear of "popery" going back to the sixteenth century. A monarchical, antepartisan attitude to politics is evident in Dryden's stanzas praising the Lord Protector. As we saw, Dryden commemorated Cromwell's imperial achievements that smote "proud Rome with dread." Belief in the imperial destiny of the Elect Nation depended not so much on a messianic leader—a new Constantine like Elizabeth or Cromwell—as upon the nation's will to resist the Antichrist. When it became apparent to them that Charles II was no Constantine, M.P.s of Marvell's persuasion banded together to oppose court policies that they suspected were advancing popery. If the king declined the fight against Antichrist, then that historic role fell to parliament and to its country members, who were the guardians of the national interest.[3]

The national surge of antipopery in 1672–74, which grew out of the third Dutch War, the Declaration of Indulgence, and the Test Act, resulted in the distrust and fear expressed by Marvell in *An Account of the Growth of Popery.* The distrust was not inspired by actual fear of England's Catholic laity, who were a tiny minority (at most 5 per cent) of the population. "Anti-catholicism," a recent scholar has said, "was not a hatred of Catholics as individuals, but a more abstract fear that tended to grow in intensity at times of political crisis." Such "abstract fear" was inseparable from millenarian hope. The fear and hope go back more than a century; they were the twin births of Marian persecutions and John Foxe's *Book of Martyrs.* Antipopery, with its quasi-mythical origin, cannot be resolved into separate religious and political elements.[4]

Readers seeking to locate Dryden's early opinions in the spectrum of antipopish sentiment will find that he usually subordinates any religious and political views he expresses in a work to its mythical pattern or plot. The theme of Protestant empire and of Antichrist's historical conflict with true religion is satirically inverted in *The Indian Emperour,* and it becomes prominent briefly in *Annus Mirabilis* and *Tyrannick Love;* after that, it leaves a diminishing trace in Dryden's other works up till the time of his conversion. By then, he had lost his enthusiasm for political action, though not for political satire. Put into the balance with his Puritan heritage, Dryden's eventual conversion and withdrawal from politics must affect our reading of his early career.

In assessing his public role in *Annus Mirabilis* and other works of the 1660s, one has to suppose that his religious opinions were no more fixed at the time than his political allegiances. Something can be ascertained of both by looking at his commitment to antipopery. Dryden's panegyric design for *Astraea Redux* rules out political or millenarian struggle; accordingly, he imagines that "the hateful names of Parties cease," and he replaces the apocalypse with a new cycle of "times whiter Series." Even so, the Protestant epic of antipopery enters the poem momentarily. The poet recalls that Charles's grandsire Henri IV was "Shock'd by a Covenanting Leagues vast Pow'rs / As holy and as Catholique as ours." Dryden is referring to, and palliating, the king's action of 1650. Charles took the Covenant and renounced his father so the Scots would acclaim him king.[5]

Dryden calls the Scottish power "Catholique" because he remembers they were a threat to England's civil order: "Treacherous *Scotland* to no int'rest true" (1:13). These were Marvell's Picts of "party-colour'd Mind" (*Horatian Ode*, 105–6) whom Cromwell subdued and civilized (*Heroique Stanzas*, 66–68). The allusion to Henri IV briefly invests Charles, elsewhere the prince of peace, in the Cromwellian role of antipopish conqueror (Henri of Navarre eventually defeated the Catholic Ligue to claim his throne). Unlike Dryden's later *Duke of Guise* (1682), which dramatizes a historical parallel, *Astraea Redux* treats popery mythically, associating it, as did Marvell in *The First Anniversary*, with the principle of disorder that the monarch overcomes by justice and of which the great symbol is the monster of primeval chaos. Dryden's panegyric cannot accommodate the Beast of Marvell's overtly apocalyptic poem, so he evokes images of "painted Ancestours" with their "lawless salvage Libertie" and blames Charles's sufferings on "the wild distemper'd rage / Of some black Star infecting all the Skies." In place of a Cromwell soaring vigorously above the chaos of "the Watry maze" to perform "in one Year the work of Ages" (above, chapter 2), Dryden's monarch brings peace to England by refraining from action in this "too too active age" (1:23, 25).

Charles is an imperial conqueror, but, to emphasize that England's renewal is providential, his role is scaled down from creator of order to dutiful propitiator of the gods:

> Tremble ye Nations who secure before
> Laught at those Armes that 'gainst our selves we bore;
> Rous'd by the lash of his own stubborn tail
> Our Lyon now will forraign Foes assail.
> With *Alga* who the sacred altar strowes?

> To all the Sea-Gods *Charles* an Off'ring owes:
> A Bull to thee *Portunus* shall be slain,
> A Lamb to you the Tempests of the Main:
> For those loud stormes that did against him rore
> Have cast his shipwrack'd Vessel on the shore.   (1:25)

This passage from 1660 may be compared with Dryden's image of heroic renewal twenty-eight years later in the figure of the Herculean infant of *Britannia Rediviva* (3:211):

> For see the Dragon winged on his way,
> To watch the Travail, and devour the Prey.
> Or, if Allusions may not rise so high,
> Thus, when *Alcides* rais'd his Infant Cry,
> The Snakes besieg'd his Young Divinity:
> But vainly with their forked Tongues they threat;
> For Opposition makes a Heroe Great.

The Apocalyptic Dragon who watches for the birth of the divine child (Revelation 12) is specifically identified by the poet in a footnote: "Alluding only to the Common-wealth Party, here and in other places of the Poem." Dryden's antipopery has come full circle. Standing on the other side after having converted, he can see that most Protestants are simply ignorant of the truth, as he had been. The real malignants—the active partisans of Antichrist—are the republicans, who, in 1687–88, had renewed their profane cry of toleration.

That Dryden should finally come to equate the Protestant epic's chief symbol of antipopery, the Dragon of the Apocalypse, with republicanism attests not so much to his conversion as to the evolution of his political views. My final chapter will argue that these had undergone a profound change by 1682, well before his conversion. In *Absalom and Achitophel, The Medall,* and *Religio Laici*—all published within the span of a year—Dryden treats republicanism and antipopish zeal as dual menaces to the public quiet. Of all the Tory propagandists, Dryden had the best reasons for remembering the success of religious toleration under Cromwell. Nevertheless, for the sake of partisanship he resolved to damn all gestures of dissent, political and religious alike. As a propagandist, he pretended that rebellion had a merely secular explanation. Instead of looking for a godly design in England's recent travails, he chose to rehash the Tory history of "sedition," forsaking, apparently, the providential mimesis of his earlier poems. Propaganda confined the poet within a narrowly Anglican uniformity. Dryden could no longer sound his earlier theme of the Elect Nation because it was now identified with spiritual radicalism and therefore dissent. His belief in the Puritan epic, upon which Dryden had based his vision of national unity in *Astraea Redux* and *Annus Mirabilis,* could not survive the partisan imperative to brand the enemy.[6]

Settling into his new role of Tory satirist at the age of fifty, Dryden managed to bury his former reputation as libertine playwright. His enemies kept alive the memory of Cromwell's panegyrist and the image of Bayes, but in spite of their detraction, the fame that Dryden suddenly acquired in 1682 was great enough to merit Scott's later epithets of "powerful auxiliary to his party" and "champion of the crown." Even today, Dryden's partisan achievement continues to bias the reading of his earlier, antepartisan works by those who stretch his Toryism back at least to the Restoration, if not before 1660. This bias comes partly from the inherent continuity of the Tory myth and partly from Dryden's success after 1680 in revising history. By insisting on an unbroken national tradition in his poems on the Restoration and by meditating frequently on empire in his plays, he sustained at least into the early 1670s his epic vision of the nation under a Protestant monarch. Between 1678 and 1682, however, Dryden's picture of a unified and continuous national history disappears from his writings. It is replaced by an alternative view of events, which he now interprets from the standpoint of a monarchy threatened by discontinuity and powerless against faction.[7]

Dryden's thoughts about a national church prior to 1680 cannot be recovered without stripping away the varnish of Toryism that was subsequently laid on them. Before a group with recognizable Tory interests was formed, first by Danby and then under pressures created by the Exclusion crisis, a thriving band of Anglican Cavaliers had made their weight felt in the church as well as parliament from the moment of the Restoration. With this faction Dryden could never be in sympathy, if only because they despised his Northamptonshire Puritan origins that implicated him, however indirectly, in the Great Rebellion. Feiling characterizes these Cavaliers as the sons of royalists, too young to have fought in the Civil War but nurtured on vivid memories of their parents' sufferings. They had been raised in the church by Anglican ministers deprived of their benefices. "They have kept their conversation apart," the Protector complained of the royalist gentry, and "have bred and educated their children by the sequestered and ejected clergy, and very much confined their marriages and alliances within their own party, as if they meant to entail their quarrel and prevent the means to reconcile posterity."[8]

Until the Convention Parliament met in April 1660, Dryden probably had little notion of the Cavalier breed or its way of life. Even the prudent George Monck was surprised by the number of young nobles who, having come of age during the Interregnum, claimed their hereditary right to enter the House of Lords in the self-convening Parliament. Monck kept them out until he might know the mood of Commons. Its Cavalier majority required them as allies against the seasoned Presbyterian royalists, who had been concerting among themselves to drive the same hard bargain with Charles that they had offered his father twelve years before (see chapter 1). Admitted to their places, these young lords, led by John Mordaunt, the royalist conspirator, swamped the crew of older Presbyterians. A year later, in May 1661, the youthful peers saw their counterparts in the Commons returned in large numbers. This was the Cavalier Parliament, destined to sit for eighteen years. With the bishops restored to the Lords, Parliament set about reversing the toleration Charles had promised in his Declaration from Breda—the promise of which Dryden made so much when he celebrated the return of mercy with "Astraea," or justice. By the end of 1661, the Presbyterians to whom Charles owed his Restoration saw their religion proscribed by the Anglican Church, now triumphant in its restoration beyond the wildest dreams of its Laudian precursor: "Within a year of Charles II's homecoming the Puritan Revolution had collapsed."[9]

Recent historians like R. A. Beddard and John Spurr have placed a new emphasis on the social and political role of the Anglican Church at the Restoration. The Church represented not just the Cavaliers but a majority of the country who were clamoring for reassurance that the Puritan experiment was at an end. The nation Milton accused of conspiring to "call back again their Egyptian bondage" were also a weary people who had long been deprived of enjoying what was rightfully their own. Although they had no particular affection for their cynical and unreliable king, he stood for legitimacy and property—for the customary ways suspended by the trauma of the Machiavellian moment. Throughout the country, many who were tired of being ruled by a military, centralized government expressed their resentment by adopting the Cavaliers' attitude of loyalty to church and king. Paul Seaward and others have demonstrated that this usually meant giving priority to the *politics* of religion, that is, putting the church even before the crown. Landowners, while not Cavaliers themselves, "had come to regard their religion as part of their birthright, a personal property on a par with their estates. It was from this identification of the Church of England with the rights of private property that the strength of the Anglican establishment derived. Henceforth the landed classes were to take unkindly any action — whether of sectary or papist, monarch or politician — which threatened to undermine their Church."[10]

In their support of the Church, Cavaliers in the Parliament made the law their excuse for rejecting every proposed compromise. This conservatism, to the extent that it was principled, was no bad thing. As the most thoughtful of Clarendon's judicial appointees said, although laws may have consequences "which cannot all by any human prudence at first be foreseen and provided for, yet . . . it is preferable before that arbitrary and uncertain rule which men miscall the law of reason." In any case, the attitude of these proto-Tories — conservative of tradition, landed, parochial — was a potent antidote to republican sentiments. Indeed, the Cavaliers played upon fears of republican anarchy to suppress the least hint of an uprising, such as Thomas Venner's feeble attempt in 1661. As late as 1665, "the established order could still feel itself under attack" from a shadow rebellion set up by *agents provocateurs*. Only this blind fear can explain the Act of Uniformity, which purged the corporations of Nonconformists, or the even more paranoid Conventicle Acts, which deported them.[11]

What is ideologically remarkable about the Cavaliers' implacability is their refusal to acknowledge any difference between religious and political dissent. The phenomenon in mass psychology known today as conspiracy theory induced those who would later form the nucleus of the Tory party to fancy themselves an embattled religious and political corporation threatened by "sedition." Cavalier conspiracy theory, by axiomatically equating dissent with subversion, closely resembled the antipopery we have already discussed. This axiomatic equation made no sense whatever to the ex-Presbyterian Dryden in the 1660s; it is entirely absent from his early works. In 1682, by contrast, he set the Cavalier axiom at the very center of *The Medall*, his "Satire on Sedition."[12]

REGICIDE AND THE ECCLESIASTICAL POLITY

Having discovered, by 1682, that British republicanism and sectarianism both originated in the sixteenth century, Dryden apparently persuaded himself that the Cavalier axiom was historical truth. He decided that the source of rebellion lay in the "talking Trumpet" of biblical hermeneutics. Dryden first set out his new theory in *The Medall* and its preface and in the preface to *Religio Laici* some eight months later. The Cavalier axiom accounts for the strong partisan thrust in the satires of 1681 and 1682. At the same time, however, it greatly complicates the providential mimesis on which Dryden's earlier productions were based. His interpretation of the nation's destiny following the Restoration will come into better focus once we have understood the ideas of church polity and dissent that he articulated more fully in 1682.

In *The Medall*, Shaftesbury is accused of having driven a populist mob, crazed with antipopery, to its opposite extreme of popery: he "Maintains the Multitude can never err; / And sets the people in the Papal Chair" (2:45, lines 86–87). Toward the end of his political attack on this new Jehu who "instructs the Beast to know his native force," the poet suddenly turns to religion and lambasts those who "plead a Call to preach, in spight of Laws":

> But that's no news to the poor injur'd Page;
> It has been us'd as ill in every Age:
> And is constrain'd, with patience, all to take;
> For what defence can *Greek* and *Hebrew* make?
> Happy who can this talking Trumpet seize;
> They make it speak whatever Sense they please!
> 'Twas fram'd, at first, our Oracle t'enquire;
> But, since our Sects in prophecy grow higher,
> The Text inspires not them; but they the Text inspire.
>
> (157–66)

By empowering the mob, Shaftesbury with his demagoguery has tapped a more dangerous source than he knows. Where "The common Cry is ev'n Religion's Test," the mob becomes the arbiter of religion, and "all are God a'mighties in their turns" (lines 103, 110). Pleading a call to preach, the zealots ignore the maxim at the end of *Religio Laici*: "*Common quiet* is *Mankind's concern*" (2:122). They subvert the polity by polarizing its members into rogues and saints grossly identified with their party ("distinguish'd by their Side"). Scripture itself is racked to confess the Good Old Cause, and the sectarian merges in the republican (2:47, lines 154–57).

This passage with its lines on "the poor injur'd Page" seems out of place in a satire directed against sedition in the political order. The impertinence of hermeneutics to this "satyre against sedition" has been overlooked because it anticipates the scriptural hermeneutics of Dryden's first poem on religion, produced later the same year. In its turn, *Religio Laici* makes a correspondingly strong *political* argument. In the first half of the poem, Dryden upholds scriptural revelation against deistic rationalism, and in the second half expounds his "Layman's Faith" in the Anglican via media between the two hermeneutical extremes identified with Roman Catholicism and antinomianism. The doctrinal arguments of *Religio Laici* have been thoroughly discussed by Sanford Budick and Phillip Harth, and it is not my purpose to rehearse them here. Instead, I shall read this public poem as a deliberation upon ecclesiology—the nature and purpose of the church—and upon how hermeneutics affects "the Common quiet." E. N. Hooker suggested that Dryden wrote *Religio Laici* as a belated response to *A Treatise of Humane Reason* (1674) by Martin Clifford, an Anglican cleric who, as client of Buckingham, was doubly offensive to Dryden. Although Clifford had died in 1677, Dryden would not have forgotten that the Master of the Charterhouse, besides viciously lampooning Dryden's plays, had busily urged toleration of religious dissent. Dryden's works of 1682 — *The Medall, Religio Laici, The Duke of Guise* —all betray their author's preoccupation with the history of sectarian dissent. Clifford's *Treatise* was probably as much in Dryden's thoughts as the tract by his friend Sir Charles Wolseley, who, like Marvell, defended Nonconformist dissent against the attacks of Samuel Parker.[13]

Like Dryden's other writings published in the twelve months that preceded it, *Religio Laici* concentrates on the political consequences of dissent. Doctrinal and theological issues are secondary to the primary question of discipline. Modern readers are apt to ignore the public perspective of *Religio Laici* and to listen intently for the note of pious awe in its famous opening lines or for the confessional humility of a poet on the threshold of conversion. Dryden's poem capped a year of reflection on England's political history. Religious doctrine pertained to that history only insofar as it affected obedience. Dryden adopts the persona of "honest Layman" to state his opinions on ecclesiastical polity, not to pour out his private thoughts. He refers throughout to the collective rather than to the individual, even when he is talking about salvation.

From the time of his initial Presbyterianism to his final Catholicism, Dryden steadily maintained this collective or corporate view of faith and salvation. He never took an interest in the archetypal Protestant scene of a soul alone with God, as did Milton and Marvell and John Bunyan. Dryden's religion was relentlessly social, even when it was not explicitly public. That is why its defining characteristic is charity—a quality that Dryden the convert found wanting in all Protestant discourse, even that of the Anglicans. If religion can be made the subject of a poem on the *public* interest, Dryden has succeeded in fashioning *Religio Laici* into a public poem. As an orator addressing his audience on the topic of their common good, he deliberates upon the summum bonum of their salvation. His social standpoint is at the extroverted extreme from the sectarian preachers in *The Medall*, who stand before their "Conventicle of gloomy sullen Saints" and threaten them with "A Heav'n, like *Bedlam*, slovenly and sad; / Fore-doom'd for Souls, with false Religion, mad."[14]

A public poet who combines charity and satire might seem even less ingratiating than the private Dryden, whose peculiar blend of deference and sarcasm evidently put off some who met him. We need to remember that his satire, just like his thinking on politics and religion, was based on a strong sense of the corporate public. The public voice first heard in 1681 and 1682 is at once minatory and cajoling, as for instance at the end of the preface to *Religio Laici* (2:108): "They ['the whole Body of Nonconformists and Republicans'] may think themselves to be too roughly handled in this Paper; but I who know best how far I could have gone on this Subject, must be bold to tell them they are spar'd. . . . The best way for them to confute me, is, as I before advis'd the Papists, to disclaim their Principles, and renounce their Practices. We shall all be glad to think them true *Englishmen* when they obey the King, and true Protestants when they conform to the Church Discipline." "Church Discipline" is a phrase from Richard Hooker, whose observations on church polity Dryden quotes throughout the preface in order to set his public confession in an orthodox historical context.[15]

"Discipline" here bears a sense quite unlike what it meant in the Hastings elegy. In 1649, Dryden thought no differently from the covenanting Presbyterians who swore to uphold "discipline and government, according

to the Word of God and the example of the best reformed churches . . . lest
we partake in other men's sins, and thereby be in danger to receive of their
plagues." Hastings's smallpox could only be a punishment for "the Nations
sin" of failing to achieve the discipline God expected of his chosen people.
Now, in 1682, Dryden has discovered that Presbyterianism is rooted in the
"republican" principle of tyrannicide. In his "Epistle to the Whigs," he cites
Enrico Davila's history of the civil wars in France: "It was a *Hugonot* Minister, otherwise call'd a *Presbyterian,* (for our Church abhors so devilish a
Tenent) who first writ a Treatise of the lawfulness of deposing and murther-
ing Kings, of a different Perswasion in Religion" (2:40). Months later, in the
preface to *Religio Laici,* Dryden has advanced another degree in historical
accuracy. He paraphrases Louis Maimbourg's recent *Histoire du Calvinisme,*
which asserts that "where-ever that Discipline was planted and embrac'd,
Rebellion, Civil War and Misery attended it" (2:107). Nearer to home, he
quotes Hooker, who voiced a prophetic *"fear, lest our hastiness to embrace a
thing of so perilous Consequence* [meaning the Presbyterian Discipline] *should
cause Posterity to feel those Evils"* that actually ensued.[16]

Classical republicanism, even in the guise in which Buchanan and Milton
present it, bears little relation to Calvinist or Presbyterian discipline. The
framework that Dryden provides for *Religio Laici* is a revealing synthesis
of history. Applying the Cavalier axiom unsparingly, Dryden yokes republicanism and nonconformity—meaning *any* departure from Anglican uniformity—as twin variants of "sedition." He then goes back beyond England's
Civil Wars to those of sixteenth-century France (having spent much of
1682 studying them in order to write *The Duke of Guise*); and, warranted
by Maimbourg, he grounds all rebellion in the desire for reform. Dryden's
more sophisticated view of popery in this preface is the clearest sign that
he is learning to historicize the national Reformation. "A General and Un-
interrupted Plot of their Clergy, ever since the Reformation, I suppose all
Protestants believe," he says, citing Rome's claim that the king of England
is vassal to the pope. Dryden attributes this claim, which had outraged the
Elect Nation since the days of John Bale and Shakespeare, to an isolated
group of Jesuits, "the worst Party of the Papists," who espouse the doctrines of popular sovereignty and tyrannicide. All the same, Dryden is Tory
enough to worry that English Catholics might hold themselves exempt from
the oaths of Supremacy and Allegiance to a "Heretick Prince." Should they
"get power to shake him off, an Heretick is no lawful King, and conse-

quently to rise against him is no Rebellion" (2:103f.). That was exactly how the covenanting Presbyterians reasoned. Compared with them, popery is less intransigent, for Dryden can report that the present pope has recently condemned the doctrine of tyrannicide.

Clearly, Dryden has been reexamining the history underlying the epic of the Elect Nation, and he has cast off the mistrust of popery that the epic continued to foster even after the Restoration. He is still using the rhetoric of antipopery made familiar by the Popish Plot, but now he sets alongside the traditional account of popery a Catholic view of the origins of Presbyterianism. The parallel between Guisards and Covenanters had first led him to question the myth of a Protestant champion. His eyes were further opened by Maimbourg, who showed him the historical roots of the myth. In the 1660s Dryden could still envision a people united under their king in the Protestant cause. Now in 1682, to the contrary, he has uncovered a history of continuous "Presbyterian" faction undermining church polity and crown alike. Dryden has learned to interpret the national experience of the past four years in the mirror of history. He finds that Tory propaganda based on the Cavalier axiom contains a large kernel of historical truth: sedition against church and crown do indeed flow from a common source. That source, however, is not the English Rebellion. It is the Reformation.[17]

From the Jesuit doctrine of tyrannicide, Dryden's preface turns immediately to "the Fanaticks, or Schismaticks, of the *English* Church" and points out that their Reformation origin lies in scriptural hermeneutics: "How many Heresies the first Translation of *Tyndal* produced in few years, let my Lord *Herbert's* History of *Henry* the Eighth inform you" (2:105). As if this slur upon one of the Elect Nation's first martyrs were not enough, Dryden baits his Whig readers with a conspectus of Reformation history calculated to rile any godly enthusiast. The millenarian vision handed down by Foxe identifies Protestantism with the primitive church. Dryden, following Maimbourg, treats English Protestantism as a casual phenomenon of recent origin: "Reformation of Church and State has always been the ground of our Divisions in *England*. While we were Papists, our Holy Father rid us, by pretending authority out of the Scriptures to depose Princes; when we shook off his Authority, the Sectaries furnish'd themselves with the same Weapons; and out of the same Magazine, the Bible. So that the Scriptures, which are in themselves the greatest security of Governours, as commanding express obedience to them, are now turn'd to their destruction; and never since the Reformation, has there wanted a Text of their interpreting to authorize a Rebel." Dryden asks his readers to link biblical hermeneutics with regicide. Nothing in the preface more strongly indicates *Religio Laici*'s political purpose.[18]

PRIVATE JUDGMENT AND DISSENT

In the context of apologetic tradition, *Religio Laici* is a defense of the faith against the three opponents named in the preface: the Deists, the Papists, and the "Schismaticks." (The heathen rationalists in the first forty lines are not considered opponents of Christianity.) From a political standpoint, however, the poem's central issue is hermeneutic responsibility. Addressing the translator, the poet says "these crude thoughts were bred / By reading that, which better thou hast read," namely, Richard Simon's *Critical History of the Old Testament* (2:116, lines 226–27). Father Simon's demonstration that the biblical text is not reliable was meant to undermine the Protestant rule of *Scriptura sola*, thereby showing the need for an infallible hermeneutic tradition. Dryden "completely misunderstood what the French priest meant by tradition," as Harth says, but that did not stop him from appropriating Simon's criticism and using it to argue that Scripture must be supplemented with "private judgment." With this weapon, Protestants since William Chillingworth had countered the papal doctrine of an infallible interpreter. As a "rule of faith," this principle of private judgment may have satisfied the needs of Anglican apologetics, but as a political principle it is dangerously ambiguous. When he appeals to private judgment as the key to hermeneutics, Dryden is inevitably drawn into contradiction.[19]

The contradiction appears in the oddly circular structure of *Religio Laici*. Centered in the question of hermeneutic responsibility, the poem initially takes up the so-called common notions of the Deist ("God-like Notions") and concludes with the decay of "The *Common* Rule" in the hands of sectaries (lines 65, 402). The commendatory verses printed before *Religio Laici* prove that some of its readers thought it freed them "from a double Care, / The bold Socinian, and the Papal Chair," while others thought it steered a via media between faction and popery and "taught us to obey, and to distrust: / Yet to our selves, our King, and God, prove just" (2:476–77). Modern readers who think the poem mediates both quarrels—that between fideist and rationalist and that between Catholic and antinomian—are content to label it Anglican. But if one starts where Dryden says he did, with the problem of how we interpret a text upon whose meaning hinges our salvation, then the poem's quest for a "common rule" of faith will look more comprehensive than these quarrels suggest. Instead of trying to mediate between variously opposed philosophical viewpoints or theological positions in order to arrive at an "Anglican" compromise, Dryden is seeking a "common rule" that embraces discipline as well as doctrine, political conduct in addition to personal belief. In the examination of *Religio Laici* that follows, I shall assume that the poet, intending to vindicate Protestant judgment against Catholic ignorance, begins by disavowing Socinian pride and ends by denouncing sectarian pride; and that this overall sweep from the rationalistic extreme of private judgment to its opposite, antinomian extreme of sectarianism results in an argument that is inconclusive.

The poet's argument relegates Gentiles and heathens to a special category so that he may concentrate on the operation of private judgment solely under the Christian dispensation. Other than the pagan philosophers, who sought the summum bonum, all the schools of thought named in the poem are actively engaged in interpreting divine revelation, whether they acknowledge God's word directly or not. The Gentiles, lacking Scripture, could contribute nothing to its interpretation, but their exclusion from hermeneutics is not simply a historical accident, for neither is the Bible known "To *Indian* Souls, and Worlds discover'd *New*" (line 179). Dryden charitably hopes that all Gentiles may be saved despite the damnation promised them in Athanasius's creed. His concern plainly shows that Dryden's object in *Religio Laici* is the salvation and judgment of humanity, not the historical continuity of its traditions. Only at the end of his poem does he recount the corruption, reformation, and abuse of scriptural hermeneutics. Up to that point, his method is not historical because Dryden is interested in the career of no particular sect, not even that of the Anglicans. Rather, he has in view the church universal and those included in its communion by virtue of the "common rule" of their faith.

What is this "common rule"? The tradition infallibly expounded by the Roman Catholic Church, says Father Simon. "Strange Confidence," replies Dryden,

> still to *interpret* true,
> Yet not be sure that all they have explain'd,
> Is in the blest *Original* contain'd.

> More Safe, and much more modest 'tis, to say
> *God wou'd not leave Mankind without a way:*
> And that the *Scriptures,* though not *every where*
> Free from Corruption, or intire, or clear,
> Are uncorrupt, sufficient, clear, intire,
> In *all* things which our needfull *Faith* require.
>
> (2:118, lines 292–300)

The last couplet characterizes Scripture in terms of what is sometimes called the Anglican rule of faith. This rule vindicates the fundamental principle of *Scriptura sola* by making tradition unnecessary: Scripture in itself is sufficient for faith. Faith is only begotten, however, at the very moment that the rule is applied by the private judgment.

That is Dryden's next point:

> If *others* in the *same Glass better* see
> 'Tis for *Themselves* they look, but not for *me:*
> For *MY* Salvation must its Doom receive
> Not from what *OTHERS,* but what *I* believe."
>
> (301–4)

Private judgment is the necessary corollary of *Scriptura sola.* This is the crucial paradox of the rule of faith: judgment of scriptural meaning is an essential act bringing faith into play. In other words, faith depends upon hermeneutics — even the faith of "Th'*unletter'd* Christian, who believes in *gross*" (line 322).[20]

Two things should be noted here. First, the hermeneutical assent to God's word is creative in a Pentecostal sense. Its prototype is Luke's story (Acts 8:26–39) of the Ethiopian eunuch whom the Evangelist Philip met sitting in his chariot reading Scripture:

> Then the Spirit said unto Philip, Go near, and join thyself to this chariot.
> And Philip ran thither to him, and heard him read the prophet Esaias [Isaiah], and said, Understandest thou what thou readest?
> And he said, How can I, except some man should guide me? And he desired Philip that he would come up and sit with him. . . .
> Then Philip opened his mouth, and began at the same scripture, and preached unto him Jesus.

Philip interprets the text typologically, explaining that Isaiah's suffering Servant (53:7–8) is to be understood as Jesus. The real agent here is not the Evangelist but the Pentecostal Spirit (Acts 2), who opens Philip's mouth and leads him to baptize the eunuch.

The second thing to note in the hermeneutical act of faith is the role of the private judgment. This Anglican phrase is conveniently ambiguous. In its obvious meaning, it serves to differentiate the believer's particular prudence from the universal agency of the Spirit in the act of understanding: without the eunuch's individual, deliberative assent, the hermeneutic effort would fall short of conversion. Private judgment, however, can also mean the practical opposite of prudent assent. It can mean factious *dissent*. That is its meaning throughout *Leviathan*, the most formidable assault ever made on the private judgment. In Hobbes's meaning, private judgment sets the individual will or conscience at odds with the customary authority of law and tradition. Private judgment exercised in this singular fashion, as opposed to the discipline of a uniform, public liturgy, leads to hermeneutic license and prophecy.[21]

In order to curb willful dissent from authority, Anglican doctrine, closely following Hobbes, insists that the mark of true judgment is obedience. The private judgment is free only to concur in "all things which our needfull Faith require." It is not free to "*talk* loudly [where] the *Rule* is *mute*." Mankind's common quiet is the overriding concern of the church, and the exercise of private judgment must therefore be qualified, as must the liberty of speaking out:

> Shall I speak plain, and in a Nation free
> Assume an honest *Layman's Liberty?*
> I think (according to my little Skill,)
> (To my own Mother-Church submitting still)
> That many have been sav'd, and many may,
> Who never heard this Question brought in play.
>
> (315–21)

The poet's ostentatious parenthetical deference is prologue to an unusually reflexive or self-conscious exposition of hermeneutical authority. The public poet steps forward as "honest Layman" to take up the debate over tradition. By reminding his audience of the summum bonum, he pronounces the whole tangled "Question" subordinate to their salvation.

Dryden is replying to the "*Objection in behalf of Tradition; urg'd by Father Simon*" (marginal gloss on lines 305–15). "Are there not many points, some needfull sure / To saving Faith, that Scripture leaves obscure?" Furthermore, are not these necessary points found in scriptural places "Which every Sect will wrest a several way / (For what *one* Sect Interprets, *all* Sects *may*)"? In paraphrasing here the preface to the *Critical History*, Dryden highlights a problem not raised explicitly by Father Simon. Those very points needful to salvation lie most open to interpretation by wrangling "Sects." Just where private judgment needs an ultimate source of appeal, the "Rule [of faith] is mute."

Dryden's outspoken critique of tradition that follows (lines 334–55) is characterized by Harth as "a precise exposition of Anglican doctrine." If it were merely that, it would fail to match the intellectual honesty of Simon's challenge. The priest's question may be restated in the form, "By what rule can we determine the truth where the meaning of Scripture is disputed?" To reply that doctrines resting on disputed passages are not "needful" for our faith is to make conformity with church polity the test of doctrine: to seek the truth, that is, in irenics instead of polemics. Notwithstanding his submissive pose, the tenor of Dryden's response is not irenic, and one may doubt whether the Anglican orthodoxy was reassured by his freewheeling demonstration of their rule of faith.[22]

Dryden assumes that the tradition Simon invokes is strictly a tradition of interpreting what has been written, Scripture. The poet wages the argument on Protestant ground, taking for granted the primacy of Scripture and its interpretation while completely ignoring the extrascriptural traditions maintained by Rome. The Church of England pretended to recognize some of the "general, old, disinteressed" councils and Fathers of the Church, but in practice it put even those authorities to the test of *Scriptura sola*. Dryden admits that "*first* Traditions," could we know them to be authentic, "were a proof alone" of the Bible's meaning; for "next [after] *Rules*," he says, come the "best *Authorit[ies]*." The crabbed orthography and syntax of line 339 hide the postulate governing his argument, namely, his premise that recovered traditions, no matter how pure, must always be imperfect by comparison with "Rules" that are independent of tradition.

That is why "men of *Wit*" who spend their lives studying "the Sacred Page" can at best reach "not *Truth* but *Probability*." They can determine "Which Doctrine, this, or that, does best agree / With the whole Tenour of the Work Divine: / And plainlyest points to Heaven's reveal'd Design" (325–31), but they cannot reveal that design to others. Its revelation belongs to private judgment and the rule of faith. This rule, Dryden ultimately implies, is none other than the truth itself, which "by its own Sinews" survives the gauntlet of corrupting transmission:

> Such difference is there in an oft-told Tale:
> But Truth by its own Sinews will prevail.
> *Tradition written* therefore more commends
> *Authority,* than what from *Voice* descends:
> And this, as perfect as its kind can be,
> Rouls down to us the Sacred History:
> Which, from the *Universal Church receiv'd,*
> Is *try'd,* and *after,* for its *self* believ'd. (348–55)

The Bible is scriptural history: both a stream and a scroll that "Rouls down to us." It is "tradition written." There is also an unwritten tradition that is received from (not *by*) "the Universal Church." Dryden makes this universal (*katholou*) church his standard throughout the rest of the poem. By this touchstone, he tries the truth of the several denominations, starting with the falsely "Catholic" Church whose oral traditions ("what from Voice descends"), he says, are lacking in authority. One unbroken tradition alone meets his test: the incorruptible "Sacred History" revealed by the Holy Spirit. The Spirit illuminates the written tradition whose text, "try'd" by the private judgment, acts as its own witness and is "for its self believ'd." The ultimate rule of faith, then, is a hermeneutic principle: the biblical text made self-authenticating.[23]

Dryden would seem to have brought his readers back from tradition to *Scriptura sola.* But the position to which he returns leaves them more anxious, not less, about "things *needfull* to be *known*" (line 369). The Anglican rule of faith has been stretched until it has become useless. The public poet, wishing to show himself a docile son of the "Mother-Church," offers a specific example of private judgment: his opinion that the Gentiles might be saved (lines 212–23). For that heterodoxy he has carefully prepared readers in his preface: "I have written, perhaps too boldly on St. *Athanasius.* . . . I am sensible enough that I had done more *prudently* to [omit it]. But then I could not have satisfied my self, that I had done honestly not to have written what was my own" (2:99). Dryden uses every rhetorical art to clear his private judgment from the taint of singularity. No show of submission, however, can undo his ultimate appeal to a universal church and its higher rule of faith or disguise the fact that his layman's religion assumes a freedom to dissent.

By exceeding the rule of "things needfull" and owning a universal church that extends beyond the Anglican pale, Dryden shifts the entire burden of hermeneutic responsibility to the private judgment of his readers. If "that vast Frame, the Church" that he goes on to discuss is more comprehensive than the Catholic Church, which is "but *part*," the same particularity limits the Anglican Church. If "The *Book*'s a *Common* Largess to *Mankind*" and does not require a Catholic exposition, if "It *speaks* it *Self*, and what it does contain, / In all things *needfull* to be *known*, is *plain*," readers cannot help asking whether it does not speak to other needs besides those of the official clergy. Presumably an Anglican or any other reader for whom "plain" means literalistic and unproblematic would not be disposed to meddle with the text at all, much less pursue the typological applications of its "Sacred History." If "plain" means self-evident and convincing, whose hermeneutics makes it so?[24]

The obvious danger in this private hermeneutics is its singularity, which feeds the pride of the interpreter. Dryden is well aware of the danger, and on first reading Simon's book he may have thought of Clifford and those like him who boasted of their rational religion. As was noted above, *Religio Laici* begins with the pride of the rationalists and ends with the willfulness of the sectarians. The only effective check on singularity that Dryden recognizes is consistency with some rule. The very reflexivity of the public poet implies this consistency. His "Layman," ranging far beyond what concerns Anglican apologetics, surveys our universal quest for the summum bonum and measures the results by the highest rule of all: divine revelation. Dismissing the Gentiles with their inadequate "Fathom" of reason (line 41), Dryden proceeds straight to the "Rules of Worship" discovered by the Deist. "These Truths are not the product of thy Mind," Dryden tells him, "But dropt from Heaven," like the other "God-like Notions" (lines 46, 65–67). He confirms this by showing that although the highest canons of natural justice are inferior to the Deist's rule of worship enjoining remorse and expiation, the Deist's rule is nevertheless imperfect because it does not teach us that man still requires justification by Christ. When the Deist asks how "This one Rule of Life" (line 132) could direct Gentiles lacking Scripture, Dryden admits that "a *Rule* reveal'd / Is *none* to *Those*, from whom it was *conceal'd*," and he quotes Paul's redeeming observation that the Gentiles "Were to themselves both Rule and Law alone" (199–210).

Having shown in the first half of his poem that even the best rules for discerning the summum bonum are imperfectly derived from revelation, the poet takes advantage of these interpretive heights to deliver a judgment inspired, he tells us, by the divine rule of charity to the heathens. Next (lines 224–355) comes the exchange with Father Simon that we have discussed, following which the poet makes his way down the hermeneutic slopes, asking the expositors the same question he debated with Simon: Whence can they "infer / A right t'interpret?" (361–62). The poet has already concluded that the only right comes from the rule of faith, defined as the self-authenticating text received from the universal church (lines 352–55). Any lesser hermeneutical rule must be grounded in the pride of singularity. Because the political and ecclesiastical forms of singularity are faction and sect, those also are the institutional sources of false interpretation. The Holy Roman Church appropriated the Book intended as "a Common Largess to Mankind" and substituted for God's word the priests', who "learn'd their knack so well, / That by long use they grew *Infallible*" (386–87). The recovery of the Bible at the Reformation is unexpectedly disparaged in Dryden's metaphors implying selfish interest and rival factions: the printed Old and New Testaments become "the *Will* produc'd" for which everyone "put in for a Share: / Consulted Soberly his private good; / And sav'd himself as cheap as e'er he cou'd" (392–97).

With the Bible in every vulgar hand, "The *Common* Rule was made the *common* Prey; / And at the mercy of the *Rabble* lay," while "men wou'd still be itching to *expound*." Dryden's short history of biblical hermeneutics concludes with a Hudibrastic caricature of the common expositor during a time when "The *Spirit* gave the *Doctoral* Degree: / And every member of a *Company* / Was of *his* Trade, and of the *Bible* free" (400–10). The Cavalier snobbery in these lines signals the poet's return to the fold of Anglican authority with its slippery via media and its Hobbesian proscription of singularity. The "Common Rule"—Dryden seems to have left it abandoned to the "common Prey"—is replaced by the Anglican rule. After assuring us that

> Faith is not built on disquisitions vain;
> The things we *must* believe, are *few*, and *plain*;

> But since men *will* believe more than they *need;*
> And every man will make *himself* a Creed,

the poet concludes that "private Reason 'tis more Just to curb, / Than by Disputes the publick Peace disturb" (431–48). The private judgment out of which the layman of *Religio Laici* has surreptitiously fashioned himself a creed is finally suppressed as "private Reason."

In the context of this public "Discourse" on religion, the scholastic principle in line 442 ("For no man's Faith depends upon his Will") echoes the civil prudence of *Leviathan.* In chapter 42, "Of Power Ecclesiasticall," Hobbes writes that "the Office of Christs Minister in this world, is to make men Beleeve, and have Faith in Christ. But Faith hath no relation to, nor dependence at all upon Compulsion, or Commandement; but onely upon certainty, or probability of Arguments drawn from Reason, or from something men beleeve already." This proposition is fully consonant with Anglican doctrine, which recognizes the three motives to faith given by Hobbes: the "certainty" of assent or conversion by the Spirit, the "probability" in rational discourse, and the testimony of written tradition (the Bible, to which Hobbes ascribes the authority of an indirect witness). Having shared the midcentury experience, Hobbes, the Church, and Dryden all realize that compulsion and willfulness have a single root, and that the problem of freedom is only magnified by dwelling on the tangled question of faith.[25]

Despite their doctrinal agreement, Hobbes unconscionably shrinks the ecclesiastical power without correspondingly enfranchising our private judgment. *Leviathan* restricts the church's role in society to that of a teacher without any legislative or compulsive authority. Hobbes deduces this role from the circumstance that the Kingdom of God, of which the clergy are ministers, lies yet in the future; "and they that have no Kingdome, can make no Laws." Hobbes wants to ensure Leviathan's absolute authority, and he cannot allow its sovereignty to be divided with the church. Accordingly, in the historical second half of his book, Hobbes argues that scriptural doctrines, put forth by Christ for his future kingdom, are intended as "Canon, or Rule of Faith," and not as laws to regulate civil society. These canons acquired the force of law only when and insofar as "the Soveraign Civill Power," in the person of the emperor Constantine, decreed their observance. Hobbes's ecclesiology is anathema to the Anglican Church on two counts.

It is Erastian in that it subordinates church to state, instead of granting the church spiritual authority over the state. Moreover, by locating its authority in a Kingdom of God not yet come, Hobbes strips the church of its power to excommunicate Nonconformists; only those who expressly deny that Jesus is the Christ can be excluded from the church: "Faith is in its own nature invisible, and consequently exempted from all humane jurisdiction; whereas the words, and actions that proceed from it, as breaches of our Civill obedience, are injustice both before God and Man." [26]

In propounding this ecclesiology obnoxious to the church, Hobbes raises the two issues identified throughout much of the seventeenth century as comprehension (inclusion of Nonconformists in the national church) and indulgence (toleration of dissenting sects). These important issues give us a means to measure Dryden's poems of 1682 against his earlier opinions. *Leviathan* belongs to 1651, and its teaching on church polity is aimed chiefly at ensuring the common quiet in a godless republican Commonwealth. Under the Protectorate also, every form of sectarian dissent was tolerated except for popery and professed atheism. Cromwell's toleration mightily frustrated the Presbyterians. It seems to have delighted a young and anticlerical Dryden, which suggests that he had already abandoned his family's originally Calvinistic ideal of comprehension: specifically, the union of all Protestants in a single church. At the Restoration, he still clung to the imperial side of this goal, alluding several times to the Elect Nation. The church, on the other hand, is seldom mentioned seriously in his works before 1682. The major exception is *Tyrannick Love* (1669), in which the church, represented by St. Catharine, appears as a defiant and persecuted sect.[27]

As we saw, the Anglican Church at the Restoration chose to enforce uniformity rather than work for the comprehension sought by old Presbyterians like Richard Baxter. It is difficult to imagine what elements of Anglican discipline or doctrine could have appealed to Dryden. He shared neither the Cavalier gentry's memory of persecution nor its respect for the clergy. He certainly did not become more zealous for Anglican uniformity than he had been for the Presbyterians' goal of comprehension. He publicly associated himself with Anglican interests for the first time in 1678, when he dedicated *All for Love* to Danby (below, chapter 7). That allegiance was political rather than religious; Dryden lacked the Cavaliers' enthusiasm for a uniformity that would exclude all Nonconformists from the official church. Four years later, in *Religio Laici*, his confession of Anglican doctrine was equivocal, as I have tried to demonstrate.[28]

If the comprehension of all believers within a visible church, whether reformed or restored, was not a serious concern of Dryden's prior to 1682, what was his attitude to the alternative of indulgence (toleration)? That touched him more immediately, for the government's intermittent policy of indulgence affected the daily life of the nation. In *Astraea Redux*, Dryden praised the king's promise of "Mercy" in his declaration from Breda. When the Anglicans, with the parliamentary backing of the Cavaliers, preempted the king's indulgence and scuttled the comprehension favored by Clarendon in 1662, Charles tried again in 1668 and was rebuffed by a surly Commons. During the parliamentary recess in 1672, he finally issued his own Declaration of Indulgence to all Nonconformists—including of course Catholics—only to be forced to repeal it when Parliament reconvened the next year.

The frustrating of the king's indulgence ought to remind us, with our tolerant indifference to sectarianism, that the seventeenth century had far too much at stake in a visibly uniform church to encourage religious diversity. At issue was the form of worship, not the correctness of what one believed. Quaker and other sectarian observances threatened to bring back anarchy. Spurr has remarked that " 'schism' was replacing 'heresy' as Rome's principal charge against the Church of England." Anglicans repeated the charge against Dissenters. "To grant an indulgence in this kind is to establish a schism by law," one M.P. objected in 1668. "If a toleration be granted to those dissenters it may probably end in Popery." Dryden's views on indulgence can be seen in the persistent anticlericalism of his plays and the *libertin* exposure of persecution in *The Indian Emperour*. His position seems close to that of the king, who would have enjoyed the playwright's bantering the clergy just as he delighted in Marvell's retort to the archdeacon, Samuel Parker. As I said, Dryden never invoked Anglican interests or the Cavalier axiom equating dissent with sedition until 1678. The real question is whether he pushed the equation so far as to identify all religious dissent with schism once he had enlisted his pen in the Tory cause.[29]

His propagandistic aims in both prefaces of 1682 are unmistakable: to brand the king's enemies with sedition and to establish the legitimacy of the church and monarchy against which they rebel. This partisan satire takes a public stand on the polity of the visible church, but it does not affirm or attack religious beliefs. For Dryden, the truth of religion—which included its moral discipline—remained above partisan dogma. The public poet never meddles with heresy or with actual schism. The Anglican doctrine of *Religio Laici* is hardly adequate to religious truth. Out of mere rhetorical expediency, the public poet conforms as "honest Layman" to the Church's minimal rule of faith: "Having laid down, as my Foundation, that the Scripture is a Rule; that in all things needfull to Salvation, it is clear, sufficient, and ordain'd by God Almighty for that purpose, I have left my self no right to interpret obscure places, such as concern the possibility of eternal happiness to Heathens: because whatsoever is obscure is concluded not necessary to be known" (1:102). Despite this pretense of conformity, the poem itself flouts the antipolemic doctrine of Anglican minimalism. As a political gesture, Dryden's public confession keeps within the bounds of church discipline. Its doctrine is another matter. The only church whose doctrine Dryden affirms in this or any of his other writings before 1686 is the church named in *Religio Laici:* "the Universal Church" with its tradition of "Sacred History." [30]

Dryden's review of religions in the final hundred lines of the poem and the historical summary in its preface make abundantly clear his belief that no "part / Of that vast Frame"—no partial sect, such as the Anglican Church—can claim to be the universal church. Dryden does not mention comprehension for the good reason that he has always doubted the Restoration Church's ability to unite believers. As for toleration of Dissenters, Dryden himself questions Anglican pretensions to adequately represent the universal church. Dissent has to be tolerated in order to preserve the full, catholic truth. The poet of *Religio Laici* is just as guilty of indulging this radical dissent as the naively antepartisan poet of *Annus Mirabilis.*

Even in his most partisan satire rooted in the Cavalier axiom, Dryden usually respects the distinction between spiritual dissent and schism. *The Medall* associates the sect with the "Conventicle" and its political counterpart, the Whig Association. As the association forms a state within the state, so the sect gathers a church without the Church. A sect is schismatic because it behaves like a faction, which, struggling with its rivals, eventually breeds anarchy. Dissent on the other hand need not be schismatic; indeed, it acknowledges the orthodoxy from which it differs. A Nonconformist is someone who conforms imperfectly. When Dryden lampoons "the Non-conformist Parson, who writ the *Whip* and Key" travestying *Absalom and Achitophel,* he scoffs, "A Dissenter in Poetry from Sense and *English,* will make as good a Protestant Rhymer, as a Dissenter from the Church of *England* a Protestant Parson" (2:42). Dryden's jeer imputes heterodoxy but not schism to his foe and censures his language more severely than his politics.

In this passing criticism of his enemy's hermeneutics early in 1682, Dryden touches on the problem of freedom in its most Hobbesian form: the tension between spiritual indulgence and secular authority. Eight months later, when he connected biblical hermeneutics with king-killing in the preface to *Religio Laici,* the poet could hardly avoid reflecting on the freedom with which he himself had treated King David in his poem a year earlier. He dignifies his license by claiming to have unwrapped the memorial sword of Goliath; but that is the sword David stole to defend himself against his own king (2:98). Like honest dissent, true hermeneutics obeys a higher rule of faith than the canons of Tory Anglicanism. Dryden aptly describes scriptural hermeneutics as a "talking Trumpet," a powerful megaphone capable of shaking the civil order. Although "fram'd, at first, our Oracle" for us to consult, "It has been us'd as ill in every Age." Dryden's historical pessimism is deeper than his contempt for the Whigs, and it suggests he was returning to the providential mimesis that had been his original inspiration. "Since our Sects in prophecy grow higher, / The Text inspires not them; but they the Text inspire," he wrote, and then later in the year accused the infallible Church of Rome and its priests of exploiting the same "talking Trumpet" until the Reformation called them to account: "At last, a knowing Age began t'enquire / If *they* the *Book,* or *That* did *them* inspire" (2:48, 121).

Like the prophet who wields them, both sword and trumpet can take on a life of their own. After two decades of paying lip service to the established church while scoffing *en cavalier* at its clergy, Dryden found that his partisan responsibility as a Tory obliged him to denounce *all* dissent from the Church of England as politically seditious, a task abhorrent to his Puritan soul. He says "the Fanaticks, or Schismaticks" have used the Bible "as if their business was not to be sav'd but to be damnd by its Contents" (2:105), yet he is nearly as reckless as they and is well aware that his satire tends like them to the shameful tearing apart of the community. "I can write Severely, with more ease, than I can Gently," he declares in the preface to his first satire. His second ends with the motto, *"Pudet haec opprobria, vobis / Et dici potuisse, et non potuisse refelli"* (it is shameful that this blame could be laid on you and that you should be incapable of refuting it). In the preface to *Religio*

Laici, he says, "I who know best how far I could have gone on this Subject, must be bold to tell [the sectaries] they are spar'd" (2:3, 52, 108).

Dryden's arrogant boast of hermeneutic authority is not easily harmonized with his professions of charity and of submission to ecclesiastical authority. Yet the pride he takes in his satirical power is matched by a Juvenalian reflexivity. The note of rhetorical self-consciousness is the voice of the public poet, still audible above the partisan denunciation. On the verge of damning his enemies for schismatics, he pulls back instead, as if he read in their excommunication a reflection of his own. He begins his declamation as a Tory propagandist but he ends it as Jeremiah. Satire turns into providential mimesis, and Dryden's highest mode of public dissent is a prophetic reflexivity.

False Freedom and Restoration

Many who were soberly bred up in religion as Dryden was may have turned away from the church, but few of those renegades were to undergo conversion in their sixth decade. In the preceding chapter, I have taken for granted the continuity of Dryden's religious thought; extrapolating it by almost a quarter-century, I have tried to fix more precisely its relation to the apocalyptic moment of renewal in the 1650s. Dryden was slow to grasp the connection that Pocock has made easy for us between republican liberty and spiritual dissent. Otherwise, the poet might have seen fit to make his confession before 1682, which would certainly have been more convenient for his critics. His example proves once again that trying to keep politics out of seventeenth-century religion is as futile as it is arbitrary. Dryden's *Religio Laici* offers a commonplace theology, whereas his ecclesiology in the poem is distinctive. The public poet aims to make the church visible, a motive that suggests he would see nothing but incoherence in our modern efforts to keep religion out of politics.

For the official Church of England, comprehension was an immediate political problem, but Dryden addresses the issue only on the theoretical plane, referring to his inherited, catholic ideal of a "Universal Church" (*Religio Laici,* line 354). At the Restoration, his response to the Act of Uniformity and the Clarendon Code was that of other freethinkers: he affirmed the more cosmopolitan view of religion found in *The Indian Emperour* (1665). The alternative to comprehension was tolerance, and here Dryden, at some point after the king's Declaration of Indulgence (1672), parted company with the

libertines. Once he understood that their demand for toleration arose not
so much from the desire for a *universal* church as from hostility to a *visible*
church, Dryden necessarily despised the secular rationalists whom he associated with republicanism: freethinkers like Buckingham, laissez-faire mer-
chants like Slingsby Bethel, and deists like Shaftesbury and Locke.[1]

The ancient, catholic ideal of a visible church ran up against formidable
rivals in the secular ideals of the mid-seventeenth century. Given Pocock's
characterization of the Machiavellian moment as the "moment at which
grace acted in history," one doubts that the young Dryden can have avoided
its elation altogether. "Bliss was it in that dawn to be alive": if he felt no
Wordsworthian zeal, he must at any rate have known Milton's sense of liberty
and must have discussed the Machiavellian ideas domesticated by Harrington
and Nedham. In some measure, he experienced a new political order whose
promise lives on, despite the dreary record of aborted innovations from that
time to ours. Lacking evidence of Dryden's response to events, I have supposed that the year of anarchy intervening between the Cromwell poem and
Monck's arrival so alarmed him as to sour whatever hopes he had for the
great secular experiment of the Interregnum. His disillusion can be read in
the couplet he wrote in 1660: " 'Twas MONCK whom Providence design'd
to loose / Those real bonds false freedom did impose" (1:26). Looking back
on the change, Dryden characterizes the republican experiment, or at least
its phase of 1659, as a "false freedom." He could not have made that analysis
in 1660 had he not harkened, however briefly, to the siren of republicanism.

My exposition of Dryden's thought has stressed up to this point his lifelong ideal of a comprehensive, visible church. In this chapter, I shall trace
his poetic career down to *Annus Mirabilis*, aligning his essentially Puritan
ideal with historical events. My argument is that he perfected his method of
providential mimesis as a means for criticizing what seemed to him the dangerous license of republican ambition. Every political theory has to come to
terms with the problem of freedom, either by imposing limits on people or
by teaching them to limit themselves. Dryden's obvious leaning to the first
theory did not blunt his keen interest in the second or check his own spirit
of free inquiry. If we keep in mind both authors' desire to interpret for their
contemporaries the *saeculum* of nature and history, we can read Dryden's
providential mimesis as a response to Harrington's secular prudence.

Pocock has analyzed the extremely rich texture of political theory from
the Civil Wars to the Revolution of 1688, distinguishing its most potent and

seminal ideas: millenarianism and the Elect Nation; antipopery, Erastianism, and the dictatorship of Leviathan; Cromwell as a Moses or as a Davidic or an English king; the popular myth of a pre-Norman, "Ancient Constitution" under whose guidance Anglo-Saxon freeholders instituted the precursor of parliament; English customary law with inherited property and rights based on prescription; the concept of "mixed government" formulated in the king's answer to Parliament's *Nineteen Propositions* of 1642; the questions of feudal tenures and the House of Lords; the ongoing debate over a standing army and civic control of the militia; Aristotelian, Polybian, and Machiavellian cycles of virtue and decay. For the purpose of shedding light on Dryden's political thought, I shall focus on those ideas most commonly ascribed to republicans in the aftermath of England's Machiavellian moment.

SECULAR PRUDENCE AND LIBERTY

In 1692, looking back more than fifty years, Dryden recalled that he had read Polybius "in *English* with the pleasure of a Boy, before I was ten years of Age: and yet even then, had some dark Notions of the prudence with which he conducted his design" (20:18). What sparked this boyish admiration was the historian's artistic prudence, not the actual virtue of *phronēsis* that Polybius commends in heroes like the younger Scipio (see, for example, *Histories*, 32.16). In dashing off this prefatory "Character of Polybius," Dryden pauses to rebuke his source, Isaac Casaubon, for daring to claim that Polybius believed in providence. Dryden insists that Polybius's whole history refutes that opinion. The Greek historian's "Irreligion" is manifest, despite his skepticism about pagan deities and superstitions: "Neither do I know any reason, why *Casaubon* shou'd inlarge so much in his Justification, since to believe false Gods, and to believe none, are Errors of the same importance. He who knew not our God, saw through the ridiculous Opinions of the Heathens concerning theirs: and not being able without Revelation, to go farther, stopp'd at home in his own Breast, and made Prudence his Goddess, Truth his search, and Vertue his reward" (20:31).

Dryden, now in his sixty-second year, knows full well that the prudence "worshipp'd" by Polybius is not the same as the narrative "prudence with which he conducted his design." But even with its meaning shifted, Dryden's use of "Prudence" is misleading here; the Greek text plainly shows that Polybius's "Goddess" is not *phronēsis* (*prudentia*) but *Tychē*, Fortuna. *Tychē* is the great object of the *Histories*. Dryden, following Cicero, has equated the historian's prudential knowledge of Fortuna with the pagan sumum bonum of wisdom. His intent is to deny that Polybius ever achieved a Boethian vision transforming Fortuna into providence.[2]

Having contained Polybian wisdom safely within the profane *saeculum* defined by Augustine, Dryden then goes on to praise the pagan's foresight: "he wonderfully foresaw the decay of the *Roman* Empire, and those Civil Wars which turn'd it down from a Common-wealth, to an absolute Monarchy: He who will take the pains to review this History, will easily perceive, that *Polybius* was the best sort of Prophets, who predict from Natural Causes those Events, which must naturally proceed from them" (ibid.). Dryden evidently took the pains to review book 6 of the translation in hand. There Polybius interrupts the narrative of the Punic Wars to insert his discourse on the Roman constitution. He expounds his celebrated theory of the mixed constitution and of its cyclical growth and decay—the notorious *anakuklōsis* through which proceed the forms of government by one, by few, and by many. Dryden says nothing about the *anakuklōsis*, a universal hypothesis he probably found just as chimerical at sixty as he had at ten. But he cannot resist bringing out the personal irony in Polybius's forecast. The collapse of Rome's republic more than a century later had its remote cause in Polybius's own day—a cause, Dryden thinks, that Polybius ought to have perceived, for its operations are still visible:

> These things were not to succeed even in the compass of the next Century to that wherein he liv'd: But the Person was then living, who was the first mover towards them; and that was that great *Scipio* Africanus, who by cajolling the People to break the Fundamental Constitutions of the Government in his Favour, by bringing him too early to the Consulship, and afterwards by making their Discipline of War precarious, First taught them to devolve the Power and Authority of the Senate into the hands of one, and then to make that one to be at the Disposition of the Souldiery; which though he practis'd at a time, when it was necessary for the safety of the Common-wealth, yet it drew after it those fatal Consequences, which not only ruin'd the Republick, but also, in process of time, the Monarchy it self. (20:32–33)

Dryden imagines that Polybius, to spare Scipio's family, "gives other Reasons" too prolix to mention. But the "other Reasons" (6.1–20) are precisely the theory of historical *anakuklōsis*. And even those chapters do not suggest that the younger Scipio's premature election to consul launched the republic on its decline. That phase, says Polybius, will not begin until the inevitable extravagance and emulation arrive to corrupt the patrician classes (6.57). The truth is that Dryden has in view not Rome's republic, but England's. He is looking back at 1653, a year "which not only ruin'd the Republick, but also, in process of time, the Monarchy it self."

His ironical retrospect of the midcentury crisis is typical of the kind of reversed prophecy in which Dryden sometimes indulged. In the politicized hermeneutics of his Jacobite phase after 1689, he struck a public pose of disengaged dissent and criticized an illegitimate government to which he refused allegiance; he even died prophesying another Stuart restoration. His later remarks are valuable because they furnish a means of limiting his earlier reflections on the Interregnum. In 1641, he saw only Polybius's authorial prudence. Fifty years of rebellion and revolution did not raise his estimate of that prudence. Since he goes out of his way to stress that the Greek historian's prophetic tact is no "Revelation" of providence, we may conclude that the Polybian *anakuklōsis* had no effect upon the stubbornly providential basis of Dryden's political thought.

This conclusion helps to determine his initial stake in the debate over Cromwellian prudence and the crisis of the Machiavellian moment. Late in his career we find Dryden misreading Polybius's cyclical theory of "Natural Causes" and missing the historian's emphasis on the relative stability of a mixed constitution. Dryden very likely understood Polybian republicanism reductively, therefore, from the outset. Constitutional change (*metabolē*) was an irrational "process of time" that would destroy "Monarchy itself." Both a monarchy and a republic are futile contrivances of human nature. "Natural Causes," left without divine intervention, tend only toward chaos. Unredeemed man cannot fathom the mystery of the state or achieve a lasting polity.

This thoroughly Augustinian, antipolitical assessment of the human condition is consistent with the elegy on Hastings (above, chapter 1), and it squares with the political voluntarism of Dryden's heroic plays. Dryden's initial poem of 1649 puts no trust in monarchy, which had just been abolished. His Restoration poems and plays, as we shall see, express a qualified trust that grows steadily more ambivalent. The accession of a *false* monarch after 1689 at last freed Dryden from his long, but always provisional commitment to a restored dynasty whose divine mandate seemed increasingly dubious. Dryden's rebellious fantasies, which he had for years diverted to the heroic plays and to *Mac Flecknoe,* could now be unleashed against William. The real target of Dryden's satire, though, was not the usurping king or a rival poet. It was the institution of "Monarchy itself." The extremes in Dryden's nature finally met: the Catholic recusant liberated the Puritan radical, and the newly mordant note in his public voice from about the time of *The Spanish Fryar* (1680; see chapter 7) proclaimed Dryden's slight regard for temporal kingship.

The Williamite Revolution raised for Dryden the old problem of obedience. Chafing once again under the need to obey the powers that be, he harked back to the Interregnum crisis. At the height of the Rebellion, the controversy over the Oath of Engagement had soon eroded customary authority. None of Dryden's works reflects anguish over having sworn to respect the Commonwealth, as do the plays of the earl of Orrery, for instance, who repeatedly apologized to Charles II for having served the rebels. Dryden's position at the Restoration needs to be differentiated, therefore, not only from that of the older generation of royalists but also from that of the forward-looking Cromwellian counselors like Edward Montague (later earl of Sandwich), Cooper (Shaftesbury), and Broghill (Orrery). The royalists were mostly Cavaliers. Among these, some courtiers—for example, Davenant and Waller—who had betrayed the cause were able in 1660 to make their peace with the new king. Others, like Cowley, failed conspicuously to do so. In his Restoration poems, Dryden carefully avoided the problem of the old royalists' divided loyalty; as a public poet, he would have been most imprudent to rake up a savage memory. Dryden's public years overlapped the Interregnum generation of Marvell, Orrery, and Shaftesbury, three men who were all born in 1621 and whose political views closely match the pattern that Wallace characterizes as "loyalism." Dryden's relative youth and isolation at Cambridge, however, kept him from directly experiencing with them the seismic transformation of the political order under the Commonwealth. Its shock nonetheless affected his career, and this chapter will trace the republican aftermath in his Restoration poems.

The Engagement controversy and its "loyalist" solution generated the classic treatise on the problem of authority, *Leviathan.* Hobbes's overriding theme is obedience to a government de facto rather than de jure. "It is testimony to the enduring strength of English conservatism under catastrophic conditions," Pocock remarks, "that so colorless a theme produced so much thought of major importance." These catastrophic conditions were caused by the radical break with tradition in 1649. The young poet of the Hastings elegy may have felt that his elders had made a mess of things, but the Regicide did not shock him as it shocked genuine royalists. As for taking the Engagement, the Machiavellian moment that Pocock—and eventually Dryden himself—would treat as a watershed seemed to call for political makeshift, as Worden has remarked: "Loyalism was elevated to the status of a political theory . . . it also reflected the widespread feeling among less articulate men that bad government was better than no government, and that it was wiser to square one's conscience with allegiance to an unwelcome regime than to leave the management of affairs solely in the hands of one's enemies."[3]

The Engagement controversy was a serious constitutional crisis. Its politically destabilizing effect should be contrasted with the millenarian radicalism of the preceding decade. After 1644, the original cause of the godly M.P.s had split up into several interests (above, chapter 1). Those religious radicals whom the newly established Presbyterians branded Independents rejected an established church, insisting that religion, far from being subordinate to the state (as "Erastians" held), was itself the basis of civil reform. Milton's tracts on reformation down through *Areopagitica* (1644) show the Independent platform. In that address to Parliament, his Independent spirit of reform catches up our civic and religious life in a single embrace:

> Liberty . . . is the nurse of all great wits; this is that which has rarify'd
> and enlightn'd our spirits like the influence of heav'n; this is that which
> hath enfranchis'd, enlarg'd, and lifted up our apprehensions degrees
> above themselves. Ye cannot make us now lesse capable, lesse knowing,
> lesse eagerly pursuing of the truth, unlesse ye first make your selves,
> that made us so, lesse the lovers, less the founders of our true liberty.
> We can grow ignorant again, brutish, formall, and slavish, as ye found
> us; but you then must first become that which ye cannot be, oppressive,
> arbitrary, and tyrannous, as they were from whom ye have free'd us.

The Levellers' *Humble Petition* to Parliament after the second Civil War in 1648 revived the spirit of *Areopagitica*. They sought egalitarian laws, democratic rights, and the franchise for most persons, matching these demands by a call for freedom of conscience in words that echo Milton's. They deprecate "the example of former tyrannous and superstitious parliaments, in making orders, ordinances, or laws, or in appointing punishments concerning opinions or things supernatural, styling some blasphemies, others heresies, when as you know yourselves easily mistaken, and that divine truths need no human helps to support them; such proceedings having been generally invented to divide the people amongst themselves and to affright men from that liberty of discourse by which corruption and tyranny would be soon discovered."[4]

Christopher Hill has written about Milton and the experience of defeat, but one could make a case for the modest success of Miltonic liberty and its political realization in the Commonwealth, which was a free republic *under* God if not *of* him. That less-than-perfect form of government consisted of a purged Parliament, its Council, and a victorious Army led by Cromwell. In chapter 2, we noted Marvell's disparaging account of the last phase of the Commonwealth and its brief successor of 1653. Writing his own prose eulogy of the Protector in 1654, Milton gave up on the vision of a Christian republic set forth in *Areopagitica* ten years before and put his hope in the individual leadership—as opposed to the civic *virtù*—of the elect few. In the end, he would abandon altogether his dream of a *vivere civile* (civic life) and, despite being haunted by the image of a Commonwealth lost, assert that the true polity was a paradise within.

By 1654, the debate on the problem of freedom had shifted away from these arguments of Miltonic liberty. Millenarian antinomianism could now be dismissed along with the precepts of the Fifth Monarchists whom Marvell ridiculed. From the time of the Protectorate, spiritual license ceased to be the political problem that it had been for Milton. The religious indifference and downright atheism of republican Commonwealthsmen, which gave way to Cromwell's benign toleration, took the sting out of religious dissent and dissipated its anarchic force. The Quakers' aggressive attempts at discipline threatened the religious peace after 1652, but they were careful not to interfere in the civil government. Ever since 1649, that government had been not only kingless but avowedly godless: rulers no longer pretended to have God's direct warrant. The change pointed far beyond the Restoration. In the end, separating religion from politics was the easiest way to evade the problem of freedom. All modern liberal governments have adopted this republican solution.

REFORM THROUGH INNOVATION

Inasmuch as the godly cause of the early 1640s had broken down into sectarianism, the decay of millenarian hope was the generation of the republic.
Civic secularism began its rapid ascent during the high noon of the Miltonic
debate over Christian liberty. A Marxist might try to explain secularism as
an emergent formation within the dominant religious culture, but the secular republicanism that appeared in England at midcentury was not a class
phenomenon, and the Great Rebellion is no more reducible to social than
religious conflicts. The best way of coming to grips with Dryden's hostility
to republicanism is to look at the new secularism that would eventually supplant religion as the basis of modern society.

Reform was the common element joining religion with politics, Puritans
with republicans, and the godly cause with the Good Old Cause. Whether
the object of reform is an institution (church and state) or the private individual, reformers appeal to our better instincts. Calvin, convinced that our
nature is wholly corrupt, nevertheless bids us expect a calling to justification
and election. Others like Aristotle regard man as essentially political and do
not find the notion of corruption or sin helpful in realizing our civic life.
Machiavelli prefers to use the term "second nature" for man (de)formed by
custom, reserving "corruption" for the breakdown of the state, not the individual; in this he follows Polybius. Machiavelli parts company with Augustine in never admitting that the republic is created by grace; neither does he
share Savonarola's enthusiasm for a religious reform that would restore us
to our *prima natura*.[5]

Short of a millennium, which *Areopagitica* warns us not to expect soon,
nobody in England prior to the Civil Wars had envisioned a transformation
of our "second nature." In fact, millenarian impatience with the penalty of
Adam soon aroused contramillenarian types like the Presbyterian William
Prynne, who came to the rescue of our "second nature" and defended it on
the grounds of customary, legal tradition. Custom is the friend and foe of reform, which it initially resists but finally confirms. Machiavelli fully exploits
this dialectic of custom and innovation in his matchless analyses of revolutionary events and their aftermath.[6]

When the Levellers at Putney affirmed the natural rights and goodness
of man, they combined their demand for the transformation of our "second
nature" with an attack on custom, especially the law. Unlike those reformers

who sought to restore the church as an "apostolic" but ambiguously timeless kingdom of the spirit, the Levellers bounded their reformation within the *saeculum*. Like Marx later, the Levellers were scornful of pretensions to transcend the world and time. They locate the nature and purpose of human existence entirely within history or the *saeculum*. Our customary "second nature" is not an effect of sin reversible only through divine grace. It is a condition brought on by ourselves and suffered by us owing to crass slavishness and lack of political will. Therefore, it is directly remediable by human action.

This kind of reform stands on its head the postlapsarian world of Augustine and Aquinas and of Dryden and Milton. Divine grace, instead of supervening upon history and upon fallen nature, inheres in us from the beginning. Our "second nature" is subsumed by imputing to us an original nature in which sin has been canceled. This recovery of an original world of natural rights is not warranted by Machiavelli, who merely assumes that humanity, having once fallen into its "second nature," can be stabilized in that imperfect condition by good laws and customs (*buoni ordini*). Machiavelli's legislative goal anticipates Hobbes. By contrast, the Levellers' transformation of the *saeculum* coincides with the millenarians' transcendence of it. That is my reading of Pocock's thesis quoted above in chapter 2: "The moment of recreating the republic, that society in which men were what they ought to be, was hard to conceive without adding the concept of the apocalyptic moment, or moment at which grace acted in history."

The republican ideal of secular reform sprang from the Civil Wars. I think Dryden was wary of republicanism because he feared its discovery of our radical prudence: of our ability, that is, to *recreate ourselves by forming a state*. What Dryden apprehended as the problem of freedom the republicans seized as an opportunity.

The Machiavellian *innovazione* of the republic in 1649 was a far more radical act than the founding of the Protectorate five years later. The Cromwellian institution was celebrated by Marvell, and Dryden praises it as a reactionary accomplishment that returned the nation to stability. In sharp contrast, the institution of the Commonwealth in 1649 destabilized customary government by completing England's break with tradition. Such a moment of confusion and opportunity is what Machiavelli calls an *occasione*. The traditional symbol of secular confusion and instability is Boethius's Fortuna, usually pictured with her wheel, and in Machiavelli's writings political stability results from a struggle between Fortuna and *virtù:* either the heroic *virtù* of the prince or the collective *virtù* of an armed and active citizenry. In the confusion of this struggle, the *occasione* deprives the contestants of their supporting habits or customary mores; they can no longer get their bearings from tradition. As Pocock says, "In the final, Boethian, analysis, the price to be paid for a life of civic activity was vulnerability to fortune; and the republic, being that community in which each individual was defined by his activity, was the community committed by its political form to contend against that vulnerability. States and nations, like individuals, might rise and fall as ambition condemned them to mount upon the Wheel, but only the republic obliged the individual to pit his virtue against fortune as a condition of his political being. Virtue was the principle of republics."[7]

The English response to this moment of vulnerability to fortune was *Leviathan* and the other writings in the Engagement controversy. Turning to these writings, one finds in them neither a Machiavellian eagerness to seize the *occasione,* nor the vicarious participation in the *kairos* offered by Marvell's *Horatian Ode.* In retrospect, the Commonwealth would seem an opportunity lost. To a reflective person living through it, however, doubts about the futility of all action were apt to overwhelm the prudential possibilities in the *kairos.* Such is the tenor of Anthony Ascham's discourse *Of the Confusions and Revolutions of Government:* "The time present is governed by the wils of men, which are mysterious one to another, and are so covert and serpentine, that they who sit in Councill together, rarely penetrate themselves." Hobbes removed the doubt by trading off prudential freedom for the man-made security of a contract. *Leviathan,* a work of sheer voluntarism in comparison with the rational wit and prudence of Harrington's *Oceana* five years later, portrays "the human individual existing at a moment of near-total delegitimation and artificially recreating authority from a state of dereliction."[8]

Dryden did not contribute to the Engagement controversy, but his later remarks about the origin and renewal of "Empire" in his Restoration poems and heroic plays make it clear that he considered the *occasione* of 1649 a crisis from which the nation was rescued by traditional authority and providence, not by civic *virtù* and prudence. Even in the *Heroique Stanzas,* Cromwell's "Heroïque Vertue" depends on "Heav'n," and its antagonist is not Fortuna but the sullen "Commons" and civil unrest: "No Civill broyles have since his death arose, / But *Faction* now by *Habit* does obey." When Dryden recalls the crisis of 1649 in *Astraea Redux,* he does not think of the republic's founding as a deed of civic *virtù* but as the act of an inflamed Commons ("the Vulgar"), whose *virtù* he symbolizes by figures of the Cyclops and the Titans scaling Olympus (1:14, 16, 22–23). Although he left only a few clues to his political reflections during the seventeen months between these two poems, I believe Dryden located the real constitutional cataclysm in 1659 rather than ten years before. It was in 1659 that he discovered the brute force of "the Vulgar" will and first grasped the full meaning of the Good Old Cause. Now he knew from experience "Those real bonds false freedom did impose" (1:26, line 152).

The secular innovation that Dryden terms chimerical had been debated in Commons throughout 1659, the *annus mirabilis* of English republicanism. M.P.s argued over the form of government and especially over the question of a senatorial Upper House, in Machiavellian language derived from *Oceana*. That model commonwealth itself was proposed for adoption in the House by Harrington's friend Henry Neville, while "a regular campaign of Harringtonian pamphlets pressed it on the public at large." Harrington and his friends made up the elegant Rota Club, whose political debates, according to John Aubrey, "were the most ingeniose, and smart, that ever I heard, or expect to heare, and bandied with great eagernesse: the Arguments in the Parliament howse were but flatt to it." This republican discussion fixed the slogan "Good Old Cause" in the public mind once and for all.[9]

ARMED CITIZENS AND THE GOOD OLD CAUSE

"The Good Old Cause" is the watchword of rebellion in *Absalom and Achitophel*, and we need to know which aspects of Interregnum republicanism Dryden meant to dismiss by the slogan. The basic Machiavellian axiom of *Oceana*, that men become free by civic participation, was originally affirmed by the Levellers at Putney, as we saw. The axiom took on a concrete meaning when the Levellers annexed to John Lilburne's demands for suffrage the Machiavellian principle that an armed citizenry (*popolo armato*) is the only enduring basis of a state. This classic idea, prized as the key to liberty by republicans as disparate as the genteel James Harrington and the rifle-toting opponents of gun control in the United States, summed up for the Army its concept of freedom. From this republican premise, Pocock traces a filiation of arguments: those against "standing armies" or mercenaries, those for the protection of property rights, and those warning of the inevitable corruption that besets a republic when its citizens become the clients or dependents of their social superiors or persons of wealth. Each of these arguments resonates in the opinions expressed by Dryden in his poems at the Restoration.[10]

All three topics—arms, property, and corruption—are correlated in the *Discorsi*, 1.55, in which Machiavelli concludes that a free republic can avoid corruption only if its citizens maintain *equalità*. By equality he means freedom from dependence or clientage, achieved by owning sufficient property; and freedom from the threat of force, which is secured by destroying the feudal nobility with their armed retainers. As Pocock comments, "There must be the political conditions which permit the arming of all citizens, the moral conditions in which all are willing to fight for the republic and the economic conditions (lacking in the case of a lord's retainers) which give the warrior a home and occupation outside the camp and prevent him becoming a *suddito, creato* or mercenary whose sword is at the command of some powerful individual. The economic independence of the warrior and the citizen are prerequisites against corruption."[11]

English republicans wanted to halt the decline that had begun when the "Norman Yoke" of monarchy and aristocracy was laid upon Anglo-Saxon freedom. Nedham's *Case of the Commonwealth* (1650) describes what can happen when "civility [civic sense: Machiavelli's *civiltà*] hath degenerated into effeminacy": "If at any time there have happened worthy resolutions in virtuous spirits to recover their freedom, they have for the most part failed in the enterprise by reason of the corruption of their party [Machiavelli's *fazione*] which causeth men at length to decline the common cause through pusillanimity, faction, treachery, or apostasy; being more superstitiously inclinable to adore the greatness of a tyrant than really affectionate to the worth of liberty." Nedham had contributed to the Hastings volume a poem from which the author of *Absalom and Achitophel* would lift a line, and Dryden likely got some notions of a military republic from the essays Nedham wrote during the years following the extinction of the royalist cause at Worcester in September 1651. Nedham's editorials in *Mercurius Politicus*, later collected into *The Excellency of a Free State* (1656), "are a blueprint, consciously Machiavellian, for a republic democratic not in anything he says about the suffrage, but in being ruled by an armed Many." The Army, Nedham says, must demand the frequent election of parliaments by the people and must guard against the revolution being taken over by an oligarchy: "Any form of entrenched power is therefore a threat to popular liberty, and *Mer-*

curius Politicus carries on a lengthy campaign against any revival of 'kingly' or 'standing' power."[12]

Dryden's opinion of the militants and their Good Old Cause in 1655 may be brought out by comparing his sentiments with Marvell's (see chapter 2). Dryden was living in London again by the time Marvell's *First Anniversary* appeared, or soon after. No doubt he too applauded Cromwell's success in bridling the radicals. In their poems on the Protectorate, however, both poets ignore the growing difficulty Cromwell had with his army, who prevented him from accepting the crown that was repeatedly offered to him. And while they praise his foreign conquests, they both shun the Machiavellian theme of imperial expansion by a *popolo armato* — Marvell because of the Fifth Monarchist danger and Dryden because the people's leader is dead. Dryden, whom the government was employing in some capacity by April, saw the army deny Oliver the customary crown that was his due. Marvell did raise concerns about the succession, but because he conceived of the great captain as the servant or the herald of Christ, he had to dodge the questions of who would inherit Cromwell's office and whether there would be an office to inherit. His equivocation arose from his confusion about the millennium, which left him unable to place Cromwell in history the way Dryden could. Marvell's chiliastic avoidance of history is akin to the army radicals' impatience with the customs and laws that grow out of secular history. Nowhere in his works does Dryden ridicule the saint's ascetic longing to outsoar the *saeculum*. What he did ridicule and did not well understand was the millenarian urge to *transform* the *saeculum* and throw off the shackles of custom. He abominated a republic that was a secularized version of the millennium because such a republic was a monstrous simulacrum of the visible church.

"England's second flush of republicanism began as a reaction against the single rule of Oliver Cromwell," Felix Raab has said. Marvell's *First Anniversary* records the beginning of that reaction, which gathered strength when Cromwell dismissed Parliament early in 1655 and which reached a climax late in 1656, at the time *Oceana* appeared. For the next five years, Sir Henry Vane and the army and finally Milton himself rallied the forces of reform against revisionary backsliding, and the Good Old Cause became their cry.[13]

It was during this Harringtonian half-decade that Dryden first encountered modern political thinking. At Cambridge, he had witnessed at most some academic hand-wringing over the Engagement, but in London, he saw the power of new ideas to shake the government. I do not believe that he initially confounded secular radicals with millenarians, or the army with Fifth Monarchists; only to gratify his Tory readers twenty years later did he adopt their Cavalier axiom. Even though the Good Old Cause, therefore, came to be identified with Cromwell by those wanting to blacken his memory, Dryden first knew the cause as a *threat* to Cromwell: a howl emitted by the "Faction" that the Protector muzzled and forced to obey. Dryden's eyes were opened when, soon after Cromwell passed from the scene, the Good Old Cause took deadly aim at customary government. Sixteen fifty-nine taught Dryden the appalling potency of Harrington's and Machiavelli's ideas.

Among Harrington's prolific outpourings in 1659 was *Axioms Political*, which included these: "XCVIII. Where there is a standing army, and not a formed government, there the army of necessity will have dictatorian power. . . . XCIX. Where an army subsisteth upon the pay or riches of a single person, or of a nobility, that army is always monarchical. Where an army subsisteth not by the riches of a single person, nor of a nobility, that army is always popular." Such axioms are prudence methodized. Like Hobbes, Harrington considered politics a science. He comes forward as Machiavelli's heroic legislator to combat Fortuna, who constantly destabilizes human institutions by corrupting them. Corrupt laws are a far greater evil than corrupt men.[14]

Laws become corrupt when they cease to reflect the underlying power structure, which Harrington calls the *balance*. His Machiavellian science cleverly neutralizes the question of our fallen nature: "The balance altering, the people, as to the foregoing government, must of necessity be corrupt; but corruption in this sense signifieth no more than that the corruption of one government (as in natural bodies) is the generation of another; wherefore, if the balance alter from monarchy, the corruption of the people in this case is that which maketh them capable of a commonwealth." The moral character of a people depends on their government. Machiavelli had observed that the subjects of a monarchy are hard to conquer but easy to rule, whereas the reverse is true of the citizens of a republic. Any change in "manners" (mores), therefore, comes from a change in the balance that determines the form of government. Harrington lays out the elements of government, using the Aristotelean/Polybian scheme of the one, the few, and the many — monarchy, aristocracy, democracy. All three forms are "mixed" in a dynamic balance that Harrington bases on property ownership. A disturbance in this mixed balance is corrected by revolution, which redistributes property in a new balance and brings government back from selfishly factional or "private unto a more public interest."[15]

Nothing better demonstrates the secular and humanistic roots of modern thought than this teleology of a rational "public interest." Harrington is saying that men improve their natural condition by human legislation: we *reinvent ourselves politically*. Harrington does away with the Boethian dualism that locates providence outside of a fallen *saeculum* that it sporadically infuses with grace. Harrington moves providence inside the *saeculum*, or secularizes it: in other words, he identifies providence with legislative *prudence*. He interprets Israel's theocracy as a commonwealth whose popularly elected leader, Moses, submitted the Ten Commandments to the people for ratifying. As a consequence of this biblical literalism, he immediately found himself charged with atheism, like Hobbes. Accordingly, he begs his "godly" reader to consider "Whether human prudence be not a creature of God, and to what end God made this creature." In thus displacing providence by prudence, Harrington does attain Hobbes's goal of reducing prophecy and the vox Dei to civil injunctions. But their authority lies in human reason, not in the Erastian state. Harrington's bold hermeneutics may well have lighted the way for Dryden to a rival style of providential mimesis.[16]

We may summarize the republican ideas in which Dryden had shown the most interest as the year 1659 began and the Protectorate was enjoying its last months of calm. He had witnessed the resistance to monarchy and the attacks on privilege (including the new Other House, a surrogate for the House of Lords). He feared the continued vociferousness of the Army and its levellers. He was probably not reassured by Harrington's plan for incorporating this radical element in a Machiavellian *popolo armato*, and he could only mistrust the alliance that was forming between godless republicans and zealous sectaries. His political thinking was still joined to religion: he viewed the Augustinian *saeculum* in a Boethian perspective, though he conceived of providence also in terms of the artist's prudence (*Heroique Stanzas*, 93–96). Machiavellian prudence—the civic *virtù* whereby men innovate and cope with instability and Fortuna—is imputed to Cromwell only providentially (lines 125–28). Harringtonian prudence, by means of which man rectifies the state according to its true balance, relied on a dangerous popularity. Later in 1659 and early in 1660, after watching John Lambert and the restored Rump crazily manipulate this balance, Dryden would characterize the Good

Old Cause and republican prudence by metaphors of the proud Titans. His titanic republicans correspond to Hobbes's "Mortal God," Leviathan, and he shunned their Erastian utopia as a mockery of the visible church.

SOBER GOVERNMENT AND MORAL KNOWLEDGE

Dryden's first three Restoration poems all concentrate on events of 1659 and 1660; thereafter he begins to widen the historical perspective. When Cromwell died, faction and Commons quickly ceased to obey. Dryden seems to have blamed most of the ensuing confusion on an army whose fanaticism was exploited by ambitious politicians. The Machiavellian topic uppermost in *Astraea Redux* is the problem of who controls the army. Over the winter of 1659/60, Monck dealt circumspectly with both the purged Parliament and the army:

> Nor could his Acts too close a vizard wear
> To scape their eyes whom guilt had taught to fear,
> And guard with caution that polluted nest
> Whence Legion twice before was dispossest,
> Once sacred house which when they enter'd in
> They thought the place could sanctifie a sin. (179–84)

The California editors, Hooker and Swedenberg, gloss the "polluted nest" as "the House of Parliament when occupied by the Rump." The gloss is typical of the anachronism that overtakes the most careful scholarship when it relies on the Cavalier axiom and partisan historiography. Dryden, who never noticed the symmetry we find in Interregnum history (Long Parliament-Rump-Protectorate-Rump-Long Parliament), would not have given the name of "Legion" to the purged Parliament in which his cousin and his uncle had served alongside at least one of his future patrons (Lord Lisle). Moreover, the "Rumpers" were "dispossest" more than twice. They were turned out by Cromwell in April 1653, by Lambert in October 1659, and finally by Monck in February 1660. And nobody would have said that Cromwell "dispossessed the Rump" when, in 1653, he *dissolved* the Long Parliament, which had survived for twelve years despite its purging in 1648.[17]

"Legion" is not Parliament or its Rump. Dryden means the army, rampaging apparently out of control and in no way reminiscent of the file of musketeers Cromwell led into the House in 1653. The army's action in 1659 shocked all of London, recalling Pride's Purge of 1648. The "sacred" House became a "polluted nest" when the soldiers rollicked inside St. Stephen's Chapel, the ancient precincts where Commons assembled. In 1653 Cromwell firmly governed his police troops, something neither Colonel Pride nor Lambert was able to do. Furthermore, in 1659 the army itself compared its action with the purge eleven years earlier.[18]

Readers of *Astraea Redux* will mistake its historical focus until they realize that its author is riveted by the events of 1659. For us, the Rebellion and Interregnum center in the Regicide. Dryden took a different view of the epoch. The "Faction" that Cromwell had taught to obey "by Habit," Dryden says, now "seiz'd the Throne" (line 22). This cannot refer to the regicides of 1649, who did not *seize* but constitutionally abolished the throne. Dryden is thinking of what happened to the throne restored by Cromwell and lost again by his son in 1659.

The passage goes on to mention the soldiers' prayer sessions and fast sermons—customs that the army kept until long after 1648. Dryden compares the troops' spiritual exercises to the "devouter *Turks* [who] warn their souls / To part" before they drink:

> So these when their black crimes they went about
> First timely charm'd their useless conscience out.
> Religions name against it self was made;
> The shadow serv'd the substance to invade:
> Like Zealous Missions they did care pretend
> Of souls in shew, but made the Gold their end.
> Th' incensed Powr's beheld with scorn from high
> An Heaven so far distant from the sky,
> Which durst with horses hoofs that beat the ground
> And Martial brass bely the thunders sound.
> 'Twas hence at length just Vengeance thought it fit
> To speed their ruine by their impious wit.   (189–200)

Dryden charges the unruly soldiers with religious hypocrisy: "they did care pretend / Of souls in shew, but made the Gold their end." He has borrowed the image of Legion from the Presbyterian Robert Wild's poem *Iter Boreale*, and he imitates Wild's description of the fanatics whom Lambert enlisted to put down the royalist uprisings and to help secure the country against both Monck and the Rumpers in the last months of 1659. "Bodies of armed men were gathering, either for self-defence or self-enrichment, which favored neither party," Ronald Hutton writes. "If there was a time in 1659 which justified the term 'anarchy' . . . this was it." Dryden's lines associate these unruly Fifth Monarchists and "Quakers" with the ideological cant of republicans like Vane who now made their grab for power. They remind Dryden of Salmoneus, the audacious demigod he numbers among the Titans. The metaphor shows that he blames the republicans for misleading the army sectaries by "their impious wit," which notoriously led the Good Old Cause to self-destruct in 1659 and 1660. Salmoneus will supply the epigraph for *The Medall*, in which again the Titan will represent Shaftesbury's religious hypocrisy or demagoguery with which he cloaks his ambition.[19]

Far from admiring the outpouring of pamphlets and expressions of civic *virtù* called forth by the collapse of the Protectorate, the poet reflects on providence and its taciturn instrument, General Monck. Dryden's prudential heroes—Sir George Booth, Monck, and the king himself—are not victors in a contest with Fortuna. They are the beneficiaries of a divine dispensation. Dryden presents their actions in a Boethian perspective utterly distinct from the secular perspective of Machiavelli and Harrington, in which providence is merely immanent. Despite the imperial echoes—Charles is "toss'd by Fate" like Aeneas (line 51) and at last assumes "Great *Augustus* Throne" (line 321)—the poem emphasizes patience rather than heroic action. Charles prospers better than Otho because he "stay'd and suffer'd Fortune to repent" (67–68). It is not his *virtù* but his *throne* that withstands "Fortunes fruitless spight" (97–104). Providence shows directly its care of the nation and the monarchy and only incidentally its care for the king.

His "early Valour" (line 73) was ineffectual, like Booth's "forward Valour" (line 145); "crost" because "Providence design'd" otherwise and chose Monck for its instrument. Dryden compares Monck's characteristic virtue of foresight with *art*, using what has become the poet's favorite prudential metaphor:

> 'Twas MONCK whom Providence design'd to loose
> Those real bonds false freedom did impose.
> The blessed Saints that watch'd this turning Scene
> Did from their Stars with joyful wonder leane,
> To see small clues draw vastest weights along,
> Not in their bulk but in their order strong.

> Thus Pencils can by one slight touch restore
> Smiles to that changed face that wept before.   (151–58)

The illusion of civic freedom under the republic imposed "real bonds" that could be loosed only by the agent of a Boethian providence. Monck's power comes from the transcendental heaven of "blessed Saints." For mortals below, the "turning Scene" controlled by Fortuna and her wheel is suddenly altered by the perception that what looked like chance is really providence. Dryden's metaphor draws an explicit analogy between providence and artistic prudence, and at the same time updates the Boethian vision by hinting that the "Scene" watched by the saints is theatrical.

Most of Dryden's Restoration poems make the "impious wit" of the republicans look dim beside the dazzling wit of a revealed providence. In the earliest poem, *To Sir Robert Howard*, Dryden calls the true wit of Howard's poetry another manifestation of providence, just like Monck's prudence:

> Of Morall Knowledge Poesie was Queen,
> And still she might, had wanton wits not been;
> Who like ill Guardians liv'd themselves at large,
> And not content with that, debauch'd their charge:
> Like some brave Captain, your successfull Pen
> Restores the Exil'd to her Crown again.
>
> (1:18, lines 45–54)

"Morall Knowledge" is the moral science of Hobbes and Davenant (see chapter 5), which emulates that of Machiavelli and Harrington. Whereas the republicans would form the character of the people by civic *virtù* and the balance of their government, Dryden derives a people's mores (including their poetry) from "A sober Prince's Government" (line 56). Under the restored monarchy, poetry again becomes the ally of providence against impious, republican wit. In the excitement of proclaiming a new "providence of wit" (line 34), however, Dryden inadvertently pays Monck a republican compliment. Dryden says his "name preserv'd shall be, / As *Rome* recorded *Rufus* memory" (95–96). This allusion to a republican hero—Rufus's civic patriotism is further emphasized in a note—was no doubt an oversight; it did not get reprinted until 1696.

Astraea Redux ends by telling Charles, "At home the hateful names of Parties cease / And factious Souls are weary'd into peace" (312–13). The next year, in Dryden's coronation panegyric *To His Sacred Majesty*, the law-lessness of 1659–60 has become an indefinite period of Deluge that preceded the Restoration (compare *The First Anniversary*). On this occasion of praise, the Machiavellian *occasione* is forgotten, and the poem does not hint at active prudence. Instead of *virtù*, "A noble Emulation heats [Charles's] breast." The royal virtue is passive—indeed, vegetative—and most readers would prefer the irreverent opening of *Absalom and Achitophel* to the trite wish for succession here:

> A Queen, from whose chast womb, ordain'd by Fate,
> The souls of Kings unborn for bodies wait.
> It was your Love before made discord cease:
> Your love is destin'd to your Countries peace. (119–22)

This tableau of connubial absorption is far removed from the vigorous Crom-well commended in the *Heroique Stanzas*.

The pretense that a timeless monarchy was now restored after a hiatus might serve the poet's ceremonial ends, but it could not satisfy Dryden's eventual need for historical explanation. The Machiavellian moment of the Interregnum had shown him the temporality of all rule. Dryden's fascina-tion with history, his effort to discover its "prudence," sets his work off from the royalist enthusiasm over Charles's providential escape from Worcester and his Restoration. The poet's real interest lay in a broader mimesis of providence, whose special care England had been. Dryden made good that claim both at Cromwell's death and at the Restoration by discovering a his-torical continuity in either event. Like the ancient constitution to which all parties clung during the crises of the 1640s, the monarchy in 1660 stood for an unbroken *custom*. Monarchy was but one of several customary symbols. Dryden transfers his admiration for Cromwell to other masters of experi-ence, prudential heroes who carry over the "Last Age" into the present. Like Monck and Howard, the figures Dryden salutes in his Restoration poems— Clarendon, Charleton, Orrery—discerned a continuity in historical actions and events where most saw nothing but chance and discontinuity.

To My Lord Chancellor is the first in a series of attempts—culminating five years later in *An Essay of Dramatic Poesy*—to reestablish continuity with the culture drowned in "that wild Deluge" (1:33). "The Muses" (1:38) remind Clarendon of the youthful Hyde's exchange of verses with his friend Davenant. Presiding in Chancery, Clarendon represents equity, which

Dryden ingeniously links to the "mercy" of Charles I. The late king's "fatal goodnesse [was] left to fitter times" through his "Legacy"—namely, the lord chancellor himself (49–64). Because Clarendon embodies the royal prudence—that which is nearest to providence—he operates like nature with unbroken continuity, so that "we might unwind the clue" to find in him a "rich and undiscover'd World" (67–78). In the same way, Cromwell was "the Confident of Nature," or alchemist, whose own "rich Idea's" were "the rule and measure to the rest" (*Heroique Stanzas*, 99–104). Either hero presents a Boethian sagacity superior to Machiavelli's Fortuna yet dependent on providence. Cromwell's providence was all but unsearchable, whereas Clarendon's is more visibly identified with the king, who boasts "A Fate so weighty that it stops" the wheel of "weary'd Fortune" (129–32). Admiring subjects are assured that the mysteries of state, like heavenly motions, suffer no breach in their prudence. Clarendon's "orb" is lesser than the king's, "Yet both are for each others use dispos'd, / His to inclose, and yours to be inclos'd" (39–42). The *arcana imperii*, like nature and art in the *Heroique Stanzas*, are a seamless continuity.

The guiding thought of this very intellectual poem appears in the conceit at the end. A *senex puer* who combines youth and age, Clarendon is the Janus of this New Year's offering: he faces backward to the Last Age and forward to "the glorious Course you have begun":

> Yet unimpair'd with labours or with time
> Your age but seems to a new youth to climb.
> Thus Heav'nly bodies do our time beget;
> And measure Change, but share no part of it.
> And still it shall without a weight increase,
> Like this New-year, whose motions never cease.
>
> (147–52)

The whole poem has been built on astronomical figures, as Dryden tries to grasp a secular mutability comprehended within the perfection of the spheres. Like those, Clarendon revolves through the years "unimpair'd." He ages without care ("weight") while measuring the times to us who mark him. Dryden sees in his ageless prudence the essence of history: alteration combined with identity. Clarendon achieves stability *through* constant change. Charles's reign, like the peace, is best secured by "restlesse motions" (line 106). Clarendon's prudence must "immortal prove" because it is guided by the king and "the Center of it is above" (153–end). In this image, Dryden offers his patron an archetype of the Boethian *saeculum* ruled by a partly visible providence.

To My Honored Friend, Dr. Charleton trumpets the historical reflexivity awakened by recent events. Dryden records England's, and Charleton's, part in the European Enlightenment, which the poet defines as a liberating of "free-born Reason" from Aristotelean scholasticism. Progress depends not on innovation but on just the reverse: on the restoration of our customary freedom suppressed by doctrinaire republicans, who taught that "the *Saxons*" (line 44) gave us our original institutions when in fact our earliest government was monarchical and Danish. Charleton's putative discovery that "Kings, our Earthly Gods, were Crown'd" at Stonehenge unearths the nation's authentic ancient constitution: not a Saxon republic crushed by the Norman yoke, but a "mixed" government of king, Lords, and Commons. Dryden projects a tripartite scene of the king, the Lords who elect and counsel him, and the common "Subjects" whose role is to confirm and admire him. Stonehenge was a "*Throne*" for investing kings,

> Where by their wondring Subjects They were seen,
> Joy'd with their Stature, and their Princely meen.
> Our *Sovereign* here above the rest might stand;
> And here be chose again to rule the Land.   (49–52)

These lines convey the providential origin of kingship "in terms of ancient English custom rather than of scriptural warrant," to use Pocock's language once more: "The immemorial monarchy was the best guarantee of the immemorial law. The Restoration of 1660 was the greatest triumph which the cult of the ancient constitution ever enjoyed." Having emphasized that custom secures English freedom better than republican doctrine can, Dryden ends his poem with a providential narrative of the visit Charles made to Stonehenge after his flight from Worcester: "His *Refuge* then was for a *Temple* shown: / But, *He* Restor'd, 'tis now become a *Throne*." [20]

ANNUS MIRABILIS

In *Annus Mirabilis*, Dryden trained his mimesis of providential history on the Dutch War and the London Fire, seeking to juxtapose human prudence and *contemporary* events. He dedicated this versified theodicy to the City of

London: "I have heard indeed of some vertuous persons who have ended
unfortunately, but never of any vertuous Nation: Providence is engag'd too
deeply, when the cause becomes so general. And I cannot imagine it has resolv'd the ruine of that people at home, which it has blessed abroad with
such successes. I am therefore to conclude, that your sufferings are at an
end; and that one part of my Poem has not been more an History of your
destruction, then the other a Prophecy of your restoration" (1:49).

To ingratiate himself with the Presbyterian citizens, Dryden adopts the
familiar note of admonitory prophecy. *Annus Mirabilis* is Dryden's final attempt as public poet to stir up the old Cromwellian enthusiasm for the
Elect Nation. Events overtook the poet: after he had spent the summer on
the heroic subject of the naval wars, the London Fire obliged him to vindicate providence from the millenarian doomsayers. He explains in the critical
preface that he has had to give up epic unity; therefore "I have call'd my
poem *Historical*" (1:50). The author's frequent meditation on the inscruta-
bility of historical providence is at least as notable as the epic action:

> In fortunes Empire blindly thus we go,
>   And wander after pathless destiny:
> Whose dark resorts since prudence cannot know
>   In vain it would provide for what shall be.
>
> (stanza 200)

"Fortune's Empire" is a fair title for the vastly enlarged, but still Boethian
saeculum of *Annus Mirabilis*. Quoting these and other examples, Hammond
observes, "Dryden introduces the point that Fortune is capricious and un-
predictable, and that we are all liable to be her victims. That this is given
eloquent expression and made to stand alongside the explicitly Providential vocabulary is a sign that during the composition of *Annus Mirabilis* he
is opening his mind for the first time to the tragic implications of classical
philosophy." [21]

This note of tragic naturalism is also in part the result of Dryden's providential mimesis. A narrative of providence is seldom auspicious, as the history of Yahweh's dealings with Israel can attest. Dryden is faithful to events
and natural detail in his poem because he offers a literal imitation of the
saeculum, not an apocalyptic interpretation. The pathos of defeat in *Annus
Mirabilis*, framed by the author's preface exalting the Virgilian naturalism
of the *Georgics*, points to the more thoroughly secularized providence of the

Fables. For example, when the Dutch lie in their shallows like "the false Spider, when her Nets are spread," waiting for the refitted English ships to run their keels into the sands, providential winds and tides come to the rescue:

> It seem'd as there the *British* Neptune stood,
>> With all his host of waters at command,
> Beneath them to submit th' officious floud;
>> And, with his Trident, shov'd them off the sand.
>
> (stanza 184)

The Virgilian image turns providence into a stereotype: the kind of deus ex machina found in the landscape painting of the next century, in which the pantheon of classical gods superintend a Kantian or deistic nature emptied of divine grace.

Despite its unpropitious subject, *Annus Mirabilis* has a brightness missing from *Absalom and Achitophel,* the next poem that Dryden would publish after a long interval of nearly fifteen years. By then, partisan satire had sharpened and deformed his public role. In this poem culminating the first stage of his career, no sedition is to be found, only epic foes — the heroic Dutch and the elemental fire — while providence watches over the nation in the person of the royal mediator. The poet does not stand upon a Tory platform or sound his "talking Trumpet" to rally the partisan mob. Its freedom from sedition gives *Annus Mirabilis* a certain political freshness, but the poem is far from cheerful. Its audience in the fall of 1666 did not need to be reminded of mortality. While the epidemic had subsided in London during the year, cities like Cambridge and Southampton continued to be ravaged. Dryden, writing in Wiltshire, had seen his first son born a year before at the height of the plague, and the pathos of a new parent can be heard in the lines on Albemarle and Rupert hastening to their ships: "Infants first vows for them to Heav'n are cast, / And future people bless them as they go" (stanza 51). Pamphlets had decried the Restoration and England's backsliding even before the fire in September, but in this poem Dryden ignores "the Nations sin" (chapter 1).

Annus Mirabilis still fits within the framework of the millenarian epic and concludes with the Isaianic vision of a renewed Protestant nation led by its "Maiden Queen," a neo-Elizabethan England (stanzas 294–301; cf. Isaiah, chs. 60–62). Besides interceding for his people like David (stanzas 265–70), Charles is their messiah ("*Cyrus,*" stanza 290) who restores them to Jerusalem and their godly prince (stanza 10) who opposes the latest Antichrist, King Louis (stanzas 7–8, 41, 299). These sparse biblical allusions, like the comparisons of the dukes of York and Albemarle (Monck) with Moses (stanza 92; cf. the prefatory "Verses to her Highness the Dutchess," lines 17–18, 28–29), are placed efficiently to keep before us the Elect Nation and its goal. Other scriptural allusions are hermeneutically uncomplicated and seem mostly adventitious: Albemarle's disabled ship is like the ark, deadly to the enemy who approaches it (stanza 94); the three days' battle might be revenged in one, could the sun stand still as it did for Joshua (stanza 118); Holmes's fleet lies in wait for the Dutch like "huge Leviathans t'attend their prey" (stanza 203); the Dutch "like fall'n Angels" in awe of Rupert dread "This new *Messiah*'s coming" (stanza 114).[22]

Dryden's references to the Apocalypse and Resurrection are properly confined to the poem's second epic action of the London Fire. His "talking Trumpet" is unwontedly silent in the action of the wars, and he may eschew Scripture deliberately. His reflections on human fate dwell more exclusively on the *saeculum* than those of any poem since the *Heroique Stanzas*. He gives special prominence to Petronius by alluding to Encolpius's ironical lament in the *Satyricon* when he sees the drowned sailor washed up on shore: "And so we suffer Shipwrack every where!" (stanzas 32–35). The question is how this literal emphasis on the *saeculum* affects Dryden's hermeneutics. Millenarianism and Scripture are virtually missing from the epic part—that is, from two-thirds of the poem. Instead of pointing his "talking Trumpet" at a visionary crowd, Dryden's metaphors direct us to cyclical phenomena: circulation of the blood, the tides and seasons, alchemical distillation and precipitation (a benign figure for taxes), and of course the vicissitudes of war and the rise and fall of commercial empires.

Dryden pauses in his narrative to review the history of navigation (stanzas 155–64). The English with their knowledge of longitudes and tides have nearly made "one City of the Universe." To go beyond "our Globes last verge" and explore our planetary "Neighbours," however, requires a greater prudence than "poor man-kinds benighted wit." Accordingly the poet turns aside to address the Royal Society:

> This I fore-tel, from your auspicious care,
>   Who great in search of God and Nature grow:
> Who best your wise Creator's praise declare,
>   Since best to praise his works is best to know.

O truly Royal! who behold the Law,
  And rule of beings in your Makers mind,
And thence, like Limbecks, rich Idea's draw,
  To fit the levell'd use of humane kind.

(stanzas 165–66)

Progress, in Dryden's view, is like alchemy: a miraculous, historical transformation but contained within the alembic of the *saeculum*. Alchemy, traditionally known as the *royal art*, has always been a symbol of transcendence. Like Chaucer and Shakespeare, Dryden regards alchemical transcendence as a physical and psychological phenomenon rather than a key to theological truth. Unlike religion, alchemical transformation is not a means for escaping the Boethian *saeculum*, but a passage to a better or more comfortable position within it. Alchemical transformation corresponds to Dryden's idea of limited (as opposed to infinite) progress. In the resolutely historical world of *Annus Mirabilis*, transcendence and progress are both transition. Dryden carefully establishes the image of Charles contemplating the *opus alchymicum*, both when the king plans to finance the war (stanza 13) and when he renews it by repairing the fleet (stanza 140; cf. 139). The alchemist scrutinizes his "Limbeck," in which mind and matter unite ambiguously. He seeks the quintessence (the philosophers' stone) empowering him to control natural processes. By virtue of this alchemical reflexivity, he attains a sublime degree of prudence, becoming, like Cromwell, "the Confident of Nature" (1:14). Similarly, the Royal Society's prudence approximates divine providence ("the Law, / And rule of beings in your Makers mind"), enabling nature's confidants to adapt God's "rich Idea's" for man's use.

Dryden's office as historian is to interpret not the *natura naturata* of the scientists but the *natura naturans* of events—"a School distinction" he makes in his prefatory "Account" (1:53). He is practicing something like hermeneutics, only he claims to be interpreting not Scripture but literal phenomena: prodigies witnessed in his own time. For this reason he has to be chary of using biblical language. He wants to keep his providential mimesis on a footing with the sober investigations of the Royal Society. Availing himself of the old typology to interpret events would not just be unscientific, it would be unhistorical.

His reflexivity as public poet, therefore, is historical as well as political. The alchemical metaphor is significant. It shows that Dryden's meditation on historical events, like the Royal Society's new way of studying nature, had not yet degenerated into modern positivism, in which the observer becomes a *subject*, standing over against an *object* that is simply posited. Dryden's historian is still part of the events—providential, epic, or commercial—that he describes, and so are his readers. As chemistry was to supplant alchemy, so narrative literalism would banish historical reflexivity.

In the first part of *Annus Mirabilis*, Dryden avoided typological hermeneutics because it defeats his aim of capturing historical particularity, but the uniqueness of historical materials makes their ordering more difficult. When he must nearly have completed his poem on the wars, news arrived of the fire of 1–4 September. The California editors think that "a subtle change in tone commences with stanza 212, containing the image, from Ovid, of the destruction of the world, with an allusion to the myth of regeneration in the figure of the Phoenix" (1:257). The figure is more than an allusion. The phoenix reborn out of its ashes became Dryden's chief symbol for reorganizing the entire poem. In dedicating it to the City, he uses the image to give them an anagogical hope: "You are now a *Phoenix* in her ashes, and, as far as Humanity can approach, a great Emblem of the suffering Deity." And he applies the metaphor to the *Loyal London*, the already symbolic ship built by the City to replace the *London*, which was blown up in 1665. Dryden's description of this "*Phoenix* daughter of the vanish'd old" (stanzas 151–54) has been located at the center of *Annus Mirabilis* by McKeon in his extended study of the poem.

McKeon explicates Dryden's eschatological and prophetic themes. In order to read *Annus Mirabilis* typologically, he divides it into two precisely equal halves that share the four stanzas (151–54) describing the *Loyal London*. On the hypothesis that "the events of the second half recapitulate those of the first from a new and more meaningful perspective," McKeon arranges the parallels between the two parts in a chiastic scheme, locating the "Phoenix" of the *Loyal London* at the convergence of two sets of events: those flowing from the poem's opening prophecy and those leading to its closing prophecy.[23]

McKeon provides this heuristic scheme in the hope of turning up a paradigm whereby the poem's meaning can be inflected. Dryden's providential mimesis creates a typological vacuum: what makes one historical event more significant than another? McKeon supplies the missing typology: "I suggest that *Annus Mirabilis* has the structure of Christian history in that

it is organized around a central event of multileveled significance and consists of historical correspondences whose component events derive their own
significance from their relations with one another." By putting the *Loyal
London*'s resurrection at the center of Dryden's history, McKeon can argue
that the poem looks back to the Civil Wars as well as ahead to the fire and
beyond. For example, when Dryden writes that the *Loyal London*'s "sanguine Streamers seem the floud to fire," he is prefiguring stanza 231: "A Key
[quay] of fire ran all along the shore, / And lighten'd all the River with the
blaze." By the same token, later events may postfigure former, as the fire and
London's new birth recapitulates the Civil Wars and Restoration.[24]

In my opinion, McKeon draws nearest to Dryden's latent typology with
his eschatological reading of the fire. In connecting the phoenix with the
fire's transforming effect, however, McKeon ignores the fact that the phoenix is a prime symbol of alchemy. It stands for the moment when the *opus
alchymicum* produces its tincture, or rainbow of fused metals, signaling rebirth and the philosophers' stone. The alchemical phoenix also represents
the risen Christ, as Dryden understands when he applies the image to the
City itself (see above). McKeon identifies Charles with the phoenix when
the king accedes to the "*Cities* request to the King not to leave them" and
their town, as the gloss reads on stanza 288:

> But so may he live long, that Town to sway,
>   Which by his Auspice they will nobler make,
> As he will hatch their ashes by his stay,
>   And not their humble ruins now forsake.

What McKeon does not say is that the phoenix-king completes an alchemical process, which the poet has made explicit in order to mark the climax of
Annus Mirabilis by these stanzas.[25]

Before the fire, the king appears in the poem as the alchemist of the
opus but—significantly—not as the product of the *opus*. Stanzas 10 to 18
show him distilling "the fair Idea's . . . Of Fame and Honour which in dangers lay," along with the necessary taxes, "like vapours that from Limbecks
rise." Dryden underscores the alchemical process by noting "two glareing
Comets" ascending in the alembic of the macrocosm, a familiar conceit of
astrologers from Paracelsus to John Dee and Elias Ashmole. The king depu-
tizes to Prince Rupert and Albemarle the active work of honor while he
superintends the "Nations fate" (stanzas 45–47). His alchemical oversight is

made explicit in stanzas 139 to 150, describing how *"His Majesty repairs the Fleet"* and how he sees the *opus* brought to a preliminary tincture or completion in the poem's first phoenix, the *Loyal London*. The stanzas on navigation that follow climax in the alchemical *"Apostrophe to the Royal Society,"* which clearly links the society's royal art to that of their master.[26]

Dryden's original design must have kept the king out of the historical action, allowing him to contemplate it reflexively like an alchemist meditating on the *opus*. The king's work in the poem—the end product of his royal art—was to be the war itself. The fire caused Dryden to alter his design by making the king an actor and sufferer in the poem. This change, throwing the king into the very historical process he had been contemplating, is the source of the new typology that invades the otherwise literal, providential mimesis of *Annus Mirabilis*. The poem's change of perspective is reflected in the king's own point of view. The alchemical reflexivity with which he oversaw the wars is cast off, and he takes on an eschatological reflexivity: an Isaianic awareness of himself as the suffering servant of his people. Abandoning the auspicious role of alchemist, he now becomes the self-sacrificing phoenix or pelican, "The Father of the people" (stanza 286) who sustains them out of his own blood. He is what alchemy calls the *rex:* the gold that, dissolved in quicksilver, represents the dying king who undergoes dissolution in order to be resurrected from the fiery crucible.[27]

The fire in the last part of *Annus Mirabilis*, therefore, is indeed a vehicle for "the profound ambiguity of the eschaton," as McKeon says, but the vehicle is specifically an alchemical retort. Instead of allowing his providential narrative to lapse into traditional apocalyptics, like most of the poems on 1666, the poet joins the king and the readers who are his subjects in a single event. He integrates them both into a new *type*, which he creates out of the literal, historical moment. This new eschaton does not transcend the *saeculum*. Like science or the alchemical *opus*, it is contained within time. It is a myth of earthly monarchy eclipsed and restored. As such, it does not prefigure the end of the world. The year of wonders is not dissipated in a vision of the millennium. Its fire is the real Fire suffered by the "Royal City" whose restoration equates *historically*, not just symbolically, with Jerusalem rebuilt by loyal Jews (stanza 290). Charles is a provisional or nonce messiah like Cyrus.[28]

If Dryden's new type prefigures a perpetual cycle of monarchy restored, it must also postfigure monarchy in its eclipse. The poet can draw parallels from the imperfect past that help him piece together and complete the still-unfinished type. Thus, the fire in Dryden's account begins as the nemesis of monarchy but then turns into its alchemical furnace. Dryden's note referring to Ovid distinguishes this earthly, cyclical cataclysm from the Apocalypse ("the death of time"). He next examines the fire's origins:

> As when some dire Usurper Heav'n provides,
>   To scourge his Country with a lawless sway:
> His birth, perhaps, some petty Village hides,
>   And sets his Cradle out of Fortune's way.
>
> (stanzas 212–13)

To read this as a simile of Cromwell is to impose a Tory typology on the poem equivalent to the scriptural typology that Dryden eschews. "Lawless sway" is an unlikely characterization of the Protectorate, and nobody would attribute low birth or mean fortune to Cromwell. The fire certainly stands for rebellion, but Dryden assigns its origin to the country, probably because he does not want to stress too literally the historical roles played by London and Parliament in the rising against Charles I.

Beginning secretly as "seeds of fire" (Ovid's *semina flammae,* as Hammond notes), the fire soon becomes an "infant monster" and murderous outlaw escaped from prison, his lust aroused by "The winds, like crafty Courtezans." With the whole town now lying prey before him, the fire is joined by "The Ghosts of Traitors from the *Bridge*" (stanzas 217–23). Some of the regicides' skulls were displayed on London Bridge, but so were those of Fifth Monarchists. The ghosts need not have participated in the historical Rebellion to be united in their deathless hatred of kings. As "bold Fanatick Spectres," they dance a witches' Sabbath, circling the fire and imparting to it their lethal, antimonarchical animus. Their awakened spirit warned contemporary readers that the threat to monarchy was imminent, not past; the much-praised stanza 223 should alert even the modern reader to the perennial sedition that would later crop up in the Whig Association and the conventicles of *The Medall.*[29]

By stanza 233, the fire walks openly through the town scattering "his longing flames," which, beginning as snakes or predatory birds, quickly grow to an army intent on despoiling Whitehall. Having been deserted in his sleep by England's guardian angel—who fled in antipathy to the revived spirits of king-killing (stanza 224)—the king now emerges from Whitehall

Palace to enter the fuliginous City, preceded by his "harbingers of smoke" and "By sparks that drive against his Sacred Face" (stanza 239; compare the alchemical *rex* plunged into the alembic). He endures his tearful immersion in this crucible until stanza 253, helpless against the dragonlike, alchemical fire and its civil analogue, the breakdown of morality and neighborhood. The low point is reached as the weary king disappears, leaving his powers with his lunar counterpart, "his Royal Brother." The nocturnal apocalypse ensuing is an alchemical *nigredo*—the point at which the despair in the mind of the alchemist corresponds to the physical occlusion of the *rex* dissolved in quicksilver:

> Night came, but without darkness or repose,
>   A dismal picture of the gen'ral doom;
> Where Souls distracted when the Trumpet blows,
>   And half unready with their bodies come.
>
>   (stanzas 253–54)

Under cover of the night, or *nigredo*, a transformation occurs. The mob, who were last seen (stanza 252) loading their backs with "the spoils of *Vulcan*," are replaced by the pitiable crowd who return to their vanished homesteads to "stir up coals and watch the Vestal fire" (stanza 257). It is their prayer for the missing king overwhelmed in sorrow that begins his regeneration:

> No thought can ease them but their Sovereign's care,
>   Whose praise th' afflicted as their comfort sing:
> Ev'n those whom want might drive to just despair,
>   Think life a blessing under such a King.
>
> Mean time he sadly suffers in their grief,
>   Out-weeps an Hermite, and out-prays a Saint. . . .
>
>   (stanzas 260–61)

This is the posture of the occulted king in the alchemical *opus*—the *nigredo* that precedes the dawn or spring of the king's rebirth as the phoenix (stanzas 284–88).[30]

When Dryden began *Annus Mirabilis*, he probably meant to end with sentiments like those in stanza 289 on the people tried by "an expensive, though necessary, War" (1:48). The truth was that "ever since February 1665, Charles and his ministers had been in the position of a soldier who continues to assault an impregnable position for fear of being executed if he retreats." Without the stanzas on the fire, Dryden's poem would probably have fallen prey to the vicissitudes of public whim, like Waller's *Instructions to a Painter.* By giving Dryden a new typology, the fire, not the Dutch Wars, allowed him to historicize *Annus Mirabilis.*[31]

The proposition that myth is a necessary ingredient of authentic history will not seem paradoxical to the twentieth-century reader. My thesis has been that Dryden's literal imitation of the Boethian *saeculum* reconstitutes history as providential mimesis. This historical hermeneutics leaves no room for the old biblical typology. As opposed to the language of revelation, providential mimesis is the language of the book of nature and history. Hammond believes that Dryden's classical language evinces his pagan skepticism; but Dryden's skepticism, I have argued, never extends as far as to question Boethian providence, on which he grounds his by now clearly defined historical reflexivity. As in the case of Shakespeare's history plays, a *radical* imitation of providence, by rejecting allegory, results in a skepticism that can be profoundly visionary.

The fire in *Annus Mirabilis* is a new type. It resembles an apocalypse but—like the Polybian prudence with which this chapter began—it refers to a cyclical reality, not to the end of the world. This historical reality is the fall and rise of monarchy. Applying hermeneutics to Dryden's new typology, we can moralize the fire as the republican spirit. Dryden brings out the monarchical tragedy of republicanism by dramatizing the pathos of the suffering king. In so doing, he creates a new myth, superficially royalist but thoroughly skeptical beneath its formal accommodation of Cavalier and Anglican beliefs. For some time after *Annus Mirabilis,* Dryden's biblical hermeneutics was silenced. Fifteen years later, he would recall the poem's mythic figuration of the problem of freedom—the unending conflict between innovation and legitimacy. On that new occasion, he would seize the "talking Trumpet" from sectaries and Anglicans alike and use it to prophesy the ironies of providential history.

The Last Age

By imitating the literal event and letting its meaning emerge from the historical context, Dryden sought to make providence explicit. I characterize this hermeneutic approach to history as providential mimesis. Dryden's purpose recalls Augustine's insistence on the literal meaning of Scripture. Both writers regard the Bible as a consummate work of *mimesis,* even in its prophetic passages. Speaking like a poet, the prophet records providential fact without interpretive comment. This motive to providential mimesis, deriving from his Puritan radicalism, only grew stronger over the course of Dryden's career. It joins his poems to sober narratives like those of Bunyan and Daniel Defoe, for instance, that adapted the secular imitation of providence to early modern fiction.

When we look for the same providential mimesis in his plays, however, we find that it has been displaced by a quite different, popular motive. In his Restoration poems through *Annus Mirabilis,* Dryden wrote as a poet (or prophet) addressing topics that concerned the public good. His plays, on the other hand, before they could advise or instruct, had to please. The theater is public to the extent that it draws the audience into a kind of ritual or communal participation, but Dryden's theater gratified a coterie, not a truly national audience. Consequently, in 1668 when he confessed, "My chief endeavours are to delight the Age in which I live" (9:7), he was pretending that the select audience who admired his kind of rhymed, heroic play represented the civilized nation. Even their sophisticated acclaim did not satisfy him, though, and he followed the path of Pierre Corneille, inventing a critical tradition to justify his success. His early critical essays, 1664–72, are the subject of this chapter; the next chapter will examine the plays themselves.

By the time he completed the last of his five heroic plays, Dryden had ceased to boast that he was one of the successful dramatists who "still conform'd their Genius to their Age" (11:201). In his prologue to *Aureng-Zebe* (1675), he offers to "retire, betwixt two Ages cast, / The first of this, and hindmost of the last." This note of epigonism—which is first heard in 1673, soon after the resounding success of *The Conquest of Granada*—has been ascribed to the playwright's disgust with a new generation of authors like Elkanah Settle, who aped the rhymed tragedy brought into fashion by Davenant, Orrery, Howard, and Dryden. Although Winn blames the playwright's disillusion chiefly on personal disappointment, I believe its causes are public and inherently professional and will argue that Dryden, having labored for a decade to portray in his drama an ideal culture, belatedly awoke to the vanity of that ambition. The 1670s brought the collapse of the political consensus that the nation had enjoyed following the Restoration and that informs Dryden's heroic plays. With the breakdown of public confidence, he no longer found heroic mimesis adequate to the historical understanding of actual, providential events.[1]

DAVENANT'S MORAL SCIENCE

To the two-part *Conquest of Granada* published in 1672, Dryden prefixed "Of Heroic Plays: An Essay," in which he recounted the growth of the new genre:

> The first light we had of them on the *English* Theatre was from the late Sir *William D'Avenant:* It being forbidden him in the Rebellious times to act Tragedies and Comedies, because they contain'd some matter of Scandal to those good people, who could more easily dispossess their lawful Sovereign than endure a wanton jeast; he was forc'd to turn his thoughts another way: and to introduce the examples of moral vertue, writ in verse, and perform'd in Recitative Musique. The Original of this musick and of the Scenes which adorn'd his work, he had from the *Italian* Opera's; but he heighten'd his Characters (as I may probably imagine) from the example of *Corneille* and some *French* Poets. In this Condition did this part of Poetry remain at his Majesties return: When growing bolder, as being now own'd by a publick Authority, he review'd his *Siege of Rhodes*, and caus'd it be acted as a just Drama (11:9).

These few pregnant remarks have called forth several theories designed
to explain the rhymed heroic play and its genesis. Embellishing Dryden's
straightforward historical account, critics have emphasized one or another of
its elements. They have argued that the plays of John Fletcher and the Cavalier dramatists anticipated Davenant; that French drama, domesticated by
Orrery, was the decisive influence; and that the form of the heroic play was
determined by Renaissance epic theory. Most recently, scholars like Joanne
Altieri have paid new attention to Davenant's innovations of music and spectacle and have found an origin for the heroic play in the masque.[2]

These accounts of the heroic play all miss Dryden's emphasis. He says
that the heart of Davenant's innovation consisted in "examples of moral
virtue, writ in verse," and that this invention was born of necessity. Dryden
is thinking of the rebellious times recalled by Davenant in his "Poem to the
King's Most Sacred Majesty" (1663), in which Davenant blames the Regicide indirectly on the Presbyterians. Their philistinism, the poet claims, was
more insidious than overt sectarianism because it undermined civil society.
What all sects fail to grasp is the civilizing effect of art, which the "froward"
Presbyterians despised as mere "Ornament":

> Yet why with Sects (whose *Congregations* are
> But Men *well disciplin'd* for *Civil War,*
> Not meek Assemblies but a sullen Crowd,
> Who out of haughty pride disdain the Proud)
> Should *Calvin*'s froward Sect be rudely bent,
> Like *Zealous Goths,* against all *Ornament?* . . .
> If they in curious Tropes and Figures Preach
> (Which were the *Ethnick* Ornaments of Speech)
> And to our Ears provocatives allow,
> Why should our Eyes th'allurements want of Show?

In this sketch of Interregnum sectarianism, one recognizes the main traits of
the polemic against Calvinism in Dryden's poems of 1682. Davenant was the
younger poet's first and most valued guide in critiquing his native culture.[3]

"Ornament" had already been connected with moral philosophy in Davenant's preface to his epic poem, *Gondibert* (1650). At that date, Davenant
hoped to mollify Puritanical morality by "wit," which is the stuff of the
poem's "ornaments." He would not "presume to call the matter of which the

Ornaments or Substantial parts of this Poem are compos'd, *Wit;* but onely tell you my endeavour was, in bringing Truth, too often absent, home to mens bosoms, to lead her through unfrequented and new ways." Modern readers are likely to balk at the equation of ornament with poetic substance, unless they recognize the radically mimetic principle underlying Davenant's rhetorical theory. The equivalence foreshadows romantic aesthetics by placing art on the same footing with religion: "As Poesy is the best Expositor of Nature . . . so Nature is the best Interpreter of God, and more cannot be said of Religion." Providential phenomena—the *saeculum* of nature and history—are divine mimesis, already accomplished, and human art is merely its "Expositor," interpreting God's creation by dressing it to advantage. Like Dryden after him, Davenant finds his materials in their literal setting, where providence left them, and he varies them freely. His "Ornament" is equivalent to Sidney's second nature, or "golden" world of wit.[4]

Such mimetic freedom assumes a high degree of moral prudence in poets. Because they track the sinuous ways of providence and light up its unexpected symmetries, "Poets are of all Moralists the most useful. . . . For Nature performs all things by correspondent aids and harmony. And 'tis injurious not to think Poets the most useful Moralists, for as Poesy is adorn'd and sublim'd by Musick, which makes it more pleasant and acceptable, so Morality is sweetned and made more amiable by Poesy." Echoing Sidney (whom he elsewhere names as an ideal type), Davenant claims that "even *Honour,* taught by moral Philosophers, but more delightfully infusd by Poets," is a sure guide to piety; "for it is as wary and nice as *Conscience,* though more cheerful and couragious." The word "conscience," together with the search for a prudential guide, unmistakably orients Davenant's essay within the Engagement controversy, while the high premium on honor is a reminder that readers of his preface included the royalists in exile at the Louvre.[5]

Davenant probably inspired Dryden's assertion that "Poesy was Queen" of "Morall Knowledge," just as Dryden got from the laureate his first light on heroic plays. Davenant's preface was closely cognate with *Leviathan,* the premier study of moral science and its bearing on authority and obedience. Hobbes's work, also published from Paris in 1651, resulted in part from discussions with Davenant. *Gondibert* and its preface had been dedicated to Hobbes the previous year, while Hobbes's "Answer to Davenant" was also printed with the uncompleted poem. Hobbes agrees with Davenant that wit or imagination is the most powerful means of inculcating civic principles and teaching the people "health of Morality":

> Whatsoever distinguisheth the civility of *Europe* from the Barbarity of the *American* savages, is the workmanship of Fancy but guided by the precepts of true Philosophy. But where these precepts fail, as they have hitherto failed in the doctrine of Moral vertue, there the Architect, *Fancy,* must take the Philosophers part upon her self. He therefore that undertakes an heroick Poem, which is to exhibit a venerable & amiable Image of Heroick vertue, must not only be the Poet, to place & connect, but also the Philosopher, to furnish and square his matter, that is, to make both Body and Soul, colour and shadow of his Poem out of his own Store.

Hobbes wants the epic poet to assume the standpoint of the philosopher and to censure his own imagination, hewing and squaring the matter supplied by his "Fancy" to ensure that it conforms to the truth. Hobbes's criterion is very like the supreme judgment Dryden imputes to Virgil and (in drama) to Ben Jonson, and it depends on the same virtue of radical mimesis. That is to say, the poet's "own Store" implies neither subjectivity nor psychological autonomy. The poet's "wit" (imagination) can only imitate the historical experience stored in his own memory and in the collective memory of his audience. Hobbes formulates the mimetic principle in a rule that is both elegant and compendious: "As truth is the bound of Historical, so the Resemblance of truth is the utmost limit of Poeticall Liberty."[6]

Both in theory and practice, the "poetical liberty" of the drama is limited by Hobbes's verisimilitude: the demand that it resemble the truth. Dryden assailed this limit with his heroic plays, but later, when he cast his response to Rymer in terms of "manners" (mores, *moeurs*), he acknowledged the moral and political roots of verisimilitude. Moral science in the end outweighed sheer wit. Dryden's science had originated in the social crisis of England's Machiavellian moment, and it remained his touchstone of political truth. In 1668, when Howard belittled the achievement of dramatists by suggesting that poets need not "study strict reason," he was dismissing their moral science as politically irrelevant. In reply, Dryden affirmed poetry's mimetic basis with all the energy of Hobbes: "I am of opinion that they cannot be good Poets who are not accustomed to argue well. False Reasonings and colours of Speech, are the certain marks of one who does not understand the Stage: For Moral Truth is the Mistress of the Poet as much as of the Philosopher: Poesie must resemble Natural Truth, but it must *be* Ethical." The new laureate did not concede a monopoly on wisdom even to the natural philosophers, and he certainly could not suffer Howard, newly turned "Statesman," to vaunt a moral knowledge truer than poetry (9:12, 10).

The pith of Dryden's remarks on the origin of heroic plays comes to this: *The Siege of Rhodes* and its descendants are the product of Davenant's moral science, which in turn rests on the mimesis of contemporary political experience. This mimetic basis needs to be kept in view, lest the Tassonian liberties that Dryden took with verisimilitude prove a red herring, as they have to some of his critics unmindful of the poet's deeper involvement in history and politics.

As documents addressed to the Commonwealth, neither *Leviathan* nor Davenant's preface could well ignore the common people as a political force. Davenant, considering that the "distemper'd State" has received no remedy from "the Four chief aids of Government, *Religion, Armes, Policy, and Law*," argues that the government, "still making the people our direct object," should apply the help of "Poesy." And Hobbes, answering the objections of fellow exiles that the vulgar lacked understanding, sounds like a Machiavellian demophile with his claim that "all men by nature reason alike, and well, when they have good principles." Both friends belonged to the Cavendish circle active at Paris and Antwerp. Besides patronizing Hobbes and Davenant, Newcastle and his brother Charles received in their salon René Descartes, Marin Mersenne, and Pierre Gassendi, while keeping up correspondence with visitors from London—notably John Pell, Sir William Petty, and Sir William Brereton, members of Samuel Hartlib's international group of reformers. Davenant's *Gondibert* and its preface digest elements of the social philosophy he discussed with these pragmatic, forward-looking thinkers. In *Gondibert*, the House of Astragon recalls the House of Solomon in Bacon's *New Atlantis*, even as the preface avouches the Baconian aim of "bringing truth . . . home to men's bosoms."[7]

Davenant's Protectorate "entertainments" and "operas" grew out of serious meditation on political reform. Recently it has been discovered that he published anonymously, at the end of 1653, a thirty-two-page octavo with the Baconian title, *A Proposition for the Advancement of Moralitie, By a New Way of Entertainment of the People.* This pamphlet, coinciding nearly with the Instrument of Government, is a directive for the new Protectorate. "As

'tis the principal Art of Military Chiefs to make their Armies civil," he begins, "so is it of Statesmen to civilize the people." After some reflections in
an Augustinian vein (and, more directly, in the vein of Fulke Greville) on
the imperfection of all government and its inevitable lapse from popularity,
Davenant proposes "the improvement of instructive *Morality; not specula-
tive Morality*, but that which is active and brought home to the senses." He
borrows Sidney's examples — the music of Orpheus, Amphion, and David,
the parables of Solomon, Menenius Agrippa, and Jesus — and, under the
same category of affective representations, he names "Discourses," by which
"we mean not intellectual School disquisitions, but smart reflections upon
manners." Noting the power of art to harmonize discord and make conflict civilized, Davenant says the "Morality" he would inculcate "excludes
debates" and therefore is a better safeguard of religious quiet than con-
frontational methods; here he undoubtedly glances at the recently dissolved
Barebone's Parliament. And he closes this argument with yet another civilizing metaphor: "The wayes to sacred Religion" can "be made more plaine
and passable by the footsteps of her usher, *Morality*." [8]

Wary of Cromwell's severely Presbyterian counselors, Davenant carefully avoids the word *plays*. He stresses that "Presentments" will divert
people from state affairs, and he notes with Hobbesian sarcasm that the
failed Commonwealth practiced "a new way to enlarge the State, by making
every Subject a States-man." Scenic "representations" leave a powerful impression, although Davenant admits that the impression will vary with the
spectator, "it being in the most refin'd and Ætherial Spirits a curiosity and
desire of knowledge; in common soules, an abject admiration." These anti-
democratic reflections are tailored to the reactionary advent of the Protectorate. At the same time, Davenant expects his entertainments to promote
the public good, not stir up faction. "The people will ever be unquiet whilst
they are ignorant of themselves, and unacquainted with those Engins that
scrue them up, which are their passions, in true characters of the beauties
and deformites of vertue and vice." The audience, according to the same
axiom of public reflexivity on which Dryden based the heroic play, would
discover their communal selves in these moral characters. [9]

It was not until two years later, after Dryden had come to London, that
Davenant finally put his theories to the test. He staged *The First Days Entertainment* at his home, Rutland House, on 23 May 1656, as was reported by
a government agent who says admission cost five shillings a head. The ele-

vated price indicates that Davenant had failed to win state support for his project but had resolved nonetheless to hire artists and musicians of the stature of Henry Lawes, Henry Cooke, and Charles Coleman. It also shows that he had given over the Hobbesian aim of qualifying the manners of the people and instead was aiming his moral science at their natural leaders, the gentry. Just before launching his project, he wrote a letter to Cromwell's secretary of state, John Thurloe, arguing that the wealthy gentry whose support the Protectorate desperately sought might be lured back to town by "pleasant assemblies." "If morale representations may be allowed," he concluded, "the first Arguments may consist of the Spaniards' barbarous conquests in the West Indies and of their severall cruelties there exercised upon the subjects of this nation." Davenant was thus laying out a vast program early in 1656. He had failed to interest the government in the "private entertainment" he was mounting, but he let Cromwell's key official know that he stood ready to assist in the Protector's grand Protestant design against Spain.[10]

Although the prologue to *The First Days Entertainment* mentions "*Opera*" for the first time in England, the music does not support anything like a plot. The only dramatic parts are the "declamations." Of its two debates, the second and longer is waged between a Parisian and a Londoner, each of whom sketches the shortcomings of the other's city. Dryden would remember this artfully calibrated *paragone* when he undertook to compare English drama with French in *An Essay of Dramatic Poesy*. The government visitor reports that the Londoner "had the better of itt," and the declamation on the whole is a fine example of the moral "Discourse" that, as Davenant had promised, "excludes debates" of a more rancorous nature. "The Curtains are suddenly clos'd" on the "entertainment," enforcing the civic moral sounded in the opening song with its pun on the Protector's name: "Did ever War so cease / That all might Olive weare?"[11]

Davenant's greatest experiment, as Dryden implies, was much more than propaganda. *The Siege of Rhodes* occupied Davenant off and on for seven years. The first part, another product of 1656, is described on its title page as "a Representation by the Art of Prospective in Scenes, and the Story sung in *Recitative* Musick." Davenant's address "To the Reader" apologizes for the cramped scenes at Rutland House and also for the play's lack of "Walks, and interweavings of design," curtailed to allow for the recitative. By June of 1659, he produced a second part at the roomier Cockpit in Drury Lane. Unlike part 1, part 2 was not published until 1663 and contains no indications for music until act 5 with its "*Symphony expressing a Battail.*" *The Rehearsal*'s elaborate parody of the scene proves how famous Davenant's "opera" became after the Restoration, when, according to Dryden, the laureate revised *The Siege of Rhodes* and produced it "as a just drama." This first occurred at the Duke's Playhouse in June and July of 1661, where part 2 alone had an extraordinary run of twelve days.[12]

Dedicating it to Clarendon when he published the entire *Siege of Rhodes* in 1663, Davenant calls particular attention to the play's chief moral example: "I have brought *Solyman* to be arraign'd at your Tribunal, where you are the Censor of his civility & magnificence." Davenant contrasts the sectarian zeal of his old, "vertuous Enemies [who] deny *heroique Plays* to the Gentry" with his more authentic, civic morality: "As others have purg'd the Stage from corruptions of the Art of the Drama, so I have endeavour'd to cleanse it from the corruption of manners; nor have I wanted care to render the *Ideas* of Greatness and Vertue pleasing and familiar." Besides shifting the word *virtue* here from its sectarian meaning of moralizing to its civic and heroic meaning, Davenant clearly distinguishes the formal improvements made to dramatic art on the Continent from his own, mimetic contribution to the stage—his more accurate portrayal of "manners." Scholars have taken the phrase "corruption of manners" in a Presbyterian or moralizing sense rather than in the literal sense of *mores:* the customary traits or characteristics of the people that the pulpit and theater both have allowed to deteriorate. Davenant, more sociologist than sectary, is proclaiming not his righteousness but his superior skill in moral science.[13]

Davenant gives a large clue to his design when he recommends Solyman's "civility and magnificence." A long poem he wrote before 1658 to his friend Orrery (then Broghill) praising the earl's "civility" lets us see which "manners" Davenant aimed to purge or restore in *The Siege of Rhodes*. He complains of the moral savagery displayed not so much by Cromwell's government, in which Broghill served as counselor, as by England's fiercely Puritanical leaders,

> Who the civility of Honour hate,
> Because they fear it is effeminate.
> They think that sullen rudeness is a grace;
> And Conquest is less brave then to deface. . . .
> They civil Government enough detest

> Because 'tis by that Epithet exprest. . . .
> All that by courage daring *Rome* or *Greece*
> Have done, these have outdone by boyst'rousness:
> Whose Rage durst break (breaking the Muses hearts)
> The ancient League between all Arms and Arts.

The Hudibrastic satire on philistine zeal here is leveled at the same target as Dryden's lines on the "wanton wits" in his poem to Howard: the "ill Guardians" who "debauch'd their charge," forgetting the moral sovereignty of art—the fact that "Of Morall Knowledge Poesie was Queen" (1:18).[14]

The Siege of Rhodes renews the ancient league between arms and arts. In large measure it restores, in a new form alternative to the masque, the moral images prized by the Caroline court. The role of Ianthe, sung by the first professional actress on the English stage, was partly based on Queen Henrietta Maria, who pawned her jewels to raise arms for the royalists. In the dozen poems he wrote to the queen and her friend the countess of Anglesey, Davenant exploits the chivalric contrast between civilizing beauty and war's rudeness. "The Countess of Anglesey lead Captive by the Rebels," for instance, builds on the very sentiments that the Sultan and later the Rhodians express toward the captive Ianthe:

> O Whither will you lead the Fair,
>   And spicy Daughter of the Morne?
> Those Manacles of her soft Haire,
>   Princes, though free, would faine have worn. . . .
>
> Run, Run! Pursue this Gothick Rout,
>   Who rudely Love in bondage keep;
> Sure all old Lovers have the Goute,
>   The young are overwatcht and sleep.

The Siege of Rhodes passed along this note of courtly gallantry to the rising bourgeois culture. It was still the badge of chivalry for the aged John Dryden at the end of the century ("Old as I am, for Ladies Love unfit, / The Pow'r of Beauty I remember yet"), and after that for Edmund Burke, when he lamented the execution of Marie Antoinette.[15]

Much like *Orlando Furioso* (also quoted in Dryden's essay "Of Heroic Plays"), *The Siege of Rhodes* is a veritable courtesy-book of moral sentiments all tending to *civility*. In the play's most heroic action, Ianthe returns with-

out escort to Solyman's camp. Her confidence in his civility converts the
very essence of power to religion, as the Sultan observes:

> Pow'rs best Religion she,
> Perhaps does civilly believe
> To be establish'd, and reform'd in me,
> Which counsels Monarchs to forgive.
>
> (part 2, II,ii,31–34)

Davenant's moral science comprises the topics essential to civilization: generous emulation, self-sacrifice to gain fame and earthly immortality, compas-
sion for those cast down and above all magnanimous exchanging of benefits.
This last virtue is Senecan, and John Wallace has argued that it is the cement
of Dryden's heroic society; but it was Davenant who, amidst the miasma of
distrust and jealousies that shadowed the end of the Protectorate, restored
heroic beneficence and reciprocity to the stage.[16]

The last and most formidable threat to heroic civilization in *The Siege
of Rhodes,* again as in Ariosto's epic, is jealousy. In part 1, Ianthe was able to
join her husband, Alphonso, in the besieged city because Solyman granted
her a free pass for both of them. When she tells him how the Sultan ad-
mires her, Alphonso grows jealous. He is the first character to waver in his
magnanimity, in the middle of the play, and his lapse demoralizes the whole
city (IV,iii,11f.). He regains confidence in Ianthe after both of them have
shed blood in the city's defense. By the end of the revised part 1, however,
Davenant reintroduces the destructive principle of jealousy in the person of
Roxolana, Solyman's imperious wife.

With these moral types, Davenant offers a new paradigm of civilization.
But are his paradigmatic characters anchored in political reality? Joanne
Altieri finds no conflict between public and private attitudes in the play
because the characters' "interior life is in full harmony with the historical
world, with public life, a state we find hard to take seriously." In part 2,
however, Davenant introduces a potentially explosive conflict without per-
mitting it to unfold. The mob is brought into the action just at the moment
the Rhodian Admiral conceives a secret passion for Ianthe, and it is he
who first characterizes "the Peoples various minds / Which are like sudden
winds" (I,i,169–70). The people in their collective will force their leaders
to risk Ianthe's life by sending her to treat with the Sultan. The ungovern-
ability of the Rhodians contrasts starkly with Turkish subordination, as the

breakdown of command in the besieged city is offset by Solyman's masterful demonstration of the *arcana imperii*. Altieri remarks that the play's private or personal action is really "public in its conception." That may be true of part 1, but for part 2 it no longer holds; not because Davenant fails to correlate public action with private sentiments, but because his moral science has not succeeded in making the sentiments and the actions explicit.[17]

Inchoate sentiments and plotting can expose the heroic play to ridicule, as the scenes of whispering in *The Rehearsal* demonstrate. The ambiguity in Davenant's play stems mainly from his flawed political conception. He cannot decide whether the people clamoring for Ianthe represent vulgar panic or the actual vox Dei. By shifting the question of obedience to the idealized Turks guided by Solyman's prudence, however, the playwright merely transposes the problem onto a subjective plane. Even so, the subjectivity remains ambiguous, bearing the quasi-public name of the Sultan's "high Interest" (II,ii,43). Solyman, who soliloquizes more than once on his weariness of state affairs, is not always clear about his intentions. This master of experience conducts the play's great experiment in moral science when he sets out to recover his wife from her frowardness, and although we see him observing Roxolana's passions with detachment (IV,i), we never do grasp the scope of his experiment. We learn rather that even he, with his supreme discretion, cannot overturn the barbarous Turkish custom that dictates succession to the throne. All of the heroic plays down to *Aureng-Zebe* project this kind of sovereign prudence shrouded in ambiguity. By 1675, the heroic sovereign had been divorced from political actuality, and his or her moral example had receded with the "private" passions into subjectivity.

ORRERY, SUCKLING, AND "QUEEN GORBODUC"

In his poem to Orrery, Davenant pretends to be Columbus discovering the vast terra incognita of the earl's virtue and civility. Dryden borrows this Columbus metaphor in his poem to Charleton discussed earlier, in which he lists Orrery among the eight luminaries who have defied Aristotle's tyranny and restored knowledge. The structure of Dryden's poem rests on a clear distinction between the natural and the human sciences (*geisteswissenschaften*). Four scientists are balanced against Columbus and three men of letters: Bacon, Charleton (in his capacity of antiquarian), and Orrery. Orrery shares an antithetical couplet with his brilliant younger brother Robert, the chemist: "And noble *Boyle*, not less in *Nature* seen, / Than his great *Brother* read in *States* and *Men*" (1:43, lines 27–28). That he thought so highly of Orrery's moral knowledge at the end of 1662 is a fact crucial for reconstructing Dryden's conception of the Last Age. Before Dryden began to work personally with Davenant in 1667, he found in Orrery the best living exponent of a vanished court and its literary culture. To help us unravel the complicated web of Dryden's historical reflexivity, the noble Anglo-Irish author must pass from oblivion for the rest of this chapter and part of the next.

Before the Restoration, Orrery had published nothing besides the first five parts of his interminable *Parthenissa*. This *roman de longue haleine*, however, broadly parades his reading in states and men. Its opening sentence introduces the reader into the world of heroic sentiments whose mimesis would dominate the stage after the Restoration. Orrery's long-winded novel begins, "The sun was already so far declin'd, that his heat was not offensive, when a Stranger, richly arm'd, and proportionably blest with all the gifts of Nature and Education, alighted at the Temple of Hierapolis in Syria, where the Queen of Love had settled an Oracle, as famous as the Deity, to whom it was consecrated." All the characters' expressions are as refined as their manners, which the author lovingly details. One of her suitors writes to the heroine, "If by the loss of the greatest part of my Blood, I have discover'd a Passion, which offends the fair *Parthenissa*, I am ready to shed the residue of it to appease her." Parthenissa herself cruelly turns an occasional sentiment to give it point: "Since his believing me guilty of change is his fault, I am resolv'd it shall be his punishment." This antithetical preciosity is adapted not to psychological analysis but to the posing of hypothetical dilemmas, as when a suitor declines to make a liar of a mistress who believes him guilty of a crime. "The revealing of my Innocency," he says, would punish him worse than if he were guilty, because disabusing her would impeach her wisdom; on the other hand, by suffering her unjust opinion, he labors in the toils of a paradox. "To continue neer her, I must be unworthy that Honour; and to make my self appear worthy of, I must be banish't from it." Politics enters midway through part 3, in which the author inserts a dialogue on the relative virtues of monarchies and commonwealths; but aside from this set piece, the political allusions in *Parthenissa*, like those to religion, are mere metaphors for love and honor.[18]

Dryden would have first heard of Orrery (then Lord Broghill) in London in 1655, when *Parthenissa* was published and received "amongst divers of the Witts a very favorable Reception." A native Munster baron who had joined Cromwell's campaign of 1649–50, Broghill had become close friend to Cromwell's son Henry and was a champion of the Irish Protestants. As a member of the Protectorate Parliaments, president of the Council in Scotland, and finally lord president of Munster, Broghill was one of Cromwell's shrewdest counselors. Despite his relative youth (he was born in 1621, like Marvell and Shaftesbury), he had experienced a lifetime of warfare in his ten years of nearly incessant campaigning in Ireland—in the long conflict that, we sometimes forget, both preceded and protracted the English civil wars. Dryden knew that the noble author of a fashionable heroic romance was also an accomplished general and governor. He may have heard too of Orrery's manuscript *Treatise of the Art of War* (not published till 1677).[19]

Orrery was a living embodiment of the manners and poetry of a court Dryden knew otherwise only through its literature. Dryden read the poems addressed to Broghill by Suckling and Cowley. He may have seen Broghill's poem "To Mr. Cowley on His Davideis," and he certainly would have known of Broghill's "Verses to His Highness on his late Victory in the Bay of Sancta Cruse in the Island of Teneriff." Dryden's cousin and probable employer, Sir Gilbert Pickering, was an intimate of Henry Cromwell, who, as governor-general in Ireland, would have communicated to his Northamptonshire associates the activities of his friend Broghill. Their communications traveled in both directions. In his first critical essay, Dryden tells the world that Orrery heretofore has requested from Ireland "all my Writings," including no doubt the *Heroique Stanzas* on the late Protector, whom both men had admired and praised.[20]

Dryden says Orrery is "read in States and Men" because the Cromwellian peer, equally at home with English and French tastes from the preceding reign, was in a unique position to gratify the wishes of a sovereign bent on refining the manners and conversation of his own court. After paying his respects to Charles, Orrery returned to Ireland late in 1660 bearing a charge from the king to write a play in the fashion then prevailing in France: a serious play in rhymed couplets. The requested play, of which Dryden probably heard something, was in the king's hands by February 1662. In the event, Orrery's first play (discussed in the next chapter) was staged instead in Dublin. None of his plays was produced in London until August 1664. By then, the Dryden-Howard *Indian Queen* had introduced the town to the novelty of a rhymed "heroic play," while Dryden's own tragicomedy *The Rival Ladies* was about to appear in print with a dedication "To the Right Honorable Roger, Earl of Orrery." This preface defines the issues in an already well-known "Quarrel," as Dryden calls it, over rhyme. The historical argument of the preface is paramount. In his maiden critical essay, Dryden is eager to proclaim Orrery not the inventor but the *restorer* of English rhymed tragedy.[21]

A modern reader has difficulty understanding Dryden's admiration for Orrery, whose uninspired and repetitive plays, as Pepys (initially among their admirers) came to realize, all have "just the same design, and words, and sense and plot." Even before his plays were staged, however, Orrery was the man to whose judgment the court deferred, as Dryden was no doubt aware. Orrery's chaplain records that the king's command of 1660 grew out of "a dispute, that arose in his royal presence about writing plays in rhyme: some affirmed it was not to be done; others said it would spoil the fancy to be so confined, but lord Orrery was of another opinion." The other parties in this "dispute" are unknown, but one of them was probably Sir Robert Howard, who would reply to Dryden's 1664 preface. Orrery's countess was cousin to Howard, just as Dryden had married Howard's sister. Dryden probably was introduced to Orrery by their common kinsman when Orrery, returning to England in the summer of 1664, took in hand the long-deferred staging of his plays.[22]

Dryden credits Orrery, as earlier he had credited Monck and Howard, with having providentially foreseen the restoration of legitimacy — in this case, England's legitimate drama. Dryden's compliments to the earl are the poet's means of displaying his own historical reflexivity. Gratified at the kindness Orrery "has continually shown to all my Writings," Dryden says, "Your favour has shone upon me at a remote distance, without the least knowledge of my Person" (8:96). Dryden's accent on *all* of his writing harks back to the *Heroique Stanzas* and its imperial moment of shared, national pride antedating the Restoration. Dryden draws his usual analogy between artistic prudence and "your daily practice in the World": "You still govern Men with the same Address, and manage Business with the same Prudence . . . with this only advantage of ease to you in your Poetry, that you have Fortune here at your command" (8:97). The analogy between providence and Orrery's intellect is pushed to an extreme, as when Dryden puffed Cromwell's "intuition" *(Heroique Stanzas, line 102)* and the "rapid motion" of

Clarendon's mind ("To My Lord Chancellor," 109–12). Orrery rules "Fortune" in the world of his heroic drama like God ruling the *saeculum*.

Dryden's remarks about propriety in language lead to the dispute over rhyme. Intimating that Orrery is keenly interested in the question, Dryden tries to raise his patron's historical awareness. He offers to arbitrate between the Last Age and the present, for he perceives that the oldest, customary ways have been misunderstood by those who talk of

> the New way . . . of writing Scenes in Verse: though, to speak properly, 'tis not so much a New way amongst us, as an Old way new reviv'd: For many Years before *Shakespears* Plays, was the Tragedy of *Queen* Gorboduc in *English* Verse [rhymed couplets], written by that famous Lord *Buckhurst*, afterwards Earl of *Dorset*, and Progenitor to that Excellent Person, who (as he Inherits his Soul and Title) I wish may Inherit his good Fortune. (8:98–99)

This notorious error reveals the bias of Dryden's historical thought in 1664. His knowledge of the Elizabethans is quite vague. Besides the mistake about "Queen Gorboduc," he ascribes the invention of blank verse to Shakespeare. He no doubt imagined that he was unveiling another historical discovery like Charleton's. Arguing at the bar of history, Dryden has found a customary precedent linking two of his noble patrons—Buckhurst would be the dedicatee of *An Essay of Dramatic Poesy*—with the dramatic practice of the Last Age. The precedent was particularly happy, moreover, because it associated Orrery and Buckhurst with John Suckling, the arbiter of Caroline taste and the source, as we shall see, of Dryden's mistake about Queen Gorboduc.

In writing his first criticism, Dryden took his standards from the practice of the last king's court. He associated both Orrery, who had attended there, and the young Buckhurst, whose mother was first cousin to Suckling, with that Cavalier poet and the refined culture he expressed. Dryden everywhere attests his admiration for Suckling. In his first comedy, Dryden appropriates lines from *Aglaura*, just as Orrery had borrowed a whole scene from Suckling's *Brennoralt*. Some ten years before, Dryden had imitated Suckling's *précieuse* love letters in an overwrought epistle to Honor Dryden, his cousin (1:8–9). Dryden may have begun by admiring Cowley, "the darling of my youth," but he soon made Suckling his touchstone for courtly refinement and the writer after whom he modeled his authorial persona. As one of the speakers in Dryden's *Essay of Dramatic Poesy* remarks, living writers "can produce nothing so courtly writ, or which expresses so much the Conversation of a Gentleman, as Sir *John Suckling*" (17:14).[23]

His mistake of "Queen Gorboduc" notwithstanding, Dryden's attempt at literary history attains its object, which is to associate the most elegant poet of the Caroline court with the "New way" of writing. Dryden's revelation that a play by Buckhurst's ancestor warranted the new rhymed drama, which was therefore "an Old way new reviv'd," amounted to an extremely deft historical compliment to his present and future patrons. The precedent, as it happened, was false, but nobody seems to have noticed the mistake before Gerard Langbaine. Dryden cannot have seen any of the three Elizabethan editions of the play he misnames, or he would not have made Sackville its sole author, in defiance of the title pages. Neither was he helped by Sackville's "Excellent" great-grandson. That nobleman's indifference or ignorance suffered the multiple error to stand through four subsequent editions of *The Rival Ladies*.[24]

Dryden's mistake is easily explained. In 1659 appeared *The Last Remains of Sir John Suckling. Being a Full Collection of All His Poems and Letters Which Have Been So Long Expected, and Never Till Now Published.* Turning to the newly published correspondence, Dryden found two letters containing allusions to Shakespeare's plays, of which Suckling was known to be a *cognoscente*. In the first (no. 39) Suckling identifies his allusion, but in the second letter (no. 48), he plays with a speech from *Twelfth Night* (4.2) without naming his favorite comedy:

Ladies,
The opinion of things, is the measure of their value, as was wisely said of a Neece of Queen *Gorbodukes*. Know then, . . .

Although the errata corrects this strange slip, Dryden evidently failed to notice both the misprint and its correction. His oversight merely shows that he was at this date more familiar with Suckling's writing than with Shakespeare. His memory was not at fault, for he had never seen *Gorboduc*, a relic of the Last Age. The virtue that Johnson admired in Dryden, his "vigilance that permitted nothing to pass without notice," in this case delivered to him a false report that he received for an inspired precedent, taking the next opportunity to present these historical reflections to his noble patron, who was the living ambassador from Suckling's court to the Restoration theater.[25]

If my reconstruction is accurate, Dryden's error allows us to assess his knowledge of the literary tradition and to delineate more precisely the two eras or temporal "horizons" he is fusing: the last Age and his own. He had not yet learned to differentiate the Elizabethan dramatists from their successors, and in fact viewed the Last Age primarily through lenses inherited from the Caroline court. At the Restoration, Dryden's immediate object would be to map the cultural horizon eclipsed by the Civil Wars. We saw above (chapter 3) that Dryden had only the slightest stake in the restored church and in Cavalier politics. But he was deeply interested in reviving the cardinal arts of "Morall Knowledge" and language, both preserved intact by the native tradition. To this historical end, classical literature was a soundly academic but limited guide. The new arbiters of culture were courtly gentlemen, and to persuade them that the restoration of native poetry was a legitimate goal, Dryden had to find convincing English precedents.[26]

Dryden suggests that the interpreting of the past requires a historical prudence akin to the political foresight he celebrates in his noble patrons. Historical hermeneutics, he implies, can help define the culture achieved by his age. He does not envisage a panegyric to the zeitgeist; neither is the public poet interested in past facts per se, like an antiquarian. He wants to bring out the past's continuing influence on the present: its "effective history" (*wirkungsgeschichte*), to use Hans-Georg Gadamer's term. At the same time, Dryden's example of practical literary history is a far cry from the twentieth century's antimimetic experiments with new historicisms that pretend to "represent" the past by reinventing it. As Dryden's experience proves, self-conscious emulation of an actual past is the only means by which the public poet can foster historical reflexivity.[27]

HOWARD AND THE QUARREL OVER RHYME

Dr. Johnson, referring to the mid-1660s before Dryden had established himself as a playwright, remarked that "Davenant was perhaps at this time his favourite author." Johnson was not thinking of the dedication to Orrery, in which Dryden praises Davenant for "the Noblest use of [rhyme] upon the Stage" (8:100). Rather, Johnson had in view "the stanza of four lines alter-

nately rhymed": the *Gondibert* quatrain. After the *Heroique Stanzas,* Dryden
did not repeat the form in his poems until *Annus Mirabilis.* He did, however,
experiment with its "noblest use upon the stage" in 1664–65. A soliloquy in
The Rival Ladies runs together two quatrains, and fifteen more are found in
The Indian Queen. When Howard published their collaborative effort in his
Four New Plays (1665), he added a preface answering Dryden's remarks on
rhyme the year before. Howard deprecates the French way of plays in rhyme
and says he has followed the new fashion only in order not to appear singular.
He objects to rhyme on the grounds of verisimilitude. So unnatural is spontaneous rhyming that "it may be concluded impossible that any [dramatic
character] should speak as good Verses in Rhime as the best Poets have writ."
On the other hand, "A Poem, being a premeditated form of Thoughts upon
design'd Occasions, ought not to be unfurnish'd of any harmony in Words."[28]

     This reply led to the debate between Dryden and Howard in *An Essay of
Dramatic Poesy,* to which their bitter exchange of 1668 was the coda. By then,
the two brothers-in-law were divided by jealousies unrelated to their clash
over rhymed plays. Before their quarrel turned acrimonious, the real question at issue between them was verisimilitude. Howard's distinction between
"premeditated" verse and direct mimesis was still respected by Dryden when
he addressed to Howard his "Account" of *Annus Mirabilis* in November
1666—at a date long after Howard's preface of 1665, yet before the publication of *An Essay of Dramatic Poesy* in 1667. Writing from Wiltshire, Dryden
entrusts his "historical poem" to his brother-in-law and asks Howard to
"make my Poem fairer by many of your blots" (1:59). His compliment recalls
the prefatory note to Howard's own *Poems* of 1660, in which Howard says he
"prevail'd with a worthy Friend to take so much view of my blotted Copies,
as to free me from grosse Errors." The complex portrait of Zempoalla in *The
Indian Queen* reflects their shared interest in Virgil and the character of Dido.
When Dryden, in the "Account," explains the difference between Ovid's
"wit writing" and Virgil's "wit written," he very likely borrows a salient distinction from the discussions he and Howard had kept up for seven years.[29]

     The "Account" is a discourse on epic poetry, modeled on the preface to
Gondibert, from which Dryden adopts his main postulate that "the composition of all Poems is or ought to be of wit." Dryden recommends Davenant's
quatrain as "more noble, and of greater dignity . . . then any other Verse in
use amongst us" (1:51). When he proclaims Virgil "my Master in this Poem,"
however, Dryden breaks with Davenant, who in his preface obliquely faulted

the Roman poet by quoting Virgil's "bold Censurers." Those say that his wit
is deficient in its monotonous gravity and that "he sometimes deprives us of
those natural probabilities in Story which are instructive to humane life."
Dryden hints that Davenant's preface limits too narrowly the scope of the
heroic poem. This is a point to which he would later return, in the essay "Of
Heroic Plays." There, after quoting Davenant's judgment that an epic ought
to be "*more like a glass of Nature, showing our selves in our ordinary habits,*"
Dryden comments, "But this, I think, is rather a Play in Narration"; that is to
say, Davenant restricts epic decorum to literal mimesis. Presumably Howard
agreed with this criticism, and the "Account" of *Annus Mirabilis* reflects a
common opinion of Dryden and Howard that an epic poem is fundamentally
different from a play—even though five years later Dryden would define the
heroic play as "an imitation, in little of an Heroick Poem" (11:11, 10).

Reserving any comments on the stage for *An Essay of Dramatic Poesy,*
on which he was working concurrently, Dryden uses Ovid as his prime example of literal mimesis. Ovid's reputed advantage over Virgil is that "he
pictures Nature in disorder," especially "the movements and affections of
the mind." But if Ovid's passions, spontaneously expressed, raise "greater
concernment," Virgil excels him in describing "Action or Persons." Virgil's
superior *enargeia,* or vividness of rhetorical effect, is repeatedly emphasized.
He "sets before your eyes the absent object, as perfectly and more delightully
then nature . . . we see the objects he represents us with in their native figures, in their proper motions; but we so see them, as our own eyes could
never have beheld them so beautiful in themselves . . . the very sound of
his words has often somewhat that is connatural to the subject, and while
we read him, we sit, as in a Play, beholding the Scenes of what he represents" (1:53–55). Dryden's simile equates Virgilian *enargeia* with *opsis,* with
visual mimesis. Presumably *enargeia* was the quality that Howard, too, prized
in the Roman poet.

In his preface the year before, Howard had roundly condemned classical dramatists and their modern imitators for substituting stage narration—
which cannot achieve the *enargeia* of a "premeditated" poem—for mimetic
representation (*opsis*). "Every thing makes more impression Presented than
Related," he says; otherwise "a whole Play might be as well Related as
Acted." This last remark is echoed by Dryden's phrase, "a Play in Narration," but here it points to the criticism currently leveled against Orrery's
successful plays. Howard may have read Sidney or François Hédelin, abbé

d'Aubignac and may have discussed theatrical effects with Dryden, Orrery, and Orrery's "old Frend Will: D'Avenant." In any case, he had discovered the principle of *decorum* and was intent on enforcing it: "I am now convinc'd in my own Judgment, That it is most proper to keep the Audience in one entire disposition. . . . I dispute not but the variety of this World may afford pursuing Accidents of such different Natures; but yet though possible in themselves to be, they may not be so proper to be Presented,—an entire Connexion being the natural Beauty of all Plays." The two hallmarks of Davenant's and Dryden's heroic plays—rhyme and variety of "accidents" (passions and actions)—are debarred because they are not "proper for the Subject," which is either "serious [and] high-born," or natural and comic.[30]

Howard's gauge of decorum was obviously verisimilitude, which was also his strong suit as playwright. *The Committee* and *The Country Gentleman* are creditable experiments in low mimesis, while *The Indian Queen* and *The Duke of Lerma*, even if they are the fruits of collaboration, both sustain a decorum as elevated as the plays of Dryden and Orrery. Like Sidney's *Apology*, Howard's preface begins and ends on a note of aristocratic *sprezzatura*, of skeptical detachment or self-mockery, but it achieves neither grace nor clarity. Howard, unable to follow Dryden's poetic flights, admired Virgil without conceiving that his *enargeia* might give light to stage decorum—without realizing that Virgil's moral science was a magazine of dramatic manners. Instead of fashioning moral types, Howard sought first and last the decorum of "an entire Connexion," an unbroken *opsis* whose plausibility rested on what audiences expected, on custom and prescription. This decorum, he insisted, could not be methodized as a moral science. Its only true measure was the play's success. Applying that immethodical test, Howard boasts of having found audiences very indulgent: "When I consider how severe the former Age has been to some of the best of *Mr Johnson*'s never to be equal'd Comedies, I cannot but wonder why any Poet should speak of former Times, but rather acknowledg that the want of Abilities in this Age are largely supply'd with the Mercys of it. I deny not but there are some who resolve to like nothing."[31]

When Dryden mentions in his "Account" that Howard is "not of the number of those . . . *qui carpere amicos suos judicium vocant* [who call it judiciousness to carp at friends]" (1:59), he may well be compensating for the portrait of Howard as Crites that he was about to publish. In *An Essay of Dramatic Poesy,* "*Crites,* a person of sharp judgment, and somewhat too delicate

a taste in wit" (17:9), quarrels with Lisideius's and Neander's presumption
that "Rhyme is proper for the stage": "I might satisfie my self to tell you,
how much in vain it is for you to strive against the stream of the peoples
inclination; the greatest part of which are prepossess'd so much with those
excellent Playes of *Shakespeare, Fletcher,* and *Ben. Johnson,* (which have been
written out of Rhyme) that except you could bring them such as were written better in it, and those too by persons of equal reputation with them, it
will be impossible for you to gain your cause with them, who will still be
judges. This is it to which in fine all your reasons must submit" (17:64–65).
Crites doggedly clings to prescriptive custom, just as Howard had done and
would do again when, in 1668, he taxed "Argumentative Poets" and "the
unnecessary understanding of some that have labour'd to give strict rules to
things that are not Mathematical." [32]

Dryden's rash retort on that later occasion was crafted to show that the
notoriously opinionated Howard, and not he, was guilty of an unfashion-
able positiveness. Nevertheless, it was Howard who stood on firmer mimetic
ground. Dryden, in his critical pursuit of a moral science that might emulate
Virgil's rhetoric, was impatient with Jonsonian realism and the traditional
decorum of the stage. The failure to mention rhymed plays in the "Account"
of *Annus Mirabilis* can be explained by supposing that the author was preparing to rehearse elsewhere Davenant's ideas on heroic drama. That Dryden
knew Howard was well acquainted with those ideas cannot be doubted, considering how familiarly the "Account" refers to the *Gondibert* preface. Whatever their opinions of drama, Davenant, Howard, and Dryden all agreed that
the highest kind of writing is the epic. At the same time, they all subscribed
to Hobbes's dictum that poetry is based on mimesis of actual experience.
Although Dryden claims that in Virgil's special case, "*Materiam superabat
opus* [the art excelled the matter]," he agrees with Davenant and Hobbes
that the greatest poetry is rooted in the nation's historical experience. The
rich subject of *Annus Mirabilis,* he says, "has given me two Harvests in a
Summer, and in both oppress'd the Reaper. All other greatness in subjects is
onely counterfeit, it will not endure the test of danger; the greatness of Arms
is onely real: other greatness burdens a Nation with its weight, this supports
it with its strength" (1:55, 52).

Heroic mimesis is Dryden's subject both in *Annus Mirabilis* and its critical preface. "I should not have written this," he says of the "Account," "but
to a Person, who has been ever forward to appear in all employments, whither

his Honour and Generosity have call'd him" (1:50). Davenant had identified honor and love as the essential ingredients of heroic mimesis. The naval wars and the London Fire left no room in *Annus Mirabilis* for love and its civilizing effect, so Dryden contrives to bring love into the end of his "Account," where he prints his verses to the duchess of York "on the Memorable Victory Gain'd by the Duke" over the Dutch. Dryden says of this poem that the "same images serve equally for the Epique Poesie," except that in their civil application "there is somewhat more of softness and tenderness to be shown in them" (1:56–58).

His final compliment to Howard sustains this note of heroic civility: "I wrong the Publick to detain you longer." Some two years later, Dryden would momentarily belie the spirit of noble mimesis and would turn the salute to his brother-in-law's public service into a sneer: "The corruption of a Poet is the Generation of a Statesman." Dryden's vicious metamorphosis of his adversary in the "Defence" erodes the very civility which is no less the principle of his moral science than of heroic society. Even in this moment of intemperance, however, Dryden remembers Davenant and the mimetic basis of the heroic enterprise. Toward the end of his polemic, Dryden uses the analogy of a mirror to refute Howard's literal objections to dramatic heightening ("The strength of his reason depends on this, that the less cannot comprehend the greater"). The mirror similitude is traditional, but the two disputants would have understood its particular allusion to Davenant's much-admired poem to the king, quoted above. The theater, says Davenant, is

> the Poets Magick-Glass
> In which the Dead in vision by us pass;
> Where what the *Great* have done we do again,
> But with less loss of time and with less pain.

Dryden wants Howard to see that drama is more than a transcript of immediate experience. It is a "magic glass" that lets us *reflect upon* experience. And the new dramatic mimesis, as Davenant suggests, depends critically on the king's own moral science:

> If to reform the publick Mirrour (where
> The Dead, to teach their living Race, appear)
> May to the People useful prove, even this
> (Which but the object of your leisure is

To respite Care, and which successivelie
Three of our last wise Monarchs wish'd to see,
And in a Century could not be wrought)
You, in Three years, have to perfection brought.[33]

DRYDEN'S "SESSION" OF THE WITS

The several distinct opinions of Davenant, Orrery, and Howard had been
actively revolved by Dryden when he retired to Wiltshire in the summer of
1665 to set down his thoughts about the stage "with the same delight with
which men think upon their absent Mistresses." Although he strikes this
jaunty pose of "amusement" in dedicating *Of Dramatic Poesy: An Essay* to
Buckhurst, his short address "To the Reader" mentions a greater ambition.
"Written in the Country without the help of Books, or advice of Friends,"
the *Essay* is merely the first part of a projected treatise on "the Vertues and
Faults of the *English* Poets" who have written in the dramatic, "the Epique,
or the Lyrique way" (17:3, 7). Both prefaces were added perhaps two years
after Dryden began the *Essay,* and taken together they fulfill his public role in
1667 and prove him eminently qualified for the laureateship he would inherit
within a year. On the one hand, he furnishes his young patron with an example of genteel civility that joins the arts with arms. On the other, he shows
his cultivated "Reader" the way to historical self-awareness by expanding
the contemporary literary horizon until it coincides with the Last Age.

Either of these public motives is wholly in keeping with Dryden's ideal
of moral science. He achieves heroic mimesis by juxtaposing the dialogue of
the *Essay* with the naval battle off Lowestoft and by recounting the "war of
opinions" as it is managed by "Gentlemen, with candour and civility" (17:6).
He attains historical reflexivity through emulation, defining for "the Reader"
the character or zeitgeist of the present age in contrast to that of the Last
Age. The *Essay* provided contemporaries with a mirror of wit, a mimesis
of the same aristocratic culture whose epic self-consciousness is reflected in
the heroic plays as well as by the poet in *Annus Mirabilis.* The speakers in
the *Essay* affect a *sprezzatura* that can be attributed largely to their historical
reflexivity. In stressing their "consciousness of historical effect," the author
wants us to imagine that they are aware, from their barge on the Thames, of
their power to shape their culture. Dryden brilliantly applies his moral science to the task of setting forth the mores of his age. The resulting *Essay* is

his masterpiece of cultural mimesis—his Restoration answer to Suckling's "The Wits," the prototype of subsequent poetical "sessions."

Charmed by the *Essay*'s literal setting, a reader is apt to forget the principle of heroic mimesis formulated by Neander: "A Play . . . to be like Nature, is to be set above it." All verisimilitude "must *be* Ethical," and Dryden has been true to the ethos he imitates in the *Essay*. But he has freely invented its literal circumstances, and no one until Malone supposed that the dialogue on the Thames actually took place. Contemporaries such as Howard assumed that Dryden was himself the origin or "Author of an Essay of Dramatick Poesie" he fabricated out of the writings of Corneille and others. Howard's sarcasm stung Dryden as an accusation of plagiarism, and he retorted in kind. The one reader who might have pursued the hints about the actual persons and circumstances of the dialogue was its dedicatee, Buckhurst.[34]

If that young nobleman ever pondered the *Essay* as he was invited to do, he must have been puzzled at the author's motive for writing it. "The Reader" is told that its drift "was chiefly to vindicate the honour of our *English* Writers, from the censure of those who unjustly prefer the *French*." Buckhurst, however, is told two quite different things. The author dedicates the *Essay* to him in the hope "that it might awaken in you the desire of writing something . . . which might be an honour to our Age and Country." But at the end of his dedication, Dryden lets fall a partisan motive. Having emphasized his own stake in the now-famous quarrel over rhyme and having warned that he will "dissent from the opinion of better Wits" in order to "defend my own," Dryden says he wants to mitigate the *public* quarrel about "Playes in verse." He will do this by recounting in the *Essay* a *private* "Dispute betwixt some of our Wits" on that subject as well as on two more topics: ancients versus moderns and "the Wits of our Nation" versus foreign writers. He will let Buckhurst "decide it in favour of which part you shall judge most reasonable."

I think Buckhurst understood that this private dispute was a fiction meant to provide an urbane diversion or an interlude in the public quarrel over rhyme. Buckhurst must have known the parties to the quarrel, and Dryden expected him to appreciate their characterization in his *Essay*. Dryden's allusion to Cicero and Atticus suggests that at least one of them— possibly Howard—was a friend whom Dryden made to "sustain the part of an Enemy in Philosophy." In sum, Dryden introduced a roman à clef element to pique the interest of his young patron and draw him into the circle of those concerned for "the honour of our *English* Writers." That circle excludes "the Reader," who is enigmatically informed that three of the speakers are persons of "witt and Quality" concealed under "borrowed names." We do not know whether Buckhurst or anyone else relished Dryden's subtle character-drawing. The only response came from an irritated Howard, which suggests that Dryden had succeeded in identifying one pair of speakers, Crites and Neander, all too blatantly, resulting in the nasty public exchange a year later. There is no evidence that the other pair were even conjecturally identified until after their originals were dead.

Because Dryden's mimetic ethos is based on an actual, historical moment, we cannot understand the *Essay* without knowing the identities of its four speakers. The views of Neander and Crites are consistent with those of Dryden and Howard, once we accept the clue found in Cicero's dialogues, where the opinions of anyone impersonated can be varied dialectically as in Dryden's example of Atticus. Eugenius has been identified, incongruously enough, as Buckhurst himself—by Matthew Prior, Buckhurst's protégé, who seems to have confused the first speaker who refutes Crites with the patron to whom Dryden appeals in his public quarrel with Howard. As for Lisideius, no historical person has been found to match up with his opinions; his identification as Sedley rests on nothing more substantial than the imperfect anagram of their two names.[35]

The fact is that ever since 1668, few of Dryden's readers have taken his fiction seriously enough to follow up the hints he dropped for Buckhurst and "the Reader." In the eyes of his contemporaries, the *Essay* remained exactly what Howard implied: a manifesto of dramatic rules with historical examples. If modern readers of the *Essay* mean to recover its mimetic intent and its basis in the author's experience, they must first sweep away Malone's web of conjecture and go back to the historical moment of 1665–67. If I have succeeded in reconstructing its temporal horizon, readers should be able to see that the actual persons whom Dryden assembled for this imaginary "session of the wits" are himself and the three older playwrights we have been discussing.[36]

Recognizing Davenant and Orrery among the speakers brings the *Essay* immediately into focus. Davenant, especially, had been the presiding genius of Dryden's first critical efforts, and the older poet is quoted in the dedication even before he appears in the person of Eugenius. He provides a vital link between the Last Age and the new generation: more forward-looking than

the severely censorious Crites and Lisideius and therefore more congenial
to Neander, who is the youngest and most enthusiastic of the company. It is
fitting that Eugenius should revere Jonson, who preceded Davenant in the
laureateship; that he should call the roll of stellar poets from the last court;
and that he particularly should want Neander to give the characters of Jonson and Shakespeare and to report the "session" held by Suckling and John
Hales comparing those two giants. Davenant is the oldest speaker present in
the *Essay*, yet he provides the hopeful lines on the spring that are applied to
the callow Buckhurst in the dedication. Buckhurst seems to have been one
of Davenant's admirers, and it is for his benefit that Dryden elaborates the
laureate's signature theme: the civilizing effect of poetry and love on noble
spirits.[37]

The dialogue of the *Essay* is so framed as to evoke an ongoing, epic contest in arms and arts. As the sounds of battle die away, Eugenius "was the
first who congratulated to the rest that happy Omen of our Nations Victory."
That is his cue to raise their captious gossip to the higher ground of literary
emulation. After Crites has championed the ancient dramatists and sustained
his part against the moderns (including the Elizabethan playwrights Howard
admired), Eugenius replies, launching his arguments from the *Gondibert*
preface. "A dull imitation" of the ancients would stifle progress, he says: "We
draw not therefore after their lines, but those of Nature." Davenant's medi-
tations on Tasso in his preface had led him to the doctrine of emulation, on
which in turn each of Dryden's four speakers comments by quoting Velleius
Paterculus. Since the dispute had been narrowed to the drama, Eugenius
is able to deny that his adversary has proved the ancients "wrought more
perfect images of humane life than we." Thereupon Eugenius removes the
entire debate to the terrain of moral science, where character, "wit," and of
course the passions are significant, whereas plot and dramatic probability are
much less so.[38]

Eugenius accomplishes this mimetic shift by a perfunctory review of the
stock fables and supposed unities from which Crites had argued the superior
decorum of classical drama. "These are Plots built after the *Italian* Mode of
Houses, you see thorow them all at once," he complains, repeating a figure
that Davenant had used in his poem to the king. His digression on wit serves
the same purpose as the discussion of wit in the *Gondibert* preface. It enables him to transcend the customary decorum of genre and *opsis* and to
concentrate instead on rhetorical mimesis ("Ornament," in the preface). The

example of Ovid, "who had a Genius most proper for the Stage," leads him to "admiration and concernment, which are the objects of Tragedy," and to love, which was the main subject of *Gondibert*. From the time he wrote its preface and his *Proposition*, discussed earlier, Davenant had insisted that the object of moral science was the truth of passions rather than actions, because audiences, by seeing their passions represented, come to understand themselves. Eugenius finds no "Love-Scenes" in classical tragedy to compare with "the excellent Scenes of Passion in *Shakespeare* and *Fletcher*." Love "is the most frequent of all the passions, and being the private concernment of every person, is sooth'd by viewing its own image in a publick entertainment." He insists that an audience watches the movements of the characters' "minds, as much as the changes of their fortunes. For the imaging of the first is properly the work of a Poet, the latter he borrows from the Historian." [39]

Eugenius thus caps his argument with a paraphrase of the central philosophical axiom for which Hobbes and Davenant had commended poetry. In controverting Crites' rules of decorum, Eugenius has established the chief end of the *Essay*. The author, through Neander, will promote rhetorical mimesis ("lively imitation of Nature") and rhyme over literal mimesis and verisimilitude, which are too much dependent on *opsis* and the unities. Lisideius, the speaker who succeeds Eugenius, had originally defined a play as "A just and lively Image of Humane Nature, representing its Passions and Humours, and the Changes of Fortune to which it is subject." Crites had objected that the definition was not properly dramatic, as well he might: not only does it fail to distinguish rhetoric from *opsis*, it says nothing about actions or plot. His jibbing at Lisideius's conception of a play recalls Howard's original dissent from Orrery and Dryden, in his preface of 1665. There he censured those who make "up their Plays with almost entire and discoursive Scenes, presenting the business in Relations. This way has very much affected some of our Nation, who possibly believe well of it more upon the account that what the *French* do ought to be a Fashion than upon the Reason of the thing." [40]

Their original quarrel flares up again just as Lisideius and Neander have ended and the author is about to close off his mimetic frame: "This, my Lord," he tells Buckhurst, "was the substance of what was then spoke on that occasion." Crites interrupts and takes them to task for assuming that rhyme is proper for the stage: "I confess I have a joynt quarrel to you both." The third debate then ensues, with Dryden and Howard barely keeping up their disguised personae. Crites' interruption brings us close to the mimetic origins of the *Essay*. I maintain that its debates were occasioned by Sir Robert's having publicly queried the practice of Orrery and Dryden, and that the real issue between them was verisimilitude. For that larger question, rhyme became a proxy.[41]

By determining Orrery's position in the quarrel, we can clear up more than one puzzle in the *Essay*. When Dryden first raised the topic in his dedication of 1664, he said rhyme sounded unnatural only if the words were viciously chosen or ill-placed. This argument from success left Howard unconvinced, and he strained pedantically to distinguish poetic license from the rational decorum of the stage. Rhyming verses "declare the labor that brought them forth"—hence the admiration for Virgil that he undoubtedly shared with Dryden. But Virgil's labored art is unnatural on the stage, where it is a distraction from the "entire Connexion" or decorum that Howard found essential for verisimilitude: "Against this I can raise no Argument but my Lord of *Orory*'s Writings, in whose Verse the greatness of the Majesty seems unsullied with the Cares." Howard implies that Orrery's achievement cannot bear close scrutiny, however: "This particular Happiness . . . does not convince my Reason, but employ my Wonder." As Howard would put it even more bluntly in 1668, Dryden has mistaken the question by "charging all defects upon the ill placing of words." Dryden's argument "is an attempt to prove that nothing may seeme something by the help of a Verse, which I easily grant to be the ill-fortune of it."[42]

Plainly, Howard thought the successful heroic plays were more rhyme than reason. Like the French Academy attacking Corneille's *Le Cid*, Howard denied that the rhymed plays had any merit besides novelty. Dryden, in seeking a rationale for his success, must have expected the support of Orrery, the Anglo-Irish Corneille who was his patron. From the fact that Howard returned to attack the rationale for rhyme as if it were Dryden's exclusively, however, we may conclude that Orrery made no reply to Howard. I suspect the quarrel evolved as follows. Dryden first hailed Orrery (and of course Davenant) for having discovered a means of improving upon the greatest drama of the Last Age. "This way of writing in Verse, they have onely left free to us," says Neander, adding from his vantage point of 1667 that "our age is arriv'd to a perfection in it" (17:73). Howard, having tried this way and judged it unnatural, claimed in 1667 that the popular verdict was the same as his. That is why Crites tells the proponents of rhymed plays that they "strive against the stream of the peoples inclination" (17:65).

Because Davenant's practice already put him on Dryden's side of the quarrel, his arguments for innovation from the *Gondibert* preface merely needed rehearsing by Eugenius. As for Orrery, despite the fact that he had produced three rhymed plays by 1667, other evidence suggests that *he agreed with Howard* in thinking his success more poetic than dramatic. Howard's brother, Edward, said that Orrery considered "his *Mustapha* &c . . . Poems, instead of Plays, for reasons that he is better able to give." Evidently the earl, with the self-deprecating irony that noble authors seem to have at their command no matter how slight their talent, had offered arguments against his own practice. This private opinion of Orrery's lends an edge to Neander's observation when, quoting Lisideius's definition, he remarks that Crites' "Argument is almost as strong against the use of Rhyme in Poems as in Plays. . . . However, the agreement betwixt them is such, that if Rhyme be proper for one, it must be for the other." Dryden means to show that his opinionated brother-in-law contradicts the Irish peer whom he professes to admire.[43]

Dryden's aim of traducing Howard is startlingly clear as Neander begins his response to Crites. Betraying his disguised persona, Dryden replies ad hominem to Howard by telling the world exactly where Orrery stands in the quarrel over rhymed plays: "I should alwayes be ready to confess, that those which I have written in this kind come short of that perfection which is requir'd. Yet since you are pleas'd I should undertake this Province, I will do it, though with all imaginable respect and deference both to that person from whom you have borrow'd your strongest Arguments, and to whose judgment when I have said all, I finally submit" (17:68). The quarrel "concerns me less then any," he says—because Dryden wanted Orrery to understand that Howard's strictures particularly concerned *him* as the author whose plays (or "Poems") came nearest the required perfection. Furthermore, by making Orrery a speaker in the *Essay,* Dryden resumed the discussion of the Last Age that he had opened with his patron in 1664.

Although Crites balks at Lisideius's ambiguous definition of a play, Howard and Orrery evidently took similar views of stage decorum, in that both playwrights strove to keep an unbroken "Connexion" and to maintain heroic manners even in villainous characters like the Duke of Lerma or Tryphon. Dryden therefore contrived to put both noble authors on the losing side of the debate over verisimilitude that dominates his *Essay*. Crites champions the decorum of the ancients and Lisideius that of the French, although he realizes that "*Crites*, in his Discourse for the Ancients, has prevented me." Lisideius's lengthy defense of verisimilitude, drawn mostly from Corneille's *Trois Discours* but significantly alluding to Sidney as well, complements the case made for the unities by Crites. Either champion of decorum is overmatched by arguments for the greater variety and rhetorical energy of the native English drama. This structural bias of the *Essay* carries beyond the quarrel about rhyme, and it prejudices the contest with the Last Age by favoring wit or heightened mimesis over verisimilitude. Neander's famous dictum ("A Play . . . to be like Nature, is to be set above it") corresponds to his celebrated characterizations of Shakespeare, Jonson, and Fletcher, whose authorial personae stand out above their works. The writers Dryden would later call "the Gyant Race before the Flood" could not be superseded until "The present Age of Wit obscures the Past." [44]

That moment had not yet come in 1667, when, as Dryden told his reader, he still needed to sort out "the Vertues and Faults of the English Poets." Four years later, in his preface to *An Evening's Love*, he bade his "Reader" expect a discourse on the topic when his *Conquest of Granada* appeared, and he could "justly claim precedence of *Shakspear* and *Fletcher*, namely, in Heroick Playes" (10:202). When his masterpiece came out in 1672, however, the promised historical discourse, assuming it existed, had gotten split up into the brief essay "Of Heroic Plays" and a "Defence of the Epilogue." The polemical "Defence" was necessitated by the author's boast that Restoration culture had finally surpassed that of the Last Age and that his plays, insofar as they imitated the new society, were therefore superior to Shakespeare's and Jonson's.

This is a surprising outcome of the debate over verisimilitude, for it compromises Davenant's original purpose of grounding drama in moral science instead of superficial decorum. The *Essay of Dramatic Poesy* had been structured so as to make progress depend on wit. Poets, like other great wits of the age, would break the mold of traditional decorum and discover "almost a new Nature" in the realm of moral science (17:15). Five years later, Dryden announces that the new nature is the refined mores he portrays, and he locates moral knowledge in the conversation of witty men and women. In contrast to the Sidneian poet creating a timeless heterocosm, Dryden claims a more passive role, saying he merely "imitates" the society in which he lives and writes (11:201). The public poet and author of the *Essay* had shown a more active reflexivity. As a mimetic "session" portraying the zeitgeist, the *Essay* parallels the heroic plays. The verisimilitude that Dryden prized most was not dramatic. It was narrative mimesis of the literal history authored by providence, a history that included the clash between the mores of the Last Age and his own. In working out a moral science adequate to both eras, he merges their horizons without losing the distinction between them.

Just how effectively Dryden fused the two horizons can be seen by comparing the *Essay* with Suckling's poetical "session," "The Wits." No matter how closely Dryden imitates Suckling, the courtly poet maintains a reflexivity superior to that of his professional admirer. When Apollo in the ballad examines each candidate for the bays in turn, he is angry to find Suckling absent:

> *Suckling* next was call'd, but did not appear,
> And strait one whisperd *Apollo* in's ear,
> That of all men living he cared not for't,
> He loved not the Muses so well as his sport;
> > And
> Prized black eyes, or a lucky hit
> At bowls, above all the Trophies of wit;
> But *Apollo* was angry, and publiquely said
> 'Twere fit that a fine were set on his head.
>
> > > (lines 73–80)

In contrast to Suckling, Dryden places himself at the center of his own literary "session." Inserting themselves reflexively into the scene they project, either writer reveals what he expects from "the Muses." The Cavalier poet flouts Apollo's authority and the renown of a laureate, setting a higher premium on his luck at sport. He knows he is not what he is; fame—that is, "whisper[ing]"—can make or unmake him. The Restoration poet is less insouciant and, in his determination to erect a pantheon for his times, more heroic and vulnerable. He records his own achievement, neatly dividing the dramatic palm among the four speakers in the order of their seniority. Audiences "are already favourable to verse," he affirms, and "no serious Playes written since the Kings return have been more kindly receiv'd by them, then

the *Seige of* Rhodes, the *Mustapha,* the *Indian Queen,* and *Indian Emperour*"
(17:73–74). Historical self-understanding always remains incomplete, however. Whether his heroic project would result in a temple of Apollo or a
tomb for Bayes—a living *mimēsis* or a monument of vanished minds—was,
as Dryden knew, a question to be decided only by the greater dialogue of
history.[45]

Masterless Men:
The Heroic Plays

Replying to his brother-in-law's attack the year after *An Essay of Dramatic Poesy* appeared, Dryden boasted that he could fit his genius to whatever humor was uppermost among audiences: "I confess my chief endeavours are to delight the Age in which I live." His confession was not strictly true. Dryden had no more confidence than Howard did in the judgment of the crowd, and he certainly did not espouse his opponent's antinomian view that "there can be no determination but by the Taste." Each of the three debates in the *Essay* hinges on a judicious contrast of tastes, and all four speakers insist that emulation colors our liking or disliking. It was ostensibly against Howard's success in comedy that Dryden matched his talent for rhyme, but he was also vying with the illustrious dead. The *Essay* was written mainly to educe the standards by which his contest with the Last Age might be decided. As the playwright in Dryden was discovering his ability to delight the age, the critic was developing a keen historical reflexivity. He knew his heroic plays were successful imitations of the zeitgeist and he said so, in 1671. Like the positions staked out in the *Essay*, however, his dramatic mimesis was problematic: success with a particular audience still left the achievement uncertain. Competing with the Elizabethans really meant emulating "the greater Dead" in a "session" that could never end, and Dryden finally grew weary of the contest.[1]

Historical reflexivity and emulation of the past are the two faces of Dryden's strong commitment to providential mimesis. In his heroic plays, even as he stretches the limits of verisimilitude, Dryden gives sharper definition to the historical circumstances and the political limitations of the restored monarchy. The unbounded willfulness of a hero like Almanzor appears to swallow up the modest prudence of an actual hero like Monck. At the same time, however, the *saeculum* in which the dramatic hero exerts his will is brought firmly under providential control. The heroic plays, recapitulating the experience of rebellion, demonstrate to their Restoration audience at once a new freedom and an old constraint. In the plays we will examine, the heroines and heroes confront a series of deliberative crises, but the acts flowing from their deliberations are never channeled into a definitive plot. Dryden's heroic plays are built on the principle of Davenant's moral science: "Wise Poets think it more worthy to seek out truth in the Passions then to record the truth of Actions." Lisideius's definition of a play (see chapter 5) replaces the plot with "Changes of Fortune" and substitutes "Passions and Humours" for actions. Yet Dryden's pursuit of "truth in the passions" led to frustration. In 1675, he disclaimed ten years spent trying to outdo the Elizabethans: "He has now another taste of wit,"

> And to confess a truth, (though out of time)
> Grows weary of his long-lov'd Mistris, Rhyme.
> Passion's too fierce to be in Fetters bound,
> And Nature flies him like Enchanted Ground.
> What Verse can do, he has perform'd in this,
> Which he presumes the most correct of his:
> But spite of all his pride a secret shame,
> Invades his breast at *Shakespear's* sacred Name:
> Aw'd when he hears his Godlike *Romans* rage,
> He, in a just despair, would quit the Stage.

Significantly, his next play returns not only to blank verse but to Shakespeare's Romans cast in a familiar historical setting. About the same time that Rymer was demanding probability in the fable or plot, Dryden was realizing that the passions yield no truth in isolation from history.[2]

I believe that his very success hid from Dryden the fact that his moral science had strayed far from its mimetic basis. The author of a heroic play, he wrote, is "to endeavour an absolute dominion over the minds of the Spectators" (11:14). Howard thought this ambition betrayed a Bayes-like conceit in Dryden ("a wrong measure of his own proportion"). I shall argue that his defiance of traditional decorum and verisimilitude has republican overtones. These are heard when Dryden replies to Howard's attack on the *Essay* and makes "Rhyme" a metaphor for the usurping imagination. He says "Prose [is] the rightful Prince" of comedy, "yet is by common consent depos'd, as too weak for the government of serious Plays; and he failing, there now start up two Competitors; one the nearer in blood, which is blanck Verse; the other more fit for the ends of government, which is Rhyme. Blanck Verse is, indeed, the nearer Prose, but he is blemish'd with the weakness of his Predecessor. Rhyme (for I will deal clearly) has somewhat of the Usurper in him, but he is brave, and generous, and his Dominion pleasing." The whimsical metaphor implies real political insight, as do the heroic plays themselves, but his subsequent attempt to label Howard a republican ("a Statesman") by whom "the Commonwealth gains" calls into question Dryden's own reflexivity (9:7, 10). While scorning Howard's commonsense decorum, Dryden was flirting with Howard's antinomianism in a different guise. In the turmoil of the 1670s, the theater became for him an evasion of the problem of freedom, and the new empire of imagination confidently proclaimed in the essay "Of Heroic Plays" proved after all, like any sectarian utopia, to be socially irrelevant.

HOBBESIAN SOVEREIGNTY

By the sixth year of the Restoration, Dryden had defined his public vocation with respect to his Elizabethan and Caroline predecessors, but he had yet to come to terms with the more immediate past — the Interregnum he had actually experienced. Notwithstanding Lisideius's (Orrery's) contrite admission to Neander that "We have been so long together bad Englishmen" (17:33), Dryden usually adopted the Cavalier position that the Rebellion was none of his doing, a stance that apparently went unchallenged until Shadwell retorted against *Mac Flecknoe* with his angry *Medal of John Bayes*. The five poems that Dryden wrote between 1660 and 1662 alluded to recent events, but in subsequent works he distanced himself historically from the Rebellion. For twenty years after *Annus Mirabilis* and *An Essay of Dramatic Poesy*, he was silent about his private experience of the 1650s. Then, in the moving *confessio* from part 1 of *The Hind and the Panther*, he owned that his "private reason," nurtured under the Great Rebellion that gave it so wide a charter, had kept him from seeing the light:

> My thoughtless youth was wing'd with vain desires,
> My manhood, long misled by wandring fires,
> Follow'd false lights; and when their glimps was gone,
> My pride struck out new sparkles of her own.
>
> (3:125, lines 72–75; cf. line 63)

His struggle to bring his private judgment under the yoke of doctrinal obedience seems to have climaxed with his conversion, about which Dryden tells us little. Nonetheless, I believe the struggle left its trace in his earlier works and particularly in his plays. The sixteen plays that Dryden produced from 1663 to 1677 often exploit the Restoration audience's keen interest in a parallel struggle: the conflict over obedience in the political sphere. His opportunistic dramatization of this conflict has led some of Dryden's critics to read the plays as propaganda or as fictions of state, the way much Jacobean and Caroline drama has been read. While I grant that Dryden aimed chiefly to please the Cavalier and reactionary element in his audiences, I cannot agree that he sought to engage them with political allegories or to flatter or satirize them with the kind of utopian fictions that political theorists characterize as counterfactual. I contend rather that even while he carried out the public orator's policy of deprecating "false freedom," as in *Annus Mirabilis* and his earlier panegyrics, Dryden meant to set forth in his serious plays an effectual providence that he tests repeatedly by dramatizing the tenacious spirit of private rebellion.

The most famous discussion of "private judgment" and its bearing on political and religious obedience is of course found in *Leviathan*, the chief product of the Engagement debate that had agitated the universities during the first year Dryden spent at Cambridge. Dryden was a "great admirer" of Hobbes, according to Aubrey, and "oftentimes makes use of his Doctrine in his Playes." Sooner or later Dryden must have discovered his affinity for the political ideas of a thinker from the Last Age who had survived to admonish the present. The year of chaos between Richard Cromwell's abdication and Charles's Restoration corresponded to nothing in Harrington's sanguine theory of a natural "balance"; on the other hand, the virtual collapse of rule drove home the Hobbesian teaching that all government is fragile. Dryden need not endorse Hobbes's prescription of a man-made Leviathan—that factitious and "Mortall God" set up in place of the divinely appointed monarch—in order to relish the philosopher's tonic argument that in our Augustinian *saeculum*, the alternative to fragile peace is perpetual war: a state of nature "where every man is Enemy to every man."[3]

Dryden's plays have been superficially interpreted as mirrors of the Hobbesian state of nature. In fact, they portray civilized men and women raised above the state of nature and chafing at those artificial laws and voluntary limitations that bind them to the commonwealth. For Hobbes, unlike Harrington, the quest for rational community runs counter to our instincts: human beings are naturally aggressive. The "generall inclination of all mankind," says Hobbes, is "a perpetuall and restlesse desire of Power after power, that ceaseth onely in Death." This general inclination hardly does us credit because we can fully indulge it only in a prepolitical state of nature, wherein we enjoy maximum liberty in a life that is "solitary, poor, nasty, brutish, and short." When we reluctantly give up this private liberty, we do so merely to gain safety and not in order to acquire the better "second nature" that Machiavelli describes—the civic *virtù* of the classical *polis*. We surrender our natural rights in exchange for artificial laws. The choice is rational only to this extent, that men normally can be expected to choose the greater interest of self-preservation over the lesser right of unrestrained license. The Hobbesian covenant whereby all men agree to incorporate themselves into Leviathan resembles not so much a federation of equals as it does a pact imposed by the victor on the vanquished. Conforming grimly to our fallen condition in the Augustinian *saeculum*, Leviathan is a compact entered into by willing slaves only when their native political apathy has been vexed by greed and fear.[4]

The far more spirited characters in Dryden's early plays claim a freedom that differs from our natural rights in that this liberty is politically defined. Regarded simply as *individuals,* they appear to be what Hobbes calls "masterlesse men," between whom "there is perpetuall war, of every man against his neighbour; no inheritance, to transmit to the Son, nor to expect from the Father; no propriety of Goods, or Lands; no security; but a full and absolute Libertie in every Particular man." Regarded in their *political* dimension, however, these dramatic personae behave more like "States, and Common-wealths" in their relations to one another: "Not dependent on one another, every Common-wealth, (not every man) has an absolute Libertie, to doe what it shall judge . . . most conducing to their benefit." The "masterlesse men" and women of Dryden's plays act like sovereign states. The relations between them often imply a primitive, natural condition; but in themselves, each of these heroes and heroines is a complex "commonwealth" of diverse impulses mustered under a single, formidable interest. Almanzor differs from a noble savage because he knows the political meaning of his nobility: "I alone am king of me." The knowledge allows him to compete with Boabdelin as a rival state. The competition would be unedifying if the rival were lacking in political reflexivity, as in the case of a rebellious mob or a primitive wild man or forester of Elizabethan romance.[5]

Restoration audiences were obsessed with sovereignty. This preoccupation was genuinely political: they were capable of looking beyond the dramatic figure of a king and of examining his office. The actual kings they had known—Charles the martyr as well as his son enfeoff'd to idleness—had proved all too mortal, with feet of clay. As a consequence, real sovereignty could be displayed more effectively in a powerful tyrant than a weak monarch. The political sophistication of Restoration audiences should make us wary of seeing historical coincidences in the plays. Davenant and Henry Bennet, Lord Arlington, or the Howards and Sir William Coventry, might be particularly caricatured in *The Rehearsal* or *The Country Gentleman*, but the king himself was never brought on stage. Nor need he be; for this audience, merely the possibility of the royal presence in the theater was enough to heighten the fascination of portraying and criticizing sovereignty.

The criticism began before the Restoration, when the throne was vacant. John Wilson's *Andronicus Comnenius*—published in 1664 but written earlier and based partly on an anonymous Caroline play—sketches with Tacitean incisiveness the rise and fall of the Byzantine usurper, who meets a Sejanus-like end when he is dismembered by the mob. Andronicus, meant to recall Cromwell, is brought in by a faction (cooperating with a very Presbyterian "Patriarch") to cleanse the court of its hated Latin officeholders. The Greek Orthodox faction discover too late that they have hatched a serpent's egg, and they rue their "crime / Of ignorance and well-meaning" when the tyrant executes the young king he was brought in to protect (IV,ii). Wilson draws verbatim on Shakespeare's *Richard III*, imitating that play explicitly in the scene (III,ii) in which Andronicus affects to abhor the crown proffered by a henchman, and again in the scene (IV,iii) in which he cynically woos the widow of the young king he has murdered. The potent mobs are testily disparaged by the royalist author, but Wilson nevertheless credits them with a political savvy beyond the reach of the plebs we saw in *Coriolanus* (chapter 1). The rabble welcome aristocracy, "Oligasky," democracy, or anarchy, so long as they have their "Liberty" (V,iii). Such a vox populi with real, historic significance had long been absent from serious drama, having disappeared with *Catiline* and *Henry VIII*.[6]

Wilson's original attempt to recover the historical realism of Shakespeare and Jonson entails a fresh look at sovereignty. Wilson was a devoted Yorkist who had already replied to Milton's *Eikonoklastes* and would later write *A Discourse of Monarchy* (1684). His control of Byzantine history gives Wilson's play a dynamic pulse absent from the Caroline masque and still quiescent in most drama of the 1660s. Plays that adopt the Cavalier myth of "regicide and restoration" invariably present a romantic, uncritical version of history. From John Tatham's *The Rump* (1660) to John Caryll's *The English Princess* (1667) and Sedley's *The Mulberry-Garden* (1668), the rightful monarch and his supporters are less fully historicized than the rebels, who, consequently, seem more contemporary. Caryll, for example, makes his usurping Richard III pertinent by having him allude to the Satan of *Paradise Lost*, a work barely off the press. The strong rulers in these plays are usually cast in the mold of a villainous Oliver Cromwell, whose bold misdeeds, as time passed, kept a stronger hold on the audience's imagination than the acts of King Charles and his son. Wilson's energetic usurper rankles at having been exiled by the great Michael Comnenus, and toward the end he rants at the gods in desperate couplets (V,vi), but he is far from being a mere humor of malignancy. His black rage, like Saul's, can be calmed by a lutanist lamenting the transience of princely estate (V,iv); he deals shrewdly with the conspiracy against him, and courageously with his assassins; and after his death, his son Manuel takes revenge on the chief conspirator. Wilson makes this son a blameless Richard Cromwell, and at the end has the legitimate King Angelus crown his restoration by an act of mercy: "I pardon him! / It is enough to me he durst be virtuous, / When Caesar, and that Caesar his father, too, / Was otherwise." Here Wilson has departed from history, apparently in order to show that the usurper's sovereign virtues, if not his illegal crown and dynasty, could inspire another generation.[7]

In stressing the significance of Wilson's unacted play, I may seem to ignore Robert Hume's caveat against looking for "profundity and high seriousness" in Restoration drama. Hume prefaces his survey of five hundred plays from the period 1660–1710 with the remark, " 'Restoration' plays are full of social and political commentary, and bits of the philosophy of the time are recognizable enough, but almost without exception they aim more at entertainment than at deep meaning. The plays are often acute, pointed, pathetic, or satiric—but very seldom do they probe character deeply or present ideas which are essentially more than commonplaces." Hume's dichotomy of "entertainment" and "deep meaning"—a disjunction of Horace's *utile dulci* that goes back to Charles Lamb—indicates his agreement with the midcentury historicism discussed in my Introduction. His phrase "the philosophy of the time" betrays an antiseptic, formalist attitude to political ideas whose vitality will be apparent to any modern reader caught up in their dialectic. Unwarranted also is the assumption that the entertainment in these plays can be clearly distinguished from "probing" analysis. The oblique and furtive psychologizing that twentieth-century criticism associates with depth of "character" is rare in playwrights before the eighteenth century and is seldom found in public or courtly scenes even in Shakespeare. On the other hand, the "commonplaces" in which a vanished society openly trafficked may often serve to mark its cultural premises off from ours.[8]

As one of these commonplaces, the topic of sovereignty underwent a striking transformation at the hands of Restoration playwrights even before the Exclusion crisis, the moment (1678–81) in which Hume locates the watershed between earlier, "Carolean" drama and the "Augustan" drama that succeeded it. How the Exclusion crisis affected Dryden is the subject of my final chapter; here I shall focus on his dramatic representation of sovereignty. He presents sovereignty in two main phases: in the serious plays leading up to *The Conquest of Granada,* and in the three tragedies he wrote or adapted between the Test Act (1673) and the end of 1677.

PROVIDENCE AND TYRANTS

In his plays down through 1671, the playwright dallies ever more boldly with Hobbes's essential concept. Like Wilson, Dryden endows his sovereign tyrants with more intellectual vigor and rhetorical authority than the representatives of legitimacy who depose them. Zempoalla in *The Indian Queen* is more charismatic than the Ynca or Queen Amexia, Montezuma and the Indians of *The Indian Emperour* are nobler than the Europeans and their religion, Maximin is more spirited than St. Catharine in *Tyrannick Love.* Why is charisma in these plays at odds with legitimacy, and what does the mismatch reveal about Dryden's political thought?

In those three plays and in *Secret Love,* the title refers to the sovereign character. Merely hereditary rulers and their officers are given inferior roles—the "Dull part of Dignity," as Rodorick notes in *The Rival Ladies:* "Often the worst Actors play the Kings" (4:160). The innovative moment of the problem of freedom is most spectacularly dramatized in bold acts of prudence, whereas the conservative phase of the problem—authority or legitimacy—can be overlooked until the final scene. Political authority is forever dissolving and renewing itself in Dryden's serious plays, which borrow from romance their reversals of state and changes of will. Nonetheless, Dryden reaches back beyond the apolitical drama of the Caroline playwrights and Fletcher to Shakespeare's histories with their authentic revolutions. A signal achievement of the heroic plays was to restore to English drama the forgotten element of historical necessity.[9]

Dryden accomplished this providential mimesis by referring to recent history. The Interregnum loomed in the mind of theatergoers until driven from memory by the new crises of the 1670s. Restoration audiences did not welcome reminders that *their* sovereign was vulnerable; staging the act of regicide would have been unthinkable for a generation not able to abide even the printing of Marvell's Cromwell ode. Dryden's plays appealed to this audience because they staged the Machiavellian moment as the crisis of a hypothetical sovereignty, not that of a historical sovereign. Dryden's masterless men and women debating with one another amidst revolutionary circumstances were radically political. His providential mimesis gave him a surer grasp of the revolutionary moment, for example, than Orrery could ever attain. Orrery's initial play was historically vague at conception, and its successors utterly forsook politics and history to pursue courtly fantasy. Orrery was the first to dramatize the crisis of 1659 in *The Generall* (produced in 1664 after *The Indian Queen* but written before it). This quasi-allegory of the Restoration illustrates the excesses of Cavalier and aristocratic faction, of which Dryden's theory of sovereignty offers a criticism.

Orrery's nameless, usurping king is endowed with Cromwell's boldness but not his prudence: he is the easy dupe of his loyalist commanders, quite unlike the Protector, whose spy system was the envy of European governments. Still less credible is the king's lust. Orrery, like Edward Howard in *The Usurper* (1664), portrays a tyrant whose ambition panders to his love: in this case Altemira, the cynosure of the play whom Orrery clumsily links with legitimate monarchy. The usurping king confesses, "You sacred powers, to whome my heart is knowne, / You knowe that cheifly I usurp the Throne / But with more hopes to have successe in Love / A Monarch's power can only gett above." Altemira refuses to become his queen, but not out of loyalty to the exiled king. Rather, she is the prize in a combat for chivalric glory, and most of the play's bloodshed involves her two rival suitors. Her fiancé, "cloaking private hate with publique wronge, / Tooke Armes" against the usurper—but not to bring back the true king. His rival Clorimun ("the General"), on the other hand, serves the usurper faithfully just as Monck and Orrery served Cromwell, until Altemira persuades him to throw off his duty and oblige her instead by freeing his captive rival. Clorimun palliates this breach of obedience by accusing the usurper of ingratitude, but his defection bespeaks a self-interest hostile to sovereignty.[10]

The truth is that Altemira is an essentially feudal symbol whom Orrery fails to render historically significant. She inclines to the loyal party, like the Cavalier heroines in *The Cutter of Coleman Street* and *The Committee* who spurn their rebel wooers. As the focus of aristocratic factionalism, however, Altemira is not a wholesome image of undivided sovereignty. When she finds that Clorimun means to switch his allegiance to King Melizer, she urges him to turn his "Conquering Army" against the usurper. But the general will not breach his feudal honor code:

> Justice herself wou'd blush, shou'd shee receive
> A right which treachery does to her give. . . .
> Disgrace I fear lesse than to be unjust.
> 'Tis such to take and then betray a trust.
> Though I my power and *Melizer* esteeme,
> Yet I love honour more than power or him.

Rather than serve historical providence, Clorimun fashions his prudence in the courtly mirror of honor. He wants to restore Melizer, "But as my case is, all brave men will owne / 'Tis sinne to talk of 't, till to do't is none." This could lead to a providential restoration in imitation of Monck's action. Orrery fails to develop the hint, however, because he identifies neither honor nor Altemira with providence. In an unwitting parody of Lucrece founding the republic on her suicide, Altemira takes poison to avoid rape by the usurper and on her deathbed adjures him to restore the King. In fact, Melizer works his own restoration by killing the usurper privately in a judicial combat at the end of act 4. King Melizer then spends the last act in concealment as a spectator at Altemira's absurd resurrection and her Platonic reconciliation of her bloody rivals: she allows Clorimun nominally to possess her just long enough to bestow her on her fiancé.[11]

Melizer's aloofness is repeated in his successors. Like Solyman in *The Siege of Rhodes*, Orrery's sovereigns—Henry V, Mustapha, the Black Prince—habitually wrap their motives in the *arcana imperii*. If they outdo their noble friend or wife in honor, their emulation reflects more credit on the nobility to whom they condescend than on their royalty. In *The Black Prince*, Orrery puts two kings into competition with the Prince and Lord Delaware, splitting sovereignty into feudal anarchy. Orrery's final heroic play, *Tryphon*, focuses again on a regicidal usurper.

Like Tryphon, the usurping Zempoalla stabs herself at the end of *The Indian Queen*. But the heroine of the play by Dryden and Howard possesses a Cromwellian *virtù* unknown to Orrery's usurpers. She enjoys the gods' favor, and her passions, while disruptive, are integrated into a darkly providential destiny over which her vows give her some control. Enthroned by her lover, Traxalla, who deposed the Mexican king because he judged Zempoalla more truly "a sovereign" than her brother, she scorns "dull successive monarchs." She justifies her rule by a de facto argument taken from Hobbes: "'Tis power to which the Gods their worship owe, / Which, uncontroul'd, makes all things just below." She displays her full-blown sovereignty when she officiates both as priest and queen. Preparing to sacrifice her captives, she identifies the gods' providence with her power to mete out political justice, arguing that her very success proves the Yncas led by Montezuma are "invaders" who pursue "false quarrels" (8:191, 204, 206, 221).

The chink in Zempoalla's armor of *virtù* is her son. Acacis is his mother's conscience, troubled by the guilt of her usurpation. He points out that she cannot execute Montezuma for disloyalty without impeaching herself. When she stands heroically firm in her vow to sacrifice Montezuma to the Mexican "God of Vengeance," Acacis violently makes an offering of himself. His immolation draws an immediate providential response in the form of a popular uprising: Amexia, the legitimate queen, leads in a crowd proclaiming Montezuma her son and king.

Derek Hughes observes that Zempoalla is "the psychological center of the play," and he thinks her career is "a general symbol of the self-annihilation to which the life of passion tends." Regarded politically rather than psychologically, however, the Indian queen, in her bid for autonomy, attempts the self-transcendence characteristic of Dryden's heroic, masterless men. Her sovereignty is compromised by her infatuation with Montezuma, which is like Dido's but is not consummated. In her suicide, she tries to preserve her sovereignty and remain "Mistress of my Destiny." "In spite of" her ominous dream and her son's bitter denunciations, she heroically exults, "How pleas'd I am to see / Heav'ns truth, or falsehood, should depend on me."[12]

The final tableau of the dead queen and her son is a harsh reminder of the providential limitations upon Zempoalla's sovereignty. She had a melancholy preview of her end in the conjuring scene of act 3. In *Astraea Redux* (lines 153–54), Dryden imagined providence as stage machinery. His plays likewise schematize the Boethian condition of their masterless men. Zempoalla's incantation scene, which is repeated with modification in *The Indian Emperour* and *Tyrannick Love*, is meant to circumscribe the sovereign, like all mortals, within the *saeculum:*

> Poor Mortals that are clog'd with Earth below
> Sink under Love and Care,
> While we that dwell in Air
> Such heavy Passions never know.
> Why then shou'd Mortals be
> Unwilling to be free
> From Blood, that sullen Cloud
> Which shining Souls does shroud?   (8:210)

"Cannot your Art find / Some means to ease the Passions of the Mind?" Zempoalla cries, berating priest and gods alike for their providential impotence in the face of love.

Zempoalla learns that she is not sovereign over her passions. In *The Indian Emperour*, Montezuma, after he encounters the conquistadors, consults the High Priest out of fear, as well as to know the issue of his love. An "*Earthy Spirit rises*" to instruct him and the priest: "In vain, O Mortal men your Prayers implore / The aid of powers below, which want it more: / A God more strong, who all the gods commands, / Drives us to exile from our Native Lands" (9:46). Because the emissaries of this "God more strong" are the Spaniards and their popish priests, we may be sure that Dryden and his audience regarded Cortez, for all his equivocal honor, much as they did "That old unquestion'd Pirate of the Land, / Proud Rome" (1:15). Dryden taps the Protestant nationalism that inspired Cromwell's Western design and Davenant's *The Cruelty of the Spaniards in Peru*. *The Indian Emperour* strikes many readers as unusually pessimistic, perhaps because its struggle for empire of the New World lies between Antichrist and a heroic pagan. Such a contest could yield no true sovereign, and the playwright did not have to insist on the limits of its hero (who loses his empire) or those of his conquerors (whose chivalry is tainted with policy and greed). While Zempoalla's "God of Vengeance" settles her score with Montezuma, Dryden aims his heaviest strokes at the invading Christians and their specious charity.

Montezuma's naive satire on the church has been set down to Dryden's anticlericalism, but this is to forget that his Restoration audience, whatever they thought of the Anglican bishops, would never confuse their national hegemony with the spiritual tyranny of the pope. "The Sovereign Priest," says Pizarro, "Who represents on Earth the pow'r of Heaven, / Has this your Empire to our Monarch given." Montezuma retorts with Hobbes's clear distinction between the Kingdom of God and the secular kingdom divinely granted to Leviathan: "Empires in Heaven he [the pope] with more ease may give . . . But Heaven has need of no such Vice-roy here, / It self bestows the Crowns that Monarchs wear." Told of the Christian priests, Montezuma is quick to see that they pretend to sovereignty: "Those ghostly Kings would parcel out my pow'r . . . They teach obedience to Imperial sway, / But think it sin if they themselves obey" (9:42–43).

In the torture scene of act 5 that Voltaire admired, the church of the conquistadors is revealed to be an arrogant monster of intolerance. Pizarro has Montezuma racked to discover his gold while the Christian priest conducts an Inquisition. Dryden is no less solicitous for the soul of his hero than for the pagans to whom he would extend his charity in the preface to *Religio Laici*. The Indian emperor becomes a martyr for agnostic freedom, as Montezuma himself ironically notes. His skeptical via media—"For though some more may know, and some know less, / Yet all must know enough for happiness . . . 'tis better in the midst to stay"—makes the Christian Priest impatient: "But we by Martyrdom our Faith avow." "You do no more then I for ours do now," comes the victim's reply (9:100).

The ascendancy of this evil that darkens Montezuma's last hours should recall the play's tragic subtitle: "The Conquest of Mexico by the Spaniards." Empire shrinks before our eyes to the spectacle of Montezuma's body racked along with his High Priest, who dies blaming the dismembered sovereign

for not protecting his people. In Montezuma's end as in Almeria's passion-
ate suicide, we see the tragedy of conquest. Cortez, who comes just too late
to prevent both of these events caused directly by himself, seems to realize
that he has destroyed the nobler spirit of the Indian empire in Montezuma
and Almeria (Zempoalla's daughter by Traxalla) and has conquered only its
timid heiress, Cydaria. Readers mistake Dryden's point when they complain
that the other two Indian survivors flee from society to an illusory happiness. Guyomar and Alibech will seek the barren north. It holds their only
chance for "Love and Freedom" because its soil yields neither gold nor rich
harvests, and "No *Spaniard* will that Colony destroy."[13]

The "Earthy Spirit" summoned to inform Montezuma of his destiny
tells him instead of "A God more strong, who all the gods commands." The
scene in the Magician's Cave dramatizes the clash between Christianity and
paganism, first recorded by Plutarch in a famous essay on the cessation of
the oracles, an event supposedly coinciding with the birth of Christ. Milton
alludes to the Plutarchan event in his ode "On the Morning of Christ's
Nativity":

> The oracles are dumb,
> No voice or hideous hum
>   Runs through the archèd roof in words deceiving. . . .
> The lonely mountains o'er,
> And the resounding shore,
>   A voice of weeping heard, and loud lament. . . .
> In consecrated earth,
> And on the holy heart,
>   The Lars and Lemures moan with midnight plaint.
>
>   (lines 173–91)

In Dryden's scene, "The Air swarms thick with wandring Deities, / Which
drowsily like humming Beetles rise / From their lov'd Earth, where peace-
fully they slept, / And far from Heaven a long possession kept" (9:46). The
truth of providence has dawned on the New World, even though the God of
mercy fails to supplant the god of vengeance.

In *Tyrannick Love,* Dryden amplifies the irony he finds in pagan incom-
prehension of providence. This time, the conjuration in act 4 is performed
to help Maximin gain Catharine's love. Chanting their disdain of mortals
who, blind to providence, "*fear such events as will ne're come to pass,*" the

astral spirits visit the sleeping Catharine with an erotic dream. After their song and dance comes this stage direction: "Amariel, *the Guardian-Angel of S. Catharine, descends to soft Musick, with a flaming Sword. The Spirits crawl off the stage amazedly*" (10:149f.). By asserting thus blatantly the supremacy of Christian providence, Dryden exposes the pagan's ignorance and defeats Maximin's intellectual sovereignty—the skepticism that initially led Maximin to brand Christianity "an execrable superstition" and to remark wittily, "Zeal is the pious madness of the mind" (10:121). Up till now he has been another Montezuma, a champion of pagan agnosticism against Christian proselytizing.

Before he finally goes mad, Maximin abuses his rational sovereignty by contriving mechanical tortures for Catharine. He does not comprehend the more subtly ruthless machinery of divine providence, which, besides dispatching angels to rescue its saint, systematically raises and allays Maximin's tyrannic love, as Catharine smugly observes, "A pow'r controls thee which thou dost not see; / And that's a Miracle it works in thee" (10:179). Having sent her to be executed, Maximin tries to bury his pangs of remorse under a Hobbesian swagger: "Who can do all things, can do nothing ill. / Ill is Rebellion 'gainst some higher pow'r: / The World may sin, but not its Emperour" (10:180). In thus traducing the insanity of the false sovereign, Dryden was paying a compliment to the temperate rule of King Charles. The compliment to Queen Catherine was more ambiguous. Her dramatic namesake makes an awkward foil to Maximin. Catharine's saintliness consists more in decorum than in act or will. She does not become an agent of providence as do the more fully secularized heroines like Almeria. She disengages herself deliberately from the *saeculum:* "I am plac'd, as on a Theater, / Where all my Acts to all Mankind appear, / To imitate my constancy or fear" (10:163). Her attention to theatrical decorum recalls Prospero in *The Tempest*, and it anticipates Lyndaraxa. It paves the way for a false or illusionary providence in the plays.[14]

SOVEREIGNTY MORALIZED

Michael Alssid notes that Maximin conceives of himself not only as god but as dramatist:

I'le find that pow'r o're wills which Heav'n ne're found.
Free will's a cheat in any one but me:

> In all but Kings 'tis willing slavery,
> An unseen Fate which forces the desire,
> The will of Puppets danc'd upon a wyre.
> A Monarch is
> The Spirit of the World in every mind.

Observing that this "tyrannic playwright" would impose his imagination on providence itself, Alssid calls Maximin "the example par excellence of the false poet of heroic tragedy." The true providential script is followed by Catharine, who can read its "Miracle" even in the tyrant's love. Quoting Dryden's remark in the preface that Maximin was designed "to set off the Character of S. Catharine," Alssid suggests that *Tyrannick Love* presents "a scale of moral experience" ranging "between these extremes of vice and virtue."[15]

In his preface, Dryden acknowledges the roughness of "this Poem . . . contrived and written in seven weeks," and the prologue makes light of any breach of decorum, saying the poet "Allow'd his Fancy the full scope and swing. / But when a Tyrant for his Theme he had, / He loos'd the Reins, and bid his Muse run mad." This sounds perilously like a dramatic recipe for Settle and Nathaniel Lee. But in late 1670, Dryden was looking backward, contrasting his play with "the Extravagancies and Impieties of the Pulpit in the late times of Rebellion." Hoping to put his moral science at the service of religion, he considered that "even the instructions of Morality were not so wholly the business of a Poet, as that the Precepts and Examples of Piety were to be omitted." When we compare the resulting extravaganza with Dryden's assertion fifteen months later that the poet is "to endeavour an absolute dominion over the minds of the Spectators," we can see what happened during the time he was composing *The Conquest of Granada*. He tried to extend his "moral science" to the supernatural. On the one hand, his preface of 1670 familiarly invokes epic "Wit" or Virgilian *enargeia* to authorize "these Heroick Representations, which . . . are not limited, but with the extremest bounds of what is credible." At the same time, Dryden boasts that he can portray genuine sovereignty in a grotesque tyrant like Maximin: "there is as much of Art, and as near an imitation of Nature, in a Lazare as in a Venus." Rather than vice and virtue, Dryden has tried to join the moral extremes of license and freedom: the *freedom* of the political and moral subject with the *license* of the imagination. Exactly like republicanism (see chapter 4), the ungoverned "wit" creates an illusory or "false freedom."[16]

Whatever its "faults of the writing and contrivance," *Tyrannick Love* is unexceptionable in its monarchical, Augustinian politics. Dryden never lets us forget the fact that Maximin is Caesar, divinely ordained and therefore punishable by God alone. Porphyrius talks much of tyrannicide and resolves to kill Maximin, but the attempt plainly shows the pagan's delusion, and he is saved from his folly by Maximin's providential death. This comes at the hand of an officer who is inspired to avenge the suicide of Maximin's daughter (and incidentally Catharine's death, although the direct consequence of her martyrdom was the tyrant's insanity). Dryden keeps his providential machinery working smoothly. The removal of an emperor, no matter how tyrannous, is never the business of "private judgment." God sends an agent in the form of a saint whose beauty drives the tyrant mad; God then picks his successor through the vox populi of the Roman Senate.

Dryden has copied his "Lazare" faithfully, cleaving to moral science. His providential mimesis allows him to telescope events so as to bring out God's purpose: for example, he moved the scene "from Alexandria in Egypt (where S. Catharine suffered) and laid it under the Walls of Aquileia in Italy, where Maximin was slain; that the punishment of his Crime might immediately succeed its execution." Dryden is proud of having wrought his materials into a powerful dissuasive against king-killing: "I am already justified by the sentence of the best and most discerning Prince in the World, by the suffrage of all unbiass'd Judges; and above all, by the witness of my own Conscience, which abhors the thought of such a Crime" (10:110f.).

Porphyrius's attempt at tyrannicide merits close examination. For modern readers, whose tenets are parliamentarian if not republican, killing or limiting the king is the only way to solve the problem of political freedom. Even Hughes, whose book is by far the best study of the heroic plays, writes that Porphyrius's "independent rebellion is the immediate, indispensable cause of Berenice's survival." But it is her *providential* cry from the scaffold that warns her tyrant husband against her lover's attempt. Providence has laid for Maximin a broader trap, which it now springs. It motivates Porphyrius, Berenice, and the suicide of Maximin's daughter, while it activates, in sympathy with them, a rebellious army and Maximin's enraged assassin.[17]

In this way, *Tryannick Love* combines freedom with license. The license appears in the spectacular stage effects, in Porphyrius's rebellion, and in the poet's (or Maximin's) "Muse run mad." The freedom is secured by a providence that the poet faithfully imitates, mainly by holding fast to the *image* of the sovereign. In our Augustinian or Hobbesian *saeculum*, this image is the sole anchor of our freedom. When it fails, we drift into chaos. Sovereignty, rather than a particular monarch such as King Charles the Martyr, was Dryden's symbol for order. No actual, living king could match the image of sovereignty that Dryden crafted for the *Heroique Stanzas* or the image he fashioned later in *Albion and Albanius*. Erasmus had observed that praise is a better corrective for princes than satire. The paradoxical effect of Dryden's praise is *to divorce the sovereign from his sovereignty*. That is why Dryden's "little Critiques," if not his king, heard a treasonable note in the poet's Maximin. The tyrant's excesses betray the sovereign image no less damningly than Mac Flecknoe's defects betray it. The poet's own imagination is a rebel (or a brave "Usurper"). Dryden was at all times aware of this. As late as 1694, when he has Aeneas describe King Priam's corpse ("A headless Carcass, and a nameless thing"), he is careful to note that the line is Sir John Denham's (5:403). Since monarchy safeguards our laws and liberty, the poet's freedom as a subject of the crown must depend on his willingness to curb the license he takes with the king's image.

My theme is Dryden's political and historical reflexivity—his conception of himself as a public poet writing in a native tradition. This reflexive conception was not primarily introspective but external, in that it was bound up with the public *fact* of his literary and dramatic accomplishments. Within perhaps seven years of his experiment of 1669, Dryden staged the coronation of Mac Flecknoe near the actors' Nursery, where "little Maximins the Gods defy" (2:56). The poet thereby disowned his mad sovereign at a time when he sought to identify his art with legitimate monarchy. This shift in Dryden's political reflexivity conceals a paradox. By the late 1670s, the figure of the sovereign in his drama would become virtually insignificant (see my final chapter). When he was writing *The Conquest of Granada*, however, Dryden still believed in sovereignty. So implicit was his belief that he did not hesitate to draw the full-length portrait of a false sovereign in compliment to his king. The portrait of Maximin, furthermore, was followed by that of another weak king, Boabdelin, who shares the play with Dryden's consummate hero. Almanzor—modeled, we are told, less on Achilles than on the king's loyal brother—is a king*maker*. By the same token, the poet's disconcerting ability to confer and take away sovereignty is on full display in *The Conquest of Granada*. In that masterpiece crowning the first decade of the Restoration, the playwright's "usurping" wit has come into its own.

FALSE SOVEREIGNS AND DECORUM

Dryden created his "Lazare" of Maximin to help audiences appreciate their true sovereign, whom providence had restored to them. Like Davenant in his "Poem to the King" nine years before, Dryden reposes full trust in Charles when, in the "Defence of the Epilogue," he credits him with refining the conversation of the court. During his exile, Charles cultivated his spirit "in the most polish'd Courts of *Europe* . . . At his return, he found a Nation lost as much in Barbarism as in Rebellion: and as the excellency of his Nature forgave the one, so the excellency of his manners reform'd the other" (11: 216). In 1672, at the very moment the king was pushing England into a bogus war against Holland and losing the trust of Parliament by his Declaration of Indulgence, Dryden was proclaiming Charles an authentic sovereign on the evidence of his "manners."

These manners obviously differed from the mores based on historical mimesis that Davenant and Dryden both were calling for at the Restoration. The newly restored king was a providential hero, and "moral science" and its "Queen," poetry, waited on him to record his exemplary actions. Sixteen years later, Dryden says he hopes to makes Charles and James the heroes of a national epic. He is vague about its historical subject, but his subsequent remarks in the *Discourse of Satire* (4:20), even though he was by then a Catholic, imply that the projected poem would have recounted an international struggle against Antichrist. This Antichrist was not necessarily the pope, with whom he had been identified only since the Reformation; primitive Christianity held him to be a demonic or false emperor.

We glimpse Dryden's vision of this older, Manichaean conflict, which involves opposing spirits and guardian angels, in Maximin's clash with God and Catharine and in Montezuma's encounter with the Spaniards and their "God more strong" than his elemental gods. Dryden's moral science, if used in conjunction with providential mimesis, could be an apocalyptic instrument. In his satires of the early 1680s, the apocalyptic element is less explicit than it has become by the time of *Britannia Rediviva* (see chapter 3). All the same, *Absalom and Achitophel* and *The Medall*—not to mention *The Duke of Guise* and *Albion and Albanius*—unmistakably subject the sovereign to a trial by providence, recalling the national judgments that Shakespeare dramatizes in histories from *King John* to *Henry V.*

Sixteen seventy, the year in which he completed his greatest heroic play, was the midpoint between the two constitutional upheavals that round off the first half of Dryden's career. The prefaces and "Defence" he published with *The Conquest of Granada* in 1672, together with the dedications to Rochester and Sedley the next year, reveal an author preoccupied with the court's manners almost to the exclusion of historical politics and history. Dryden uses the dedication to Sedley to inform the vulgar world that "our Genial Nights" are proper symposiums, not debauches: "the Cups onely such as will raise the Conversation of the Night, without disturbing the business of the Morrow. And thus far not only the Philosophers, but the Fathers of the Church have gone, without lessening their Reputation of good Manners, or of Piety." This sketch of himself surrounded by courtly wits should be contrasted with the dialogue imitated in *An Essay of Dramatic Poesy.* Dryden now employs his moral science to scandalize the "Pedants" beyond the pale of his coterie, likening his new friends "the Wits (as they are pleas'd to call them)" to the Church Fathers (11:321).

Had sovereignty itself become a mere question of "manners" for Dryden by 1673, the year of the Test Act? The evidence of his plays is ambiguous. In *Secret Love* (1667), which dramatizes the clash between obedience and private judgment in Philocles, Dryden had proved to his king that he could explore the mysteries of sovereignty without evoking the specter of a false sovereign. This romantic play offers an emblem of the *arcana imperii,* although its exotic, Fletcherian politics are insulated from history. That is probably why the king "grac'd it with the Title of His Play," as Dryden reports in the preface. The genre obligated the playwright to aim at courtly epideixis instead of the public deliberation of the heroic plays. The bourgeois hero is stripped of his prudence by being kept ignorant of the Queen's love for him. Not only is Philocles' "private judgment" thus neutralized; he cannot rebel as a lover. His one act of disobedience is instigated by Prince Lysimachus in order to incriminate him with the Queen. Philocles hesitates to join the coup, solemnly protesting that "Int'rest makes all seem reason that leads to it. / Int'rest that does the zeal of Sects create, / To purge a Church, and to reform a State." But when he and Lysimachus then imprison the Queen in order to secure her from the designs of her rumored bourgeois lover (Philocles himself, of course), his confusion of the public good with his private interest comically diminishes him (9:115, 174).

Philocles' behavior is made a foil to set off the heroic Queen's struggle to recover her "prudence" and "sense of glory" that she feared had been lost to love. Her self-restoration is dramatized in the final scene in an intriguing duel of *bienséance* (public decorum) with Lysimachus. Her fault has not been her passion but its disclosure to her confidante. Fame has broadcast her love, like Dido's, and her strong-willed show of decorum enables her to conquer vulgar rumor, Lysimachus, and Philocles all at once. She publicly commands Philocles to marry his fiancée, simultaneously declaring her intention never to marry. By this act privately renouncing her "secret love," she achieves glory as the Maiden Queen. Dryden's title thus makes explicit the Queen's private emotion. He does not hint that her agonizing passion continues beneath her public decorum. She becomes what she seems: the image of a complex yet perfect sovereignty (9:148).

Prospero stands for a different kind of sovereignty in *The Tempest* as revised by Dryden and Davenant. He is frustrated in his attempt to manage the lives of others, not because he is the tyrant of a tragedy but because he tries to second-guess providence. Davenant and Dryden accent his limits by inventing a non-Shakespearean crisis. After only two acts, they have removed the original cause of Prospero's rancor. His speech of forgiveness ("with my nobler / Reason 'gainst my fury I will take part") is advanced from where Shakespeare placed it at the end of act 4 to the beginning of act 3. The adapters are careful moreover to excise Shakespeare's only dangerous threat to monarchy, the conspiracy against the sleeping Alonzo. Even the combination of Trinculo, Caliban, and Stephano against Prospero becomes a drunken antimasque, a toothless satire on republicanism. Sebastian's role is dropped and the guilt of Antonio and Alonzo blithely expunged by showing them a pageant in act 2. The figures of Pride, Fraud, Rapine, and Murther dance round them while they listen to songs on the punishment of usurping kings. In 1667 the authors clearly had no intention of recalling the actual Rebellion, by now fading from the public memory. Their moral science aims at the Augustinian rebellion of our wills against providence.[18]

Having foreshortened Prospero's private ordeal and relegated politics to a carnival, the adapters precipitate the real catastrophe they had been holding back. Exiled with Prospero was the infant heir of Mantua, Hippolito, whom Prospero has bred up in isolation from his *two* daughters because he has learned from Hippolito's horoscope that the young duke will be harmed if he encounters a woman. By the end of act 3, however, Hippolito has seen and fallen in love with Prospero's younger daughter, Dorinda. Relieved that no harm comes to the young man, Prospero wonders if perhaps his art has misled him. He tags Shakespeare's celebrated theme, "We are such stuff as dreams are made on" with Augustinian couplets (10:64). When the jealous Ferdinand wounds Hippolito mortally in a duel, Prospero sees the horoscope's truth and his own folly. "How much in vain doth feeble Art endeavour / To resist the will of Heaven!" he moans; all his designs are ruined. "No pleasure now is left me but Revenge." Denouncing Ariel for not presaging the accident, he decides that "I'm curs'd because I us'd it [magic]" (10:84f.).

This central crisis is elaborated operatically. Prospero tries to recover his sovereign decorum, reassigning his spirits to the roles of "Ministers of Heaven, / Whilst I revenge this Murder," but his magical prudence is in vain. Everybody falls out with their friend: Prospero with the repentant Alonzo, Antonio with old Gonzalo (they had just made up); even Miranda and Dorinda cease to share one bed. Ariel, sounding like Puck, surveys all this mortal discord, taking in also the monsters and drunken sailors: "Each wou'd to rule alone the rest devour. / The Monsters *Sycorax* and *Caliban* / More monstrous grow by passions learn'd from man." The illusion of sovereignty can make a political beast of clown or sage; like masterless men, the beast may devour the commonwealth. Spectators at this play as well as those who purchased the operatic version framed by a regal frontispiece might see their political condition mirrored in the demonstration that all mortal sovereignty — individual or collective, spurious or legitimate — requires, as Prospero emphasizes, subjection to "kind Heaven." That is also the political lesson of the benediction he bestows as he leaves "this Isle": "On my retreat let Heaven and Nature smile, / And ever flourish the *Enchanted Isle*." The touch of political reflexivity in this romantic play is the hallmark of the public poet.[19]

Even as rewritten, *The Tempest* keeps much of the political realism of Shakespeare's original conception. Little of that realism is found in Dryden's second romantic tragicomedy, *Marriage à la Mode*. The state plot taken from Mme de Scudéry is handled exactly like the "high designe" of *A King and No King*, Dryden's favorite play from the Last Age. In Fletcher's play, the old counselor Gobrias, holding the key to the hero's and heroine's fate, waits for the right moment to disclose their true identities. Because this moment entirely depends, however, on a change of wills, Fletcher's play lacks a historical crisis. Its politically innocent title reflects the naive view, sustained also in *Marriage à la Mode*, that sovereignty can be patently manifested at any time. We shall see that a later tragicomedy of state, *The Spanish Fryar* (1680), has lost this simple trust.[20]

In contrast to the heroic plays and tragedies, Dryden's four tragicomedies adopt the political insouciance of his comedies, and audiences would not have taken very seriously their protean heroes and sovereigns. *The Rehearsal* made fun of such casual sovereignty by mocking the two kings of Brentford, and the mobile condition of Prince Pretty-man evidently caricatures Leonidas, the hero of *Marriage à la Mode:* "What oracle this darkness can evince? / Sometimes a fisher's son, sometimes a prince. / It is a secret, great as is the world, / In which I, like the soul, am tossed and hurled" (III,iv). The last phrase parodies the metaphors of tempest, sea, and flood that Dryden liked to use. In *The Rival Ladies,* he plunged his characters into a chaotic *saeculum* with an echo of Petronian shipwreck, and they are still toiling in the Nile's flood and ebb as *All for Love* opens. *The Rehearsal*'s effective parody relies less on language, however, than on a clever and telling indecorum, as Bayes's comic heroes make fun of Leonidas and Almanzor with their brittle heroic propriety.

Leonidas is a model of *pietas*—the respect for gods, fatherland, and parents exemplified by Virgil's Aeneas. Along with love, *pietas* complements the aggressive *virtù* of Montezuma or Almanzor, and Dryden's minor heroes and heroines of a gentler spirit, from Orazia, Guyomar, and Alibech to Ozmyn and Benzayda, fall back on *pietas* as a response to fortune and to moral dilemmas. The *pietas* of Leonidas foreshadows the more complex virtue of Aureng-Zebe, which is again exercised in connection with sovereignty.[21] The hero's exhibition of *pietas* in *Marriage à la Mode* must compete with another decorum—namely, the à la mode observance of marriage vows. Sovereignty is treated just like marriage: mocked and flouted, it nevertheless proves indispensable, and in the end it is renewed. Its success depends on the hero's laborious decorum. With each discovery that alters his identity, Leonidas kneels to a new father, transferring his duty from fisherman to usurper, and from exiled courtier to deceased king. The occasional outbursts of the masterless man are balanced by his pastoral reminiscences of private love, a topic that dominates the spirited subplot. Leonidas is anxious to behave in a manner that does credit to his station, whatever that may turn out to be. When he learns that he is not the usurper's son after all, he apologizes to his latest putative father for unknowingly having neglected his duty. "He bears it gallantly," the usurper remarks, while his newfound daughter, Palmyra (whom Leonidas loves), says, "I almost grieve I am a Princess, since / It makes him lose a Crown." The whole scene—which was surely meant to emulate Arbaces' famous discovery in *A King and No King*—is an affecting display of the hero's nice decorum as he adjusts his relations with most of the principals and excuses his insubordination to the usurper:

> And next, to you, my King, thus low I kneel,
> T'implore your mercy; if in that small time
> I had the honour to be thought your son,
> I pay'd not strict obedience to your will:
> I thought, indeed, I should not be compell'd,
> But thought it as your son.   (11:270–72)

In tragicomedy at least, decorum ought to overrule the will. Leonidas's refusal to marry as his parent demanded was behavior worthy of a sovereign prince, but not of a déclassé subject who, like Palamede in the subplot, ought to take the bride his father chose for him. The usurper, too, learns to assume a decorum if he has it not. When Leonidas, proven the rightful heir at the end, spares the usurper and embraces him as a father-in-law, the usurper's stern ambition melts in gratitude: "O, had I known you could have been this King, / Thus God-like, great and good, I should have wish'd / T'have been dethron'd before. 'Tis now I live, / And more than Reign" (11:312).

"I ALONE AM KING OF ME": HEROIC DECORUM

To punish her for loving the prince, the usurper had ordered that Palmyra be fitted with "a Player's painted Sceptre, / And, on her head, a gilded Pageant Crown" (11:267). The false sovereign did not realize that he was making a false queen of his true daughter, who would prove unable to bear a real crown's burden and would swoon upon seeing her lover unseat her father. In *The Conquest of Granada*, Lyndaraxa is of a fiercer temper and better equipped for her public role. This wicked mistress of decorum instructs Almanzor himself in *bienséance*, whereas Almahide can teach him only the ways of the heart. Hughes has carefully analyzed Lyndaraxa's command of illusion. He suggests moreover that "she is Almahide's spiritual shadow," and he calls attention to "the unconscious affinities that bind the heroine to the villainess."[22]

Instead of the complex psychology uncovered by Hughes, I want to stress what *The Conquest of Granada* reveals to be the political roots of illusion, particularly the dream of sovereignty. In Lyndaraxa's case, this dream begins as a public vision and ends in solipsism or madness: exactly the career Dryden projected for the republicans in 1660 and again in the 1680s. In the heroic plays, the first character to be caught up in the delusion of public *virtù* is Alibech in *The Indian Emperour*. While her elder sister Almeria vows to avenge their mother, Zempoalla, Alibech's *pietas* takes the form of patriotism. Wooed by both of Montezuma's sons, she refuses to say whether she favors Odmar or Guyomar: " 'Tis true my hopes and fears are all for one, / But hopes and fears are to my self alone . . . I but his Love, his Country claims his Life." Finally she reveals her love to Guyomar, at the same time asking him to prevent bloodshed and yield the city to the Spaniards while Montezuma sleeps. She argues that "When Kings grow stubborn, slothful, or unwise, / Each private man for publick good should rise." The shocked Guyomar points out that these are the sentiments of a rebel: "Take heed, Fair Maid, how Monarchs you accuse: / Such reasons none but impious Rebels use." When Odmar agrees to do her bidding, Alibech feels a mad elation, for she secretly detests him: "Fantastick Honour, thou hast fram'd a toyl / Thy self, to make thy Love thy Vertues spoyl" (9:53, 80f.).

Dryden has sketched a guileless princess led by patriotic motives to judge her sovereign and betray her love. By the courtly, heroic code ambition can take up its abode in the heart of either sex. Valeria in *Tyrannick Love* proves herself an emperor's daughter by shielding her unwilling suitor from the tyrant after he has rejected her love. Her act in concealing her love is more admirable than the Maiden Queen's because Valeria is willing to pay the price of suicide for her disobedience. All of Dryden's great-souled women have a political dimension that makes them formidable. When the Phaedra-like Nourmahal and Roman Octavia confront their more timorous sisters, they can make them quail. The dovish Cydaria has only her love—of her father, and later of Cortez—to protect her from Almeria, who inherits the imperious spirit of Zempoalla.

Lyndaraxa dominates the gallery of magnanimous heroines, and we should note what raises the soul of this villainess above the rest. Endowed with intelligence and beauty, she withholds these gifts from the service of love. When Alibech first separated public from private desires, she invented the *heroic decorum* that Lyndaraxa adopts and perfects as her trade. When Lyndaraxa tells her rival suitors that she will take the man who proves to be king, she does not let herself in for Alibech's compunctious visitings of nature. She is cut from the same bolt as Corneille's heroines: an *honnête femme* whose external reflexivity has freed her from groping after a psychologically indeterminate self. Almanzor is her counterpart until he falls in love. She is superior to him, though, because she can set finite bounds to her love. It is true that Lyndaraxa identifies her fate with Fortuna, enemy of *virtù*. But that is only a Machiavellian flourish; like her wish to appear as Abdalla's "better Fortune," it is calculated to alarm the patriarchal custodians of sovereignty:

> I my self scarce my own thoughts can ghess,
> So much I find 'em varied by success.
> As in some wether-glass my Love I hold;
> Which falls or rises with the heat or cold.
> I will be constant yet, if Fortune can;
> I love the King: let her but name the Man.

(11:53, 65)

This reflexive speech matches the dynamic proposition of Almanzor, "I alone am king of me," although his saying is politically inchoate. He does not yet know his kingdom, whereas Lyndaraxa has full intelligence of hers and can gauge its passions as coolly as if they were another's.

As a masterless woman, Lyndaraxa seeks political autonomy, but her determined quest for sovereignty should not be confused with unformed ambition. If she were an incarnation of the boundless will, she would come across as a woman of passion. Instead, she is a mistress of decorum who keeps her private emotion (love) separate from her ambition. To make this public or heroic decorum a little clearer, we can look at its roots in Hobbes. The Hobbesian individual is cognate with the sovereign state. That is to say, the individual member of a constitutionally totalitarian state is *defined by rights that the state creates*. (A Hobbist like Dryden scoffs at the inalienable natural rights of Harrington and Locke.) To bring Leviathan into being is to invent ipso facto the individual subject. Whereas the citizen of a republic acquires an active, civic *virtù*, the Hobbesian subject is more passive and selfish, mainly because that is how Leviathan has conceived him or her. Yet this selfish individual is generic. She has been shorn of her natural liberty and rights, but in return, she participates in the collective sovereignty. Her ego is a potent *I* that can identify itself with the monarchical *we*. Here is why the image of sovereignty fascinated Restoration audiences. When Dryden presents Lyndaraxa as a masterless woman, he draws on political ideas for his prepsychological analysis of the modern individual who, like the modern state, is *self-legitimating*. By perfecting her heroic decorum, she creates her public self.

Heroic decorum is based on self-legitimation. It puts the *will* first, just as the republicans did whom Dryden earlier figured as Titans and just as Lucifer, that master of decorum in *The State of Innocence* will also do. What political theory describes in the abstract can be forcefully embodied on the stage. *The Conquest of Granada* offers an illusion of heroic will in Lyndaraxa and Almanzor, but it is a concrete illusion because it grows out of the historical spirit of rebellion—the spirit enacted by the republicans and guiltily shared by Dryden and his audience. If the problem of freedom must be resolved through political self-knowledge, as Machiavelli teaches, then heroic drama is an intricate machinery for evading the problem. The heroic decorum that it glorifies is really an escape from moral science.

"MY HEART'S NOT MINE, BUT ALL MY ACTIONS ARE": THEATRICAL SUBJECTIVITY

The first part of *The Conquest of Granada* ends with Almanzor leaving Almahide without having attained the heroic decorum of which Lyndaraxa is the undisputed mistress. The second part opens with a scene that foreshadows the resolution of the public action as well as the private emotions in the play. Ferdinand's speech on the triumph of Christianity and the fall of empires assures us that the Moors and their king will no longer stand in the way of the dynastic union of hero and heroine. Queen Isabella takes Ozmyn and Benzayda under her wing, looking ahead to the final scene in which the queen brings her "shining train" of ladies to the battlefield and tempers heroic arms by her arts of religion and love (11:193). Like Ariosto's Ruggiero, Almanzor discovers true *pietas* with the defeat of the Saracen kingdom, of which Lyndaraxa is made queen just in time to share its cataclysm. Almahide is saved from infidelity to religion by Isabella, who bestows her Christian name on the Moorish queen, and from infidelity to wedlock by Almanzor, who in vindicating her from the charge of adultery acts like Ariosto's Rinaldo. As the play's masterless men and women finally recede into history and triumphant Christianity, the heroic decorum that sustained them is folded into the poet's epilogue. "Some before him writ with greater skill," he allows, but "In this one praise he hath their fame surpast, / To please an Age more Gallant than the last" (11:202). For all his heroic decorum, Dryden took care to saturate the gallantry with pathos, thereby anticipating the kind of political drama ascendant about the time of the Exclusion Bills and the Popish Plot. Indeed, the weak sovereign is a main trait in Dryden's new idiom of the passions, and in the doomed Boabdelin of part 2, we get a preview of Marc Antony. The Moorish king's Othello-like doubts of Almahide echo his public helplessness, as "the many-headed Beast" is stirred up by leaders who "vail with publick good their discontent." "Kings who rule with limited Command / Have Players Scepters put into their Hand," Boabdelin sighs. His sovereignty is ebbing from him; to regain it he must jeopardize his wife's fidelity by calling back Almanzor — the banished rival who is "greater than a Monarch on his Throne" (10:111f.).

Dryden shows the love of Almahide and Almanzor in a perspective that had never been tried on the Restoration stage. This new perspective is imported from the epic with its descriptions of the supernatural that Dryden admired in Virgil and other poets. Davenant "heightn'd his Characters" after the French manner, according to Dryden, but that was not enough; this French manner was perfected by Orrery, whose characters are fond of elaborating on their passions with antithetical monotony — "literal mimesis with a vengeance," Altieri calls it: "not so much what would reveal to us expressly the moral response of the speaker as what Descartes has told us in detail goes on in the soul." Dryden, as he claimed in 1671, sought to add to "the fulness of a Plot" in a heroic play, as well as to "the beauty of the stile," by letting "himself loose to visionary objects, and to the representation of such things, as depending not on sence [empirical knowledge] may give him a freer scope for imagination" (11:9f.).[23]

Dryden would complain four years later that "Nature [passion] flies him, like Enchanted Ground." The simile does more than link his own heroic drama to *The Tempest*. From *The Indian Queen* on, he had supplemented the rhetorical passions of his heroes with contemplative scenes removed from public view. In the conjuror's cave, an audience sees exactly what Zempoalla, Montezuma, and Catharine see; the same holds for the vision narrated to Maximin of his son's doom. The characters' melancholy or passions give them a unique perspective, but that perspective is accessible to the audience, too, *so long as it knows the characters' sentiments.* The audience counts on the playwright to make these theatrically explicit, as in the case of the Maiden Queen. The royal or noble sponsor of a masque may have the best view of its performance, but his perspective, being a matter of public knowledge, is at the same time common. By contrast, the new perspective introduced into part 2 of *The Conquest of Granada* defeats the audience's common knowledge by hinting at an incommunicable subjectivity in the experience of the characters and in their passions.

Dryden seems to have invented this private perspective as a kind of supernatural correlative to the heroic decorum upheld by Lyndaraxa. He lamely tries to ground it in moral science, finding his warrant in the fact that "in all ages and Religions, the greatest part of mankind have believ'd the power of Magick, and that there are Spirits, or Spectres, which have appear'd. This I say is foundation enough for Poetry." Dryden overextends the mimetic capabilities of the public poet. "Spectres and Magique," like the passions, can be dramatized within a conventional perspective if their significance is commonly understood. To introduce a private vision or a passion whose *meaning* is new and surprising, however, is to flirt with the solipsism of Bayes. The quasi-novelistic subjectivity found in Virgil, Tasso, and Spenser, the poets Dryden names, was a solecism in the theater: it could not be brought on stage without breaching the decorum familiar to Restoration audiences (11:12f.).

Dryden's violation of decorum occurs in the scene in part 2 in which Almanzor is blocked from entering Almahide's chamber by his mother's Ghost. The passion being dramatized is Almanzor's desire, branded as "lawless Love" by the Ghost (11:169). A conventional—if melodramatic—perspective frames most of this scene "varied with Accidents": when Almanzor threatens to force her, the heroine's attempted suicide restores him to his virtue; his lust is theatrically displaced on the two Zegry brothers, who were about to rape Almahide when Almanzor arrived; and finally, the hero's mixed passions are sublimated by making him her champion against the false Zegrys, who are her accusers. The same episode in *Orlando Furioso*, or its analogue in *Much Ado About Nothing*, demanded a perspective that was multiple but nonetheless steadfastly determinate. With the vision of the Ghost, however, Dryden tries to present a more elusive, subjective aspect of the Ariostan and Virgilian epics. He dramatizes a private experience akin to Aeneas's vision of his goddess mother and to his encounter with the metamorphosed Polydorus, or to Ruggiero's or the Redcrosse Knight's similar encounters.

The poet casts doubt on what the hero's experience means by shifting the ground of Almanzor's identity. We have been looking for a conventional, romance discovery as we near the final, *tenth* act. When all is done, however, the poet omits the public discovery and gives us Arcos's bare narrative. Dryden's design is more ambitious. He wants the spectator to share the hero's uncertainty. Almanzor learns from the Ghost that he is *other* than what he thinks he is. The Ghost tells him only that his lineage is royal and that he was born and baptized a Christian, and warns him that being "bred in errors" cannot excuse his adultery: "'That Crime thou know'st, and knowing, doest not shun, / Shall an unknown, and greater Crime pull on: / But, if thus warn'd, thou leav'st this cursed place, / Then shalt thou know the Author of thy Race" (11:168). At this moment, the epic hero is without a compass to point his course. His crisis of obedience here is entirely private. His dilemma mirrors to us our own will trapped in the passions, unable to gain freedom by conforming our acts to the public decorum or even to drive our thoughts into a rational form of discourse:

> Oh Heav'n, how dark a Riddle's thy Decree,
> Which bounds our Wills, yet seems to leave 'em free!
> Since thy fore-knowledge cannot be in vain,
> Our choice must be what thou didst first ordain:
> Thus, like a Captive in an Isle confin'd,
> Man walks at large, a Pris'ner of the Mind:
> Wills all his Crimes, (while Heav'n th'Indictment draws;)
> And, pleading guilty, justifies the Laws.   (11:170)

While he is in this dark ignorance, Almahide enters "*with a Taper*" and demands who it is that interrupts her privacy. His despairing reply, which *The Rehearsal* ridicules as the subjective sublime, is actually a futile gesture of self-definition by a hero whose heroic decorum has failed him: "He who dares love; and for that love must dy, / And, knowing this, dares yet love on, am I."

Almahide was the first to see beyond the hero's public decorum. Even as she gave Almanzor up at the end of part 1, she bravely told Boabdelin, "There is a private greatness in his wife" (11:93). In part 2, knowing that life with her jealous husband will become more hellish if Almanzor is recalled, she cannot square her duty with her desire. Her soliloquy reveals the same impairment of her public role or heroic decorum that we see later in Almanzor. First she tries to believe that heaven intends her to be "th' oblation for my People":

> Yet, for *Almanzor* I in secret mourn!
> Can Vertue, then, admit of his return?
> Yes; for my Love I will, by Vertue, square;
> My Heart's not mine; but all my Actions are.
> I'le imitate *Almanzor*, and will be
> As haughty, and as wretched too as he.   (11:117)

"I scarcely understand my own intent," she confesses. These confused sentiments bear no resemblance to Lyndaraxa's wholehearted—albeit demonic—embrace of fortune. By the final act, not even Almahide's actions are her own. Her reputation is under a cloud, and her life depends on the outcome of a judicial combat. Deprived of all hope (except for Esperanza—her maid, whose timely words work her conversion) Almahide speaks from the heart of despair. Let no wife trust in chastity or innocence, she says, for "Mine has betray'd me to this publick shame: / And vertue, which I serv'd, is but a name" (11:181). In attempting to shadow Almahide's supernatural promptings, or her dimly providential fate, Dryden obliterates her public self altogether.

IMAGINATIVE AUTONOMY

Their flawed heroic decorum sits uneasily on Almanzor and Almahide, presumably because Dryden reserves them to the greater destiny for which their love is the providential vehicle. Their lot is not necessarily less tragic for being dynastic, considering that Dryden's model is the union of Bradamante with the doomed Ruggiero at the end of *Orlando Furioso*. Were he able to free them from this dynastic action with its epic decorum, the playwright might concentrate on the heroes' love and dramatize their sentiments within the private, indeterminate perspective we just examined. Something like that happens in *All for Love*, in which the world of public honor is well lost. Antony forfeits heroic decorum but gains the auditor's sympathy, tearfully owning (sans couplets) that he "dares love, and for that love must dy, / And, knowing this, dares yet love on." The political significance of Dryden's aesthetic innovation is worth emphasizing. In these scenes of indeterminate passion, he is trying to dramatize not so much our free will as our boundless *imagination*. He thus runs into the problem of freedom in its Kantian guise of the autonomous imagination, discussed in my Introduction.

Dryden's experiment in aesthetic subjectivity coincides historically with the rise of the Hobbesian political subject. When all of us become equal subjects of an impersonal Leviathan, all of us become equally sovereign as individuals. That is why Hobbes pays so much attention to obedience and private judgment. Theoretically, every individual member of the commonwealth is capable of representing the whole, an inference that Locke would make explicit. This political consequence had a theatrical counterpart in the novel aesthetics of stage sovereignty. Individual members of the audiences who were not yet accustomed to asserting their freedom as political subjects could nevertheless exercise their new power of conceptual sovereignty. Leviathan *subjected* each individual; but in recompense, it also *invested* each individual with an imagination that breathed the spirit of the omnipotent Leviathan.

When he said that the poet must "endeavour an absolute dominion" over this imagination, Dryden had no inkling of the theatrical subjectivity to be unleashed in the next decade by Settle, Samuel Pordage, John Crowne, John Banks, Thomas Otway, and Lee. Dryden was quick to follow *The Rehearsal* and make unconditioned subjectivity the note of the bad poet. His postscript to *Notes and Observations on the Empress of Morocco* sketches the "Phanatick in Poetry," who is the opposite of the "excellent Poet" adept in moral science. The bad poet "writes by an inspiration which (like that of the Heathen Prophets) a man must have no sense of his own when he receives" (17:182). The type soon became familiar as the mad poet of the Augustans and, with the triumph of subjectivity, the inspired Romantic poet.

Whether or not he contributed in the way I have shown to the rise of theatrical subjectivity, Dryden confronted the particular problem of imaginative freedom in his unperformed opera *The State of Innocence* (1674). A rhymed and drastically truncated *Paradise Lost*, the play starkly outlines the struggle between our obedience and our subjective or imaginative autonomy. Adam and Eve are not Bayes and Settle, but they are preoccupied with imaginary change to a degree not hinted at by Milton. In the poem, Eve's

dream of transgression in book 4 disturbs her, but without causing guilt. She
and Adam innocently sing a canticle on the goodness of God's creation, and
Heaven responds by sending Raphael. In the opera, the angelic tempter of
her dream appears with *"a Woman, habited like* Eve*"* and they watch *"other
Spirits dance about the Tree in deform'd shapes"* (12:118); when the angel gives
them the fruit, they too turn into angels. By dramatizing this vision of defor-
mity and change, Dryden indicates that his Paradise is already postlapsarian,
unlike that in *Paradise Lost,* in which Sin and Death do not bring radical
change into a perfect world until after the Fall. Milton's readers of course
are not innocent; we take our first view of Paradise, appropriately, through
Satan's eyes. But the opera violates the decorum of our common view by
intimating the subjective perspective of Eve's dream. She lies asleep onstage
to indicate that we are seeing her dream; but its meaning *for her* depends
on private and indeterminate sentiments that the author leaves unexpressed
because they elude "the decorum of the stage."²⁴

The opera omits the Wars in Heaven and the account of the Creation that
occupy the middle third of the poem. Books 5–8, often called the education
of Adam, are drastically foreshortened to a hundred lines of dialogue on free
will between him and the two angels, Raphael and Gabriel. The angels try
to teach Adam the difference betwen God's "boundless pow'r" and man's
"boundless libertie of choice," but their pupil clings stubbornly to Hobbes's
rational monism. If human choice is merely the final link in a chain of causality, he argues, then obedience and disobedience are meaningless: "For he
[God], before that choice, my will confined." In vain does Raphael try the
Deist argument based on expectation of "reward or punishment." Finally,
enjoining Adam to obey and be blessed, the angels *"fly up in the Cloud,"*
leaving him to meditate on our labile nature and to formulate the problem
of freedom:

> Hard state of life! since Heav'n foreknows my will,
> Why am I not ty'd up from doing ill?
> Why am I trusted with my self at large,
> When hee's more able to sustain the charge?
> Since Angels fell, whose strength was more than mine,
> 'Twould show more grace my frailty to confine.

Adam's questions obviously pertain to our condition in the Augustinian
saeculum rather than to Paradise, just as Eve, entering next, turns this post-

lapsarian scene into Marvell's "The Garden": their paths are so lavishly strewn with flowers that "With pain we lift up our intangled feet" (12: 124, 126).

If Dryden's Eve is more flirtatious than Milton's, she is also more intellectual. On first acceding to Adam's love, she had said, "I well foresee, whene'er thy suit I grant, / That I my much-lov'd Soveraignty shall want" (12:112). Lucifer (Dryden's biblically correct name for Satan) has to persuade her that she and Adam by right are masterless men, since they were formed spontaneously, as was the "Power" who pretends to command them. Dryden ingeniously neutralizes the sexist bias of Milton's temptation scene by having Lucifer tempt her in his own person. His winning speciousness overcomes our discernment equally with hers. Eve watches a dumb show in which "*A Serpent enters on the Stage, and makes directly to the Tree of Knowledge, on which winding himself, he plucks an apple; then descends and carries it away.*" As she marvels at his impunity, Lucifer enters "*in a humane shape*" and tells her that he was the "speckled serpent" (12:130). This is an excellent example of Dryden's skill in moral science, and it corresponds to the providential mimesis of his narrative poems: the specious, allegorical image is rejected in order to charge the natural form or event with greater meaning. In giving Lucifer the human attractiveness of a nobleman like Rochester, Dryden turns "Poetique Licence" into *literal* hyperbole.

In Dryden's version of the fall, our will rebels against obedience with the help of the imagination, which gives substance to our dream of masterless sovereignty. *The State of Innocence*, like *Mac Flecknoe*, works to curb individual subjectivity by exposing the falsehood of heroic decorum, but it does little to build up a genuinely political reflexivity. Dryden's opera for the most part lacks direct political reference. The first scene of the consult in hell, with its antirepublican satire on the Dutch, is closer to Joost van den Vondel than to Milton; both here and in Adam's vision of a naval battle at the end, Dryden repeats the jingoistic politics of *Amboyna*. The one effort he makes to place the opera in the context of England's republican aftermath comes in the dedicatory epistle to Mary of Modena, in which he asserts that the sovereign beauty of the Estense princess dazzles beholders when it is unveiled like "the Magical Shield of your *Ariosto*." "You have subverted," he tells her, "even our Fundamental Laws; and Reign absolute over the hearts of a stubborn and Free-born people tenacious almost to madness of their Liberty" (12:83). The last two clauses suggest that Dryden was already thinking of the "Headstrong, Moody, Murmuring race" of "*Adam*-wits, too fortunately free," whom he would describe four years later in *Absalom and Achitophel.*

"'TIS ALL A CHEAT": THE MELANCHOLY PRINCE

Only recently has the decorous hero of Dryden's *Aureng-Zebe* been called a hypocrite. That he was spared for so long is a little surprising, in view of the historical model Dryden chose. The last ruler (1658–1707) of the crumbling Mogul empire, Aureng-Zebe was a religious zealot indifferent to political stability and suspicious of his nobility. In conceiving him as a distinctly melancholy type, Dryden may reflect the figure of a divided monarch. Yet until recently, no one suspected irony in Dryden's choice of monarchs or doubted that he meant to dramatize "the triumph of the ideal prince over a variety of physical, emotional, and spiritual obstacles," as Alssid put it. Alssid considered Aureng-Zebe "the poet's ultimate ideal, his 'mirror' of the great monarch whose private happiness is fused to the public good."[25]

The notion that Aureng-Zebe is a kind of Restoration Hamlet, too high-minded for the times that are out of joint, is now generally challenged. Hughes brands Aureng-Zebe "another of Dryden's naïve idealists, blind to his own frailties but always ready to magnify and deplore the slightest hint of frailty in others. . . . His life is a life of theatre, dedicated to the cultivation of simple, conventional roles that in no way answer to the complex frailties of his character." Hughes imagines Aureng-Zebe to hide a seething volcano beneath his stoic decorum—a hero whose "private intention flatly contradicts the public boast."[26]

Where can one find Aureng-Zebe between these extremes of heroic solemnity and comic irony? The polarized readings may be a clue to the playwright's ambition of portraying a hero who is more contemplative than active. Hamlet is indeed the closest model for Aureng-Zebe's pronounced melancholy. To understand this Renaissance phenomenon, however, Dryden's reader must shun the psychological trap of mistaking the author's deliberate ambiguity for unconscious ambivalence. Aureng-Zebe is a type of the same melancholy that Dryden describes in himself (9:8). This intellectual melancholy bears no relation, however, to the reflexivity of the public writer conscious of historical and political change.

Instead of invoking a psychology dependent on the modern convention of an autonomous psyche, Dryden used the older, Cartesian method based on the generic analysis of the passions mysteriously generated in the soul. Dryden's psychology is his moral science, with its mimesis of events and passions that are regarded as providential.

Melancholy dominates Aureng-Zebe's character and behavior. Besides having him listen to music as he utters his famous speech, "When I consider Life, 'tis all a cheat" (beginning of act 4), the playwright unmistakably identifies the melancholic by his fitful activity. Aureng-Zebe oscillates between paralysis and manic action. The prospect of death most elates him. He comes fresh from battle at the opening of act 2, after "*a Warlike Tune is plaid, shooting off Guns.*" He pours out a libation as he goes to taste the poisoned cup (12:214). At the end of the act, he leaves a yielding mistress and a submissive father at the first sounds of combat: "I feel th'inspiring heat, and absent God return" (12:227). This demonic elation, which also drives him to a reckless confrontation with his guilty father and his usurping brother, is artfully contrasted with Indamora's fear of death, which Dryden discusses in his preface. Aureng-Zebe bullies her timid spirit because it could not make her die for him, yet he recoils in horror from Nourmahal's wild spirit, which can and does.

Melancholy also produces Aureng-Zebe's awkwardly self-conscious decorum. Initially he emulates the familiar, heroic *pietas,* which is complicated by the first of his quarrels with Indamora when she tells him about his father's lust (he quarrels with her each time they meet). Containing his passion with an effort, he closes the first act by reminding himself, "I to a Son's and Lover's praise aspire: / And must fulfil the parts which both require." He describes the passions of his soul while acting them out. Despite his stiff manner, Aureng-Zebe can be almost loquacious when he has an occasion for these rhetorical passions, as when he woos Indamora in fulsome lines describing sexual culmination (12:225). Aureng-Zebe's decorum gets him through crises of duty or honor. For example, even when the Emperor has taken Indamora and the crown from him and has left the hero alone to blaspheme virtue—"Barren, and aery name! . . . The World is made for the bold impious man"—Aureng-Zebe withstands the temptation to rebel and rejects the offer of support from his troops (12:191).

He also displays his *pietas* to great effect against his combined foes in a scene at the middle of the play (12:198). The Emperor has agreed to hand over the empire to Nourmahal and Morat while keeping Indamora for him-

self. The hero walks boldly into their presence: "With all th'assurance Innocence can bring, / Fearless without, because secure within, / Arm'd with my
courage, unconcern'd I see / This pomp; a shame to you, a pride to me." He
then spars with Morat in an aggressive duel of *bienséance* matched only by
the confrontation between Octavia and Cleopatra. "When thou wert form'd,
Heav'n did a Man begin; / But the brute Soul, by chance, was shuffl'd in," he
tells his brother, who retorts by calling him "preaching *Brachman.*" Morat's
very indecorum and directness make him an attractive foil to the hero, and
we are pleased that Indamora, who descries in Morat "a Soul irregularly
great," by her catechism and love wins over a noble villain whom the hero
can only browbeat with his hateful "Self-denying Cant."

Aureng-Zebe's heroic decorum serves him well in his public conduct
and in scenes with his father, and with Nourmahal, in which he must play
Hippolytus to her Phaedra. His stoic *pietas* is of no avail against his melancholy, however. This saturnine quality winds up his "passions of the soul"
to their antithetical heights: glory and shame, hope and fear, confident love
and jealous despair. "Believe yourself your own worst Foe," Indamora tells
him at their first interview, and her final, gently mocking words to him are
even nearer the truth: "You would but half be blest!" If Aureng-Zebe sometimes looks like a self-portrait, that is because Dryden the playwright is
fascinated by melancholy: not the clinical despondency of modern psychology, but the demonic or cosmic force that Aristotle identified with genius.
Behind Aureng-Zebe's superficially stoic self-reliance, his melancholy resembles more than anything else the proud self-legitimation we met in
such characters as Zempoalla and Maximin or Lyndaraxa and Lucifer. His
heroic decorum of self-denial is Aureng-Zebe's characteristic way of rebelling against the *saeculum,* our world of Faustian illusion in which, "Fool'd
with hope, men favour the deceit." [27]

Such a rebellion is more philosophical than political, and *Aureng-Zebe,*
Dryden's one serious play on a contemporary subject, more often recalls the
spirit of Rochester's *Satyr against Reason and Mankind* than the misogyny
of *Samson Agonistes* (to which it alludes). *Aureng-Zebe* is Dryden's first play
to show not just a contempt for the mob, but fear and disgust toward popular power. In a hundred lines, the opening council scene combines historical
exposition with a masterful review of state prudence and its limitations. As
"Fortune labors with the vast event," the ministers, unable to keep up an
active intelligence of affairs, "In corners, with selected friends, withdraw: /

There, in deaf murmurs, solemnly are wise." At such a Machiavellian moment of innovation, "Th'impatient crowd" is a formidable, unreliable force: "In change of government, / The rabble rule their great oppressors' fate, / Do sovereign justice, and revenge the state." This general collapse of prudence in the public realm is what Dryden himself, in his dedication of the play, wishes to escape. He introduces a hero who must find his self-legitimation in that realm while armed, like the poet, with Montaigne's stoicism but additionally beset by domestic jealousies.

Indamora might seem to express the author's sentiments in her soliloquy closing act 3: "Whom Heav'n would bless, from pomp it will remove, / And make their wealth in privacy and love." Yet her wish is merely the decorum of the love-crossed sovereign. As the captive Queen of Kashmir, she represents a paradox: sovereignty subjected and, by that very token, made into a desirable object. Dryden's heroine has nothing to associate her with the public realm except her status and her name. Making Indamora politically insignificant brings the predictable consequence that in loving her, each of her four lovers is prepared to forgo the public life.[28]

Hughes complains that Indamora, forced by Morat to choose between loving him and consigning Aureng-Zebe to death, "reveals a clear disparity between heroic façade and human nature." She first says she esteems both her life and Aureng-Zebe's less than honor, but then she temporizes by flattering Morat's hopes. Her fault does not lie entirely in weakness of character, however. The hero magnifies her wavering constancy by volubly disparaging it; the dark glass of his melancholy deforms her malleable nature.[29]

We saw Dryden venture beyond traditional stage decorum with its common, shared perspective when he tried to communicate Almanzor's and Eve's private sentiments. Aureng-Zebe's subjectivity in the final scene is similarly presented by letting his melancholy distort the perspective. Dryden's remarks on the passions in prologue and dedication imply that he was aware of his innovation and may have discussed it with the king, who had admired the double perspective of *Secret Love*. Possibly "the most considerable event [that was] modeled by his royal pleasure" was this curiously private scene of unfathomable jealousy, in which Aureng-Zebe, whose death had been announced at the hands of rebels, returns victorious to find the dying Morat cradled in the arms of Indamora.

He sees Morat kiss her hand and hears her prayer, "Oh stay, or take me with you when you go; / There's nothing now worth living for below." According to the stage direction, "*She turns and sees* Aureng-Zebe *standing by her, and starts.*" His glacial decorum and irony as he orders Morat's body carried off stage make his boiling passion evident: "I go, to take forever from your view / Both the lov'd Object and the hated too." She pleads with him to "Leave off your forced respect, / And show your rage in its most furious form." But Aureng-Zebe retreats into a paroxysm of self-torment that carries him to the zenith of his melancholy decorum. He has seen Indamora worship Morat in death (as Morat's widow also will do when she immolates herself), and he fixes in his soul this vision of "the lov'd Object." The whole scene is refracted through his mute and indeterminate subjectivity. A signature of the new perspective is nostalgia—the trick of rehearsing passions dramatized earlier. Aureng-Zebe, after digressing to recount the generous death of his rival, Arimant, returns to the love scene he has just witnessed: "I heard his words, and did your actions view; / You seem'd to mourn another Lover dead: / My sighs you gave him, and my tears you shed." He deplores her human weakness as "Nature's fault." In fact, Indamora's clinging to Morat proved how highly she "valu'd life." For that, his melancholy soul cannot forgive her.[30]

"IS IT FOR THEE TO SPY UPON MY SOUL?"

"I never writ any thing for my self but *Antony and Cleopatra*," Dryden recalled in 1695. He was contrasting *All for Love* with his tragicomedies—plays "given to the people" because their comic plots made them generically inferior (20:76). His favorite play turned solely upon the grand passion of "Antony and Cleopatra," those "famous patterns of unlawful love" (13:10). Two years after fretting that natural passion "flies him like Enchanted Ground," Dryden at last caught and transfixed the fleeting passions, mainly in the overwrought Antony. When Cleopatra's favorite eunuch watches to see how the hero will take the news of her death, Antony snaps at him, "Is it for thee to spy upon my Soul, / And see its inward mourning?" Alexas is not the only spy. When Antony first appears, Ventidius steps back to "observe him first unseen, and find / Which way his humour drives" (13:101, 30). Charmion describes to the queen how Antony tearfully received her gift while Ventidius stood by frowning. Dollabella and Ventidius interpret Octavia's feelings to Antony, Ventidius and Octavia misinterpret Cleopatra's flirtation with Dollabella, and, entering as Mars and Venus in their masque,

Antony and Cleopatra interpret themselves. The playwright has scrapped the decorum of a common perspective along with his rhyme. Writing "for my self," he was ready to pay the hefty price of dramatic ambiguity to achieve a greater depth in the passions.

The literal mimesis of the passions called for by Lisideius / Orrery reaches its limits in *All for Love*. Apart from the multiple suicides that create the illusion of closure, the whole action of the play is weeping, embracing, and declamation. The prologue promises a hero who "Weeps much; fights little; but is wond'rous kind," and his condition is elaborated for a hundred lines by Ventidius and others before the hero enters, "*walking with a disturb'd Motion, before he speaks*" (13:20, 30). Throwing himself down on the stage, Antony presents the icon of fallen *virtù* that is dwelt on exhaustively for five acts. Dryden has borrowed this Elizabethan icon from George Chapman— no doubt one of the "glaring Colours which amaz'd me in *Bussy Damboys* upon the Theatre" (14:100). Dryden emulates the Last Age much the way his hero strives to recover his *virtù*. By the end of this scene, which the poet preferred "to any thing which I have written in this kind," Antony has been roused to stirring reminiscences. Such lines as "O, thou hast fir'd me; my Soul's up in Arms," however, are more apt to make us think of Timotheus's ode than of Shakespeare's Brutus and Cassius (13:19, 38).

The author has endowed Alexas with his own skill in reading the characters, a reflexive device so heavily used as to suggest that the rhetorical passions have reached a dead end in this play. The eunuch foretells to Cleopatra the course of Antony's love; undertakes to smooth her way by tying her bracelet on the martial lover; and, of course, falsely reports her death, thereby causing Antony's botched suicide. The author, no less busy than Alexas, places everyone except the audience at a privileged angle for observing Antony. Like Samuel Daniel and Shakespeare, Dryden robes Antony in the grandeur of the Roman past. Having vouchsafed us the historical frame, however, the author refuses to define the meaning of the actions or passions it contains. Dryden presumably indicates "the excellency of the Moral" by his subtitle (13:10). The world of honor that Antony has lost matters less than the fact that he has lost it *well*—for love. But this love, unlike the antagonistic friendship of Ventidius, lies mostly in the inaccessible past. Instead of using moral science and the fable or plot to explicate the lovers' passions, Dryden relies on a rhetoric of nostalgia. Dollabella admits to Cleopatra that he lied about Antony's feelings for her:

> Oh, had you seen
> How often he came back, and every time
> With something more obliging and more kind,
> To add to what he said; what dear Farewels;
> How almost vanquisht by his love he parted,
> And lean'd to what unwillingly he left:
> I, Traitor as I was, for love of you,
> (But what can you not do, who made me false!)
> I forg'd that lye; for whose forgiveness kneels
> This self-acccus'd, self-punish'd Criminal.   (13:78)

The passion of love described here and elsewhere in the play is the quin-
tessentially Petrarchan agony of parting and renunciation. As Aureng-Zebe
makes love to Indamora by quarreling with her, so Antony is always on the
verge of leaving Cleopatra—even though Alexas rightly assures her to the
very end, "Believe me, Madam, *Antony* is yours. / His heart was never lost."
Such lovers can never possess each other this side of death. At the end of
act 4, after they have wept with Dollabella—who will simply be excised from
the play, like Antony's oppressive jealousy—their doleful reunion breaks up
with the joyless stage direction, "*Exeunt severally*" (13:94, 92).

In theory, dramatic characters might live entirely by their passions,
so long as we can see that these really do modify their circumstances or
lebenswelt. Without practical actions and a plot, however, it is hard to show
this modification. The rhetoric of *All for Love* is in the perfective tense, so to
speak. All the actions have been passed over, not as a concession to Lisideius
and the unities, but so that Antony and his friends may rehearse them in a
private, subjectively indeterminate perspective. On the classical and Elizabethan stage, the *narratio* supplies a common perspective by setting down
the experience or event narrated, not the feelings of the narrator and his
auditors. When Gertrude, for example, describes the silvery undersides of
the willow leaves, she helps us imagine the last things Ophelia saw as she
drowned. We never ask how Gertrude knows this or whether she witnessed
the scene she describes so affectingly. In *All for Love,* on the other hand,
the rhetorical reminiscences that clot the flow of the action create a world
of passions increasingly hard for an audience to take in. What is the point,
for instance, of Ventidius's misreading the interview of Dollabella and Cleopatra? He uses this specious evidence to insinuate that she is false and so to

arouse Antony's jealousy. Dryden cannot mean that the honorable Ventidius has turned into honest Iago, bent on destroying Antony. The wicked genius behind the plot to make Antony jealous is Alexas, and he, too, stumbles when Ventidius and Antony press him (a "Witness / From Hell") to prove Cleopatra fickle. Alexas admits that she is, enraging Antony and estranging him from wife and mistress alike. Afterward, Alexas bitterly regrets with Cleopatra "my ill-tim'd truth"! Evidently both of them have forgotten that her love for Dollabella was merely faked (13:83, 93).

This Bayesian disregard for a consistent perspective may come from too much "poetique licence," the Virgilian, rhetorical freedom that Dryden had long been claiming for the dramatist who sought truth in the passions. At the same time, these scenes of indeterminate emotion recall Hobbes's warning against the "palpable darkness" of Metaphysical wit and "strong lines," or "the ambitious obscurity of expressing more then is perfectly conceived." Dryden strains too far the decorum of stage characterization when—for example—he asks us to swallow Antony's self-description:

> Why was I fram'd with this plain honest heart,
> Which knows not to disguise its griefs and weakness,
> But bears its workings outward to the World?
> I should have kept the mighty anguish in. . . .
> But I am made a shallow-forded Stream,
> Seen to the bottom: all my clearness scorn'd,
> And all my faults expos'd!   (13:86)

His ecstatic transparency may be *actable,* but it reads more like bombast than moral science.

These unruly passions that fly the bounds of a fixed perspective are suited to the political world of *All for Love.* Dryden has pitched his legendary model of "unlawful love" in a guttering Roman republic where sovereignty has yet to emerge (Octavius does not appear in the play). In the political limbo at the end, Serapion and the priests are left to establish authority. Unlike Machiavelli, Dryden saw little difference between democracy and anarchy; like Shakespeare, he could conceive of the Roman republic only as a civic arena of feudal nobles whom a weak senate could not control. This left him without a public object for *pietas.* That political virtue is mocked in the heroine's name: Cleopatra joins the words "glory" and "fatherland." In losing the "world," Antony gives up family and friendship, but not much besides. Does its lack of a clear political moral mean that *All for Love* has no claim to moral science?

Its love and honor are aristocratic values of questionable worth without a heroic society to uphold them. Antony is left alone to carry the burden of loyalty, which is the irreducible feudal virtue. No mobs are active in this play, but the troops who betray Antony care as little as a mob does for *pietas* and loyalty. The real tragedy that *All for Love* presents is the death of the courtly ideal: the heroic civility distilled in Davenant's phrase "Arms and Arts" (chapter 5). Harrington, analyzing the causes of the Civil Wars, had put his finger on what the erosion of chivalric values meant for politics. A monarchy requires either an aristocracy or an army to stand between itself and the people. When the House of Lords lost its parliamentary leadership, the crown was abolished and a Commonwealth set up: "The house of peers, which alone had stood in this gap, now sinking down between the king and commons, showed that Crassus was dead and Isthmus broken." Harrington's principle must have been getting fresh attention in 1678. When Dryden dedicated *All for Love* to Danby, he hailed him as the last nobleman to "stand like an Isthmus bewixt the two encroaching Seas of Arbitrary Power, and Lawless Anarchy." [31]

Our Author Swears It Not: Satire

Like the five heroic plays, *All for Love* locates the private passions in the midst of a disintegrating empire in which the growing power of Rome dismantles the legacy of Alexander. For sixteen years after *The Indian Queen*, Dryden portrayed fallible sovereigns. Whatever autarchy they have is enervated by love. Only by keeping in the background of the play, as Octavius does, can a true sovereign avoid the quagmire of the *saeculum*. The chief political lesson to be gained from Dryden's unsovereign princes is the exquisitely democratic moral that love and the passions level us all. As audiences grew more hungry for such regal pathos, other playwrights were glad to feed the new appetite, but Dryden was not. His complimentary epilogue of 1671 later gave way to revulsion when he derided passages from the heroic plays: "I knew they were bad enough to please, even when I writ them" (14:100).

This disillusion with the theater, which followed close on the success of *The Conquest of Granada* and the reflected éclat of *The Rehearsal*, may have been born of Dryden's misgivings at having squandered his talents. He had succeeded in amusing the crowd with rhetorical passions instead of providential (or even Longinian) mimesis. The whining note of the prologue to *Aureng-Zebe* can be heard intermittently for another four years until the end of 1679, when the infamous Rose Alley assault occurred. During the two years that followed, Dryden learned to put his talents at the service not of drama but satire, and in that service managed to recover his moral science.

"CLAM'ROUS CRITIQUES" AND MALCONTENTS

Dryden's satire began with the casual swipes at competitors in his prologues and epilogues and with more focused attacks on Howard, Shadwell, and Settle in his prefaces, where he used the irony and meiosis of *An Essay of Dramatic Poesy* and its "Defence." His satire of personal rivals reaches its maturity with *Mac Flecknoe*, written sometime in the two years after mid-1676. Because this poem was not published until 1682, *after* Dryden had emerged as satirist of his "True-Blew-Protestant" (or Whig) rivals (2:53), it can reveal nothing of the public poet on the threshold of the national crisis. Indeed, a parenthesis like "The fair *Augusta* much to fears inclin'd" (line 65) could not have been added before the fall of 1678, and Dryden would have warmly rejected any attempt to read his poem as a public comment on the growing debate over exclusion or the politics of succession to the throne. Unlike the earlier quarrel over rhyme, his private quarrel with Shadwell was not something he judged to be in the public interest, and the partisan motives that led to the poem's publication in 1682 did not exist at the time Dryden published *All for Love*, probably in March 1678.

Two of Shadwell's aristocratic patrons did provide Dryden with a public target, however. Exactly a year before this date, Buckingham had been sent to the Tower with Shaftesbury for trying to dissolve the Cavalier Parliament. Always an engaging figure, the duke was freed, says Marvell, at the suit of "Nelly, Midlesex [Buckhurst], Rochester, and the merry gang, [and] layd constantly in Whitehall at my L: Rochester's logings leading the usuall life." Dryden's score against him went back to *The Rehearsal*. As for Buckingham's merry host, Rochester had praised Shadwell's comic genius in his *Allusion to Horace* (1675–76), a satire that accused Dryden of being "such a vain, mistaken thing / To wish thy works might make a playhouse ring / With the unthinking laughter and poor praise / Of fops and ladies, factious for thy plays." Besides endorsing Shadwell's plays, the *Allusion* draws freely upon their many caricatures of Dryden as "Drybob" and other taciturn, melancholy figures unapt for comedy. Dryden had waited two years to strike back at Rochester. His chance came to retaliate against both him and Buckingham when *Timon of Athens* was staged in January. Shadwell's play opens with a travesty of Dryden and his "damn'd Panegyricks" and closes with a plug for Buckingham (to whom it is dedicated) as a popular leader. Buckingham was in fact "the only one of Charles's ministers who pursued a career for amusement . . . and set a standard of ducal independence and vagary never since approached."[1]

Dryden published *All for Love* two months later and dedicated it to Danby, a former protégé of Buckingham and now his great enemy with whom he was vying for control of the government's French policy. It was probably Buckingham's recent notoriety that prompted Dryden, nearly five years after *Amboyna* and the Test Act, to step once again before the public. Winn calls the dedication "more explicitly political than any piece of prose he had yet written," but Dryden's grasp of the political situation, as we shall see, was very shaky. He knew that Buckingham, who had moved into the City and stood for alderman, wanted to bring down Danby's government so he might replace him as prime minister, using his French connections to treat with Louis, who was now completing his six-year conquest of Belgium. Dryden had first mocked Buckingham in a letter of 1673 inviting Rochester to laugh "at the Great Duke of B—— who is so oneasy to [him]self by pursueing the honour of Lieutenant Generall" in the Dutch wars. The dedication and preface of 1678 are unified by their allusions to Buckingham's French ambitions, which are literary as well as political and therefore, Dryden implies, no less vexatious to himself than to Danby. "Steadiness of temper" like the lord treasurer's is "requisite in a Minister of State" (13:5). By the same token, the future Zimri's known instability disqualifies him as a sober critic of drama or a judge in the kingdom of wit.[2]

The attack in *The Rehearsal* on Dryden's heroic style (repeated in the *Allusion to Horace*) had sent him back to his dream of an epic, first disclosed in the preface to *Aureng-Zebe*. In 1677, *The State of Innocence* appeared with Lee's commendatory verses urging Dryden to shame his "clam'rous Critiques" by singing "The troubles of Majestick CHARLES" and with "The Authors Apology for Heroique Poetry and Poetique Licence" (12:538, 86). In this critical preface Dryden, armed by Longinus, counterattacks his critics of the past five years. The "Apology" is an important milestone in his return to the moral science from which he had wandered ever since the quarrel over rhymed plays. As he had done in *An Essay of Dramatic Poesy*, he appeals to a "Universal Tradition" of poetry "which has pleas'd the most Learn'd, and the most Judicious." In praising the epic genius, he does not mean "to undervalue the other parts of Poetry," such as comedy, Buckingham's particular talent: "Let every Man enjoy his tast: but 'tis unjust, that they who have not the least notion of Heroique writing, should therefore condemn the pleasure which others receive from it, because they cannot comprehend it" (12:90, 89).

Like Rymer, whose *Tragedies of the Last Age* later in the year would revolutionize English criticism much the way *Leviathan* had radicalized political theory, Dryden studies to avoid singularity of opinion. Longinus has taught him the difference between "snarl[ing] at the little lapses of a Pen" and criticizing justly — observing "those Excellencies which should delight a reasonable Reader," including poetic license when it conveys heightened passion: "It requires Philosophy as well as Poetry, to sound the depth of all the Passions; what they are in themselves, and how they are to be provok'd: and in this Science the best Poets have excell'd" (12:87, 91). He quotes a line from Cowley that he would mock in *Mac Flecknoe* — "Where their vast Courts the Mother Waters keep, &c." — and shows "How easie 'tis to turn into ridicule, the best descriptions, when once a man is in the humor of laughing, till he wheezes at his own dull jest!" (12:96).

The Ciceronian motto on the title page of *All for Love* is likewise aimed at Buckingham's gang of critics: "It is easy to single out some flaming word (if I may use this expression) and ridicule it when the fires of the soul have cooled" (13:2; Loeb translation, modified). A year later, in *Troilus and Cressida*, Dryden imposes the image of Buckingham, known for his skill as a mimic, on Ulysses' description of Patroclus:

> Ev'n thee, the King of men, he does not spare
> (The monkey Authour) but thy greatness Pageants,
> And makes of it Rehearsals: like a Player
> Bellowing his Passion till he break the spring
> And his rack'd Voice jar to his Audience . . .
> Tickling his spleen, and laughing till he wheeze. (13:254)

Dryden consistently imagined Buckingham as a raucous "Player." Even after Buckingham's death he would say of *The Rehearsal*, "I knew the Author sate to himself when he drew the Picture, and was the very *Bays* of his own Farce" (4:8). The stinging wit of that farce still rankled in 1679. In "The Grounds of Criticism in Tragedy," published that year as a critical preface to *Troilus and Cressida*, Dryden made Rymeresque fun of his own, undramatic similitudes while belatedly offering his response to *The Rehearsal*. Against Buckingham's capricious detraction he raises the shield of moral science. As in 1668, when he testily gave Howard to understand that poetry "must *be*

Ethical," Dryden now, with Longinian aplomb, declares that the mores or "Manners" of tragedy are grounded on "the Principles of Moral Philosophy" and not on a mistaken "pathetic vehemence" or "the roar of passion." Those effects "will move no other passion than indignation and contempt from judicious men." Dryden chastises the duke, who, as mimic and "monkey" playwright, vainly seeks "approbation from sober men" (13:241f., 14).

All for Love is armed against Buckingham in its prologue mentioning its "Heroe, whom you Wits his *Bully* call," and against Rochester in its epilogue, which trusts that the author has not disappointed the taste of "some antiquated Lady" (see Rochester's *Allusion,* quoted above). The dedication notes that the overtaxed French conquer abroad only to be poor at home, and the preface rejects French decorum—the placid *honnêteté* of Racine—as unfit for the English stage: it is unjust "that the *French* should prescribe here, till they have conquer'd." Dryden forbids mere wits to disturb poetry's hierarchy with their "smattering of *Latine*" or their "*French* version" of Horace. "Those who are allow'd for witty men, either by the advantage of their quality, or by common fame," Dryden has "disdain'd to answer, because they are not qualified for Judges . . . neither are they qualified to decide Sovereignly, concerning Poetry" (13:6, 13, 18).

Polishing further the image of the future Zimri as a blest madman and splendid buffoon, Dryden turns against him Horace's wry observation on the universal restiveness of men and asks, "Is not this a wretched affectation, not to be contented with what Fortune has done for them, and sit down quietly with their Estates, but they must call their Wits in question, and needlessly expose their nakedness to publick view?" The last phrase may hit at Rochester's escapades, and Dryden implies that the earl tyrannizes over poets just as Dryden feared he might do in 1673. The taunt that the Laureate wrote for popular applause was more than Dryden could bear from a crony of the histrionic Buckingham, and he diminishes Rochester to one of the duke's "little *Zanies*" who are "Persecutors even of *Horace.*" He warns Buckingham that the earl's satire "falls most heavily on his Friends" whose talents Rochester mistakenly praises (13:14f.).

After he had put Buckingham among dunces in the schoolroom, exposed him for one of Horace's bores who pester an author with their conversation, and made him the buffoon of his own farce, Dryden wrote the dedication, in which he placed his victim on the greater stage of political affairs to which he fatuously aspired. This was an ominous move by the public poet. Widely circulated in manuscript, *Mac Flecknoe* had demonstrated its author's gift for personal lampoon, and Buckingham could not have been more wrong when he wrote of Dryden in 1677, "That drone has left his sting upon the stage." One of the duke's cohort noticed about this time that Dryden "begins to aim at the renown / Bestow'd on satirists, and quits the stage / To lash the witty follies of our age" and advised him to go back to his harmless playwriting. Surely neither of these wits had actually read *Mac Flecknoe*, or they would have marveled at its suavely caustic blend of a Virgilian style from the heroic plays with the Horatian manner that Dryden had perfected in his prologues.[3]

Dryden traduces Buckingham in the dedication, but to achieve dynamic satire he needed to fit Zimri into a historical narrative. In the great satires of 1681–82, he would return to providential mimesis and to moral science. He would bring Horace and Virgil, Milton and Shakespeare, Corneille and Longinus to share the historical present with Moses and Korah, Buckingham and Danby and Charles. In early 1678, the moment had not yet come out of which a historical present might be fashioned. At certain points in the dedication, Dryden speaks as prophet or public poet, but his conception of events lacks the brilliant reflexivity with which *An Essay of Dramatic Poesy* mirrors the Last Age in its own. Dryden sees well enough Buckingham's folly and malcontent, but he understands neither Danby's parliamentary imbroglio nor the constitutional crisis on the horizon. He could not foresee that by the end of the year, the lord treasurer, addressed here as a bulwark of the monarchy Buckingham assails, would cave in together with his Cavalier Parliament.

Does the address to Danby commit its author to the Cavalier axiom and consequently to the Tory partisanship that would beget *Absalom and Achitophel?* I argued in my third chapter that Dryden, as late as 1681, had still not adopted the Anglican equation of dissent with sedition that was axiomatic with Sir Roger L'Estrange and other propagandists. By the time he wrote the "Epistle to the Whigs" early in 1682, Dryden had figured out that the "talking Trumpet" of biblical hermeneutics was the origin of Presbyterian dissent, which he now historicized as Calvinistic republicanism, or, in *The Medall*'s phrase, "Republique Prelacy" (2:52). He branded that dissent politically culpable, yet only months later, his public confession of a layman's religion implied that a similar Puritan radicalism was his private rule of faith: the Dissenters' criterion of "the Universal Church" (2:120).

Since Dryden persisted in approaching public affairs from the side of religion in 1682, we can assume that questions of ecclesiastical polity were uppermost in his thoughts on the state of the nation in 1678, just as the Protestant epic — the historical narrative that he preferred to an apocalyptic millennium — had guided his thinking at the Restoration. In my preceding chapter on the heroic plays, I tried to correlate the problem of religious freedom, which centers in private judgment, with the problem of heroic decorum, which tends toward a subjective or imaginative autonomy of which the political counterpart is anarchy. The vanishing point of Dryden's view of monarchy lies on the horizon where the autonomous, psychological self takes its rise. For this reason, Dryden's twin harbingers of political chaos are a weak sovereign and solipsistic fantasy — the willfully subjective decorum that he creates for Almanzor and subsequent heroes. It was the autistic Bayes, we may recall, who found out the blessing of dual kingship.

When Dryden warns the lord treasurer of "Disturbers of his Country" like Buckingham, he is really advising Danby on the religious polity. The Puritan Laureate is trying to sound like a good Anglican. "Malecontents amongst us," he says, "wou'd perswade the People that they might be happier by a change." As in his immediately preceding publication, *The State of Innocence,* he fears that Satan may

> seduce Mankind into the same Rebellion with him, by telling him he might yet be freer than he was: that is, more free than his Nature wou'd allow, or (if I may so say) than God cou'd make him. We have already all the Liberty which Free-born Subjects can enjoy; and all beyond it is but License. But if it be Liberty of Conscience which they pretend, the Moderation of our Church is such, that its practice extends not to the severity of Persecution, and its Discipline is withal so easie, that it allows more freedom to Dissenters than any of the Sects wou'd allow to it. In the mean time, what right can be pretended by these Men to attempt Innovations in Church or State? . . . If their Call be extraordinary, let them convince us by working Miracles; for ordinary Vocation they can have none to disturb the Government under which they were born, and which protects them. (13:7)

By "Malecontents" Dryden plainly means religious demagogues. Because he adds that "He who has often chang'd his Party, and always has made his Interest the Rule of it, gives little evidence of his sincerity for the Publick Good," commentators have assumed that Dryden here refers to Shaftesbury, despite the fact that Shaftesbury had been in the Tower for a year.

Even upon his release shortly after this dedication, "there is no satisfactory evidence that he had yet a very great following either inside or outside Parliament," according to his most definitive biographer.[4]

The prime target of the dedication is more likely Dryden's and Danby's common foe, Buckingham. As late as 1682, Dryden still associated Buckingham and Clifford with rational religion and toleration, issues that disturbed the country's "Common Quiet." Clifford, author of *A Treatise of Humane Reason*, was now dead, but his patron Buckingham, besides writing what Douglas Atkins calls a "spirited defense" of Clifford's tract, had introduced a bill in Parliament supporting a general toleration of all the sects. Dryden fears "severity of Persecution"—the political consequence of toleration in a preliberal society not yet schooled to Lockean indifference.[5]

Like Hobbes, Dryden makes the government a *refuge* from those whom today we would call ideologues. The church was less dogmatic than any sect, just as the king was freer from self-interest than any doctrinaire republican. Dryden says he has "a loathing to that specious Name of a *Republick:* that mock-appearance of a Liberty, where all who have not part in the Government, are Slaves." Reaching into his memory of the Interregnum, he bids those who "intend a Reformation of the Government" to weigh what happened to the Commonwealth: they will find that those "who began the late Rebellion, enjoy'd not the fruit of their undertaking, but were crush'd themselves by the usurpation of their own Instrument." And he tries to get a handle on the constitutional agitation by reviving Harrington's metaphor of England as a mixed monarchy with its "Isthmus" of the nobility—represented here by Danby—standing between king and Commons (13:5f.).[6]

Dryden makes his return to the political scene as a public poet by comparing Danby's ministerial dilemma with the private quarrel between Buckingham and the poet. Government propaganda had joined Buckingham with Shaftesbury, so that if Dryden included the earl among the "Malecontents," he did so without taking a right measure, at this date, of his power to unsettle a king "whom God made happy by forming the Temper of his Soul to the Constitution of his Government" (13:5). When Dryden called Danby "a Copy, an Emanation of" Charles, he could not know that the king's model servant was about to despatch to Louis an offer to betray the army for money; that before the year was out an astonished Parliament would hear proof that the lord treasurer was conspiring with France; and that Charles would have to dissolve the Cavalier Parliament to rescue Danby from impeachment after Ralph Montagu, Dryden's Westminster School rival, read Danby's treasonable letter in the House of Commons.

By the end of this momentous year, Dryden would begin to see that the real "Emanation" of "The Nature of our Government . . . and the Temper of the Natives" was neither the prime minister nor his rival the monkey duke. It was the "formidable Cripple" whose spirit reflected the magnanimity of Dryden's heroes better than James or any of the certified Cavaliers managed to do. The wits—Buckingham, Rochester, Mulgrave—encouraged Dryden to despise popular applause, but it was Shaftesbury who would teach him that a far greater danger lay in ignoring the vox populi.[7]

A PROTESTANT IN MASQUERADE

In the dedication and preface to *All for Love* and in *Troilus and Cressida* a year later, Dryden tried to present Buckingham as a comic actor on the political stage. Before this, Dryden had alluded to topical events and persons in his prologues but never in his plays. I argued in chapter 6 that his weak and usurping kings represent the office of the sovereign, not Charles himself. In the sense that sovereignty also stood for *the nation*, however, the dwindling image of monarchy in the plays does reflect the waning of England's international presence, to which Cromwell had given such a luster and which was now, owing to Charles's bankrupt foreign policy, in shameful eclipse. The integrity of the sovereign steadily degenerates, from Montezuma, Maximin, and Boabdelin to the senile Emperor in *Aureng-Zebe* and, finally, no emperor in *All for Love*. In the plays from 1678 to 1680, Oedipus as monarch despoils himself, Agamemnon and Priam are mere heads of factions, and King Sancho, discovered alive in prison at the very end of *The Spanish Fryar,* is kept off the stage. Evidently the public poet had lost his ability to project on stage the political nation.

The political nation consisted of king, lords, and commoners. From each of these orders in turn, Dryden chose his patrons. My argument that his Cavalier partisanship in 1678 was more hypothetical than political accords with Harth's recent finding that Dryden's commitment to the Tory cause cannot be dated earlier than the king's speech dissolving the Oxford Parliament in March 1681. "As a professional man of the theater," Harth says, "Dryden's primary interest at this time was in ensuring the success of his plays . . . by avoiding overt political partisanship." Harth neatly observes that Dryden covered the political spectrum by dedicating *All for Love* to a Tory, *Troilus and Cressida* to the moderate Robert Spencer, second earl of Sunderland, and *The Spanish Fryar* to a scion of the Whigs.[8]

Dryden wrote a fourth serious play coinciding with the political crisis, *Oedipus,* on which he collaborated with Lee during 1678 and which he published without a dedication. Judging from its topical prologue, *Oedipus* must have been staged before the Popish Plot broke in October. The characterization of Tiresias and Creon suggests nonetheless that Dryden had been pondering the constitutional crisis. In the first and third acts, which Dryden said he wrote, these two figures compete to win over the crowd. Previously, the mob had appeared in Dryden's plays for the same purpose it does in Fletcher's: to preserve custom and legitimacy against aristocratic rebels and their factions. In *Aureng-Zebe,* one of those factious nobles scoffs that "In change of Government, / The Rabble rule their great Oppressors Fate: / Do Sovereign Justice, and revenge the State" (12:164). This feudal view disclaims the populism of Machiavelli and Harrington and rates the people incapable of upholding the political ideals of justice and sovereignty.

After *Annus Mirabilis,* Dryden had paid little heed to basic republican concepts in his works. He knew Shaftesbury only from Cavalier propaganda, which mocked him as "Sir Popular Wisdome" and "Mephistophiles" but gave no hint of the titanic force he was to become when he undertook to rid the nation of its popish governors. In *Oedipus,* Dryden modeled Creon on Richard III, a hypocrite of quite another stripe from the republican Shaftesbury. When Creon addresses the mob as "Fellow Citizens," the nobles snicker: "Fellow Citizens! there was a word of kindness!" Creon insinuates to them that "the Gods might send this plague among you, / Because a stranger rul'd." The people are about to "satisfie our Consciences, and make a new King," when Tiresias dissuades them, saying the plague is punishment for their crimes, to which they would add by rebelling against Oedipus (13:129f.). The community that shares his tragedy is Senecan rather than Sophoclean, and the adapter strangely doubles Oedipus's sense of doom in Creon's private melancholy, which Creon indulges at length just before the Ghost of Laius makes its horrific visit. This play without a sponsor lacks any clear political reference, unless the prologue, in its lines about laying "Tradition wholly by" in favor of "the private Spirit," applies to rebels as well as critics in the fall of 1678.

In the epilogue to *Troilus and Cressida,* produced the following April,

Thersites does refer to the Popish Plot, but only after some private digs at Sedley and Rochester. In view of the Rose Alley assault eight months later, Thersites' lines have a pathetic irony: "Ye expect a Satyr, and I seldom fail, / When I'm first beaten, 'tis my part to rail." The adapter of Shakespeare's obscurely satirical play seems to bear his own grudge against the political community. When Hector asks Troilus to give up Cressida for "the publick" good, Dryden exaggerates the hero's disgust:

> And what are they that I shou'd give up her
> To make them happy? let me tell you Brother,
> The publick, is the Lees of vulgar slaves:
> Slaves, with the minds of slaves: so born, so bred:
> Yet such as these united in a herd
> Are call'd the publique: Millions of such Cyphers
> Make up the publique sum.   (13:354, 305)

In reply, Hector twists one of Shakespeare's ideas (cf. 13:266) to fit the heroic context: " 'Tis adoration, some say, makes a God"; heroes need "inferiour creatures here on Earth." Like Creon and maybe the playwright, Troilus is cynical about heroic glory and frustrated in love, and he pours out his bitterness on "the publique." Also like Creon—and like Aureng-Zebe or Antony—the hero traps himself in the private perspective of his heroic decorum. His delusion costs him Cressida, and he finds the truth too late.

Dryden heightens the treachery that closes Shakespeare's play, making the cowardly Achilles butcher Troilus along with Hector. Ulysses tops off this atrocious action with a brutally glib moral: "from homebred Factions ruine springs," he says; "Publique good was urg'd for private ends, / And those thought Patriots, who disturb'd it most" (13:353). The deeper moral conveyed here is that of *All for Love:* the betrayal not just of Troilus's faith but of heroic loyalty. The *political nation* has somehow let the poet down, but rather than directly criticize king or nobility, he blames the fickle crowd. That tack is not only bad moral science, it is politically a dead end. Wallace, in his essay on Dryden's conception of a heroic society, argues that an aristocratic society needs trust so that it may freely reciprocate benefits. Wallace neglects to observe, however, that this heroic (or stoic) ideal cannot subsist without trust in the common people, who, Machiavelli warns us, are the sole basis for a relatively stable polity. These "vulgar slaves," as Troilus calls them, are the natural custodians of the "publique good," and that is why Ulysses' moral rings hollow and why Dryden's moral science is even less compelling than Shakespeare's.

By the middle of 1679, Dryden realized that the people were a significant element of the political nation, but he no longer shared with them a common good as their public poet. Yet he still kept aloof from partisanship, in spite of his overture to Danby, now in the Tower. Dryden permitted himself to satirize Buckingham and to lampoon Shadwell in manuscript; otherwise, he was chary as usual of bringing his private views on stage. But as the nation grew more politicized, Dryden was losing the advantage of his antepartisan restraint. The public poet is defined by his reflexivity: his ability, on all occasions, to locate himself in the mirror of the historical present. The revolution in the political nation raised havoc with Dryden's historical reflexivity. He would have to undergo a corresponding revolution in his private outlook before rediscovering his public role. He had toyed dangerously not only with the characters of his two noble foes but with the image of sovereignty, putting Buckingham on stage as king-mocker and crowning Shadwell as a mock-king. For all his wit, Dryden forgot at last that he, too, was on the public stage—that the laureateship was a historical role.

It was the vox populi that reminded him, at the end of the year, of his political role. With its terrifying and casual impersonality, it singled him out for physical chastisement. Late in the autumn, with all London frantic over the Popish Plot and the question of who would succeed King Charles, the poet was nearly beaten to death by hired thugs. A newspaper account of the beating says it was "thought to have been the effect of private grudge." Gossip immediately blamed the duchess of Portsmouth, the king's French mistress who had been rudely handled in an anonymously circulated satire written not by Dryden, but by his patron Mulgrave. Ward suggested that the Rose Alley attack was politically motivated, and Winn combines Ward's conjecture with a more traditional supposition: "The leaders of the opposition, to whom the Laureate's court and Catholic connections were no secret, can hardly have enjoyed being compared to the 'Rebels' of 'Forty Eight' in his last prologue; having him beaten and blaming that attack on the King's unpopular Catholic mistress would have been an effective and ironic way of killing two birds with one stone." Winn is referring to the prologue spoken at Nahum Tate's play *The Loyal General*, produced in December. Winn quotes part of it:

> The Plays that take on our Corrupted Stage,
> Methinks resemble the distracted Age;
> Noise, Madness, all unreasonable Things,
> That strike at Sense, as Rebels do at Kings!
> The stile of Forty One our Poets write,
> And you are grown to judge like Forty Eight.
>
> (1:163)

Dryden's lines cleverly adapt a historical parallel. He compares the Whigs' demand for an Exclusion Bill to the Grand Remonstrance orchestrated by John Pym in the Long Parliament in 1641. "To judge like Forty Eight" refers to the trial and Regicide of January 1649 (Old Style 1648).[9]

Apt as they are, I don't believe these lines by themselves were likely to outrage Whig sympathizers among the audience. The historical parallel had grown hackneyed with frequent use by L'Estrange and other Tory propagandists. Dryden's prologue is significant for reasons that Winn does not mention, although he is certainly right about the animus the poet's attackers bore him. Until the beating, Dryden evidently had no idea he was offending political foes. Even allowing for Harth's sensible reminder that Dryden's consequent satires are Tory propaganda rather than the outpourings of private scorn, I maintain that the Rose Alley attack caused a total upheaval in Dryden's orientation toward politics and religion and left him ideologically aligned with neither Whigs nor Tories. The beating made him far more anxiously attuned to the voice of the people.

The pageant of the pope-burning on November 17, the anniversary of Queen Elizabeth's coronation, was celebrated this year with unusual fanfare, winding up a feverish three months of civic frenzy. In late August, the king fell seriously ill. James, exiled to Flanders because of the Whigs' attempts to exclude him, rushed back to London in September. Thereupon Shaftesbury's supporters in London took alarm. A leading Whig member for the City, Sir Thomas Player, who had been the first to move in Parliament for "a Bill for excluding the Duke of York by name, and all Papists whatsoever, from the Crown of England," now gave two inflammatory speeches at the Guildhall calling for the doubling of the City guards because of the danger raised by James's presence. In October, a lurid pamphlet called upon Londoners to imagine "the whole town in a flame . . . troops of papists ravishing your wives and your daughters, dashing your little children's brains out against the walls . . . and cutting your own throats, by the name of heretic dogs. . . . Also, casting your eye toward Smithfield, imagine you see your father, or your mother . . . tied to a stake in the midst of flames."[10]

At this juncture Monmouth, whom Charles had sent for a long stay in Holland, unexpectedly returned to London. This was a signal for the Whigs to act. On 7 December, sixteen opposition peers led by Shaftesbury (including the father of young Lord Haughton, to whom Dryden would dedicate *The Spanish Fryar*) presented a petition to Charles as he was coming from chapel, and two days later petition forms were circulated throughout the City, demanding that the king summon Parliament forthwith to exclude from the throne any popish successor. Charles immediately sent for the lord mayor and aldermen and told them to punish the distribution of these "libels," as he called them. These petitions are what Dryden's prologue equates with the Grand Remonstrance to Charles I by the rebellious Parliament of 1641.[11]

The prologue to *The Loyal General* refers to these petitions and more. It opens:

> If yet there be a few that take delight
> In that which reasonable Men should write;
> To them Alone we Dedicate this Night.
> The Rest may satisfie their curious Itch
> With City Gazets or some Factious Speech,
> Or what-ere Libel for the Publick Good,
> Stirs up the Shrove-tide Crew to Fire and Blood!
> Remove your Benches you apostate Pit,
> And take Above, twelve penny-worth of Wit;
> Go back to your dear Dancing on the Rope,
> Or see what's worse the Devil and the Pope!

These lines are a direct insult to Sir Thomas Player and his brethren, the stalwart tribunes of Guildhall. These City Whigs or any of their friends in the audience—such as Player's bullying cohort Sir Thomas Armstrong, who was also Monmouth's chief agent—would feel the vocal barbs keenly owing to the following circumstances, first pointed out by the California editors.

"Factious Speech" is an express censure of Player's address to the mayor in September. A pamphlet was published in the City summarizing Player's two speeches and the lord mayor's reply. This pamphlet drew a sneering Tory response entitled *An Answer to the Excellent and Elegant Speech Made by*

Sir Thomas Player. The author, who signs himself "H.B.," chides Player for his disrespect towards James in "bringing an hundred persons at his heels [to Guildhall]. I must take the boldness to tell him, that it lookt more like a tumultuous number of Apprentices doing execution upon Bawdie-houses, than any solid considerate way of advising good for the Citie or Kingdom."[12]

As the California editors note, here is Dryden's allusion to "the Shrovetide Crew." What they do not quote—although they cite its title in shortened form—is a third pamphlet, entitled *A Vindication of Sir Thomas Player and Those Loyal Citizens Concerned with Him: In a Seasonable Reply to a late Sawcy and Dangerous Pamphlet, pretending to be an Answer to the said Sir Thomas's Speech.* Its author is particularly incensed at H.B.'s simile of carnival rampage. "What resemblance," demands the irate burgher, "had the appearance of so many *Grave Citizens* to an Hubbub of *Prentices:* or a *peaceable* humble Application to their Chief Magistrates, to the *madness* of pulling down *Brothel-houses?* . . . The man sure is afraid his Mother, the *old Whore of Rome,* should receive some prejudice by it."

Such language comes from a mind that, like Player's, bears the impress of apocalyptic Presbyterianism. Player had said that those persons who cast doubt on the plot were "the most dangerous, and had been deservedly styled *PROTESTANTS IN MASQUERADE.*" Player's vindicator takes his epigraph from Donne: "Sir, *By your Priesthood tell us who you are?*" He suggests that H.B. is "some *Ghostly Citizen* of *Rome,* A Papist in *Masquerade,*" whose aim is to "*Lull* us asleep in supposed Security, till these Popish *Butchers* may gain an opportunity to Erect their old Parisian *Shambles* in our *London* streets." H.B., he goes on, has written "a scurrilous *Libel* (for 'tis no less in Effect upon the *whole City*). . . . But what pretence is there for this *scandal?* Is every *large Assembly* a Tumult? in good time he'l call our Parliaments *Routs,* our Courts of Judicature, shall be Indicted for *Riots,* and my Lord Mayors *Show* stigmatized for a *Conventicle.*"

That is an apt summary of the rhetorical program for *The Medall.* Dryden first invoked these incendiary metaphors in December of 1679, and I think some outraged citizen in the audience learned who the author of the prologue was and had him beaten.

If Dryden never found out who ordered the personal assault, he knew what quarters bred him. In *The Spanish Fryar,* produced a year after the Rose Alley beating and published with its "Protestant" dedication to a Whig peer, Dryden shows an unwonted caution in portraying the City mob. As

McFadden remarks, "A new and surprising development, most worthy of comment, is the respect Dryden begins to show for the power of the London mob." McFadden quotes Raymond's speech urging Queen Leonora to rely on her city trainbands:

> You do not know the Virtues of your City,
> What pushing force they have; some popular Chief,
> More noisie than the rest, but cries Halloo,
> And in a trice the bellowing Herd come out;
> The Gates are barr'd, the Ways are barricado'd,
> And *One and All*'s the Word; true Cocks o'th' Game,
> That never ask for what, or whom, they fight;
> But turn 'em out, and show 'em but a Foe,
> Cry *Liberty*, and that's a Cause of Quarrel.   (14:172)

"London's passion for liberty is shared by Dryden," comments McFadden. "It may be surprising in one so devoted to a hereditary monarchy, but it is true nevertheless that liberty is Dryden's highest political value." That may be so. I see no evidence, though, that Dryden—here or anywhere else in his works—resolved the problem of freedom into a Machiavellian trust in the *popolo* or in the City's "passion for liberty." On the contrary, Raymond's ambivalent speech suggests rather that its author had become, at the end of 1680, a Protestant in masquerade.[13]

FALSE PROPHETS AND THE VOX DEI

Mob outrage levels its victims, as *The Medall* stresses repeatedly: "Almighty Crowd, thou shorten'st all dispute, / Pow'r is thy Essence; Wit thy Attribute! / Nor Faith nor Reason make thee at a stay" (2:45). Dryden's "Satyre against Sedition," written a little more than two years after the Rose Alley assault, adopts a Tory style that Harth calls the "rhetoric of outrage." Nonetheless, in the declamatory *ethos* of the public poet it is easy to detect private anger. Dryden cannot forget the wild injustice of the faceless mob who beat him. He had dedicated *Annus Mirabilis* to the City, but his plays ignored the crowd for ten years down through *All for Love*. Compared with Marvell's *Account of the Growth of Popery*, which also appeared at the end of 1677, the one play that Dryden "writ for my self" seemed agoraphobic. Each of the next five autumns yielded a traumatic event that sank deeper into his imagination than the pope-burnings that he ridiculed in his prologues. He first alluded to those in the epilogue to *Oedipus,* just before the cataclysm of the Plot and Danby's fall. The Rose Alley attack of 1679 was followed precisely a year later by the execution of the Catholic Lord Stafford, cousin to Dryden's wife. *Absalom and Achitophel* coincided with Shaftesbury's trial late in November 1681, and a year after that came *The Duke of Guise,* Dryden's and Lee's sensational indictment of the Whig Association.[14]

Dryden spent much of this five-year period revolving its events in his memory and seeking the right historical perspective for their providential mimesis. He found a parallel with the treasonable Whig Association in the Guisard *ligue,* and he translated Maimbourg's *History of the League* in 1684. In his postscript to that work, he decides that the critical moment for Shaftesbury was the two years 1679 and 1680, "when the City had taken the alarm of a Popish Plot, and the Government of it was in Fanatique hands, when a Body of [Monmouth's supporters] was already appearing in the West . . . then was the time to have push'd his business: But Almighty God, who had otherwise dispos'd of the Event, infatuated his Counsels, and made him slip his opportunity" (18:414). These pious reflections on divine providence fall short of the historical reflexivity he had achieved in *Absalom and Achitophel,* but they are enough to send the reader back to the scene of Dryden's encounter with the vox populi. In the two years between *Oedipus* and *The Spanish Fryar,* he rediscovered the providential mimesis that informs his great satires and inspires his sometimes prophetic irony.

The disgruntled poet of *Troilus and Cressida* lacked a truly public, satirical purpose. His uncertainty vanished after he was assaulted for his prologue to *The Loyal General.* From 1680, Dryden's writings recover their Boethian focus on the *saeculum,* and his moral science takes on a new edge of irony. Whenever he refers to the *crowds* in a poem addressed to the public, his reflexivity can be very complex. Contrast for instance Thersites' naive epilogue (13:355) yoking persecuted Levellers and papists with the prologue Dryden addresses to a civilized Oxford audience the next summer after his beating:

> But 'tis the Talent of our *English* Nation,
> Still to be Plotting some New Reformation:
> And few years hence, if Anarchy goes on,
> *Jack Presbyter* shall here Erect his Throne,
> Knock out a Tub with Preaching once a day,

And every Prayer be longer than a Play.
Then all you Heathen Wits shall go to Pot,
For disbelieving of a Popish Plot.   (1:160)

Four years earlier, he had hoped for a post at the same university among its "last, Provincial Band" (1:156). Now he warns them that their academic retreat cannot secure cryptopapists from the zeal of Guildhall's Presbyterians, who would maul scholars of Aquinas as gladly as "Pope *Joan*."

These allusions from the summer of 1680 tell us that the poet has acquired a skeptical view of the Reformation from his doctrinal studies traced above in chapter 3. By reviewing the development of the religious polity, he was historicizing the connection, long axiomatic for Anglican Cavaliers, between republicanism and dissent. About two months after the Rose Alley attack, Tonson published some translations of Ovid made earlier. Besides the Oxford prologue, Dryden's only work datable to 1680 is *The Spanish Fryar*, which premièred in the fall. This play alone is enough to demonstrate a decisive change in his conception of himself as public poet. To advertise his Protestantism, he offers a comic plot traducing Friar Dominic, while the serious plot—Dryden's most original variation on *A King and No King*—has been crafted to exploit London's preoccupation with the Exclusion debate, now coming to a head. Dryden leaves no handle for his enemies to wrest the play's meaning to their own use. For example, he makes a regicide of the queen, who is in love with Torrismond, the hero whom we are never quite allowed to identify with Monmouth. Ignorant that he is himself the true heir, Torrismond tells the queen, "You are so beautifull, / So wondrous fair, you justifie Rebellion." And he reaffirms this private delusion in the face of Raymond's public demand for justice (14:155, 189f.).

Dryden preempts any partisan moral by falling back on the radically Puritan position that the confusion over monarchical legitimacy in the play is a nation's punishment for regicide, as in *Oedipus*. "Blood shall never leave the Nation more!" cries Torrismond, echoing the juvenile despair of the Hastings elegy. In the play, the regicide is averted, and our misgivings prove tragicomic. Yet the author's private doubts of the monarch's authority are real enough. Having commanded the regicide, Queen Leonora finds that her sovereignty is more drastically undermined by guilt than by love. Dryden gives the audience even less ground for identifying the wavering Leonora with Charles than he did in the case of the Maiden Queen. Confident that his complaint will safely go unheeded by the king, Dryden utters a grievance he had nurtured for two years. When Bertran reports that he has executed the imprisoned king, the queen disowns the deed:

> *Bert.* If Princes not protect their Ministers,
> What man will dare to serve them?
> *Queen.*   None will dare
> To serve them ill, when they are left to Laws;
> But when a Counsellor, to save himself,
> Would lay Miscarriages upon his Prince,
> Exposing him to publick Rage and Hate;
> O, 'tis an Act as infamously base . . .
> It shews he onely serv'd himself before.   (14:170)

McFadden hears a reference to Danby here and surmises that the lord treasurer's having countenanced the Plot "might have lost him Dryden's approval." He mistakes the actual reference. The "Counsellor" who "serv'd himself" by exposing Charles was Ralph Montagu, the self-seeking companion of Monmouth whom not even Shaftesbury and the opposition could trust.[15]

Dryden betrays his deepest private involvement in the play when Torrismond, not knowing the imprisoned king is his father, describes the old man in a dungeon like the Tower,

> Bound in with Darkness, over-spread with Damps:
> Where I have seen (if I cou'd say, I saw)
> The good old King majestick in his Bonds,
> And 'midst his Griefs most venerably great:
> By a dim winking Lamp, which feebly broke
> The gloomy Vapors, he lay stretch'd along
> Upon the unwholesom Earth; his Eyes fix'd upward:
> And ever and anon a silent Tear
> Stole down and trickl'd from his hoary Beard.   (14:154)

The indeterminate, Bayesian pathos of this speech creates once again the subjective decorum analyzed previously (chapter 6). The play's overtly heroic theme is the *pietas* that keeps Torrismond loyal both to the succession and to his father. Here, however, the hero is made the unsuspected vehicle for the sorrow of old Lord Stafford, who lay in prison waiting to become the next victim of the Plot. The hero's *pietas* has a private meaning that goes beyond dramatic irony. The public poet induces the unfeeling audience to share his personal grief for the "poor Lord Stafford" whom they are about to martyr (14:323). Dryden's providential mimesis here approaches the satire of a prophet.[16]

The playwright's vigorous, Boethian irony gives *The Spanish Fryar* the look of a political puzzle. Instead of showing the Whigs bent on Exclusion, Dryden presents them loyal to succession. When Torrismond, the legitimate heir, is restored to the crown, he promptly subverts it by refusing to let justice take its course upon his regicidal queen. Against this failure to uphold the law, Raymond harnesses the force of the people for an end that is unimpeachably loyalist. "How darst thou serve thy King against his Will?" Torrismond demands. Raymond's answer epitomizes for a century to come the dispute between Whigs and Tories: "Because 'tis then the onely time to serve him." Torrismond calls in the troops, but the vox populi has the better of the argument; it is not hard to imagine the audience's thrill at hearing the exasperated hero denounce Raymond as "Thou stubborn loyal Man." The loyal rebel even brings in the stock republican metaphor from the *Vindiciae contra tyrannos* of "a Ship tost in a Tempest / Without the Pilot's Care" (14: 188; see chapter 2). Although meant as a gesture of monarchist populism, Raymond's civil disobedience veers dangerously close to the unvarnished republicanism of Achitophel: "When shoud People strive their Bonds to break, / If not when Kings are Negligent or Weak?" (lines 387–88).

It would not be too paradoxical to claim that *The Spanish Fryar* succeeded by virtue of its satire on politics per se: Dryden flatters Whig loyalism even as he mocks its republican basis. A century later, Johnson praised the play's "happy coincidence and coalition of the two plots" and said its first popularity as well as "the real power both of the serious and risible part" had kept it "long a favourite of the publick." I suspect that the play appealed to its original audience by reassuring them about the Exclusion crisis, and that after the Revolution it afforded new audiences—apart from Queen Mary, who was pained by it—a chance to look back on the dangers they had passed. *The Spanish Fryar* does what most satire aims to accomplish: it brands the enemy while cheering the faithful. Dryden plied his moral science to great effect. He identified the crowd and their undoubtedly sincere professions of loyalty with the vox Dei.[17]

Dryden's providential mimesis is equally lucid in his celebrated poem

written a year later. *Absalom and Achitophel* often leaves its reader at a loss to
sort out the history from the satire. In his portrait of Jotham, the poet recalls
a turning point of the Exclusion crisis and seems to be giving credit for an
act of loyalty. Halifax, whom James distrusted as a leader of the opposition,
had surprised the government by speaking forcefully against the Exclusion
Bill. Dryden appears to praise Halifax's conversion from republicanism:

> *Jotham* of piercing wit and pregnant thought,
> Indew'd by nature, and by learning taught
> To move Assemblies, who but onely try'd
> The worse awhile, then chose the better side;
> Nor chose alone, but turn'd the balance too;
> So much the weight of one brave man can doe.
>
> (lines 882–87)

The allusion is to Judges 8 and 9. Jotham was the son of Gideon, the heroic
judge who refused the crown in words that have rung ever since in the ears
of antimonarchists: "I will not rùle over you, neither shall my son rule over
you: the Lord [Yahweh] shall rule over you" (8:23; see above, chapter 2).
Gideon's son Abimelech seeks to become king and kills all his brothers except the youngest. Jotham escapes to the top of Mount Gerizim, whence he
denounces the fratricide and warns Abimelech's followers against choosing
him or any other man as their king. Jotham's parable (9:7–20) of the bramble
that accepts the crown after the nobler trees all refuse it is justly thought one
of the cleverest satires ever spoken against monarchy. By naming Halifax
Jotham, Dryden slyly records the republican views that would earn Halifax
the title of Trimmer.[18]

Dryden's political vision in *The Spanish Fryar* matches the ironical detachment of his narrative poems of 1681–82, which give an account of the
saeculum from a Boethian standpoint. Like the play, *Absalom and Achitophel*
is an allegory by means of which the public poet makes a radical criticism
of the monarchy he seems to uphold. Providential mimesis slides easily into
satire. It finds its materials indifferently in written or actual history and in
politics or the Bible. Montagu ruined Danby and the king's government in
1678, but Dryden waited two years to stigmatize him as Bertran. As the literal event of 1678 further unfolded its meaning, the self-serving counselor
was transformed into one of the Whig "Lords, below the Dignity of Verse":

Wits, warriors, Common-wealthsmen, were the best:
Kind Husbands and meer Nobles all the rest.
And, therefore in the name of Dullness, be
The well hung *Balaam* and cold *Caleb* free.   (lines 570–74)

The hitherto unexplained allusion to Balaam is easily understood in the light of Dryden's providential mimesis of a specific event. The story of Balaam, the prophet who was hired to curse Israel (Numbers 22–24), tallied perfectly with the blasting of Danby in the House of Commons in 1678. Unlike his biblical prototype, Ralph Montagu, the opportunistic, notoriously philandering ambassador to France, did his job only too well.[19]

Among the events of these two years of madness, Dryden was unlikely to forget his own suffering at the hands of Guildhall thugs. We heard Raymond's ambiguous description of a loyalist Protestant mob. That mob of City Presbyterians reappears in *The Medall* as the willful, "Almighty Crowd" whose consciousness ("Wit") is a mere attribute of its power. Yet Dryden from his youth had been imbued with the Calvinistic teaching that the voice of the people must be heeded as the vox Dei. His beating by a distracted mob certainly did not make it easier for him to know when God was speaking through the vox populi. The only handle by which this mob could be controlled was its *interest.* Shaftesbury's keen appreciation of that fact is underscored in *The Medall:* he "Maintains the Multitude can never err; / And sets the People in the Papal Chair. / The reason's obvious; *Int'rest* never lyes" (lines 186–88). That "Crowds err not" over the long run is also the key postulate of republicanism. Machiavelli holds that the citizens alone can safeguard the prudence of a republic; princes and nobles will fall slaves either to passion or ambition. If Machiavelli is right, then the interest of the people—its prudence—is the same as the providence of the vox Dei, which is what Raymond maintains in *The Spanish Fryar.* To set the people in the papal chair is to acclaim the vox populi for an infallible prophet.

Achitophel is another Raymond, without the sentimental loyalism that suffuses everybody in *The Spanish Fryar* except the titular rogue. Achitophel seeks to put Absalom on the throne, not to dismantle it. When he designed *Absalom and Achitophel,* Dryden felt no personal animus against Shaftesbury and evidently needed prompting from the king to darken his portrait of him. In 1680, he probably considered the earl an overzealous patriot but not necessarily a religious hypocrite or self-serving Balaam (Montagu was loathed by James, who put the highest premium on loyalty). Left to his own devices, the poet might have bade Shaftesbury to "Curb your ill manner'd Zeal," denouncing him in Torrismond's vein: "Hear this thou Tribune of the People: / Thou zealous, publick Bloud-hound" (14:192f.).[20]

Only in 1682 does the Cavalier idiom with its "rhetoric of outrage" overtake Dryden's opinion of Shaftesbury. In *The Medall*, the earl has become something worse than a treacherous vassal whose ambitions compass the throne. He still "preaches to the Crowd, that Pow'r is lent," but never relinquished, to monarchs (line 82). Beneath this republican doctrine, however, the public poet now finds a more serious problem of freedom, as he explains:

> Too happy *England*, if our good we knew,
> Wou'd we possess the freedom we pursue?
> The lavish Government can give no more:
> Yet we repine; and plenty makes us poor.
> God try'd us once; our Rebel-fathers fought,
> He glutted 'em with all the pow'r they sought:
> Till, master'd by their own usurping Brave,
> The free-born Subject sunk into a Slave.
> We loath our Manna, and we long for Quails;
> Ah what is man, when his own wish prevails!
>
> (lines 123–32)

The allusion in line 126 to Ovid ("inopem me copia fecit") equates the pursuit of freedom with the vain rapture of Narcissus; otherwise, the poet's thoughts recur to the collapse of the Commonwealth and to Exodus. Dryden is no longer thinking of David, but of Israel before the monarchy (compare the "Epistle" with its allusion to the Israel of Judges). This regression to Israel murmuring against the leadership of Moses is a sign that the poet may be calling the providence of the Stuart Restoration in question, if not God's care of the English throne itself. Any sustained reference to Moses and the Exodus in political discussion tended to destabilize a settled monarchy.[21]

The Medall is more direct in applying the Cavalier axiom: Shaftesbury heads a faction that hypocritically exploits religious zeal. In *Absalom and Achitophel*, however, as in Exodus and Numbers, political faction is not the cause of revolution. The worst rebellions originate in the collective spirit of the people. As a political strategist, Achitophel was ready to stir up that spirit and steal the crown (see 2 Samuel). While following the biblical narrative, Dryden constantly alludes to *premonarchical* Israel and to the catastrophic revolution that befell the nation before Samuel made the first king. The poet goes back to Israel of the Exodus and to the rebellion led by Korah against Moses and God.

Fundamental rebellion in the religious polity is of course Dryden's oldest concern, and his fears were not to be allayed by adopting the Cavalier axiom or even by taking part in the Tory revenge from 1681 to 1685. Until the preface to *Religio Laici*, he seems not to have realized "that the Doctrines of King-killing and Deposing" originated with "the worst Party of the Papists" (2:108; see chapter 3). Jesuits like Robert Bellarmine and Juan de Mariana grounded the right of tyrannicide firmly on the principle that the vox Dei speaks through the vox populi. In *The Spanish Fryar*, Dominic offers to accuse a husband of regicide in order to free the wife for her lover. "He has rail'd against the Church, which is a fouler Crime than the murther of a Thousand Kings," Dominic reasons. "He that is an Enemie to Heaven, wou'd have kill'd the King, if he had been in the Circumstances of doing it; so it is not wrongfull to accuse him" (14:162). To a modern reader, this malicious nonsense seems remote from fundamental issues of religious polity and spiritual rebellion. But Dryden knows his audience, and he knows the *crowd*. Their zeal made them sensible of the least skepticism about the Plot. Having suffered as a cryptopapist for jeering at this zeal, Dryden now follows a safer tack and ridicules its object instead.

The bulk of Dryden's City audience missed the connection, as he trusted they would. He lets Dominic steal the argument that Titus Oates invoked to hang his innocent victims. Inventing a rogue friar to mask a direct criticism of Oates, the former seminarian, was a stroke of genius: it shows how nicely Dryden had learned to calibrate his dialogue to suit the temper of his City audience in the ten months since he had rashly lampooned them. In a play in which even the villainous Bertran proves loyal, Dryden makes a scapegoat of the friar. It was his lone sally into pope-burning, a piece of dramatic irony that hoodwinked both the City Presbyterians and their noble sponsors to whom the play is dedicated.[22]

No one had to tell Dryden, in 1680, that belittling the Plot and its chief witness was a risky thing to do. A skeptical cryptopapist was the nation's foe, as Dryden would note a year later: "Let *Israel*'s foes suspect his [Corah's] heav'nly call, / And rashly judge his writ Apocryphal; / Our Laws for such affronts have forfeits made" (lines 664–66). Earlier in the poem the author goes into the matter of the Plot's credibility:

> Succeeding times did equal folly call,
> Believing nothing, or believing all.
> Some thought they God's Anointed meant to Slay
> By Guns, invented since full many a day:
> Our Author swears it not; but who can know
> How far the Devil and *Jebusites* may go?   (lines 128–33)

"Our Author swears it not": his demurrer echoes Sidney's famous apology for the poet accused of lying ("he nothing affirms"). The public poet of *Absalom and Achitophel* claims to affirm nothing, yet he fully intends his providential mimesis to expose false prophets.[23]

Dryden did not dare call Oates a liar until the end of 1681, when the king appeared to have saved the nation. By then, Stafford had been executed on evidence given by the now-discredited Archwitness, who had been turned out of Whitehall but had safely ensconced himself among the City Presbyterians. Dryden reflects on the bitter irony: the martyr, Stafford, witnessed to the truth with his blood, whereas the hypocrite whose false testimony belied Stafford now enjoys the reputation of a saint with all the comforts of the City. Dryden plays on the literal meaning of *martyr* (witness). Oates is called "This Arch-Attestor for the Publick Good." He is self-made, or self-erecting, a phallic serpent who boasts the power of averting the Jesuit plague visited on Israel; thus he is another false Moses (as Aaron's brazen serpent was a simulacrum of the crucified Christ). He is a comet but titanic and earth-born, capable of "Prodigious Actions," and at the same time a humble priest or Levite by trade, one of "Godalmighty's Gentlemen." Worst of all, though, Oates is a false *witness:* "Who ever ask'd the Witnesses high race, / Whose Oath with Martyrdom did *Stephen* grace?" The true witness seals with blood his testimony to that very Kingdom of God that the false martyr defiles. The first Christian martyr, Stephen, was stoned to death; the witness for "the Publick Good" gains a coat of arms for his family. The true martyr is slandered by the false, whose subsequent prosecution for slander is a ghastly mockery of heroic martyrdom, just as the biblical Korah perished in an unclean cause. The deluded nation stands "secure beneath [the] shade" of Oates, a bastard *pater patriae* who "By that one Deed Enobles all his Bloud" (633–49).[24]

For nearly two years, Oates enjoyed the stature of a Savonarola, backed by the zeal of the City against which Dryden rails in *The Medall*. For a terrifying interval, Corah swayed people's imaginations like "the pregnant enemy," as Shakespeare calls our archdeceiver. In its providential mimesis, *Absalom and Achitophel* follows the Exodus narrative, in which Israel was led not by a king but by its greatest prophet. As the historical period of the Exodus brought Israel closer to Yahweh than it would ever be under Saul and David, so the false Moses of Dryden's poem is a more radical type of evil than the false king and his counselor named in the title.

Korah's rivalry with Moses raised him above the other pseudoprophets of the Old Testament. Korah was a member of the nobility from the same Levite tribe as his cousins Moses and Aaron. His rebellion against Israel's divinely inspired leader was the most acute political crisis of the forty-year journey to Canaan. Korah incited the whole tribe to challenge Moses' authority. Dryden's poem reflects in the historical present the biblical encounter between true and false prophecy, thereby making Korah's rebellion an archetype of the problem of freedom. History, no less than the Protestant epic, reminds us that delusions and lies thrive best when God's spirit is abroad. Such was the case in 1679 and 1680, when Oates, endowed with a formidable lying spirit, enjoyed a prophetic ascendancy as satanic then as it now seems comic.

The reign of this false prophet is what Dryden recalled in his retrospect of 1684 (above) when he said the City "was in Fanatique hands." London's government, unstable ever since the Guildhall furor that Dryden imprudently ridiculed in the prologue of 1679, fell into antigovernment hands in July of 1680, when the City elected its new sheriffs, Henry Cornish and Slingsby Bethel. In *Absalom and Achitophel*, the portraits of Shimei (Bethel) and Corah (Oates) are drawn at full length. Their oddly paired figures take up lines 583 to 681, nearly a tenth of the poem. This proportion equals the space allotted to the king himself. Bethel, a sixty-four-year-old merchant holding public office that year for the only time in his life, was a republican throwback who "taught *Jerusalem* to curse" (line 932). That is, he brazenly uttered what no one since the old republicans had dared to say publicly: that prudent citizens owed a duty to the civic order and need not respect kings. Still, this bourgeois blasphemy hardly seems to make Bethel the "Fanatique" double of Oates.

What Dryden has done is to merge Oates and Bethel in the single figure of Samuel, the powerful but vindictive Judge and prophet who defied the selfsame King Saul he had earlier anointed as Israel's first monarch. The poet combines Shimei and Corah into a monstrous simulacrum of earthly injustice that loudly bespeaks Dryden's private rancor. Under Bethel's shrievalty, lying witnesses throve in the City, like the "sons of Belial" (1 Kings 21) who had the innocent Naboth stoned to death: "During his Office, Treason was no Crime; / The Sons of *Belial* had a glorious Time" (597–98). Shimei's temporal injustice leads straight to the spiritual tyranny of Corah, whose description follows. At the end of Corah's portrait, Dryden joins both men in a biblical reference to Agag. Agag was the conquered Amalekite king, spared by Saul only to be delivered up as captive to the overzealous Samuel, who hacked him to death:

> And *Corah* might for *Agag*'s murther call,
> In terms as course as *Samuel* us'd to *Saul*.
>
> (676–77)

Agag is old Lord Stafford, whom the sheriffs Bethel and Cornish executed in December 1680. With a grim brilliance, Dryden has paired Stafford's circumstances and those of Agag, whose last thought when he is led before the angry prophet is "Surely the bitterness of death is past" (1 Samuel 15). Those who query Agag's identification have objected that we cannot equate Oates with Samuel because Oates never "hewed Agag in pieces before the Lord in Gilgal."

Bethel, however, wanted to do just that. The Whig sheriff defied his king as Samuel defied Saul. Robert McHenry describes the situation at the end of 1680, when Bethel and his fellow sheriff "became notorious for their role in the case of Lord Stafford . . . convicted by the House of Lords of treason and sentenced to death. The sheriffs had questioned the King's right to commute Stafford's death sentence (which they were charged with carrying out) from the usual hideous punishment—to be hanged, cut down while still alive, disemboweled, and finally beheaded and quartered—to a mere beheading. Their motives were republican: to question the King's right to alter judgments made by Parliament." Remembering Bethel's public call for the "stoning"—the castrating or drawing that followed the half-hanging—of his wife's aged kinsman exactly a year after the beating he himself suffered as the king's servant, Dryden has conflated Oates and Bethel with the lying spirits whom God in his providence suffers to abuse the nation as false prophets and patriots.[25]

Dryden's providential mimesis in the poem invites a reading of its biblical hermeneutics at odds with his official aim of presenting the king as the nation's savior. England's reign of terror under false prophets is a judgment on what the youthful Dryden called the nation's sin. The frightening glimpse of a deluded "Samuel" who had the power to destroy kings as well as to make them reveals Dryden's misgivings about Stuart rule *jure divino*. Charles no longer seems a ruler after God's own heart. Spiritual license and republican liberty, having infected the public realm, usurp his justice by claiming the warrant both of human law and divine writ. When the king lost his monopoly of justice, the judicial proceedings against Shaftesbury became a primitive trial by combat. The nation's ordeal, as in Shakespeare's histories or the Protestant epic, becomes an appeal to God. And God's judgment, as in every trial prosecuted on the slaughterbench of history, is delivered through the vox populi.

In *Absalom and Achitophel,* that voice makes no reply to the king's triumphant speech. Instead, the laureate closes his narrative with a Tory prophecy: "Once more the Godlike *David* was Restor'd, / And willing Nations knew their Lawfull Lord." As Dryden well knew, however, the narrative that was his source does not stop with monarchy reestablished. Once David has been restored to his throne, 2 Samuel with the ensuing book of Kings resume the deeper rhythm of Exodus and the Deuteronomist redactors. In the ongoing revolution of Israel that Dryden has chosen to reflect in the historical present, after King David has successfully upheld his throne against Absalom's rebellion, new voices are raised foretelling the demise of monarchy (2 Samuel 20): "We have no part in David, neither have we inheritance in the son of Jesse: every man to his tents, O Israel!" The author officially proclaims a restoration, but in his providential mimesis we can read a prophecy of revolution.

Notes

Abbreviations

Complete Prose: The Complete Prose Works of John Milton, ed. Douglas Bush et al., 8 vols. (New Haven: Yale University Press, 1953–82).

Gibbs: *Sir William Davenant: The Shorter Poems, and Songs from the Plays and Masques,* ed. A. M. Gibbs (Oxford: Clarendon Press, 1972).

Hirst: Derek Hirst, " 'That Sober Liberty': Marvell's Cromwell in 1654," in John Wallace, ed., *The Golden & the Brazen World: Papers in Literature and History, 1650–1800* (Berkeley: University of California Press, 1985), 17–53.

Hughes: Derek Hughes, *Dryden's Heroic Plays* (Lincoln: University of Nebraska Press, 1981).

Kenyon: *The Stuart Constitution: Documents and Commentary,* ed. J. P. Kenyon (Cambridge: Cambridge University Press, 1966).

Leviathan: Hobbes, *Leviathan,* ed. Richard Tuck (Cambridge: Cambridge University Press, 1991).

McFadden: George McFadden, *Dryden: The Public Writer 1660–1685* (Princeton: Princeton University Press, 1978).

McKeon: Michael McKeon, *Politics and Poetry in Restoration England* (Cambridge: Harvard University Press, 1975).

Margoliouth: *The Poems and Letters of Andrew Marvell,* ed. H. M. Margoliouth, 3d ed. rev. by Pierre Legouis with E. E. Duncan-Jones, 2 vols. (Oxford: Clarendon Press, 1971).

Pen for a Party: Phillip Harth, *Pen for a Party* (Princeton: Princeton University Press, 1993).

Pocock: J. G. A. Pocock, *The Machiavellian Moment: Florentine Political Thought and the Atlantic Republican Tradition* (Princeton: Princeton University Press, 1975).

Spingarn: J. E. Spingarn, ed., *Critical Essays of the Seventeenth Century*, 3 vols. (rpt. Bloomington: Indiana University Press, 1963).

Underdown: David Underdown, *Pride's Purge: Politics in the Puritan Revolution* (Oxford: Clarendon Press, 1971).

Wallace: John Wallace, *Destiny His Choice: The Loyalism of Andrew Marvell* (Cambridge: Cambridge University Press, 1968).

Winn: James Winn, *John Dryden and His World* (New Haven: Yale University Press, 1987).

Works: *The Works of John Dryden*, ed. Edward Niles Hooker, H. T. Swedenberg, et al. (Berkeley: University of California Press, 1956–).

Introduction

1. Samuel Johnson, "Life of Dryden," in *Lives of the English Poets*, ed. George Birkbeck Hill, 3 vols. (rpt. New York: Octagon Books, 1967), 1:400. The journal *Representations* has been a chief organ of the new literary history that seeks an alternative to mimetic historiography.

2. *Works* 13:125. In my text, parenthetical citations of this edition refer to the volume number followed by a colon and the page number.

3. *Oratio de dignitate hominis*, tr. Elizabeth Livermore Forbes, in *The Renaissance Philosophy of Man*, ed. Ernst Cassirer, P. O. Kristeller, and J. H. Randall, Jr. (Chicago: University of Chicago Press, 1948), 224–25.

4. Quoted from H. R. Trevor-Roper, *Religion, Reformation, and Social Change* (London: Macmillan, 1967), 223. Following Voltaire and Gibbon, Trevor-Roper labels the three periods of enlightenment "the age of Erasmus, the age of Bacon and the age of Newton" (200).

5. The phrase "radical Protestantism" is quoted by Trevor-Roper, 194, from Christopher Hill. For Dryden's description of his grandfather, see "To My Honour'd Kinsman, John Driden of Chesterton," lines 193–94 (*The Poems and Fables of John Dryden*, ed. James Kinsley [Oxford: Oxford University Press, 1962], 610).

6. Paul Hammond, *John Dryden: A Literary Life* (New York: St. Martin's Press, 1991), 1.

7. *The Works of John Dryden*, 18 vols. (London, 1808), 1:428, 2, xviii.

8. Thomas Babington Macaulay, *History of England from the Accession of James II* (1848; rpt. Everyman's Library, 1966), 2:28; W. D. Christie, ed., *The Poetical Works of John Dryden* (London, 1870), lix. Christie was also the biographer of the arch-Whig Shaftesbury, Dryden's Achitophel. Other than Scott's multivolume edition (reedited by George Saintsbury between 1882 and 1893), Christie's Globe volume remained the only annotated British edition of Dryden's poetry until the 1950s. George R. Noyes's American edition (Boston: Houghton Mifflin, 1909) relied on Scott's commentary.

9. Bredvold, *The Intellectual Milieu of John Dryden* (1934; rpt. Ann Arbor: University of Michigan Press, 1956), 5, 71. See T. S. Eliot, "John Dryden" (1921; rpt. *Selected Essays of T. S. Eliot* [New York: Harcourt, Brace & World, 1932]); Mark

Van Doren, *The Poetry of John Dryden* (1920; rpt. Bloomington: Indiana University Press, 1960).

10. Bredvold, *Intellectual Milieu*, 134, 150–51; Keith Feiling, *A History of the Tory Party, 1640–1714* (Oxford: Oxford University Press, 1924).

11. Hugh Macdonald, *John Dryden: A Bibliography of Early Editions and of Drydeniana* (Oxford, 1939; rpt. London: Dawsons of Pall Mall, 1966); James M. Osborn, *John Dryden: Some Biographical Facts and Problems*, rev. ed. (Gainesville: University of Florida Press, 1965); Charles Ward, ed., *The Letters of John Dryden* (Durham: Duke University Press, 1942); and Ward's *Life of John Dryden* (Chapel Hill: University of North Carolina Press, 1961).

12. James Kinsley, ed., *The Poems of John Dryden*, 4 vols. (Oxford: Oxford University Press, 1958); A. Alvarez, "The Public Poet," *New Statesman* 57 (3 January 1959): 18–19.

13. Hamilton, *John Dryden and the Poetry of Statement* (University of Queensland Press, 1967; American edition, East Lansing: Michigan State University Press, 1969), vi, viii.

14. Philip Harth, *Contexts of Dryden's Thought* (Chicago: University of Chicago Press, 1968); Earl Miner, *Dryden's Poetry* (Bloomington: Indiana University Press, 1967); Paul Ramsay, Jr., *The Art of John Dryden* (Lexington: University of Kentucky Press, 1969). Miner's book remains the most ambitious reading since Van Doren of Dryden's various corpus and is as much concerned with the content of the poet's ideas as with the shape he gives them.

15. Bernard N. Schilling, *Dryden and the Conservative Myth: A Reading of Absalom and Achitophel* (New Haven: Yale University Press, 1961), 5, 8–9; Miner, *Dryden's Poetry*, 4, xiv, 12. See Hannah Arendt, *The Human Condition* (Chicago: University of Chicago Press, 1958), part 2.

16. Alan Roper, *Dryden's Poetic Kingdoms* (Princeton: Princeton University Press, 1965), 1–14, 28, 189.

17. L. C. Knights, *Public Voices: Literature and Politics, with Special Reference to the Seventeenth Century*, The Clark Lectures for 1970–71 (London: Chatto & Windus, 1971), 98–101, 15; italics Knights's. A concern for the politics of language runs throughout midcentury liberalism, of which another trait is the appeal to moralized, partisan history reminiscent of Macaulay's Whiggery. See below, chap. 2

18. Steven N. Zwicker, *Dryden's Political Poetry: The Typology of King and Nation* (Providence: Brown University Press, 1972), 120. For Saintsbury, see above, n. 8.

19. William Myers, *Dryden* (London: Hutchinson University Library, 1973), 9, 94, 124. This distinctive book sets forth the tensions in Dryden's view of the Augustinian *saeculum* of time and nature (in other words, secular history).

20. Hayden White, *Metahistory: The Historical Imagination in Nineteenth-Century Europe* (Baltimore: Johns Hopkins University Press, 1973), xii. For a succinct account of the Kantian underpinnings of modernism and of Kant's equation between history and prudence, see Stanley Rosen, *Hermeneutics as Politics* (New York: Oxford University Press, 1987), 19–49. Because Kant understood quite well "the now-fashionable

thesis of the link between scientific rationalism and [political] domination," Rosen
argues, "the distinction between postmodernism and modernism is absurd" (3, 17).
21. McKeon, 1–2.
22. Ibid., 12–17, 33–38.
23. Ibid., 13, 40, 271–74.
24. Besides McFadden and Winn, see Ward, *Life*, vii. In calling attention to a
political reflexivity that these scholars ignore, I do not mean to slight their illumina-
tion of Dryden's irony and self-criticism. Their most positive conjectures, however,
bear upon Dryden's unconscious motives rather than his political and historical self-
definition.
25. McKeon, 17, 31.
26. McFadden, 13, 88, 171–72.
27. McFadden, 263 and chap. 6; Winn, 272–84, 345–63.
28. McFadden, 101; Winn, 218.
29. Hammond, *John Dryden*, ix–x, 130.

Chapter 1. Praise and Deliberation under the Republic

1. McKeon, 17. The concept of an ideology, if it is to mean anything more than
a primitive suspicion of those whose thought seems alien, needs to be limited to error
attributable to social causes. Ideologies cannot exist until distinct social classes have
emerged, each with its own *interest* rivaling the good of society as a whole. Dryden's
contemporaries had at best a rudimentary notion of class interest and social causality;
Dryden himself associates "interest" with individuals and fails to comprehend the
economic theory, for example, of his railing Shimei (Slingsby Bethel, who wrote about
the mercantile interest). Karl Mannheim's work is still the best historical account of
the advent of ideologies; see *Ideology and Utopia*, tr. Louis Wirth and Edward Shils
(New York: Harcourt, Brace & World, 1936), 59–83.
2. The fragment from Cato's lost discussion of rhetoric is quoted in the Elder
Seneca's *Controversiae* 1, par. 9. See George Kennedy, *The Art of Rhetoric in the
Roman World* (Princeton: Princeton University Press, 1972), 55–57. See also book 2
of Aristotle's *Rhetoric*: chapter 1 deals with the speaker's own character, and chapters
2–11 with the several emotions (*pathē*) aroused in the audience; and then, in chapters
12–17, Aristotle shifts to the characters (*ēthē*) of those who make up the audience —
their age, wealth, experience, interests. Consequently, ethos is closely bound up with
pathos, and an orator skilled in reading the ethos of his audience can employ the ethical argument to good effect.
3. Sir Philip Sidney, *An Apology for Poetry*, ed. Geoffrey Shepherd (Manchester:
Manchester University Press, 1973), 100; Thomas Hobbes, *Answer to Davenant's Preface to Gondibert*, in Spingarn, 2:60. For Kant's view of the primacy of the imagination
in transforming the world through culture, see his remarks in the introduction to his
third critique as well as its closing sections (pars. 83 and 84) on teleological judgment

(*Critique of Judgment*, tr. J. H. Bernard [rpt. New York: Hafner Press, 1951], 12, 279–86).

4. Hans Blumenberg, *The Legitimacy of the Modern Age*, tr. R. M. Wallace (Cambridge: MIT Press, 1983), 97. Blumenberg's radical thesis is that modernism is not just a rebellion against tradition but legitimate in its own right: its legitimacy consists, paradoxically, in its rejection of traditional authority in favor of an authority that comes from recognizing its own, problematic contingency: "The modern age does not have recourse to what went before it, so much as it opposes and takes a stand against the challenge constituted by what went before it" (75). Rosen notes that Blumenberg's "legitimation of modernity is compatible with the subsequent claim of postmodernity to an analogous spontaneity" (*Hermeneutics as Politics*, 48–49).

5. Aristotle, *Nicomachean Ethics*, 1177b, in *The Basic Works of Aristotle*, tr. Richard D. McKeon (New York: Random House, 1941), 1105; Arendt, *The Human Condition*, 56–57.

6. On the ideal decorum of panegyric, see James Kinsley's article, "Dryden and the Art of Praise," *English Studies* 34 (1953): 57–64; and especially James Garrison, *Dryden and the Tradition of Panegyric* (Berkeley: University of California Press, 1975).

7. On the *kairos* moment, see John E. Smith, "Time, Times, and the 'Right Time'; *Chronos* and *Kairos*," *Monist* 53, no. 1 (1969): 1–13. Smith distinguishes three senses of *kairos* which shade into one another. *Chronos* is by contrast mere duration—uniform and quantifiable time. For Hotspur's *sententia* on the nettle of safety, see the opening of *1 Henry IV*, II, iii . All of my Shakespearean quotations and allusions follow the text in *The Riverside Shakespeare*, ed. G. B. Evans et al. (Boston: Houghton Mifflin, 1974).

8. Of Marvell's three poems on Cromwell, only *The First Anniversary* was printed during Marvell's lifetime—anonymously, in a quarto of 1655. His echoes of it in his Restoration poems suggest that Dryden, as an employee in Cromwell's government, had access to *An Horatian Ode*. For Waller's *Panegyric to my Lord Protector* (c. 1653), see *The Poems of Edmund Waller*, ed. G. Thorn Drury (rpt. New York: Greenwood Press, 1968), 143, 145.

9. See Douglas Bush, *English Literature in the Earlier Seventeenth Century, 1600–1660*, rev. ed., Oxford History of English Literature (Oxford: Clarendon Press, 1962), 169. Cromwell's letter referring to the battle of Dunbar (3 September) is quoted in Christopher Hill, *God's Englishman: Oliver Cromwell and the English Revolution* (rpt. Harmondsworth: Penguin Books, 1972), 133. I follow Wallace's interpretation of *An Horatian Ode* as a deliberative work. See Wallace, 94–105, for the pamphlet debate on the "just war" against Scotland—an issue that caused the Presbyterian Fairfax to resign as Parliament's general—and for the subsequent attacks on Cromwell as a dictatorial threat to the republic. The prudential maxim closing the poem, Wallace shows, had "attached itself naturally to a usurper" ever since Velleius Paterculus.

10. See "Tom May's Death" 43–46, 67–70 (Margoliouth, 1:95). May had early declared his allegiance to Parliament and had written a *Breviary of the History of Par-*

liament. See Gerard Reedy, " 'An Horatian Ode' and 'Tom May's Death,' " *Studies in English Literature* 20 (1980): 137–51.

11. Lucan, *The Civil War,* tr. J. D. Duff, Loeb Classical Library (1962), 19–23; Wallace, 72–74. Wallace adds, "Marvell might be, like Lucan, the laureate of a madman he detested as the disturber of the peace, but on the other hand he is also writing an ode, the normal vehicle of praise for victorious generals." If Marvell is invoking Horace—as well as Lucan—reflexively, he no doubt considered Horace's stylized account of his own callow service at Philippi, when he fled the battlefield in *"celerem fugam" (Carm.,* 2.7). Horace wished to show that he had never been a formidable opponent of Augustus.

12. Strictly speaking, the term *extroversion* is anachronistic because it implies a psychological theory of the individual who is not necessarily a citizen. With Arendt and Hobbes, I assume that the state and its public life precede the autonomous psyche logically as well as historically: the self is always derived from some form of the state.

13. On the background of the doctrine, see William Haller, *The Elect Nation: The Meaning and Relevance of Foxe's "Book of Martyrs"* (New York: Harper & Row, 1963); and, for its seventeenth-century development, William Lamont, *Godly Rule: Politics and Religion, 1603–60* (London: Macmillan, 1969).

14. *Complete Prose* 3:228. Milton's tract brought him a position in the new government as secretary for foreign tongues. *Eikonoklastes* (1649) and the *Defense of the English People* (1651) followed. See n. 18 below on the Engagement; Winn, 61–62, on Dryden's election to Trinity.

15. Addition IID, lines 92–95 of the facsimile in the Riverside edition. Compare *Absalom and Achitophel,* 799–800: "All other Errors but disturb a State; / But Innovation is the Blow of Fate" *(Works* 2:29). *Revolution,* on the other hand, until well after Shakespeare's death, still kept the cyclical sense of restoration and "interchange of state" (sonnet 64).

16. *Complete Prose* 3:209–10. Inasmuch as the commonwealth speaks with the vox Dei, its well-being is our highest good. Milton therefore grounds its preservation in the natural law of self-defense. This law may be invoked by the state as well as by an individual to punish someone who tries to harm it, "seing all kind of justice don, is a defence to good men, as well as a punishment to bad; and justice don upon a Tyrant is no more but the necessary self-defence of a whole Common wealth" (254). Shaftesbury, Locke, and Marvell would later use the identical argument: Whigs opposed the government in the name of the people's self-defense.

17. *The Foundations of Modern Political Thought. Volume 2: The Age of the Reformation* (Cambridge: Cambridge University Press, 1978), 348. See Skinner's pages (340–48) on Buchanan and Mariana, two "monarchomachs" quoted by Cromwell in vindication of regicide. On the secular liberalism of the humanists from which Puritan radicalism derived its political ideas, see my Introduction, above, and the essay by Trevor-Roper quoted there, note 4.

18. For the brief text of the Engagement, see Kenyon, 341. The Engagement of

1650 should be compared with the earlier "solemn league and covenant for reformation" taken by Parliament in September 1643 (ibid., 263–66). As Presbyterian M.P.s later reminded their republican foes, when the Commons participated in this covenant, they swore to preserve the honor and power of the king, not to diminish or remove him. For the Engagement's application to Busby, see ibid., 330n.; and John Sargeaunt, *Annals of Westminster School* (London, 1898), 64, who says that one of the fellows at Eton who refused to sign it, John Hales, was deprived.

19. See C. V. Wedgwood, *The King's War 1641–1647* (London: Collins, 1958), 339. Winn, 8, notes that Hill's proximity haunted Dryden through his years at Westminster and Trinity until Hill's death in 1653. Winn quotes extensively from Hill's sermons and writings and infers that Hill was "a more tolerant Presbyterian" whom Dryden's father might expect to wipe off "the taint of Busby's Royalism" (62). Winn here confuses religion and politics. In their belief that the king was head of the state, Busby and Hill were both political royalists, in opposition to Independents such as Oxford's John Owen, head of Christ Church. Both had to subscribe to the Engagement, which was probably a greater shock to Hill's monarchist sentiments than to Busby, long inured by then to rebellion. At the same time, Winn's suggestion that Dryden must have wearied of Hill goes far to explain the poet's deep-seated anticlericalism.

20. "Presbyterian" and "Independent" are put (initially) in quotation marks to indicate political groups as distinct from religious affiliations. The labels were attached to M.P.s by the Scots, who thought their friends and enemies in Parliament corresponded to the ministerial rivalry in the Westminster Assembly. See the revision of Hexter's essay of 1938 in his *Reappraisals in History* (Evanston: Northwestern University Press, 1961), 177f. See also Valerie Pearl, "Oliver St. John and the 'Middle Group' in the Long Parliament: August 1643–May 1644," *English Historical Review* 81 (1966): 490–519; "The 'Royal Independents' in the English Civil War," *Transactions of the Royal Historical Society,* 5th series, 18 (1968): 69–96; and the first part of Underdown. Of the six "royal Independents" examined closely by Pearl, the M.P. whose votes and opinions most nearly reflected those of Dryden's family was John Crewe, who sat for Brackley in Northants. A moderate who opposed Strafford's attainder in 1641, he allied with the peace party until the Scots entered the war, at which time he went over to the "middle group" and urged Manchester to sink his differences with Cromwell (see below) for the good of the cause. After going to treat with the king at Uxbridge early in 1645, he took a harder line and began to vote with the Independents against the Scots. In 1646 he told the County Committee of Northamptonshire that Parliament was wary of letting the king come to London lest he join with the Scots and their Presbyterian followers in the City to overwhelm the Commons. Pearl's summary of Crewe's position in the crucial years 1647–48 quite probably describes the position of Pickering and Sir John Dryden as well: "Like his colleagues, Crewe preferred to support the army in 1647 rather than risk a Scottish-royalist settlement. In February 1648, Whitelocke referred to Crewe as 'in great repute with Cromwell and his party.' Yet with other men of like mind, he struggled in

that last despairing effort to secure an agreement with Charles at Newport" (" 'Royal Independents,' " 84–85). See note 26, below.

21. Montague's depression of spirits at this time no doubt reflected the second thoughts of the Presbyterian, or peace, party: "If we beat the King 99 times, yet he is King still; but if the King beat us once, we shall all be hanged." To this lament Cromwell replied, "My Lord, if this be so, why did we take up arms at first? This is against fighting ever hereafter." Quoted in Hill, *God's Englishman*, 69.

22. Underdown, 104; 79–87. Derek Hirst, *Authority and Conflict: England, 1603–1658* (Cambridge: Harvard University Press, 1986), chapter 9, dates the reaction from the recruiter elections of 1646, which reinforced the "peace" party by returning non-militant members from "pacified, but still largely royalist, counties like Cornwall" (267). Pearl describes the formidable counterrevolution staged by Presbyterian mobs demanding peace with the king and a union with their Scots brethren. See "London's Counter-Revolution," in G. E. Aylmer, ed., *The Interregnum: The Quest for Settlement, 1646–1660* (London: Macmillan, 1972), chapter 1.

23. Hirst, *Authority and Conflict*, 280. Pickering stood out among Cromwell's council for defending the Quaker James Naylor in 1657. His brother, Colonel John Pickering, was something of a fanatic who preached to his troops. See Winn, 552n.

24. Underdown, 98.

25. Ibid., 123–31.

26. Ibid., 135–39. The only speech by an M.P. connected to the moderate Independents with whom Dryden's uncle and cousin had formerly voted was that by Crewe's brother-in-law. On the basis of newspaper reports, Underdown reduces the familiar arguments "to the moderates' contention that the King could be relied on to keep his agreements, and the radicals' equally strong conviction that he could not." After the purge, this crucial vote on whether to treat with the king was made a shibboleth: only members who subsequently entered their *dissent from the resolution to continue negotiations* were allowed to take their seats in the purged Parliament. So politically sensitive were these dissents that the official record of them was erased early in 1660 (ibid., 214). Pickering, who was nominated one of Charles's judges but stayed away from the trial after the first week, entered his dissent only on 12 February, after the Regicide. Sir John Dryden did not enter his dissent (and so return to the purged Parliament) until April 1652, more than three years later. Since Pickering and Sir John both avoided Parliament the next day (6 December), it is impossible to know how they voted and whether the army had marked them for purging. Six of the seven M.P.s from Northamptonshire boroughs were purged, bringing to an end their parliamentary careers; the seventh, Edward Harby, joined Pickering and Dryden by later dissenting and resuming his seat. The most one can safely conclude from all this is that although Pickering and Dryden did not support those army radicals and republicans who were pressing for Regicide, they nonetheless fall into the small group of greater gentry (about one-fourth of their total number) who endorsed the revolution. Probably they were among those who, like Fairfax, believed that the king should

not only be curtailed in his power but further chastised as well, short of execution. See Underdown's Appendix, 364–90; C. V. Wedgwood, *The Trial of Charles I* (London: Collins, 1964), 89–91.

27. Underdown, 142–43; cf. *Astraea Redux*, 183–84 (*Works* 1:27; discussed in chap. 4, below).

28. See the California editors' note (*Works* 1:171–73), which quotes Lucy's affecting couplets. Their son's death dashed the hopes of the impecunious earl and his countess for Hastings's match with the wealthy daughter of Sir Theodore Mayerne, physician to King Charles. Michael Gearin-Tosh, "Marvell's 'Upon the Death of the Lord Hastings,' " *Essays and Studies* (1981): 105–22, argues that *Lachrymae Musarum* was a kind of cryptoroyalist publication commemorating the late king but admits that the earl of Huntingdon himself was notoriously cold in the royalist cause after 1645. I suspect the volume was gathered by "R.B." (probably Richard Brome) for the countess. Dryden's poem, included in an appendix with contributions by five other Westminster scholars and by Marvell, may have been written in emulation of Baron Montagu's two sons Edward and Ralph.

29. Lines 30–42. See Milton, *The Reason of Church Government Urged Against Prelaty*, in *Complete Prose* 1:751; and compare Calvin's *Institutes*, 4.12.

30. Opponents of the Regicide considered it a republican deed, as did many of the regicides. "It was not a thing done in a corner," declared one of them at his execution. "I believe the sound of it hath been in most nations." See Wedgwood, *Trial*, 222. As for insurrection by commoners, the most explicit political statements in the *Lachrymae Musarum* are those of Marvell ("the *Democratick* Stars did rise, / And all that Worth from hence did *Ostracize*") and Nedham ("It is decreed, we must be drain'd (I see) / Down to the dregs of a Democracie"—this last being a figure Dryden borrowed twice in his later poetry). Both these comments refer not to the Regicide but to the abolition of the Lords that followed. See the poem on page 29 by "Jo. Joyner" mentioning "Th' opprest, and now quite ruin'd House of Peers."

31. See Pepys's diary entry under 1 November 1660. Pepys was at St. Paul's School. The Westminster alumnus was the court preacher, Robert South; quoted in Wedgwood, *Trial*, 197. King Charles was indicted as "that man of blood" by the army in 1648; see Kenyon, 319.

32. Kenyon, 294; Underdown, 145. Hirst's emphasis on legitimacy is notable for the insight it gives into Cromwell's deliberation no less than Ireton's. "In succumbing to the promptings of those desperate for a semblance of continuity he [Ireton] took the incipient revolution the first of its many steps towards conservatism" (*Authority and Conflict*, 286). For the possibility that a similarly reactionary wish overtook the final session of the Long Parliament, see Underdown, who detects a startlingly conservative motive behind the majority's fatal vote of 5 December. "Ostensibly the Commons had voted that the partial agreement reached at Newport [Isle of Wight] provided a basis for further negotiations; they had in fact voted for a restoration, eleven years too early" (Underdown, 139).

Chapter 2. Cromwell and the Millennium

1. Pocock, chaps. 10–12; see also his introduction, vii–ix. The standard account of the reception of Machiavelli in England, from the time of Thomas Cromwell down to the seventeenth century, is Felix Raab, *The English Face of Machiavelli* (London: Routledge, 1964).

2. Pocock, 395–96.

3. Ibid., 374–75; Kenyon, 291–92.

4. Wallace, 105.

5. Until recently, scholars habitually broke Marvell's career into chronological stages of lyrical contemplation, political commitment, and partisan satire. These phases were then correlated with moments in an ongoing political crisis; for example, George deF. Lord, "From Contemplation to Action: Marvell's Poetical Career," *Philological Quarterly* 46 (1967): 207–24. In her introduction to *Marvell and the Civic Crown* (Princeton: Princeton University Press, 1978), Annabel Patterson notes the disintegrative effect of such periodization and suggests that the resemblance between Marvell's "political" and "lyrical" personalities is best accounted for on the basis of "a pattern of alternating commitment and retreat, of rash involvement followed by self-doubt or apology, of changes of mind and direction" (10). Those who have challenged the assumption that Marvell's lyrics date from before the Restoration include Joseph Summers, "Private Taste and Public Judgment: Andrew Marvell," in *The Heirs of Donne and Jonson* (New York: Oxford University Press, 1970), 160–62; and Barbara Everett, "The Shooting of the Bears: Poetry and Politics in Andrew Marvell," in *Andrew Marvell: Essays on the Tercentenary of His Death*, ed. R. L. Brett (Oxford: Oxford University Press, for the University of Hull, 1979), 63–64. See also R. I. V. Hodge, *Foreshortened Time: Andrew Marvell and Seventeenth Century Revolutions* (Totowa, N.J.: Rowman and Littlefield, 1978), 2.

6. Warren Chernaik, *The Poet's Time: Politics and Religion in the Work of Andrew Marvell* (Cambridge: Cambridge University Press, 1983), 5.

7. Ibid., 43–44, 53, 58–59.

8. Joseph Mazzeo, "Cromwell as Davidic King," *Renaissance and Seventeenth-Century Studies*, 183–208; Ruth Nevo, *The Dial of Virtue: A Study of Poems on Affairs of State in the Seventeenth Century* (Princeton: Princeton University Press, 1963), 109–14; Wallace, 106–44 (quotations from 143 and 126).

9. Zwicker, "Models of Governance in Marvell's 'The First Anniversary,'" *Criticism* 16 (1974): 1–12.

10. Patterson, *Civic Crown*, 70–82.

11. Ibid., 87. For Milton's gloss on Rev. 17–19 at the end of *Eikonoklastes*, see *Complete Prose* 3:598–99. Marvell's prophetic deference gives Wallace pause, and he concludes that Marvell is *not* hailing the millennium but deliberating on a Protestant campaign that must commence with Oliver's coronation (121–22). Wallace (137) analyzes the poem into its parts as a deliberative oration.

12. Hirst, 32–34. A. J. N. Wilson, "Andrew Marvell's 'The First Anniversary of

the Government under Oliver Cromwell': The Poem and Its Frame of Reference,"
Modern Language Review 69 (1974): 254-73, had already connected the line on Israel's
silence with Cromwell's reference to "the breaking of the Rump" (266).

13. Wilson, ibid., 270; Hirst, 22-25. Hirst is able to cite other panegyrics from
1654 to prove that Milton's praise of Cromwell as *pater patriae* in the *Second Defence* ("Your achievements . . . surpass every title") was hardly unique. Marvell need
not have found there his compliment, as Patterson suggests, although she too notes
Cromwell's speech (*Civic Crown*, 71-72; cf. Nevo, *Dial of Virtue*, 88-92). Marvell
probably does allude to Cromwell's speech, but I believe none of the critics reviewed
has fully explained Marvell's lines; see below.

14. Hirst, 34, 41-45; Chernaik, *The Poet's Time*, 46, for the phrase, "poetically
inert."

15. Hirst, 41-42. For Cromwell's phrase *dominium in gratia* (rule founded on
grace) and its vital connection with the succession and with Cromwell's proposed
coronation, see Wallace, 122-24.

16. Hirst, 43-46. To describe the constitutional position Marvell is recommending to Cromwell, Hirst borrows Evelyn's contemptuous word, "unkingship." For an
exposition of Marvell's supposedly "mainstream eschatology," see Margarita Stocker,
Apocalyptic Marvell: The Second Coming in Seventeenth-Century Poetry (Athens: Ohio
University Press, 1986), 10-25. Cf. Daniel 7:13, "The Son of man came with the
clouds of heaven," and Matthew 24:30, "They shall see the Son of Man coming in
the clouds of heaven with power and great glory."

17. Hirst, 35-37. Hirst attempts to distinguish between Marvell's civic role as
publicist and his quasi-courtly role as domestic counselor to Oliver. Compare Margoliouth's objection (320) to Wallace's thesis that the poem is deliberative: "It would
have been rather presumptuous of Marvell to aim at influencing Cromwell's policy
while he was practically the dependant of William Dutton's *de facto* guardian."

18. Hirst, 39, 32.

19. Wallace, 132-34; Wilson, "Marvell's 'The First Anniversary,'" 267; Patterson, *Civic Crown*, 83-83; Hirst, 25-27. Patterson, citing Bishop Hall, thinks Noah
symbolizes "the perpetually unregenerate nature of man." Wallace notes that Cham's
(Ham's) descendants were compared with rebellious subjects, and both he and Hirst
realize that the invoking of Noah must somehow bear on the topic of legitimate succession (although Hirst thinks "the more obvious reference to the succession appears
with the ascent of Elijah").

20. Marvell associates both metaphors with political chaos throughout the poem.
Compare the Amphion passage on the "tedious Statesmen . . . Whose num'rous
Gorge could swallow in an hour / That Island, which the Sea cannot devour" (69-
71). The Creation in Genesis is based upon (Canaanite) myths of a god conquering
the sea-dragon. Marvell and his audience were familiar with this metaphorical conquest from Psalms 74:13 and 89:9-10; Job 7:12 and 26:12-13; Isaiah 51:9 and 27:1.
At the Apocalypse, of course, the dragon emerges from the sea as the Beast defeated
by Christ (Revelation 12-13; 16:13-14; 20:2-10); see below.

21. Lines 343–46. Besides borrowing the "beaked Promontories" (line 358) from *Lycidas,* 94, Marvell may echo *Lycidas,* 168–71 (beginning "So sinks the day-star in the ocean bed").

22. For an analysis of the Hobbesian elements in the edifice constructed by Cromwell as "Amphion," see Hodge, *Foreshortened Time,* 107–11.

23. See Revelation 13:7 and 10, in which "the patience of the saints," possibly a sarcastic phrase, was taken in a retaliatory sense by militants: "he that killeth with the sword must be killed with the sword"; cf. also 14:12.

24. Wallace, 133–34.

25. Lines 211–20. As Margoliouth notes, Marvell echoes *Lycidas,* 177: "The blest kingdoms meek of Joy and love." The passage may echo as well the following lines from *Lycidas:* 15–17 (Milton's chorus of lamenting Muses); 100–02 (the sinking of the ill-rigged ship); 163 ("melt with ruth"); 172 ("So Lycidas sunk low, but mounted high"). See note 21, above. On the rent mantle, Margoliouth (1:324–25) comments that "the poet, like many other Englishmen, felt concerned about the political void that Cromwell's sudden disappearance might create, but this does not prove that he favoured hereditary succession as yet."

26. Wallace, 129–30; Hirst, 30–31. Patterson (*Civic Crown,* 84) quotes a sermon of 1643 to Parliament recommending Elijah as a pattern for reformers because "millennial prophecy foretold a second coming" for him, but she does not explain what Elijah's second coming meant.

27. This double tradition accounts for John's awkward narrative of the Apocalypse (Rev. 19:11–22:5). On the one hand, John follows Jewish messianic doctrine centered on a day of judgment; at the same time, he has promised (1:7) to reveal the resurrected God. In trying to accommodate a messiah who is also God, John describes *two* final wars, two victories over Satan, two resurrections, two judgment scenes. The Christian Apocalypse, in short, takes place on an earth that has been made over into Heaven. Several incompatible concepts of the millennium grow from this ambiguous root: Christ might appear before or after the thousand years, which might be a period of peace or of continuous warfare, ending only when Christ transfers his sovereignty to God (1 Cor. 15:24–28: "The last enemy that shall be destroyed is death").

28. *The City of God,* trans. Marcus Dods (New York: Random House, 1950), 762.

29. Lines 7–10. Hirst, n. 31, quotes the above sentence from Trapnel's *The Cry of a Stone,* 66.

30. *Works* 1:12. On the signs of Cromwell's regality during his last fifteen months (i.e., from his reinvestiture as Protector in June 1657), see the appendix in Roy Sherwood, *The Court of Oliver Cromwell* (Totowa, N.J.: Rowman and Littlefield, 1977), 158–67. An imperial crown was placed on the head of Cromwell's funeral effigy, and the Jacobean ceremony was carefully observed. Sherwood concludes that "the reason for strict adherence to the procedures followed at the obsequies of King James I for Oliver's funeral was not simply that those who surrounded Cromwell were interring a head of state, it was because they were burying a king." At his reinvestiture, Cromwell

had taken the oath and received election and recognition by his subjects, neglecting only the anointing and crowning (163). Compare the coronation in *MacFlecknoe*.

31. *Works* 1:11, 14. Zwicker, *Politics and Language in Dryden's Poetry* (Princeton: Princeton University Press, 1984), 70, denies that a definite political principle informs the *Heroique Stanzas*.

32. Lines 31–33. The bergamot is a fine kind of pear, possibly associated here with royalty. Dryden uses no more of *The Prince* than its final paragraph, before Machiavelli's closing "Exhortation": "la fortuna è donna . . . e però sempre, come donna, è amica de' giovanni" (Fortune is a woman . . . and therefore, like women, is always friendly to young men).

33. Blair Worden, "Andrew Marvell, Oliver Cromwell, and the Horatian Ode," in Kevin Sharpe and Steven N. Zwicker, eds., *Politics of Discourse: The Literature and History of Seventeenth-Century England* (Berkeley: University of California Press, 1987), 172, 165.

34. Ibid., 150. For an interesting argument that the Cromwell ode demonstrates Marvell's commitment to the republican experiment, see David Norbrook, "Marvell's 'Horatian Ode' and the Politics of Genre," in *Literature and the English Civil War*, ed. Thomas Healy and Jonathan Sawday (Cambridge: Cambridge University Press, 1990), 147–69. Norbrook shows that Marvell criticizes the royalism of "Horace himself and revises him in a republican direction" (153).

35. This echo was first pointed out, so far as I know, by Barbara Everett in "The Shooting of the Bears," 73 (see note 5, above). Dryden is, of course, remembering Cowley's *Davideis* as well, but *Mac Flecknoe*'s closing allusion to Elijah and Elisha seems to me to clinch Everett's suggestion that Dryden borrowed from *The First Anniversary*.

Chapter 3. This Talking Trumpet

1. See Paul J. Korshin, *Typologies in England, 1650–1820* (Princeton: Princeton University Press, 1982), 44–56; Gerard Reedy, S.J., *The Bible and Reason: Anglicans and Scripture in Late Seventeenth-Century England* (Philadelphia: University of Pennsylvania Press, 1985), 13–19, 79–83. The basic discussion of figural typology is still Erich Auerbach's "Figura," conveniently translated in *Scenes from the Drama of European Literature* (rpt. Minneapolis: University of Minnesota Press, 1984). Auerbach observes that for Church Fathers like Augustine, the literal narrative in Scripture "was pure phenomenal prophecy" (39).

2. *Works* 10:110–11; Macdonald, *Bibliography*, 33, n. 2; McFadden, chapter 2.

3. On the elect nation, see above, chap. 1, n. 13. Because "country" signified opposition to court interests, the name became a badge of those too honest, or too backward, to accept a bribe. I coin the word *antepartisan* to characterize a view of the state that denies the significance of political parties. The American word *nonpartisan* is misleading here because it means transcending the factional interests of parties whose existence nobody denies.

4. Tim Harris, *London Crowds in the Reign of Charles II* (Cambridge: Cambridge University Press, 1987), 30; and, for the estimate of Catholics in England, John Miller, *Popery and Politics in England, 1660–1688* (Cambridge: Cambridge University Press, 1973), 9–25.

5. *Works* 1:25–31 (lines 312, 292, 101–02). Dryden is not alluding here "to the Solemn League and Covenant" (1:224n.). That Covenant, signed by the English commissioners to Scotland in August 1643, was extremely unpopular at Westminster. Before confirming it in September, Parliament struck the clause describing the Scottish Church as established "according to the word of God." The Covenant, like the Westminster Assembly it entailed, was resented by the "Independent" group with whom the Drydens were most closely allied (above, chap. 1, n. 20).

6. Recently Phillip Harth, in his *Pen for a Party*, has argued convincingly that Dryden did not become an active propagandist for the Tories until 1681. Harth declines to draw biographical inferences from Dryden's new career, however. In an earlier paper read at the Clark Library Conference, February 1981, "Dryden's Public Voices" (printed in *New Homage to John Dryden* [Los Angeles: The William Andrew Clark Memorial Library, University of California, Los Angeles, 1983], 3–27), Harth dissents from scholars who contrast the Restoration poems with the satires of the 1680s as varying "chapters in the biography of Dryden's mind." Dryden's new partisanship in 1681 is a departure from his previous stance as public poet, however, and cannot be explained on the basis of *ethos* or formal expediency, as Harth maintains. See chap. 7, below.

7. Phrases adapted from Scott's *Life of Dryden*, in *Miscellaneous Prose Works* (1834), 1:204–06.

8. Cromwell's *Declaration of His Highness* (1656) is quoted by Feiling, *History of the Tory Party*, 84.

9. R. A. Beddard, "The Restoration Church," in *The Restored Monarchy, 1660–1688*, ed. J. R. Jones, 155–75 (London: Macmillan, 1979). See Ronald Hutton, *The Restoration: A Political and Religious History of England and Wales, 1658–1667* (Oxford: Clarendon Press, 1985), 117–18, on the "Presbyterian Knot."

10. *Complete Prose* 7:325; Beddard, "Restoration Church," 158–59. For other accounts, besides Hutton, *Restoration,* see Harris, *London Crowds;* Paul Seaward, *The Cavalier Parliament and the Reconstruction of the Old Regime, 1661–1667* (Cambridge: Cambridge University Press, 1989); and John Spurr, *The Restoration Church of England, 1646–1689* (New Haven: Yale University Press, 1991).

11. Sir Matthew Hale, quoted in Seaward, *Cavalier Parliament,* 44. Hale, the opponent of Hobbes, had been a judge during the Interregnum and was an original student of feudal and customary law who criticized the Ancient Constitution. On the government's fear of Quaker and other risings even during the plague, see Hutton, *Restoration,* 169–71, 231–33.

12. See Beddard, "Restoration Church," 163–64, on the "irresistible Anglican reflex" from 1660 on that led to religious nonconformity being treated as a criminal offense. "After Venner's desperate Fifth Monarchy insurrection, in January 1661, few

disputed the Cavaliers' axiom that religious dissent and political subversion were indistinguishable; soon it was to be elevated to the status of a legislative principle."

13. Harth, *Contexts;* Sanford Budick, *Dryden and the Abyss of Light: A Study of Religio Laici and The Hind and the Panther* (New Haven: Yale University Press, 1970); E. N. Hooker, "Dryden and the Atoms of Epicurus," *ELH* 34 (1957): 177–90. Harth regards *Religio Laici* as a work of Anglican apologetic, undertaken owing to "the growing disquiet in Anglican circles" over the rational religion of the "Enemies of Piety" like Charles Blount (*Contexts,* 88). For this part of his argument, Dryden seems to have used Wolseley's *Reasonableness of Scripture-Belief* (1672), as Harth shows (ibid., chap. 4 and Appendix). In Harth's analysis, Dryden, after demonstrating the necessity of biblical revelation, next proceeds to answer the objection by "the *Deist*" that revelation is not universal, as well as Father Simon's criticism that the Protestant trust in *Scriptura sola* founders on doubtful texts.

In his carefully documented exposition of Dryden's arguments, Harth leaves aside the question of their political coherence, and he doubts Hooker's suggestion that Dryden was replying to Clifford's *Treatise:* "To see *Religio Laici* as a political poem and its publication as a political act is to fail to appreciate" the distinction usually made when politics and religion became topics for discussion (228). Few Tories were capable of maintaining this distinction, however, and Dryden's rhetoric in 1682 was not designed for a context of dispassionate religious discussion, despite his remark at the end of his preface that "A Man is to be cheated into Passion, but to be reason'd into Truth" (2:109). See G. Douglas Atkins, *The Faith of John Dryden* (Lexington: University Press of Kentucky, 1980): "Harth is mistaken in thinking that 'every one of [Clifford's] opponents concentrates on the religious issues he has raised, either ignoring or briefly dismissing the political corollary of his position' " (184, n. 63; cf. *Contexts,* 237).

14. *Works* 2:51 (lines 284–86). At the end of his "Defence of the [duchess of York's] Paper" (1686), one his first writings as a Catholic, Dryden says he has found "not one Original Treatise [on] that Christian Vertue of Humility" (17:323).

15. An edition of Hooker's works including *Of the Laws of Ecclesiastical Polity* had appeared in 1666 (*Works* 2:356).

16. Kenyon, 264 (for the "Solemn League and Covenant"). Enrico Davila's history of the French civil wars, which Dryden owned, refers (without naming it) to the *Vindiciae contra tyrannos* (1578) by Duplessis-Mornay. In the earlier preface of 1682, Dryden taxes the Whigs with disloyalty, saying they follow Calvin and Buchanan, who "set the People above the Magistrate; which if I mistake not, is your own Fundamental." The later preface links the doctrines of the people's sovereignty and tyrannicide with Jesuit thought ("the worst Party of the Papists"). Making that historical link opens up for Dryden the larger problem of the Reformation and biblical hermeneutics. In 1660, when he drew the superficial parallel between Charles II's experience in Scotland and Henri de Bourbon's troubles with "a Covenanting League," Dryden had not yet learned to historicize the Reformation; he was still under the spell of the millenarian doctrine of an Elect Nation.

17. This historical explanation seems obvious enough today, but it did not con-

vince the most sophisticated historian among Dryden's contemporaries. In the preface to his *History of the Rebellion and Civil Wars in England*, Clarendon writes, "I am not so sharp-sighted as those who have discerned this rebellion contriving from, if not before, the death of Queen Elizabeth, and fomented by several Princes and great ministers of state in Christendom." Like the youthful Dryden harping on "the Nations sin," Clarendon assigns the final cause of the Rebellion to providence (Macray, ed. [1888; rpt. Oxford: Clarendon Press, 1969], 2–3). Royalist historians like Sir William Dugdale and John Nalson considered the Rebellion a feudal uprising against the king on the part of factions who used religious reform as a cloak for their ambitions. See Royce MacGillivray, *Restoration Historians and the English Civil War* (The Hague: Martinus Nijhoff, 1974).

18. See the note in *Works* 2:355. Swedenberg quotes, from Edward Herbert's *Life and Raigne of King Henry the Eighth*, Henry's speech urging the people to "be not Judges of your selves, of your phantastical opinions and vain Expositions." Swedenberg also notes the indignant reply to Dryden by the Whig journalist Henry Care, who is amazed that any Protestant should disparage Tyndale or "brand this good and holy mans endeavours with causless Aspersions, as Mr. Dryden (the Play-maker) has lately done in a Preface."

19. Harth, *Contexts*, 206–07. For Simon, tradition is not simply a resource for interpreting Scripture, but the repository of extrascriptural and prescriptural authority, such as Apostolic doctrine. He calls these traditions *non scripta* not because they are oral—as Dryden, following Hooker, mistakenly supposes—but because even if written, they are not among the Scriptures (which they sometimes antedated).

20. When Dryden says his "Salvation must its Doom receive" from his own belief, he illustrates what Chillingworth means by *private judgment* of scriptural truth. Dryden does not use the phrase in his poem or preface, but refers three times to "private Spirit"—always in connection with hermeneutics. I pass over some basic issues of epistemology here in order to pursue the hermeneutical consequences of Dryden's argument. On the complicated mechanism of assent, wherein the Holy Spirit actually assists the rational judgment by representing revealed truth with the force of direct testimony (i.e., the living presence of Christ), see Reedy, *Bible and Reason*, 57–62. For an incisive account of *Religio Laici*'s relation to the Cambridge Platonists and doctrines of innatism, see Budick, *Dryden and the Abyss of Light*, chaps. 4–6.

21. Both meanings of private judgment are found in *Leviathan*. In chapter 29, Hobbes says, "a mans Conscience, and his Judgment is the same thing." In the second half of the book, Hobbes canvasses the question of scriptural authority, and in chapter 36 ("The Word of God, and the Prophets"), he insists on the hermeneutical responsibility of every individual: "Every man then was, and now is bound to make use of his Naturall Reason, to apply to all Prophecy those Rules which God hath given us, to discern the true from the false. Of which Rules, in the Old Testament, one was, conformable doctrine." See *Leviathan*, 223, 298.

22. Harth, *Contexts*, 214.

23. See Budick, *Dryden and the Abyss of Light*, *passim*, for the variations on the

metaphor of the candle of the Lord that is both illumined and illuminating; and Reedy, *The Bible and Reason*, chaps. 2 ("The Argument from Internal Evidence") and 3 ("Testimony and Other Arguments"), for the several proofs of the Bible's authenticity. In the second part of *The Hind and the Panther*, when the Panther objects on grounds of *Scriptura sola* to Catholic tradition, the Hind refutes her opponent by pointing out that the Anglicans, too, take on infallibility whenever they disallow a specific tradition on the basis of their own scriptural hermeneutics:

> The Council steer'd it seems a diff'rent course,
> They try'd the Scripture by tradition's force;
> But you tradition by the Scripture try;
> Pursu'd, by Sects, from this to that you fly,
> Nor dare on one foundation to rely.
> The word is then depos'd, and in this view,
> You rule the Scripture, not the Scripture you. (*Works* 3:145, lines 181–93)

24. The Restoration Church's demand for a "plain" reading of Scripture was in part a reaction against the kind of exegetical redundancy satirized in *Hudibras*. Hobbes's exegeses in the second half of *Leviathan* reduce mysteries to metaphors (e.g., everlasting hellfire is derived from Gehenna, Jerusalem's smoldering garbage dump), and typology to history (Satan is any *earthly* enemy of the church). In his chapter on "The Unresolved Conflict of Dryden's Layman's Faith," Atkins, *Faith of John Dryden*, 90–95, notes the radically anticlerical thrust in Dryden's argument of *Scriptura sola*. As Atkins says, plainspeaking "in a Nation free" evidently means free of priestly control, and "Dryden must once more indicate his willingness to submit 'still' to his church. . . . The tension found elsewhere in the poem is not resolved here, however" (178n.).

25. *Leviathan*, 342. Dryden uses the word *discourse* four times in the poem and preface. *Discourse* could imply a questing intelligence, stirred up and coursing to and fro (*discurrere*) by the daylight of revelation. See Budick, *Dryden and the Abyss of Light*, 100, on the discursive reason's "synergistic capacity for providing saving truth." Budick also discusses (20) the apparently contradictory values assigned to *discourse* in the poem and illustrates the word from Hooker (58n.) and especially Chillingworth (63).

26. *Leviathan*, 359–60. On these grounds, Hobbes denies Rome's power of excommunication, which, he says, "was grounded on two errours; one, that the Kingdome of Christ is of this world, contrary to our Saviours owne words, *My Kingdome is not of this world;* the other, that hee is Christ's Vicar, not onely over his owne Subjects, but over all the Christians of the World; whereof there is no ground in Scripture" (ibid., 353–54).

27. The faith that Dryden presents in this play, far from being corporate or Anglican, is sectarian and individualistic; see chap. 6, below. The church in *The Indian Emperour* is of course the persecuting and false Church of Rome.

28. Harth, *Contexts*, 155–61. In the opinion of Harth, Dryden's charitable hope

that the heathens might be saved is characteristic of the "Latitudinarians," who alone among the Anglican clergy embraced comprehension. John Spurr, " 'Latitudinarianism' and the Restoration Church," *Historical Journal* 31 (1988): 61–82, finds that the tag of "Latitudinarian" was probably a "nonconformist slander" against clergy who had played the trimmer and conformed when the universities were dominated by Presbyterians. As to the positive meaning of "Latitude," Spurr concludes, "In the quest for salvation holy living was now held to count for more than an experience of conversion" (80–81). This smug neo-Arminianism was unlikely to sit well with the intellectually restive author of *Religio Laici*.

29. Spurr, *Restoration Church*, 114; Caroline Robbins, ed., *The Diary of John Milward* (Cambridge: Cambridge University Press, 1938), 214. The king himself was as indifferent as any *libertin* to religion (he once told Burnet that Presbyterianism was no religion for a gentleman) and promulgated his Indulgence not so much to aid Catholics or fulfil his secret Treaty of Dover as to undermine the powerful faction of Cavaliers and Church. That faction positively depended on *intolerance*, as Beddard observes: "Lay intolerance, the joint product of experience and indoctrination, was the decisive factor in restoring the Church of England to its old form and its old ascendancy" ("The Restoration Church," 165; cf. 170).

30. Dryden's eventual conversion is enough to prove that he did not really believe that "points not clearly known, / Without much hazard may be let alone" (*Religio Laici*, lines 443–44). Commenting later as a Catholic on James's Declaration for Liberty of Conscience to Dissenters, Dryden can drop the irenic mask of the public poet and use more congenial, Hobbesian metaphors for the private judgment: "I may safely say, that Conscience is the Royalty and Prerogative of every Private Man. He is absolute in his own Breast, and accountable to no Earthly Power, for that which passes only betwixt God and Him ("To the Reader," *The Hind and the Panther* [*Works* 3:120]).

Chapter 4. False Freedom and Restoration

1. For a full account of the Church's struggle for uniformity, see Spurr, *Restoration Church*, chaps. 2 and 3.

2. See W. R. Paton, ed., *Polybius: The Histories*, Loeb Classical Library, 6 vols. (London, 1922–27), index under *phronēsis*. For an analysis of the Polybian *anakuklōsis* (next paragraph), see G. W. Trompf, *The Idea of Historical Recurrence in Western Thought from Antiquity to the Reformation* (Berkeley: University of California Press, 1979), chaps. 1, 2. The best discussion of Dryden's cyclical ideas of history is Achsah Guibbory, *The Map of Time: Seventeenth-Century English Literature and Ideas of Pattern in History* (Urbana and Chicago: University of Illinois Press, 1986), chap. 7.

3. Pocock, 377; Worden, *The Rump Parliament 1648–1653* (Cambridge: Cambridge University Press, 1974), 44. Wallace, 5, defines *loyalism* as the fidelity to central, parliamentary government shown by Clarendon and quotes John Hall, who argued in 1656 that Cromwell should be elected king: "So then we may see the way to be a constant Royalist, is to be a constant Loyalist; not to respect the power or place for the

persons sake, but the person for the place and powers sake." Next to Hobbes, the profoundest thinker of the Engagement controversy was Anthony Ascham (ibid., 30–48). Ascham's melancholy, searching meditation on force and authority following the Regicide is found in *The Lawfulnes of Obeying the Present Government*. This tract earned its author an ambassadorship to Madrid, where, on his arrival, Ascham was murdered by vindictive royalists. Cf. Ludlow's remark at Pride's Purge (end of chap. 1, above).

4. *Complete Prose* 2:559; Kenyon, 323.

5. See Calvin, *Institutes*, 3.14, 24. On Machiavelli and grace, see Pocock, 213–15.

6. See particularly book 1 of the *Discorsi*. For Prynne, see Lamont's *Godly Rule* and also his *Marginal Prynne 1600–1669* (London: Routledge, 1963). Prynne was a legal historian, adamantly Erastian, who eventually came to identify the church with the Ancient Constitution, thereby magnifying English tradition as a catholic institution from which Prynne brooked no departure. Prynne's voluminous writings all display the Presbyterian outlook that must have given Dryden his first light on the relations between religion and politics.

7. Pocock, 349–50. See also Machiavelli's chapter on Fortuna in the *Discorsi*, 2.29. In his dialogue *De Consolatione Philosophiae*, Boethius learns from Philosophy that Fortuna, who seems to control the *saeculum*, is herself under the governance of providence.

8. Ascham is quoted by Wallace (36). See Pocock, 380; and, for an illuminating comparison between Hobbes and Harrington, 396–400.

9. *Aubrey's Brief Lives*, ed. Oliver Lawson Dick (Harmondsworth: Penguin, 1962), 209. The Harringtonian pamphlet campaign is described by Austin Woolrych in his volume of Milton, *Complete Prose* 7:102. Woolrych's introduction (dated 1980) is the best survey of the republican debate in 1659. Perez Zagorin, *A History of Political Thought in the English Revolution* (London: Routledge, 1954), 155, calls 1659 "republicanism's *annus mirabilis*, as England seemed a *tabula rasa* upon which any constitution-maker might try his hand."

10. Pocock, 381–83.

11. Pocock, 210.

12. Pocock, introduction to his edition of *The Political Works of James Harrington* (Cambridge: Cambridge University Press, 1977), 34–35. Pocock adds that Nedham's "target throughout is any revival of hereditary, or establishment of entrenched aristocracy, which Nedham, far more stringently than Machiavelli, sees as the principal cause of strife between patricians and plebeians at Rome" (ibid.). On Dryden's use of Nedham, see chap. 1, n. 30, above.

13. Raab, *Machiavelli*, 179–80. Raab says the first phase of republicanism failed "to achieve a viable political reality," as may be seen from the fact that King Charles was "replaced by King Nol." In his introduction to Harrington, Pocock thinks that 1656 brought "a crisis in the relations between Army and nation, Protectorate and Army, which was apparent enough to idealists of the Good Old Cause in the summer when Cromwell was abandoning the major-generals, summoning a Parliament, and moving towards the conservative experiment of the *Humble Petition and Advice*" (38).

14. Harrington, *Political Works*, 775. In *Oceana*, Olphaus Megaletor, standing for Cromwell, holds the office of Archon. He draws up the legislation for the commonwealth and then retires, like Solon.

15. Harrington, *Political Works*, 202.

16. Ibid., 175-77, 373-79, 422, 496. See *Leviathan*, part 3, chap. 32.

17. *Works* 1:228. The note on lines 151-52 (226) wrongly says, "the English army leaders, Fleetwood, Lambert, and Disbrowe," turned out the Rump. In fact, it was Lambert alone, soon to be at odds with Fleetwood and Desborough, who surrounded Parliament's own regiments on the morning of 13 October. After holding out for nearly twenty hours, the M.P.s within capitulated. As Parliament's regiments "marched out of Westminster Hall they gave Lambert an ovation. The opposing troops entered, and, twenty-two weeks after it had unlocked the House of Commons [i.e., since May, when Richard's Protectorate collapsed], the army fastened it again" (Hutton, *Restoration*, 66). Not until after 1659 was the name Rump widely used for the purged Parliament.

18. See *The Army's Plea for their Present Practice* and *A Declaration of the General Council of the Officers;* and, in reply, the *Remonstrance of the Well-Affected People of London*—all pamphlets of late 1659 cited by Godfrey Davies, *The Restoration of Charles II, 1658-1660* (San Marino: Huntington Library), 165 and 167n. For Cromwell's dissolution of the purged Parliament, see Worden, *Rump*, 335-37.

19. Hutton, *Restoration*, 83. See *Iter Boreale*, lines 176ff., in *Poems on Affairs of State: Augustan Satirical Verse, 1660-1714, Volume I: 1660-1678*, ed. George deForest Lord (New Haven: Yale University Press, 1963), 11. For the title page of *The Medall*, see *Works* 2:37. Swedenberg (289) quotes Dryden's *Aeneis*, 6.782-803 but neglects to mention his earlier use of the figure in *Astraea Redux*.

20. J. G. A. Pocock, *The Ancient Constitution and the Feudal Law: A Study of English Historical Thought in the Seventeenth Century* (Cambridge: Cambridge University Press, 1987), 156. See also Pocock's introduction to Harrington, *Political Works*, 20.

21. "Dryden's Philosophy of Fortune," *Modern Language Review* 80 (1985): 771-72. See the companion article by Hammond, below, n. 29. Readers should appreciate that the first political simile of *Annus Mirabilis*, in stanza 5, comes not from the Roman empire but the republic. The contest with Carthage/Holland, the poet says, "may prove our second Punick War"—the first having been fought by the Commonwealth's fleet in 1652-54.

22. The last allusion is less biblical than Miltonic (*Paradise Lost* was not published till later in the year but had been completed by 1665). One of Dryden's biblical similes, the canceled stanza 105 comparing Rupert's appearance to Jesus's resurrection, probably was dropped because it trenches on blasphemy.

23. McKeon, 146, 172; for the scheme, 163.

24. McKeon, 172, 164, 182.

25. McKeon, 180.

26. All of the alchemical figures in the poem relate to the king. Two earlier pas-

sages describing the blowing up of the Dutch admiral Opdam (stanzas 22–23) and the explosion of a merchant ship at Bergen (stanza 29) are Ovidian rather than alchemical; stanza 29, in particular, recalls Ovid's Phoenix (see the *Fables*, "Of the Pythagorean Philosophy," lines 578–611).

27. The pelican feeding its young with its blood is an alternative symbol to the self-immolating Phoenix. Dryden could not dwell literally on the alchemical process of the *rex* (i.e., the gold dissolved in quicksilver) disappearing in the solution. The king's dismemberment is expressed indirectly in his grief for his maimed City.

28. McKeon, 178.

29. Hammond, "The Classicist as Sceptic," *Seventeenth Century* 4 (1989): 176. On stanza 223, see the note in *Works* 1:311.

30. In the poem's closest approach to biblical typology, the king's prayer (stanzas 262–70) momentarily identifies him with David because Dryden needs to credit him with a miracle. The cessation of the fire is described in the often-ridiculed stanza 281, in which Dryden tries unsuccessfully to combine "firmamental waters" and hooded flames—both alchemical concepts. Dryden makes a last allusion to the alchemical *rex* freed from his occlusion in stanza 292: "high-rais'd *Jove* from his dark prison freed." Readers mindful of this alchemy would hear an echo of Donne's *The Exstasie:* "Else a great prince in prison lies."

31. Hutton, *Restoration*, 275.

Chapter 5. The Last Age

1. See Winn, 231–42. Winn heads his narrative "Shipwreck."

2. See *Works* 8:284–89, for a summary of the theories put forward down to 1960; and Joanne Altieri, *The Theatre of Praise: The Panegyric Tradition in Seventeenth-Century Drama* (Newark: University of Delaware Press, 1986). Altieri's important book is the best treatment of Davenant and Dryden in relation to the masque tradition.

3. Gibbs, 95 (lines 181–96).

4. Spingarn, 2:23, 48. See Sidney, *Apology*, 100, for the heterocosm or second nature.

5. Spingarn, 2:49. Davenant, who had served Fulke Greville (probably as the nobleman's secretary), took over Greville's worship of "God-like *Sidney*'s" memory. See the ideal type of Sidney in *Madagascar* (Gibbs, 14) and in Davenant's poem on Colonel Goring (Gibbs, 71–72).

6. Spingarn, 2:65, 60, 62.

7. Spingarn, 2:44; *Leviathan*, 35. In dedicating his *Essayes* (1625) to Buckingham, Francis Bacon says, "they come home to men's business and bosoms." On Davenant's relation to the Cavendish circle and the English reformers, see the article (on which I base this paragraph) by James R. Jacob and Timothy Raylor, "Opera and Obedience: Thomas Hobbes and *A Proposition for Advancement of Moralitie* by Sir William Davenant," *Seventeenth Century* 6 (1991): 205–50. Jacob and Raylor were the first to ascertain the authorship of this anonymous pamphlet.

8. Ibid., 242, 244–45, 247; for the parallels, see Sidney, *Apology*, 96, 102, 108–09, 114–15. See the commentary by Jacob and Raylor at 212–14. They reprint (242–48) Davenant's pamphlet and reproduce, from the Hartlib Papers in the Sheffield University Library, Davenant's holograph summary, with a transcription.

9. Ibid., 247, 246, 244. In his holographic summary, Davenant recommends exploiting, for the current Dutch War, "acts of Cruelty (like that in Amboyna)." Eighteen years later, Dryden would improve the hint into his propaganda play *Amboyna*.

10. The letter was printed by C. H. Firth, "Sir William Davenant and the Revival of the Drama during the Protectorate," *English Historical Review* 18 (1903): 319–21. See also Mary Edmond, *Rare Sir William Davenant* (Manchester: Manchester University Press, 1987), chapter 8.

11. Gibbs, 243. Compare Marvell's lines on "thine olive" in *The First Anniversary*, 257–64. For the government visitor's report among the State Papers at the Public Records Office, see Edmond, *Davenant*, 234, n. 7. Davenant's propagandistic efforts in the last years of the Protectorate are discussed by Susan Wiseman, "History Digested: Opera and Colonialism in the 1650s," in Healy and Sawday (above, chap. 2, n. 34), 189–204; and by Janet Clare, "The Production and Reception of Davenant's *Cruelty of the Spaniards in Peru*," *Modern Language Review* 89 (1994): 832–41.

12. Edmond, *Davenant*, 127–29, 134–35, 159–62. My quotations of the play and its prefaces are from *Sir William Davenant, The Siege of Rhodes: A Critical Edition*, ed. Ann-Mari Hedbäck, Studia Anglistica Upsaliensia 14 (Uppsala: University of Uppsala, 1973), 1–3.

13. Ibid., 5.

14. "Poem To The Earl of Orrery," Gibbs, 119–20 (lines 501–22).

15. Gibbs, 125. Compare *The Siege of Rhodes*, pt. 1, II,ii,47f. and pt. 2, III,i,67f.; and the Rhodians' conjuration in pt. 2, IV,ii. See Hedbäck, ibid., li–lv, for the plausible suggestion that the bond between Ianthe and Alphonso is based on that between Henrietta and Charles, whose marriage Davenant had idealized in *Salmacida Spolia*. Dryden's "*Poeta loquitur*" at the opening of *Cymon and Iphigenia* (*Poems*, ed. Kinsley, 815).

16. John Wallace, "John Dryden's Plays and the Conception of a Heroic Society," in Perez Zagorin, ed., *Culture and Politics from Puritanism to the Enlightenment* (Berkeley: University of California Press, 1980), 113–34.

17. Altieri, *Theatre of Praise*, 122–23. Among the Rhodians, Villerius despairs of governing the crowd's inscrutable voluntarism; the Admiral's Iago-like envy of Alphonso comes to nothing; and Alphonso's jealousy, revived by a letter from Roxolana, is unconvincingly sublimated by his joining a conspiracy against Solyman. This last scene carries republican overtones, despite its chivalric vows.

18. For example: "That noble Virtue, Chastity, is like the Fundamentals in our Religion; the highest are not to be prov'd, but believ'd." Quotations are from the folio of 1676, 1, 249, 376, 289. Parts 1–4 of *Parthenissa* appeared in 1655, followed by parts 5 (1656) and 6 (1669). The political dialogue in part 3, book 3, favors monarchy, on balance, as might be expected from a counselor who urged Cromwell to accept the

crown. For example, in a "Commonwealth a Man is seldom famous without Envy, nor lov'd without Fear," whereas a prince is above fear and can encourage merit, which is the cardinal point for an aristocrat (349).

19. See Kathleen M. Lynch, *Roger Boyle, First Earl of Orrery* (Knoxville: University of Tennessee Press, 1965), 20–26, 71–109.

20. *Works* 8:96. For Broghill's manuscript poems, see Lynch, *Orrery*, 27, 90. In addition to his verses on Broghill's wedding, Suckling's famous *Ballade upon a Wedding* was thought to refer to the same occasion, but this is shown to be impossible by Thomas Clayton, ed., *Sir John Suckling: The Non-Dramatic Works* (Oxford: Clarendon Press, 1971), 280–81. Cowley's "Ode upon Occasion of a Copy of Verses of my Lord Broghill's" was printed in his *Verses on Several Occasions* (1663; but printed earlier in Dublin); see A. R. Waller, ed., *Abraham Cowley: Poems*, 406–09 (Cambridge: Cambridge University Press, 1905). For Pickering's intimacy with Henry Cromwell, see *A Collection of State Papers of John Thurloe*, ed. T. Birch, 7 vols. (1742), 6:37.

21. Lynch, *Orrery*, 146–47; see also Nancy Klein Maguire, *Regicide and Restoration: English Tragicomedy, 1660–1671* (Cambridge: Cambridge University Press, 1992), chap. 6.

22. Pepys's diary entry for 8 December 1668; *Works* 17:361.

23. *Works* 8:85 and note (260) on *The Wild Gallant;* William S. Clark, ed., *The Dramatic Works of Roger Boyle, Earl of Orrery*, 2 vols. (Cambridge: Harvard University Press, 1937), 1:101, 2:768; Lynch, *Orrery*, 171–72, 181.

24. See Gerard Langbaine, *An Account of the English Dramatick Poets* (1691), excerpted in Spingarn, 3:140. Oldham repeats Dryden's mistake; see *Horace's Art of Poetry, Imitated in English*, in *Poems of John Oldham* (London: Centaur Press, 1960), 154. Compare also Pope's letter to Digby of 2 June 1717, in Sherburn, ed., *The Correspondence of Alexander Pope* (Oxford: Clarendon Press, 1956), 1:408. Modern readers will probably not need to be told that *King Gorboduc*, in blank verse, was coauthored by Sackville and Thomas Norton.

25. Johnson, *Lives* 1:417. See also the note in Clayton, ed., *Suckling's Non-Dramatic Works*, 330. Compare Feste's clowning speech in the person of Sir Topas the curate: "*Bonos dies*, Sir Toby; for as the old hermit of Prague, that never saw pen and ink, very wittily said to a niece of King Gorboduc, 'That that is is' " (*Twelfth Night*, IV,ii,12–14).

26. Hans-Georg Gadamer describes the encounter with tradition as a "horizontverschmelzung." "Since Nietzsche and Husserl," he writes, the word *horizon* "has been used in philosophy to characterize the way in which thought is tied to its finite determinacy, and the way one's range of vision is gradually expanded. . . . Working out the hermeneutical situation means acquiring the right horizon of inquiry for the questions evoked by the encounter with tradition." See *Truth and Method*, 2d ed., translation revised by Joel Weinsheimer and Donald G. Marshall (New York: Crossroad, 1989), 302–04.

27. "Historical reflexivity" includes awareness of tradition's ongoing effects, or what Gadamer, in an exuberant verbal synthesis, calls "wirkungsgeschichtliches

bewusstsein." This reflexivity accompanies any genuine "fusion of horizons." The new horizon thus realized "is not set in motion by historical consciousness," Gadamer insists, "but in it this motion becomes aware of itself" (ibid.). Gadamer respects Heidegger's existential axiom that our historical condition, or the tradition into which we find ourselves "thrown," *precedes* our self-consciousness. See also Joel Weinsheimer, *Gadamer's Hermeneutics* (New Haven: Yale University Press, 1985), 182–84.

28. Johnson, *Lives* 1:425; Spingarn, 2:103, 101.

29. See the note in *Works* 1:207–08. Dryden's commendatory poem (1:18) praises Howard's eloquent expression of "*Elisa's* [Dido's] griefs" in his translation of Virgil's book 4. On the distinction between "wit writing" and "wit written," see above, chapter 4. For a full account of Dryden's falling-out with Howard, see McFadden, chap. 2.

30. Spingarn, 2:100, 102. In a letter of 1662, Orrery says he has promised his next play to his old friend, Davenant (Clark, ed., *Dramatic Works* 1:25).

31. Spingarn, 2:104.

32. Spingarn, 2:106.

33. *Works* 9:10, 19; Gibbs, 99–101 (lines 371ff.).

34. *Works* 17:75; 9:12. The only references to the *Essay* by name come from Martin Clifford and from Langbaine, who also call Dryden a plagiary (Spingarn, 2:107; 3:146); and from *The Censure of the Rota* (1673), a pamphlet that quotes from "his *Dramatique Essay.*" Buckingham's insertion in act 3, sc. 1 of *The Country Gentleman* may spoof the *Essay*'s method of "debate alternative." Winn, judging from "the references that now began to bristle forth from the prefaces and prologues of rival playwrights," calls the *Essay* "a critical sensation" (191). But even an admiring disciple like Oldham was inclined to borrow its examples while disregarding their context in the dialogue. See his *Prologue to Satires Upon the Jesuits*, 28–31 (*Poems*, 81).

35. Dedicating his *Poems* to Dorset's successor in 1708, Prior tells him that his father, the former Buckhurst, was consulted for his judgment by writers like Waller, Butler, and his good friend Buckingham; and that "Dryden determines by Him, under the Character of Eugenius; as to the Laws of Dramatick Poetry" (*The Literary Works of Matthew Prior*, 2d ed., ed. H. B. Wright and M. K. Spears [Oxford: Clarendon Press, 1971], 249). The phrase "Lawes for Dramatick Poesie" is Howard's, and it provokes Dryden in his "Defence" to remind Howard that their different opinions were "defer'd to the accurate Judgment of my Lord Buckhurst" (*Works* 9:15). Since Eugenius seems "to have the better of the Argument" against Crites, and since Neander appears as his client in the *Essay* much the way Dryden leans for support on Buckhurst in the dedication, Prior merely drew an inference that has been made subsequently by Malone and others (ibid., 17:33, 55). In "The Persons in *An Essay of Dramatic Poesy*," *Papers on Language and Literature* 2 (1966): 305–14, Stanley Archer reaffirms Malone's identifications, but he also demonstrates Prior's confusion about the occasion of the *Essay*. I discuss the names of the personae in the final note of this chapter.

36. Davenant and Orrery, especially, were part of Dryden's conception of the Last Age. At the end of the *Essay*, Eugenius and Lisideius go off "to some pleasant appointment they had made" (*Works* 17:81). Davenant was fifty-nine and Orrery forty-four, and Dryden was far more likely to imagine "Eugenius" and "Lisideius"

going to wait on their friend Clarendon than to one of the bouts of dissipation for which Buckhurst (twenty-three) and Sedley (twenty-six) were notorious.

37. *Works* 17:14, 55–56, 5. Years later, dedicating his Juvenal to Dorset in 1692, Dryden recurs to the metaphors of discovery and Columbus that he and Davenant had originally applied to Orrery: "I made my early Addresses to your Lordship, in my *Essay of Dramatick Poetry;* and therein bespoke you to the World: Wherein, I have the right of a First Discoverer . . . When thus, as I may say, before the use of the Loadstone, or knowledge of the Compass, I was sailing in a vast Ocean, without other help, than the Pole-Star of the Ancients, and the Rules of the *French* Stage amongst the Moderns" (4:4–5). A little further on, Dryden excuses his garrulity by reminding the earl of what Davenant used to say about talkative old men (4:16). One would like to think that Buckhurst—who, as a follower of Buckingham's politics, was estranged from Dryden soon after the *Essay* came out—appreciated its skillful historical mimesis. Unfortunately, Prior's error probably owes more to Dorset's vanity and forgetfulness than to his knowledge. Dryden had carefully reprinted the *Essay* in 1684.

38. *Works* 17:9, 12, 22; Spingarn, 2:7, 11. Eugenius's analysis of a play into four parts follows Scaliger (*Works* 17:23 and 369n.), but he is repeating Davenant's analysis from the preface to *Gondibert* (Spingarn, 2:17–18).

39. *Works* 17:25, 30–32; Spingarn, 2:16, 61, 11. In his "Poem to the Kings most Sacred Majesty" (Gibbs, 100), Davenant compares the simple classical plots to small houses with

> Two low Rooms upon a Floor:
> Whose *thorow lights* were so transparent made,
> That Expectation (which should be delai'd
> And kept a while from being satisfi'd)
> Saw, on a sudden, all that *Art* should hide. (376–86)

40. *Works* 17:44, 15; Spingarn, 2:99.

41. *Works* 17:64. The second edition omits "my Lord" but retains the comma after "This," almost certainly indicating a printer's error. Dryden has now arrived at the public "encounter with my Adversaries" that he named at the end of the dedication, in which he distinguished the original quarrel from the other two incidental topics that the speakers "mingled, in the freedom of Discourse."

42. Spingarn, 2:102–03, 108. In the latter preface, Howard sneers at Dryden's "absolute triumph declared by his own imagination" and suggests that the author (like Bayes) loses his reflexive awareness of time and occasion: the exaltation of his "Fancy" is the cadence of his reason "and gives the deceiv'd person a wrong measure of his own proportion" (ibid., 111).

43. Edward Howard, preface to *The Women's Conquest* (1671), sig. a$_2^r$; *Works* 17: 75. By the time the *Essay* appeared in print, Howard had exasperated Orrery with his bill against importing Irish cattle. In his preface, Edward Howard argues, like his brother, for traditional blank verse.

44. *Works* 17:34, 75; "To my Dear Friend Mr. Congreve" (*Poems,* ed. Kinsley, 489).

45. Three of the four speakers' "borrowed names" are commonly said to be Greek (cf. *Works* 17:355), but that is strictly true only of "Crites" (*kritēs*, umpire or judge). Dryden's invention, "Neander," is unattested; *neandros* is a young warrior, and Dryden probably meant the *neos* to convey the sense of fresh (sc. playwright), rather than the social meaning of *arriviste*.

Several editors have adopted Malone's gloss of "Eugenius" as meaning "well born." That may have been Prior's interpretation, but Dryden's Greek was too fastidious for him to confuse the essential root, *gene-* ("race," *genea;* cf. Latin *genera*) with the Latin word "genius." Rather, he intends a hybrid of the two languages: "good wit." He may allude to the hero of *The Silent Woman*, Sir Eugenie Dauphine, who overreaches his clever friend Truewit. Davenant admired Jonson enough to appropriate his epitaph ("O Rare Sir William Davenant"), and Dryden's coinage of "Eugenius" matches his later tribute to Davenant as "a man of quick and piercing imagination . . . nothing was propos'd to him, on which he could not suddenly produce a thought extreamly pleasant and surprizing . . . He borrowed not of any other; and his imaginations were such as could not easily enter into any other man" (*Works* 10:4).

The hybrid "Lisideius" involves yet another language. *Lis* is a Gaelic word meaning "fortified hill" or "castle," as in the name of Orrery's estate of Lismore. The Latin addition, therefore, simply identifies Orrery as "lord of the castle" (literally, "the castle it [is] his").

Chapter 6. Masterless Men: The Heroic Plays

1. *Works* 9:6, 11:201 (*2 Conquest of Granada*, epilogue), 12:159 (*Aureng-Zebe*, prologue); Spingarn, 2:106.

2. Spingarn, 2:3; *Works* 12:159. Dryden read Rymer in 1677 shortly after completing *All for Love* (*Works* 13:369n.).

3. *Brief Lives*, 236; *Leviathan*, 223 (on private judgment), 120, 89. Dryden admired Hobbes's magisterial style and compared it with that of Lucretius (*Works* 3:10).

4. *Leviathan*, 70, 89, 120.

5. Ibid., 149; *Works* 11:30.

6. Only the Caroline antimasque preserves something of the popular mob. Citations by act and scene refer to the text edited (without line-numbering) by Maidment and Logan, *The Dramatic Works of John Wilson* (Edinburgh, 1874; rpt. New York: Benjamin Blom, 1967).

7. Ibid., V,viii. The historical Isaac Angelus had Manuel's eyes bored out. See also Maguire, *Regicide and Restoration*, 77–78; Harold Love, "State Affairs on the Restoration Stage, 1660–1675," *Restoration and 18th Century Theatre Research* 14 (1975): 1–9.

8. Robert D. Hume, *The Development of English Drama in the Late Seventeenth Century* (Oxford: Oxford University Press, 1976), 30. Apart from minimizing the importance of political ideology, this judicious survey is invaluable.

9. Plays that sensationalize topical events, like *Sir John van Olden Barnavelt* (1619) and *A Game at Chess* (1624), do not impart a coherent view of history; quite the reverse. A glance at Harbage's *Annals of English Drama, 975–1700* (rev. Samuel Schoenbaum [London: Methuen, 1964]) reveals that history plays disappeared from the public stage after Shakespeare. The only surviving exceptions are Robert Davenport's *King John and Matilda* (1631) and John Ford's *Perkin Warbeck* (1633). Suckling's tragedy of *Brennoralt* (1639), with its shrewd political and historical analysis, is an important link between Shakespeare's histories and Dryden's heroic plays.

10. Clark, ed. *Dramatic Works* 1:137, 159.

11. Ibid., 1:135, 152, 158f.

12. *Works* 8:230; Hughes, 37. Hughes (42) remarks on "the longing for self-sufficiency that animates so many of Dryden's characters." Compare the self-apotheosis of Nourmahal in the final scene of *Aureng-Zebe*, when she declares null the gods' authority because they have failed to protect her image in Morat, her son who lies fatally wounded. Dryden's poem to Howard praises Howard's skill in translating Dido's passion, and Zempoalla's role may be the work of the same hand.

13. *Works* 9:111. Hughes thinks the lovers' self-exile completes a "movement from fruition to unfruition [and] from Paradise to the wilderness" (42). Although he exposes the conquistador's false ideals, Hughes may give him too little credit for his irony. Cortez achieves a Boethian detachment from his passions when he contemplates the effect of Almeria's visit: "More than I wish I have, of all I wish bereft! / . . . We toss and turn about our Feaverish will, / When all our ease must come by lying still; / For all the happiness Mankind can gain / Is not in pleasure, but in rest from pain" (end of act 3).

14. Hughes analyzes the theatrical metaphors in the plays. Referring to Michael Alssid's book (see the following note), Hughes says that Maximin's scheme to establish a successor and to win Catharine "are those of a dramatist seeking to abolish the real world and enthrone that of his imagination" (63). Hughes considers Lyndaraxa the supreme mistress of illusion (99).

15. Michael Alssid, *Dryden's Rhymed Heroic Tragedies: A Critical Study of the Plays and of Their Place in Dryden's Poetry*, Salzburg Studies in English Literature (Salzburg: Universität Salzburg, 1974), 2:279, 1:163; *Works* 10:156, 179, 110.

16. *Works* 10:109–12, 114; 11:14. *Tyrannick Love* was performed by June 1669 and published with the preface around November 1670. *The Conquest of Granada* appeared early in 1671 and was published a year later with the essay "Of Heroic Plays" and the "Defence of the Epilogue."

17. Hughes, 61. Hughes thinks that Dryden has altered his French model, Porphire, who "despite his hatred of Maximin's cruelty, indignantly refuses to join Maxime's conspiracy" (78). But Dryden, while raising the pagan's *will* to rebel, clears him of the tyrannicidal *act*.

18. *The Tempest*, prepared for the fall season of 1667 and therefore coinciding with the publication of *Paradise Lost*, is much closer in theme to *The State of Inno-*

cence (1674) than to *Tyrannick Love,* whose providential agency is spectacular but unimaginable as opera.

19. For a reading of Ariel's resourcefulness as a type of Dryden's authorial prudence, see Katharine Eisaman Maus, "Arcadia Lost: Politics and Revision in the Restoration *Tempest,*" *Renaissance Drama* 13 (1982): 189–209. See also Matthew Wikander, " 'The Duke My Father's Wrack': The Innocence of the Restoration *Tempest,*" *Shakespeare Survey* 43 (1991): 91–98.

20. See below, chapter 7. Herrick notes the "high designe" of *A King and No King* in his commendatory verses before the Beaumont and Fletcher Folio of 1647. Lisideius (Orrery) praises their "excellent play" because "the whole unravelling of the Plot is done by narration in the fifth Act" (*Works* 17:42). In *Love Triumphant,* the queen, exactly like Fletcher's Gobrias, encourages an apparently incestuous passion. Dryden varied this situation in *The Spanish Fryar,* and he gave it a tragic turn in *Don Sebastian.*

21. On Dryden's *pietas,* see James D. Garrison, *Pietas from Vergil to Dryden* (University Park: Pennsylvania State University Press, 1992).

22. Hughes, 103.

23. Altieri, *Theatre of Praise,* 163. See also chapter 5 above.

24. *Works* 12:118. In visibly projecting Eve's intimation of change and death, Dryden may be trying to bring out the implications in her dream of "flight and change / To this high exaltation" (*Paradise Lost* 5.86–91). Like the Ghost of Almanzor's mother unable to scale the walls of Heaven (10:168), Milton's Eve suddenly "sunk down"—an effect that would be disconcerting onstage, where two angels "*take the Woman each by the hand, and fly up with her out of sight*" (12:120).

25. "The Design of Dryden's *Aureng-Zebe,*" *Journal of English and German Philology* 64 (1965): 452–69. At that date, only D. W. Jefferson and Bruce King took a comic view of all the heroic plays. Further historical irony arises from the fact that, six years after Dryden's play—in 1681, the year of *Absalom and Achitophel*—Aureng-Zebe's son revolted against his father's government and died in exile.

26. Hughes, 127, 132–33. See also Robert S. Newman, "Irony and the Problem of Tone in Dryden's *Aureng-Zebe,*" *Studies in English Literature* 10 (1970): 439–58.

27. *Works* 12:174, 246, 210. On the tradition of Aristotelian melancholy, see Raymond Klibansky, Erwin Panofsky, and Fritz Saxl, *Saturn and Melancholy* (London: Nelson, 1964).

28. According to the exposition in the opening scene, Indamora is to be Aureng-Zebe's "recompense" for defeating his rebellious brothers. His father, brother, and Arimant become his rivals, but Indamora's dowry per se never enters their political deliberations. Critics have adopted Allsid's suggestion that Indamora stands for India (or for patriotic love), but her name probably comes from the platonic heroine of Davenant's masque *The Temple of Love.*

29. Hughes, 126–27.

30. For a good example of this nostalgic perspective, see *Venice Preserved,* beginning of act 5.

31. Harrington, *Political Works*, 198; *Works* 13:5. The play's closing moral ("No Lovers liv'd so great, or dy'd so well"), spoken by Serapion, outraged the republicanism of at least one Whig. Novak (ibid., 376) quotes John Dennis: "Was ever any thing so pernicious, so immoral, so criminal, as the Design of that play? . . . That Priest could not but know, that what he thus commended, would cause immediately the utter Destruction of his Country, and make it become a Conquer'd and a Roman Province. Certainly never could the Design of an Author square more exactly with the Design of White-Hall."

Chapter 7. Our Author Swears It Not

1. Margoliouth, 2:355; *The Complete Poems of John Wilmot, Earl of Rochester*, ed. David M. Vieth (New Haven: Yale University Press, 1968), 124–25; David Ogg, *England in the Reign of Charles II*, 2d ed. (Oxford: Oxford University Press, 1956), 329.

2. Winn, 305; *The Letters of John Dryden*, ed. Charles Ward (Durham: Duke University Press, 1942), 9. His speedy release from the Tower lost Buckingham his standing as a leader of the opposition in contrast to Shaftesbury, who endured prison for a year rather than submit to the government. Marvell (Margoliouth, 2:355) reports that the earl refused an offer from James, conveyed to him by the Catholic Lord Stafford. The story indicates that Shaftesbury was gaining stature as the champion of antipopery, although the government caricatured him as a self-seeking *Anglican* rather than a Dissenter. See K. H. D. Haley, *The First Earl of Shaftesbury* (Oxford: Clarendon Press, 1968), 431–32, 435. Haley notes (444) that a month after Dryden's preface and the fall of Ghent, Buckingham remained the only peer that the French ambassador thought Louis might bribe to undermine Parliament's anti-French policy.

3. *Poems on Affairs of State*, ed. Lord, 1:388, 394.

4. Haley, *Shaftesbury*, 441. Novak correctly points out that Dryden echoes Nedham's *Pacquet of Advices and Animadversions . . . to the Men of Shaftesbury* (1676), which calls Shaftesbury "Mephistophiles, the Faery Fiend that haunts Both Houses" (*Works* 13:395–96, 462–63). Novak's commentary on *All for Love* is indispensable, but I reject his inference that Dryden already discerned Achitophel in the earl whom Cavalier propaganda made out as a self-interested demagogue (above, n. 2). Dryden had no clear sense of the very fluid parliamentary opposition, and neither did Shaftesbury himself as yet take an apocalyptic view of James's Catholicism. Marvell's *Account of the Growth of Popery* had just appeared at Christmas, but the last thing anybody expected was the volcano of national hysteria and antipopery that would erupt in October when Godfrey was found dead. In February, Dryden thought the danger lay in "every Remonstrance of private men . . . and Discourses which are couch'd in ambiguous terms." He was more alarmed at the effect of Clifford's *Treatise* on the religious polity than by the constitutional impact of the Harringtonian *Letter from a Person of Quality* (1675), written by Shaftesbury and Locke.

5. Atkins, *The Faith of John Dryden*, 114–19, sketches the controversy generated

by Clifford's *Treatise* and quotes from Buckingham's defense of it, which "no doubt circulated in manuscript until its posthumous publication in 1705" (ibid., 183n.). See above, chap. 3, n. 13.

6. Dryden refers to the Instrument of Government on which Cromwell based his Protectorate that put an end to the Commonwealth (above, chap. 2). Harrington adapts the "Isthmus" figure from Lucan, where it applies to Crassus standing between Caesar and Pompey. The Civil War broke out when "the house of peers . . . now sinking down between the king and commons, showed that Crassus was dead and Isthmus broken. But a monarchy divested of her nobility hath no refuge under heaven but an army" (Harrington, *Political Works*, 198).

7. *Works* 13:6; 2:52 (*The Medall*, line 272). Haley, *Shaftesbury*, 346, remarks that Shaftesbury "was the only non-Royalist who attained the front rank among Charles's advisers, [but] in the long run he was separated from them because for him loyalty to the King was not an end in itself."

8. *Pen for a Party*, 54–59. Harth does not claim that Sunderland was already a trimmer in 1679, but see the important article by Alan Roper, "Dryden, Sunderland, and the Metamorphoses of a Trimmer," *Huntington Library Quarterly* 54 (1991): 43–72.

9. Ward, *Life of Dryden*, 144; Winn, 328. When Harth suggests (*Pen for a Party*, 296n.) that these politically divisive "similes of rebels and regicides [soon] would become too highly charged," he postdates a response that nearly proved fatal to Dryden. See my note in *Cithara* 30 (1991): 10–17; and Susan J. Owen, *Restoration Theatre and Crisis* (Oxford: Oxford University Press, 1996).

10. *An Appeal from the Country to the City*. The author may be Charles Blount. On Player, see J. R. Jones, *The First Whigs* (London: Oxford University Press, 1961), 66.

11. The prologue must therefore have been delivered between 9 and 18 December. For an analytical narrative of these weeks, see Haley, *Shaftesbury*, 552–64.

12. For the note by Hooker and Swedenberg, see *Works* 1:366.

13. McFadden, 224. In 1683, alarmed at being accused of attacking London's charter in *The Duke of Guise*, Dryden wrote *The Vindication:* "A wise man I had been doubtless for my pains, to raise the *Rabble* to a *Tumult*, where I had been certainly, one of the first men, whom they had *limb'd*." In the dedication, he says his desperate writing adversaries "assault us like Foot-padders in the dark" (14:321, 209).

14. *Pen for a Party*, chap. 4, recounts how Shaftesbury's abortive indictment brought to light the illegal "Association" that seemed to confirm the government's suspicions of a Protestant Plot. For "rhetoric of outrage," see 163. In an appendix, Harth lists some thirty prologues and epilogues by Dryden performed or published from the autumn of 1678 to the spring of 1684.

15. McFadden, 225n.

16. Winn, 336, notes that Stafford was attended in his last days by the Benedictine James Corker, who "published an account of Stafford's trial and death" that certainly bore on Dryden's conversion.

17. Johnson, *Lives* 1:356–57.

18. The California editor says that Jotham spoke against "Abimelech and his murderous seizure of the crown" (2:280). The point of the allusion, however, is that in the Israel of Judges there was no crown to seize. The Book of Judges ends with the formula, "In those days there was no king in Israel: every man did that which was right in his own eyes." The same allusion underlies Dryden's apostrophe to London in *The Medall:* "But still the *Canaanite* is in the Land" (line 178; cf. Judges 1:27-32). And he goads the Whig leaders in his "Epistle": "Who made you Judges in Israel?" (2:39).

19. Ever since a contemporary, Narcissus Luttrell, in his copy of *Absalom and Achitophel* glossed "well-hung" as a reference to the earl of Huntingdon "who hath a swinging P—— as is said," scholars have tried to identify Balaam from the epithet (*Works* 2:260-61). Dryden of course wanted to stress the historical parallel but chose the epithet "well-hung" to fit Montagu. His rival who knew him well, Sir William Temple, remarked of his physical endowments that the ladies were always Montagu's "best friends for some secret perfections that were hid from the rest of the world" (Burnet's *History of My Own Time*, ed. Osmond Airy [1897], 1:599).

20. Dryden's lines 180-91 praising Shaftesbury as a lord chancellor "content to serve the Crown" were canceled, probably by Charles. See *Works* 2:411-12; and Edward L. Saslow, "Shaftesbury Cursed: Dryden's Revision of the *Achitophel* Lines," *Studies in Bibliography* 28 (1975): 276-83.

21. See *Metamorphoses*, 3.466, for Ovid (not noted in the California edition). On the Exodus metaphor, see Michael Walzer, *Exodus and Revolution* (New York: Basic Books, 1985).

22. McFadden (221) sees the connection but gets it backward: "The audience could detect an allusion here to Titus Oates, but in literary fact the Friar is an entirely different figure." On the contrary, Dryden uses the literary (or dramatic) fact to hide his cryptopapist doubts of the Plot.

23. *Apology*, 123. I have repositioned these lines as Harth suggests, being convinced by his demonstration that they were misplaced when a cancel leaf was substituted for the original C1 (*Pen for a Party*, appendix 2; see also above, n. 20).

24. See the California editor's note on the passage (2:267) explaining how Oates had a coat of arms fashioned for himself. One should note that Dryden would have linked Korah's fate in Numbers—he is swallowed when the earth opens up—to the fate of the Roman patriot Curtius.

25. Robert McHenry, "Dryden's History: The Case of Slingsby Bethel," *Huntington Library Quarterly* 47 (1984): 253-72. See also McHenry's article, "'The Sons of Belial' in *Absalom and Achitophel*," *English Language Notes* 22 (1984): 27-30. McHenry does not connect Bethel's gesture of "republican" cruelty with the lines on Agag's murder, but he does note that Dryden associated Oates with Bethel's shrievalty.

Index

Index of authors, titles, historical persons, and significant topics. Names and works mentioned only in the notes are omitted, as are characters from plays and poems.

277

Bredvold, Louis I., 5–8, 10, 15
Brereton, Sir William, 145
Broghill. *See* Orrery, Earl of
Brome, Richard, 41, 253n28
Buchanan, George, 3, 32, 91, 250n17,
   259n16
Buckhurst, Lord (Charles Sackville,
   later Earl of Dorset), 155, 163–167,
   268–69nn35, 36, 37
Buckingham, Duke of (George Villiers):
   89, 108, 217, 218–24, 227, 273n2; *The
   Country Gentleman*, 268n34. *See also*
   Bayes (*The Rehearsal*)
Budick, Sanford, 89, 259, 260–61nn20,
   23, 25
Bunyan, John, 90, 140
Burke, Edmund, 6, 149
Burnet, Thomas, 30
Busby, Richard, 33, 37, 39, 43, 251n19
Bush, Douglas, 26
Butler, Samuel (*Hudibras*), 100, 149,
   261n24
Byron, Lord (George Gordon), 7

Calvinism: and humanism, 3–4; and
   comprehension, 34–35, 102; and disci-
   pline, 37, 41–42; reform and resistance
   in, 32–33, 37, 115, 259n16; and repub-
   licanism, 91, 221; and the vox Dei,
   237
Cameron, John, 3
Caryll, John, 179
Castlemaine, Countess of (Barbara
   Palmer), 81
Catherine of Braganza, Queen, 187
Cato the Elder, 19–20, 41, 67, 248n2
Casaubon, Isaac, 109
Cavalier axiom: defined, 259n12; 84–88,
   91–92, 103, 121, 221, 233, 238–39
Chapman, George, 212
Charles I: and Dryden's family, 37, 49,
   251–53; and Parliament, 34, 39–40,
   109; Regicide of, 30, 37, 39, 41–44, 76,
   79, 128, 178
Charles II: in Dryden's Restoration
   poems, 82–84, 86, 103, 125–28; in
   Annus Mirabilis, 131, 133, 135–138;
   compared with David, 105, 238, 241,
   243, 265n30; sponsor of plays, 153,
   192, 210; Dryden's epic about, 16, 191,
   218; arbiter of refined mores, 162–63;

compared to stage sovereigns, 178–79,
   187, 190; Dryden's misgivings about,
   223–24, 233–37, 243
Charleton, Walter, 12, 81, 127, 129, 151,
   155
Chaucer, Geoffrey, 133
Chernaik, Warren, 50, 54, 254, 255n14
Chillingworth, William, 3, 93, 260n20,
   261n25
Christie, W. D., 5, 246n8
Cicero, 13, 15–16, 21, 110, 164–65, 219
Clarendon, Earl of (Edward Hyde),
   81, 103, 127, 128, 148; *History of the
   Rebellion*, 30, 260n17
Clifford, Martin, 89, 99, 223, 259n13,
   268n34
Clifford, Sir Thomas, 81
Comnenus, Michael, Emperor, 179
Constantine, Emperor, 29, 80, 82, 101
Coleman, Charles, 147
comprehension, catholic: a Presbyterian
   idea, 34–35; and chiliasm, 47; in *Levia-
   than*, 102; Dryden's ideal of, 102–04,
   107
Cooke, Henry, 147
Corneille, Pierre, 140, 141, 164, 168, 221
Cornish, Henry, 241
Coventry, Sir William, 178
Cowley, Abraham, 16, 48, 49, 112, 153,
   155, 219, 257n20, 267n35; *Cutter of
   Coleman Street*, 182
Crewe, John 38, 251–52nn20, 26
Cromwell, Henry, 153, 267n20
Cromwell, Oliver: ch. 2, *passim*; provi-
   dential role of, 25–29; Commonwealth
   radical, 33, 114, 137; Dryden's family
   and, 36–39, 44–45, 252nn21, 22; as
   Protestant emperor, 79–80, 82–84,
   109; antirepublican reaction by, 120–
   24, 263n13; prudence of, 111, 27–
   28, 133, 181; in Restoration drama,
   178–79, 181–82
Cromwell, Richard, 124, 176, 179
Crowne, John, 204

Danby, Earl of (Thomas Osborne), 71, 81,
   85, 102, 215, 218, 221–223, 227, 234,
   236–37
Daniel, Book of 47, 255n16
Daniel, Samuel, 212
Davenant, Sir William: friend of Claren-

Dryden, John, works of (continued)
Dr. Charleton," 12–13, 129, 151–52; *To His Sacred Majesty*, 127; "To My Dear Friend, Mr. Congreve," 10, 170; *To My Lord Chancellor*, 127–29, 155; "To Sir Robert Howard," 126, 143, 149, 271; "To the Memory of Mr. Oldham," 44; "To the Pious Memory of Anne Killigrew," 44; *Troilus and Cressida*, 219, 224–27, 232–33; *Tyrannick Love*, 81, 82, 102, 180, 184, 186–91, 197, 201, 209, 224, 261*n*27; preface, 188; "Upon the Death of the Lord Hastings," 4, 31, 37, 41–44, 72, 90–91, 111, 113, 233; "Verses to the Dutchess," 132, 162; *Vindication of the Duke of Guise*, 274*n*13; Virgil's *Aeneis*, 190
Dryden, Sir John, 33, 36, 38, 251–52*nn*
Duplessy-Mornay, Philippe, 60, 235, 259*n*16

Eliot, T. S., 5–7, 246
Elizabeth I, 34, 59, 82, 228, 260*n*17
Engagement Oath, 30, 33, 112–13, 117, 143, 176
Erasmus, Desiderius, 3–4, 34, 72, 190, 246*n*4
Essex, Earl of (Robert Devereux), 36, 38

Fairfax, Sir Thomas, 39, 40, 249*n*9, 252*n*26
Feake, Christopher, 54, 62, 66, 70
Feiling, Keith, 6, 7, 85, 258*n*8
Fifth Monarchists, 28, 114, 120–21, 125, 137, 258*n*12; attacked by Marvell in *The First Anniversary*, 46–47, 54–55, 60, 63–66, 69, 80
Fiennes, Nathaniel, 38
Filmer, Robert, 17, 56, 61
Firth, Charles H., 70, 266*n*10
Fletcher, John, 142, 161, 167, 170, 181, 192, 225; *A King and No King*, 194, 196, 233, 272*n*20
Foxe, John, 82, 92, 250*n*13

Gadamer, Hans, 157, 163, 267*nn*26, 27
Gassendi, Pierre, 145
Good Old Cause, 37, 44–45, 63, 89, 115, 118–21
Greville, Fulke, 146, 265*n*5
Grotius, Hugo, 33

Hale, Sir Matthew, 30, 87, 258*n*11
Hales, John (of Eton), 166, 251*n*18
Haley, K. H. D., 223, 273*n*2, 274*n*11
Halifax, Marquis of (George Savile), 236
Hamilton, K. G., 7–8
Hammond, Paul, 4, 18, 130, 137, 139
Harrington, James: Machiavellian *innovazione* in, 46, 63; the "balance" and revolution in, 121–22, 176, 215, 274*n*6; immanent providence and prudence in, 50, 121, 122, 125; on popular rights, 33, 198, 225; moral science of, 126, 177; and the republican *annus mirabilis* of 1659, 118, 263*n*9; *Oceana*, 31, 108, 117, 264*n*14
Harris, Tim, 82, 258*n*10
Harrison, Thomas (regicide), 60, 253*n*30
Harth, Phillip: on *Religio Laici*, 8, 89, 93, 97, 259*n*13, 261–62*n*28; on Dryden's Tory writings, 224–25, 231, 258*n*6, 274*nn*, 275*n*23
Hartlib, Samuel, 145, 266*n*8
Hegel, G. W. F., 14, 23
Henri IV, 83, 259*n*16
Henrietta Maria, 149, 266*n*15
Henry VIII, 29, 260*n*18
Herbert, Edward Lord, 92, 260*n*18
hermeneutics: and historiography, 9, 22, 80, 111, 115–16, 129, 133, 157; and deliberative prudence, 53; and the problem of freedom, 105; the Anglican rule of faith and, 95–96, 99; and pseudoprophecy, 65–66, 111, 239–42; alchemy and, 134–38; linked to regicide, 92–93, 105
Herrick, Robert, 41, 272*n*20
Hexter, Jack H., 35
Hill, Christopher, 26, 114, 246*n*5, 249*n*9, 252*n*21
Hill, Thomas, 35, 251*n*19
Hirst, Derek, 38, 53–56, 65, 68, 252*n*22, 255*n*17
Hobbes, Thomas: primacy of the state in, 250*n*12; the Kingdom of God in, 102, 185; on private judgment, 96, 100–01, 260*n*21; Engagement controversy and, 112, 117; compared with Machiavelli, 116; compared with Harrington, 121–22; individual autonomy in, 198–99, 204; on personal sovereignty, 176–77, 183; on the mimetic basis of moral